Divine Guidance

Divine Guidance

*Lessons for Today from the World
of Early Christianity*

JOHN A. JILLIONS

OXFORD
UNIVERSITY PRESS

Oxford University Press is a department of the University of Oxford. It furthers
the University's objective of excellence in research, scholarship, and education
by publishing worldwide. Oxford is a registered trade mark of Oxford University
Press in the UK and certain other countries.

Published in the United States of America by Oxford University Press
198 Madison Avenue, New York, NY 10016, United States of America.

© Oxford University Press 2020

CIP data is on file at the Library of Congress
ISBN 978-0-19-005573-8

1 3 5 7 9 8 6 4 2

Printed by Sheridan Books, Inc., United States of America

For Denise

Contents

IV. REPRISE: DIVINE GUIDANCE IN THE FIRST AND 21ST CENTURIES

Acknowledgments

This book has been decades long in the making, going back to the mid-1980s, when I first began to think about divine guidance, discernment, and delusion as topics of academic and spiritual interest while serving as parish priest for a tiny Orthodox congregation in Brisbane, Australia. In its present form it is a thoroughly revised version of a doctoral dissertation completed in 2002 under the supervision of Professor Petros Vassiliadis in the Faculty of Theology at the Aristotle University of Thessaloniki in Greece.

It has been a full and interesting life of balancing academic work and pastoral responsibilities since beginning this project in 1994. My wife and I moved from suburban New Jersey to Greece with three young sons for the first year of study, but then went on to spend the next seven years in Cambridge, England. There I gratefully attended Professor Morna Hooker's lectures on Paul and did most of my research at Tyndale House and the libraries of the University of Cambridge. At the same time as serving a small parish in Cambridge, I became involved in founding the Institute for Orthodox Christian Studies in 1999 with scholars from around the United Kingdom and the support of the Cambridge Theological Federation and the Faculty of Divinity of the University of Cambridge. In 2003 I moved to Ottawa, Canada, to teach at Saint Paul University and the Sheptytsky Institute of Eastern Christian Studies, while continuing to serve as a parish priest. In 2011 I was appointed chancellor of the Orthodox Church in America; I left that position in 2019 to return to pastoral ministry, teaching, and writing. I currently serve as pastor of Holy Ghost Orthodox Church in Bridgeport, Connecticut, and as an adjunct professor at Fordham University and St Vladimir's Orthodox Theological Seminary.

Only recently did I have the time to return to the manuscript and prepare it for publication. I am especially grateful to Cynthia Read, executive editor at Oxford University Press, for her warm reception in making this possible. I would also like to thank the external peer reviewers who recommended publication and gave helpful advice. Others at OUP guided the book's production, including Hannah Campeanu, Tharani Ramachandran, Leslie Johnson and copy editor Judith Hoover.

I am deeply conscious of the debt of gratitude I owe to scores of people living and departed over the years and in several parts of the world, without whose inspiration, advice, encouragement, and support in many and various ways—academic, financial, social, and spiritual—neither the dissertation nor this book would have been started or completed.

Among those who most encouraged and assisted me in the academic endeavor are Professor Vassiliadis and Professor John Karavidopoulos of the University of Thessaloniki; the Rev. Dr. Bruce Winter (who acted as codirector of my research) and the community of scholars at Tyndale House in Cambridge; the Very Rev. Dr. John Breck, Professor Veselin Kesich (+), the Very Rev. Dr. Thomas Hopko (+) of Saint Vladimir's Seminary in New York; and Dr. Philothei Kolitsi of Cambridge and Thessaloniki, who supervised the translation of the English text into Greek for formal submission to the University of Thessaloniki.

I would also like to thank many others who with friendship and prayer assisted me and my family along the way with this project.

In Australia, Brian and Lorna Lightowler introduced me to divine guidance in the life and thought of Frank Buchman.

In the United States, I have had the help and counsel of my close friend the Very Rev. Dr. John Shimchick over many years. Others who were there at the start were Archbishop Peter L'Huillier (+), Dr. John Boojamra (+), and Sotiri and Xanthi Kotopoulos. Most recently Michael Hyatt, former CEO of Thomas Nelson Publishers, gave me valuable advice and an encouraging review of my book proposal.

In Thessaloniki, various forms of support came from Professor Antonios Tachiaos, the Rev. Dr. Nicholas Loudovikos, Rev. Athanasios Gikas, the clergy of St. George's Church (Panorama): Fr. Alexios, Fr. Panagiotis, and Fr. Nicholas (+); Anna Petridou (+); Amalia, Haris, and Mattos (+) Papadopoulos; James, Anne, and John Lillie; Angela and Panagioti Salpistis; the Very Rev. John (+) and Niki Sarantos of the American Farm School; and Peter Baiter and the Pinewood School.

In England, I appreciated the advice and encouragement from Metropolitan Anthony Bloom (+); Metropolitan Kallistos Ware; Basil Osborne; Dr. Elizabeth Theokritoff and Dr. George Theokritoff (+); Professor Marcus Bockmuehl, who spoke with me on several occasions about his father's work on divine guidance (Professor Klaus Bockmuehl, 1931–1989); the Rev. Dr. John Binns; the Very Rev. Raphael, Carolyn, and Nicholas Armour; David and Samantha Goode; Howard Fitzpatrick and Laurie Graham; Dr. Dimitri Conomos and his family (Oxford and Thessaloniki); Archimandrite Theonas Bakalis; and Dr. Gene Green (Tyndale House and Wheaton College), with whom I had a memorable research trip to ancient Corinth.

I want to express thanks to a number of departed family members whose support for this long academic journey was deeply appreciated, although they have not lived to see the fruit of their encouragement: my parents, Alla and John Jillions (my skeptical father, always intrigued by people of faith, helped keep me honest); my in-laws, Alice and Spero Melligon; Alexander Anagnos and Micheline Chevrier; my sister, Alla.

All of my large extended family has been supportive over the years, and I hope they will forgive me if I don't mention them by name. I am especially grateful for the love of my wife, Denise, my sons, Anthony, Alexander, and Andrew (and now his wife, Alice, and our grandchildren, Eloise and James), who willingly (more or less) accompanied us geographically and/or emotionally on the adventure through the decades as we moved around the world.

But above all I am grateful to Denise, for her sharp editorial skill in reading draft after draft, for her steadfastness, self-sacrifice, and wisdom. And to her I dedicate this book.

Abbreviations

General

KJV	King James Version
LXX	Septuagint (the Greek Old Testament)
MT	Masoretic Text
NT	New Testament
NRSV	New Revised Standard Version
OT	Old Testament
RSV	Revised Standard Version
UBS	United Bible Societies

Biblical Books

Hebrew Bible/Old Testament

Gen	Genesis
Exod	Exodus
Lev	Leviticus
Num	Numbers
Deut	Deuteronomy
Josh	Joshua
Judg	Judges
1 Sam	1 Samuel
2 Kgs	2 Kings
2 Chr	2 Chronicles
Ps/Pss	Psalm(s)
Prov	Proverbs
Isa	Isaiah
Jer	Jeremiah
Ezek	Ezekiel
Dan	Daniel

New Testament

Matt	Matthew
Rom	Romans
1, 2 Cor	1, 2 Corinthians
Gal	Galatians
Eph	Ephesians
Phil	Philippians
Col	Colossians
1, 2 Thess	1, 2 Thessalonians

1, 2 Tim	1, 2 Timothy
Phlm	Philemon
Heb	Hebrews
Jas	James
1, 2 Pet	1, 2 Peter
Rev	Revelation

Septuagint Additions

Sus	Susanna
Jdt	Judith
1, 2 Macc	1, 2 Maccabees
3, 4 Macc	3, 4 Maccabees
Pr Man	Prayer of Manasseh
Ps 151	Psalm 151
Sir	Sirach
Tob	Tobit
Wis	Wisdom of Solomon

Classical and Ancient Jewish and Christian Writings

1QS	Community Rule (Dead Sea Scrolls)
Apol	Plato, *Apology of Socrates*
CD	Damascus Document (Dead Sea Scrolls)
De prov	Seneca (the Younger), *De Providentia* (On Providence)
Div	Cicero, *On Divination*
Nat	Pliny (the Elder), *Naturalis Historia* (Natural History)
Gen Socr	Plutarch, *De genio Socratis* (On the Sign of Socrates)
Tim	Plato, *Timaeus*

Secondary Sources

ABD	*Anchor Bible Dictionary.*
ACCS	*Ancient Christian Commentary on Scripture.*
ANRW	*Aufstieg und Niedergang der römischen Welt*
ASCSA	American School of Classical Studies at Athens
JBC	The Jerome Biblical Commentary
JSNT	*Journal for the Study of the New Testament*
LCL	Loeb Classical Library
LSJ	Liddell, Scott, and Jones, *A Greek-English Lexicon.*
NETS	*A New English Translation of the Septuagint.*
NJBC	The New Jerome Biblical Commentary
NPNF	*The Nicene and Post-Nicene Fathers*, series 1
OAB	*The Oxford Annotated Bible*
OCD	*The Oxford Classical Dictionary*
SVTQ	*St Vladimir's Theological Quarterly*
TDNT	*Theological Dictionary of the New Testament,*
UBS-4	Aland et al., *The Greek New Testament*
ZNW	*Zeitschrift für die Neutestamentliche Wissenschaft*

Introduction

Divine Guidance in the First and 21st Centuries

Divine Guidance Today: September 11 and Mother Teresa

How God's guidance is perceived when making decisions has implications far beyond the borders of churches, synagogues, temples, and mosques, as September 11 and its aftermath provide ample evidence.

Destructive decisions often have their source in someone's claim to be following divine revelation. This is not limited to the followers of Osama bin Laden, Al Qaeda, the Taliban, or ISIS. In 1993, as David Koresh prepared the Branch Davidians in Waco, Texas, for an apocalyptic battle against the armed marshals of the US government, he and his followers were fully convinced that they were acting in response to God's personal revelation. Divine revelation led the followers of Jim Jones into the jungle of Guyana and mass suicide in 1978. And revelation inspired Shoko Asahara's religious sect to release sarin nerve gas in a crowded Tokyo subway station in 1995. Jewish terrorism in Israel is a pervasive problem.[1] Buddhist monks in Myanmar and Hindu zealots in India have stirred up anti-Muslim and anti-Christian violence.[2] And in the US, most domestic terrorism is perpetrated by those who claim to be motivated by Christian, right-wing, or nationalist values.[3]

Current events repeatedly confirm what experts on terrorism have long agreed, that the most dangerous and unpredictable terrorist groups are most likely to be religious. "God directs us in everything we do. God is in control of everything," as one member of a violent Christian cult reported to Jessica Stern, author of *Terror in the Name of God*.[4]

Divine revelation has been used throughout Christian history—even by some of the best intentioned—to justify decisions at which conventional codes of morality recoil. William Tyndale (1494–1536), for example, the pioneering translator and martyr for the English Bible, added this comment at the end of his translation of Genesis: "Jacob robbed Laban his uncle: Moses robbed the Egyptians: and Abraham is about to slay and burn his own son: and all are holy works, because they were wrought in faith at God's commandment. To steal, rob, and murder are no holy works before worldly people: but unto them that have their trust in God: they are holy when God commandeth them."[5]

Divine Guidance. John A. Jillions, Oxford University Press (2020). © Oxford University Press.
DOI: 10.1093/oso/9780190055738.003.0001

While perceived divine guidance can lead some to destroy, it can lead many others to create beauty and practice mercy, justice, peace, and works of sacrificial charity. Indeed creativity and sacrificial service in response to divine guidance are much more a part of normal life than horrific examples of violence in the name of God. If there is a philosophical "problem of evil," there is also a "problem of good."

How many works of art and music have been inspired by faith? How many hospitals, schools, and universities? The abolition of slavery in Britain and the US was largely fueled by a sense of Christian purpose, especially from William Wilberforce, who felt called by God to remain in public life to carry on the decades-long fight in the face of constant opposition. Mother Teresa's work in India was likewise inspired by divine guidance. As a nun, on September 10, 1946, during a train ride from Calcutta to Darjeeling, Mother Teresa experienced what she termed her "call within a call." She heard Jesus calling her to abandon a quiet life of teaching and to start out on a new path to care for "the poorest of the poor." She later would often speak about God's voice being accessible to all who create the inner space to hear: "God speaks in the silence of the heart, and we listen." And yet Mother Teresa's diaries also reveal years of darkness, carrying on her vocation without any encouraging words of divine guidance.

Besides the extremes of good and evil, there is also the spirituality that percolates through daily life in all societies to one degree or another and inspires personal and public decisions of all kinds. Although the United States is becoming increasingly secular and religiously unaffiliated, 53% of Americans still claim that religion is "very important in their life." Of the countries in Europe and North America only Greece is more traditionally religious than the US, with 56% assigning this much importance to religion in shaping their lives.[6] This concerns practical questions of personal life: Where should I live? What job should I take? Whom should I marry? Belief in God also motivates decisions around a host of social and political issues: abortion, contraception, same-sex marriage, bioethics, capital punishment, foreign policy (Israel and the Palestinians). In the late 1990s Pat Robertson's Christian Coalition was one of the 10 most powerful lobbying groups in the US, and they were firmly against any form of Palestinian state, on biblical grounds that the land was given by God to Israel. This view has support from many evangelical Christians in Congress, as *Newsweek* reported in an article entitled "A Nation Bound by Faith." Most large religious groups, such as the US Conference of Catholic Bishops and the American Christian Lobbyists Association, have offices in Washington, DC. Divine guidance is a fact of American decision-making at the highest levels: "When it comes to matters of might and right, Americans look to the heavens in a way that bewilders much of the rest of the world—especially Europe."[7]

If Europe is less prone to publicly invoke divine guidance in political decisions, faith still plays a major role in the lives and decision-making of millions of Europeans. In Britain, for example, on any given Sunday more than twice as many people attend church than go to soccer (football) matches. In 2017 aggregate Sunday church attendance was some 37.5 million (722,000 on a Sunday), while attendance at football matches was 15.5 million (298,000 weekly).[8] And in the rest of Europe, as in the United States, an increasingly pluralistic society exhibits a wide array of private practices related to divine guidance. These diverse beliefs, rites, and rituals live comfortably side by side without apparently troubling others at all. This pluralism is now far more complex than the simple 1950s mix of Protestant-Catholic-Jew. Now Muslim, Hindu, and Buddhist are in the mainstream. And so are a host of newer spiritualities. Here a suburban witch living outside London reflects on her community of pagan friends:

> The astonishing fact about magic is how routine its practice becomes, with what little effort. These are, after all, pension plan managers, industrial engineers, and teachers. They meet every few weeks to call upon the "Horned One" while standing naked in an Islington sitting room, and talk about contacting Isis, evoking dragon-power and receiving a message for a friend from a hallucinated monk. Even in tolerant London this is not commonplace. Yet it becomes quite normal for its practitioners. Magicians talk about different planes and separated worlds, and they seem to try to maintain the aura of mystery around their practice, but the therapist who sets aside Friday evening for her ritual group is on Friday morning more likely to be worried about roasting the group's supper chicken than about entering the magic circle. And she is not at all flummoxed by a conversation about generating power with a tarot card.[9]

Such views, and the pluralism of which they are a part, are not so far removed from the thought-world of Greco-Roman first-century Corinth, strange as this may sound. Corinth at that time was a multicultural crossroads made up of immigrants from the diverse populations of the Roman Empire. Jews and Gentiles with a wide range of religious and philosophical outlooks mixed relatively easily in the Corinthian streets. This is one reason this study may have particular relevance in the present.

This book aims to contribute to current discussion on religion and decision-making by looking at the roots of Western attitudes toward divine guidance in the first century CE. Early Christian (Pauline) approaches to divine guidance will be examined alongside the dominant Greco-Roman and Jewish views circulating at the same time. On what basis did people make the practical decisions that shaped their lives? What was the role of divine guidance? Of human initiative? Of religious texts? Of individual conscience? Of other spiritual forces (e.g., angels, demons)? What forms did guidance take? How did one discern this to be "divine" guidance and not human imagination or spiritual deception? What room was allowed for human initiative? What about making decisions when there is no apparent divine guidance? In the process of discernment and decision-making, what were the roles of rational thought, human guides, and community wisdom? These are the sorts of questions that will be addressed.

We know more about Corinth than about any other New Testament community, so this is a useful place to begin study of how Paul and his contemporaries— Gentiles and Jews—understood the role of divine guidance in decision-making. In writing to the Corinthians Paul repeatedly deals with decisions that the ecclesiastical community or individuals have made or will make. In this study I will argue that the issue of guidance was one of the threads linking all of Paul's many concerns. At virtually every point, how guidance is understood has a direct bearing on Paul's argument.

If much recent study on Paul has focused on the social and rhetorical background to the questions he addresses, I will focus instead mainly on the *theological* presuppositions regarding the nature of human and divine interaction in the process of making decisions. These are presuppositions and attitudes in the Greco-Roman and Jewish worlds in which Paul's own views on the subject of guidance were formed. Paul's fledgling community of Corinthian Christians was drawn from both these worlds, with people whose attitudes on divine guidance had been shaped consciously or unconsciously by one or the other, or both.

Numerous studies on religious practices and beliefs in the Greco-Roman world show abundant evidence for the role of divine guidance in private and public life: oracles, astrology, interpretation of dreams, divination in a multitude of forms— analyzing the flight of birds, the feeding patterns of chickens, the livers of sacrificed lambs, chance remarks, random passages drawn from Homer or Virgil. But few studies focus on *attitudes* toward divine guidance and decision-making, and none at all on this issue in first-century Corinth. The aim of this book is to help fill this gap.[10]

In part I, chapters 1–2 present what can be known about local practices and attitudes in Corinth, mainly through archeological evidence. But archeology cannot tell the whole story, so chapters 3–7 survey the literary and philosophical evidence from the Greco-Roman world to demonstrate the range of attitudes that may have been present in a cosmopolitan city like Corinth. This includes the works of Homer, Virgil, Lucretius, Cicero, Seneca, Plutarch, the philosopher Posidonius, and others whose ideas were in circulation.[11] I argue that the issues of divine guidance were a central topic of concern and debate in the first century and that even the most vehement despisers could not avoid addressing them. At the same time, while there was a wide range of views regarding the extent to which God or the gods or spiritual powers were involved in the day-to-day decisions of individuals and states, the doubters were certainly in the minority.

In part II, chapters 8–12 survey Jewish attitudes toward divine guidance by looking at the writers Philo and Josephus, Qumran, early rabbinic writers, and other intertestamental literature. They shed a bright light on how the Hebrew scriptures—at the heart of Judaism and filled with examples of divine guidance— were understood. For first-century Judaism in its various expressions, the question was not whether God guides, but how, and the main issue was discernment of truth from falsehood. This was especially important in order to maintain spiritual sobriety in a Gentile world that, in the view of most Jews (and many Gentiles), had abandoned simple virtue and gone mad over the interventions of spiritual forces into the mundane affairs of home and state. Jewish thought on divine guidance was especially interested in the interplay between God and human initiative in taking responsibility for the world God had given into the care of human beings.

Part III, chapter 13, looks closely at Paul's first letter to the Corinthians to explore early Christian attitudes toward divine guidance. In the process I hope to demonstrate that issues of divine guidance are woven throughout the letter from beginning to end in the varied topics Paul addresses.[12]

Part IV, chapter 14, brings the various strands of research together to draw some conclusions about first-century attitudes toward divine guidance and how these might be understood in the context of contemporary research on religious experience and 21st-century questions about divine guidance, decision-making, discernment, and delusion. It is worth remembering that perception of direct experience of God or spiritual forces is a virtually universal human phenomenon that cuts across history, religions, and cultures. Gathering evidence for this has been at the heart of a decades-long project by the Religious Experience Research Centre, founded at Oxford University in 1969.[13] Now based at the University of Wales, the Centre continues to do research and publish in the field of religious experience and has collected over 6,000 accounts of people from across the world who had a spiritual or religious experience that was significant to them in shaping their lives. The final chapter draws on some of this research in suggesting approaches for understanding and evaluating claims to divine guidance in the 21st century.

Throughout this study, in surveying a very wide range of historical sources, I will be asking two very basic questions: (1) In which ways is divine guidance perceived? (2) What criteria are proposed for distinguishing true from false guidance? As will be seen, the modes of perceived divine guidance are many and various and shouldn't be oversimplified or homogenized. But there are a number of repeated patterns in the ways divine guidance is experienced across cultures and history:

1. Through sacred texts, scriptures.
2. Through tradition (written and oral).

3. Through personal experience (events, visions, a heavenly voice, dreams, etc.).
4. Through the use of reason.
5. Through worship and communal religious life.
6. Through fellow human beings (family, friends, sages, elders, clergy, etc.).

Although it would be somewhat artificial to systematically process every chapter through these six categories, it will be helpful to keep them in mind.

The Biblical "Community of Discourse" and Western Scholarship

It is worth speculating on why divine guidance has been a neglected area of study among biblical scholars. The reasons may stem from the fact that biblical scholarship on the whole, as James Dunn has written, has been "content to stand outside the community of discourse" within which these documents belong:

> Our guild as a whole has been remarkably insensitive to the reality and power of allusion within our documents. Despite our best efforts we have on the whole been content to stand outside the community of discourse within which our documents emerged and flourished and to which they gave expression. We have been like people trying to listen to other people's conversation, and indeed sometimes unsympathetic. That so much of their conversation consequently passes us by should cause no surprise.[14]

Raymond Brown, the influential late Roman Catholic biblical scholar, admitted that modern biblical studies has been largely shaped by anti-supernatural biases.[15] The New Testament scholar Veselin Kesich (Eastern Orthodox) describes this anti-supernatural bias at work in the approach of many Gospel critics: "They often rely upon their own estimate of what is morally, theologically, and psychologically probable, and separate Jesus of Nazareth from the Christ of faith. Criticism based upon an essential division between 'Jesus' and 'Christ' often derives from the critic's desire to eliminate the supernatural, and to deny the interference of the supernatural in the historical process."[16]

The notion of divine presence and direction in the details of life was an essential area of discourse—if not agreement—in Paul's world. But such an outlook is far removed from the contemporary world of biblical scholarship: "For neither Paul nor his audience was the understanding of God as an actor in the world a problem. On the other hand, such an understanding is deeply difficult within contemporary culture and theology."[17]

The antimystical bias in Western religious scholarship was the main point in Andrew Louth's seminal book, *Discerning the Mystery* (1983). While admitting that it may indeed be "deeply difficult" to enter the mystical world of the Bible and other religious texts, unless religion scholars, biblical interpreters, and general readers make an effort to appreciate and enter into a world where divine guidance is regarded as possible, they will be incapable of interpreting the Bible in any way that remains faithful to the presuppositions of the text itself.

The New Testament—in continuity with the Hebrew Bible—is full of examples of people making decisions under the guidance of God. In Acts, for example, this is one of the most striking features of life in the early church, and examples one after another can be brought forward: the choice of Matthias to replace Judas comes in response to a casting of lots (Acts 1:23–26), Philip and the Ethiopian eunuch are miraculously brought together (8:26–40), as are Ananias and Saul (9:10–19) and Peter and Cornelius (Acts 10). Paul's decision to abandon his mission in Asia Minor and go instead to Greece is a direct result of "a vision in the night": "A man of Macedonia was standing beseeching him and saying, 'Come over to Macedonia and help us.' And when he had seen the vision, immediately we sought to go on into Macedonia, concluding that God had called us to preach the gospel to them." Paul's perception was that God was guiding him by closing one door and opening another (Acts 16:9–10 RSV).

In Corinth Paul's decision to remain in the city in spite of anxiety and strong opposition is similarly motivated by direct divine guidance: "The Lord said to Paul one night in a vision, 'Do not be afraid, but speak and do not be silent; for I am with you, and no man shall attack you to harm you; for I have many people in this city' "(Acts 18:9–10 RSV). On other occasions the immediacy of the guidance is less apparent. In 1 Corinthians, for example, Paul says, "Now concerning the unmarried, I have no command of the Lord, but I give my opinion as one who by the Lord's mercy is trustworthy" (1 Cor 7:25 RSV). He has no direct divine guidance but gives his informed apostolic opinion (compare 2 Cor 8:8). In all this it is apparent that Paul inhabits a mystical world that assumes the possibility of communion with God in the most practical ways.

How did the "guild" of scholars lose its sympathy for an earlier age in which the intertwining of divine and human in the day-to-day life of the world was a respectable, even if debated assumption? Klaus Bockmuehl (1931–1989) in *Listening to the God Who Speaks: Reflections on God's Guidance from Scripture and the Lives of God's People,* a little-known work written in the last months of the author's life, provides a thought-provoking direction to look for an answer.[18] It is a deceptively simple book, written for a general, mainly Protestant readership and is not addressed specifically to biblical scholars. Indeed Bockmuehl himself was a philosopher, not a biblical scholar.[19] The book surveys the scriptures and a few leading figures from the history of the church in the West (St. Augustine,

St. Francis, Thomas à Kempis, Johannes Tauler) to demonstrate the role that listening and responding to God's direction have played in the lives of individuals and communities. But the book also provides a clear and convincing analysis of why divine guidance was largely regarded with suspicion and avoided by mainline Protestants in the centuries following the Reformation.[20]

Bockmuehl traces the roots of this outlook to Reformation debates concerning direct divine illumination. He shows that Luther and Calvin in their early Reformation days both shared the notion of an inner witness of the Holy Spirit acting alongside God's "objective" guidance through the scriptures (and for Luther the sacraments as well).[21] But they, and more especially their followers, gradually retreated from this position in the face of the extreme subjectivism of Thomas Muntzer and Andreas Bodenstein (Karlstadt) and others. Muntzer, for example, is "reported to have countered Luther's reference to Scripture with, 'What Bible? One must withdraw into a corner and speak with God.'"[22]

Bockmuehl summarizes Luther's conclusion as follows: "No one receives faith or the Spirit *without*—only *through*—the Word written and proclaimed."[23] After Luther's death, the *Formula of Concord* (1577) ensured that this position became the norm.[24] The result was that to this day "the concept of God speaking 'immediately,' without mediation is frowned upon, as is listening to God."[25]

John Calvin adopted a similar position.[26] "Generally, Calvin felt that as there were no longer oracles or visions from heaven—that the Holy Spirit was exclusively given *through* Scripture—Christians were to meditate on the promises of the Scripture and find illumination there."[27] But even this, in Calvin's view, is fraught with danger if left to the individual: "Calvin is so apprehensive of the subjectivism that can be generated when an individual believer interprets (or receives) divine revelation that, on occasion, he even frowns on private Bible study. He advocates, rather, that people are to gather in the tabernacle and listen to the authorized exposition of Scripture through the minister of the Word. For him this takes the place of prophecy in the Christian church: the Holy Spirit speaks to and guides believers through preaching."[28]

The elevation of scripture as the almost exclusive means of divine guidance in Reformation orthodoxy avoided the dangers of subjectivity by casting out individual divine guidance entirely and putting all channels of guidance in the hands of the clergy as the authorized interpreters of the Word of God. Bockmuehl concludes that "the Lutheran and Calvinist versions of the Reformation both consisted of a rejection of and warning against the idea that God could—and would—speak to humans without an intermediary."[29] While he concedes that this approach may at one time have "safeguarded" the identity of Protestantism, in the same way that a similar emphasis on the authority of the bishop in the second and third centuries protected the integrity of the early church against the excesses of Montanism and its New Prophecy (to be discussed shortly), its ultimate effect was to introduce "regimentation of thought—and the loss of freedom that the apostles Paul and John granted the churches for which they felt responsible."[30]

In reaction, says Bockmuehl, the Enlightenment thinkers went to the other extreme and rejected entirely all "tutelage"—of God, of scripture, of church, of clergy—and adopted the rule of individual reason. In Kant's words, "*Sapere aude!* [Dare to know!] Have the courage to use your own reason! That is the motto of the Enlightenment."[31]

Modern biblical studies has largely been shaped by these Reformation and Enlightenment presuppositions. These have made it much more difficult for later readers of the Bible to appreciate not only the importance given to the question of divine guidance in the first century but to enter that world sympathetically.

Bockmuehl urges, "We must go back to the stance held by the Christian faith *before* the split over Reformed orthodoxy and the Enlightenment."[32] In that pre-Reformation and pre-Enlightenment world, subjective and objective divine guidance are not mutually exclusive. As with Paul's own conversion, objective revelation always begins as one person's subjective perception that God has in some way revealed Himself, and only later, as this individual perception is confirmed by the experience of others, does it gain momentum and become "objective."

Bockmuehl's conclusion raises the question of *how* divine guidance is heard and through what presuppositions it is filtered. As Rudolph Bultmann famously said, "It is impossible to use electric light and the wireless and to avail ourselves of modern medical and surgical discoveries, and at the same time to believe in the New Testament world of spirits and miracles."[33]

While many biblical scholars would no longer follow Bultmann and state their attitude quite so baldly, it remains true that it is "deeply difficult" for modern interpreters to enter the New Testament world in which divine and human, spiritual and material, rational and mystical are all intertwined and not mutually exclusive.

Christian History and Divine Guidance

Skepticism about divine guidance is not a new problem for biblical interpreters and scholars of religion. Long before the Reformation, the church both East and West was also cautious, as I hinted earlier at the mention of third-century Montanism and its New Prophecy. In late second-century Asia Minor (Phrygia) a recent Christian convert named Montanus and his two female colleagues, Prisca and Maximilla, claimed to have received new revelations from the Spirit, and they believed that this superseded the teachings and authority of the apostles and current church order. The movement had a mixed reception initially and in many places was tolerated, but their increasing rigorism and intolerance for mainstream Christianity raised concerns about how perceptions of prophecy and divine guidance should be discerned and evaluated in the Christian community.

The early church from the start had understood the messianic age as the age of the Spirit inaugurated at Pentecost (Acts 2:1–47). While careful discernment of truth from falsehood was required, it was also assumed that manifestations of the Spirit would be a normal part of life in the church. This presupposition was the major challenge posed in Montanism. When Montanists said that they had experienced a new outpouring of the Holy Spirit taking the church in new directions, who was to say they were wrong? Who was to say that this was *not* a genuine movement of the Spirit? This pushed third-century Christianity toward (1) greater skepticism about prophetic phenomena and (2) a stronger role for the episcopate as the sober upholders of Tradition and discerners of the voice of the Spirit. But as Jaroslav Pelikan points out, the role of the Spirit became an area of ambiguity in church life. Awareness of the Spirit's direction and claims of speaking "on behalf of the Holy Spirit . . . continued among the clergy, and especially among the monks."[34] In other words, the earlier church's sense of accessible divine guidance was not easily jettisoned because Christianity already had a strong living tradition about the presence of the Spirit. Indeed Justin Martyr (100–165) had "based his case against Judaism partly on the claim that 'among us until now there are prophetic charismata,' while they had died out among the Jews; and Irenaeus described the many brethren in the church of his day who had these charismata."[35]

Even when questions were later raised about why some extraordinary phenomenon like speaking in tongues had disappeared, no one questioned the basic assumption that at the heart of Christian life there was meant to be an easy and natural direct communion with God in the Spirit that would organically influence one's thoughts, words, and deeds. Divine guidance in this way was simply normal Christian life. In fact the absence of God's presence and inspiration would be cause for spiritual distress. "Most orthodox writers in the second and even in the third century maintained that such inspiration by the Holy Spirit was not only possible, but present and active in the church. In meeting the challenge of Montanism, they could not, for the most past, take the approach that the age of supernatural inspiration had passed."[36]

Ultimately, dominant Christianity countered Montanism with an expanded understanding of the scripture, tradition, and apostolic authority within the church as the guarantee of the Spirit's teaching.

And by its adoption of the threefold norm for the church's life and teaching, orthodox Christianity fundamentally altered a conception of the activity of the

Holy Spirit that had figured prominently in its earlier history. To validate its existence, the church looked increasingly not to the future, illumined by the Lord's return, nor to the present, illumined by the Spirit's extraordinary gifts, but to the past, illumined by the composition of the apostolic canon, the creation of the apostolic creed, and the establishment of the apostolic episcopate. To meet the test of apostolic orthodoxy, a movement or idea had to measure up to these norms.[37]

Nevertheless, despite the checks and balances provided by creed, canon, and episcopacy, Eastern Christianity—and Western Catholic Christianity to a lesser degree—was insistent that direct communion with God remained the ideal norm and that the lives of the saints testified to this. This was the conclusion of the 14th-century *hesychast* controversy that pitted a medieval Latin rational theology against Eastern monastic experience. (The term *hesychast*, from the Greek, *hesychia*—stillness, rest, quiet, silence—refers to a monastic.) St. Gregory Palamas and the monks of Mt. Athos insisted that the experience of God could be direct and immediate. Nor was this seen as an exception for certain privileged mystics. Mystical communion was to be the norm to be recovered by all human beings, leading to the total transfiguration of human life. Human beings were to be so suffused with divine life and light that they could be described as divinized. This *theosis*, or deification, was the very purpose for which God had created human beings. Palamas argued—and the Byzantine church councils later confirmed this—that human beings are created to be in direct personal communion with God and with each other, not in autonomous isolation. Unmediated participation in divine life is accessible to all.[38] This remains the claim of the Eastern Orthodox Church to this day.

One of the difficulties of researching the phenomenon of divine guidance is the many names given to it and the range of conceptual frameworks within which it is treated in Greco-Roman, Jewish, early Christian, and modern literature. Prophecy, divination, private revelation, special revelation, personal revelation, occasional revelation, ongoing revelation, divine direction, divine leading, divine command, divine suggestion, divine disclosure, and of course divine guidance, all—with varying connotations—have been used to describe what is perceived as God-given insight and direction to individuals and groups. But whatever the term used, the main contention of this study is that divine guidance, far from being secondary, was central to day-to-day thought and action in the "community of discourse" that shaped Paul's Corinth. It is my hope that by digging into the rich mix of ideas and debates that circulated in first-century Corinth, I will be able to contribute to 21st-century thinking on a topic that remains deeply alive, personal, public, and controversial.

PART I

DIVINE GUIDANCE AMONG GREEKS AND ROMANS: CORINTH AS A CASE STUDY

1

Roman Corinth

The single question this section of the book seeks to answer is this: What views of divine guidance might St. Paul have encountered among Gentiles when he first came to Corinth with the Christian message around the year 49 CE?[1] In sifting the literary and archeological sources I will be looking for evidence of (1) the existence of a belief or practice that admits that God, the gods, or some other spiritual force or agent has a perceived role in motivating the thoughts and actions of individuals and groups and (2) the attitude shown in the source toward this perceived phenomenon.

After reviewing sources and methodology, I will survey the early history of Roman Corinth and consider how Greece and Rome both shaped the outlook of its population. Against this background the remainder of this chapter and the next will be devoted to looking at evidence of first-century Corinthian attitudes toward divine guidance.

Sources and Methodology

Literary sources are essential and will be used extensively here alongside archeological evidence to document religious attitudes. But if literary works mainly represent the views of the upper classes, archeology can give a broader picture of popular piety that reflects the "endless diversity of regions and classes" in the Roman Empire at that time.[2] (Figure 1.1 depicts the Roman Empire, 117 CE.)

Ramsay MacMullen underlined this diversity in his acclaimed study on paganism in the Roman Empire.[3] This means that it is impossible generalize about *the* attitude of Corinthian Gentiles to divine guidance. What can be more safely determined is the mix of attitudes and the relative weight of particular attitudes in Paul's Corinth.

The sources for this study reflect as closely as possible the situation in Corinth at the mid-first century CE. Unfortunately, with the exception of Paul's letters, the Corinth of his day is almost entirely silent when it comes to written records.[4] For a view of Corinth independent of Paul's we have to look at the archeological evidence. Here we are fortunate that excavations over the past hundred years have systematically unearthed inscriptions, coins, sculpture, pottery, and building remains that give us invaluable evidence for the life of ancient Corinth. Yet the

Divine Guidance. John A. Jillions, Oxford University Press (2020). © Oxford University Press.
DOI: 10.1093/oso/9780190055738.003.0001

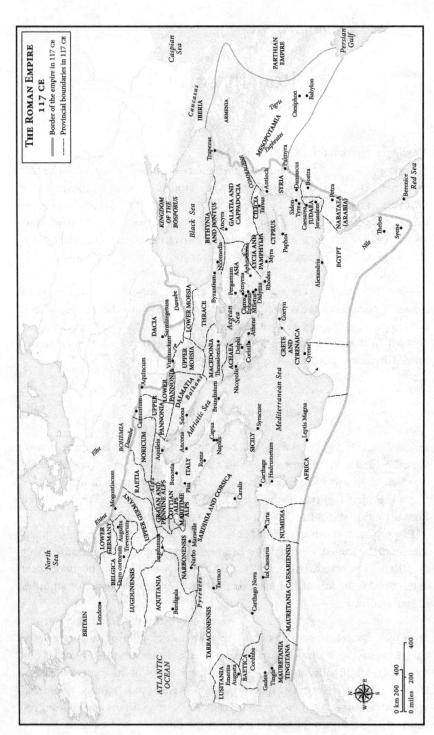

Fig. 1.1. The Roman Empire, 117 CE. Based on *Oxford Classical Dictionary*, http://oxfordre.com/classics/page/maps-tiberius-to-trajan.

Fig. 1.2. Temple of Asklepios, Corinth. Courtesy of HolyLandPhotos@comcast.net.

archeological evidence must be carefully separated to exclude those findings that do not belong to the specific period we are seeking to document. Scholars have pointed to inaccuracies in New Testament studies resulting from the indiscriminate use—as well as neglect—of archeological data.[5]

Two cautions are in order here. First, the archeological data alone rarely present a complete picture.[6] Second, there is a temptation to use archeological discoveries without due attention to their physical location and dating. Take, for example, one of the most intriguing finds in Corinth, a striking collection of clay (terracotta) body parts—arms, legs, eyes, ears, genitals—found during excavation of the main healing temple in Corinth, the Asklepeion, dedicated to the god of medicine, Asklepios. (Figure 1.2 shows the remains of the temple of Asklepios; Figure 1.3 is a display of the clay figurines in the museum at Corinth.)

Teachers and pastors have used these figures to reach conclusions about the healing cult in first-century Corinth and have assumed that St. Paul would have seen such displays and found in them the inspiration for his "body of Christ" analogy for the church (1 Cor 12:14–27). However, none of these terracotta votive offerings dates any later than the fourth century BCE, so we can't assume that they stand behind Paul's analogy. Of course the absence of such finds does not *exclude* the possibility that the practice continued or was revived sometime later. Even today visitors to Orthodox churches in modern Greece will be struck by the small silver plaques of body parts hung on icons in thanksgiving for healings.

Fig. 1.3. Terracotta body parts as votive offerings to Asklepios, Corinth. Courtesy of HolyLandPhotos@comcast.net.

Accurate dating and reading of the archeological and literary evidence is important because scholars have shown that the Roman flavor of Paul's first-century Corinth differentiates it significantly both from its Greek past and from its second-century character during the revival of Hellenism under Hadrian.

The Roman Character of First-Century Corinth and Its Impact on Religious Culture

By the time Homer's *Iliad* was written in the eighth century BCE Corinth had a proud and legendary history as a Greek city-state that was already known as "wealthy Corinth," according to Pausanias (*Description of Greece,* 2.2:570). But that all came to an end when the city was destroyed in 146 BCE. Roman legions under General Leucius Mummius leveled Corinth after it led a group of cities in Achaia to rebel against Rome. Strabo says they "paid the penalty, for a considerable army was sent thither, and the city itself was razed to the ground" (*Geography* 8.6.23a).

When Cicero visited Corinth about 75 years later, around 79–77 BCE, the city was still in ruins. It was partly inhabited by Corinthian slaves—living fairly well it seemed to him, looking "like freedmen" and "no longer chanting dirges"—but the overall impression was pitiful: "The sudden sight of the ruins had more effect on me than upon the actual inhabitants, for long contemplation had had the hardening effect of length of time upon their souls" (*Tusculan Disputations*, 3:53).[7] The wrecked city and countryside may have had scattered inhabitants, but Corinth was destroyed and had ceased to exist as a civic entity. Its numerous functions as a commercial, cultural, and religious center had been broken up and handed over to surrounding towns.

Shortly before his assassination Julius Caesar founded the new Corinth in 44 BCE as a Roman colony. In his honor the city was named Colonia Laus Iulia Corinthiensis, Colony of Corinth in Honour of Julius. The new settlers were mostly Italian freedmen with their families and slaves—shopkeepers, artisans, teachers, secretaries—plus a small number of veterans of Caesar's wars and a few freeborn entrepreneurs with capital for the new commercial venture. Among these settlers there may have been some of Greek origin, and as time went on others came from neighboring Greek towns. Jews and Syrians from the East were also attracted to the colony.[8] Aided by the legal and commercial privileges of being a Roman colony, they came to rebuild Corinth on its old strategic site with the vision to make it once again "wealthy Corinth." But there was no doubt about who was in charge. "Even if many of these may have been 'Graeculi' in origin, only Roman citizens could be citizens of the new colony; non-Romans were legally considered *incolae* [resident aliens], unable to undertake political or religious liturgies."[9]

The Roman color of the colony becomes especially vivid when seen against the background of Roman-occupied Greece. Until relatively recently scholars had accepted the view that the Roman occupation was neither offensive nor intrusive, that in fact the Romans and their well-ordered empire were welcomed by the local Greeks: "People had long felt the lack of a genuine ruler and of an empire with which they could identify."[10] In this view, Rome exerted no coercion; on the contrary, it was Rome that was captured by the glories of Greek culture, its religion, its philosophers, and its artists. As the Roman poet Horace wrote in a much-quoted letter, "Greece, the captive, took her savage victor captive and brought the arts into rustic Latium" (*Epistles* 2.1.156). The historian Susan Alcock in her highly regarded *Graecia Capta*, however, overturned this scenario, arguing convincingly that the image of Greece and Rome willingly captured by each other is precisely that: an image, an ancient Roman spin purveyed by propagandists like Horace, the favored poet of the Augustan Age. In actuality, Rome was able to exert clear political, cultural, and religious domination in ways that were keenly felt as oppressive in Greece. Alcock's research demonstrates the extent of the Roman occupation and its impact on Greece through the "external interventions" of the Romans and the "internal adaptations" these provoked among the local Greek populace. This deliberate reshaping left Greece markedly different from its ancient and Hellenistic past.

Rome had already had a long and destructive history in Greece by the time Roman colonists arrived in Corinth. Macedonia and Epirus as well had felt the Roman boot. That Corinth, the pride of Greek Achaia, would be turned inside out to become a Roman colony of former Roman slaves must have been a bitter cultural humiliation, apart from the economic loss that this new and privileged colony would potentially inflict on Greek cities. Crinagoras of Mytilene (70 BCE–18 CE), a Greek scholar and ambassador who lived in Rome, was bitter about the new settlement: "What inhabitants, O luckless city, have you received, and in place of whom? Alas for the calamity of Greece! Would Corinth that you be lower than the ground and more desert than the Libyan sands, rather than wholly abandoned to such a crowd of scoundrelly slaves who afflict the bones of the ancient Bacchiadae [the ruling family of Corinth in an early golden age, seventh to eighth century BCE]."[11] Many Greeks would have shared his feelings.

Corinth was the leading city in Roman Greece. It was the only "free and immune" city in its immediate region;[12] it was awarded the prestigious Isthmian and Caesarean Games (connected vitally with the imperial cult) and was named capital of Achaia around 44 CE. In this new Roman colony all Italians had privileges, but Romans were the most favored. This would have been felt not only on the level of the political and commercial elites but also in the working class, where Romans and Italians were well represented. Roman civic values dominated, and "social advancement and prestige were identified with the Latin language and Roman culture."[13]

The archeological evidence for the Roman character of Corinth is substantial. This is especially true for the early history of the colony, at least through the time that St. Paul was there.[14] As will be seen, this also has a bearing on how Corinthian thinking about divine guidance is to be understood. Here is some of the most intriguing evidence of this Roman character:

1. The layout and construction of new and reconstructed buildings were most often patterned on Italian models. Among the reconstructed temples only the healing shrine—the Asklepeion—preserves the Greek form, and this most likely was simply because the first colonists were anxious to rebuild this most important temple quickly.[15]
2. Written inscriptions in the early period are thoroughly Latin. Prior to Hadrian (98 CE), of the 104 Roman-period inscriptions found, all but three are in Latin. This shows that even in the period of growing Hellenization, it was Roman citizens and their descendants who dominated Corinthian

society. Latin names were retained among the elite. Even most tombstones were inscribed in Latin until the late third century. For the rest of the population—Jews, Greeks, Anatolians, Phoenicians—very little evidence survives.[16]

3. The coins of Roman Corinth are "remarkable for their early and strong preference for Roman types, their fast response to dynastic change, and their fidelity in conforming to Augustan monetary denominations."[17] The most obvious connection of coins to Rome are those showing the temple of the Gens Julia in Corinth (the shrine devoted to the ancestors of Julius Caesar). But coins also illustrate the Roman metamorphosis of traditional Greek religion. For example, the figure most often represented on the Corinthian coins is Aphrodite, from ancient times associated with Corinth as the goddess of sexual love but also of the sea, protection, and commerce. According to scholars, her link with Corinth as a town of sensual pleasure has been exaggerated: "From the point of view of sex, Corinth was no better or worse than any other Mediterranean port-city."[18] Indeed Corinth may even have been better than most—at least publicly, in the first century—given the morally conservative Augustan Roman values, which transformed Aphrodite into Venus, the founder of the Gens Julia. The dominant theme in the cult of Venus now becomes the imperial cult, and Venus's image in the Augustan period becomes more maternal, even matronly.[19] The temple of Venus was the most elaborate and prominent temple in Corinth, but its purpose was to honor Venus as foremother of the imperial family: "She is placed at the centre of the city as Mother of the Roman Nation, and as such as Mother of the Roman colony."[20]

4. The Roman imperial cult was active throughout the East but was especially active in Corinth (more on this later). The Roman colony "assiduously cultivated its ties with the emperor and his family,"[21] and the archeological evidence shows that the "majority of extant dedicatory inscriptions or records of priesthoods are aimed at Roman gods and imperial cults."[22]

5. There is an early preference for Italian pottery and artistic influence, as seen in local production and in the taste for imports in the new colony, "whose colonists were of Italian origin, and who would naturally maintain contacts with their homeland."[23]

6. It was the first Greek city to have Roman gladiatorial contests (Dio Chrysostom, *Discourses* 312.121).[24]

7. The colonists' ransacking of the Greek graves in Corinth shows that the colony was little interested in the ancient Greek city (Strabo, *Geography* 8.6.23c). "Indeed it is unlikely that the first colonists, having recently attained Roman citizenship with all its privileges, would wish to be associated with the Greek past, now represented by provincials of inferior

status."[25] Roman disregard for Greek sacred sites can be seen as early as 146 BCE, when Corinth was sacked and Polybius wrote "of the disregard shown by the army to the works of art and votive offerings" (Strabo, *Geography* 8.6.23).

Other Greek cities were hostile toward Corinth because of its special Roman commercial status, and underneath these commercial disputes simmered resentment and cultural disdain.[26] Several smaller Roman colonies in Greece also reinforced Roman superiority: Patrai and Nikopolis ("Victory City," opposite Actium) founded by Augustus, and possibly Dyme, founded by Julius Caesar. These colonies illustrated the pattern of studied Roman domination rather than passive assimilation. For example, while Patrai and Nikopolis are known to have had Greeks among the founding colonists, they were not locals but Greeks forcibly displaced from elsewhere in Achaia as part of the Roman policy of population redistribution. It takes little historical imagination to picture the effects of forced abandonment of ancestral lands, homes, and sacred sites. This policy also weaponized religious domination: objects of worship were often removed from Greek towns and installed in the Roman temples of the new colony.

Not only did this undercut previous territorial loyalties and promote new ties and dependencies—especially with Rome—but it had a powerful demoralizing effect on a deeply religious populace that regarded defeat as their punishment by the gods. The Romans made their power abundantly clear in the Greek geographical, political, cultural, and sacred landscape: "The direct and indirect effects of the imperial incorporation reached deep within Greek society, to a degree not previously acknowledged, transforming not only the way in which people lived and interacted with each other, but also their civic image and self-perception, their reading of the past, and their plans for the future."[27]

The Romans obviously used Greek religious culture extensively, but they transformed it as their own ends dictated. We know that the colonists often built new temples directly over the site of the old Greek cult to the same god or goddess.[28] However, the colonists adapted these sites and cults,[29] making every effort to transform rather than accept as given the Greek cults they found in Corinth: "Roman modernization seems to have been much preferred to ancient Greek authenticity."[30]

Corinth gradually re-Hellenized from the beginning of the second century. But the city Paul knew was far more Roman than Greek.[31] And in this way first-century Corinth helped promulgate Roman rule, Roman interests, Roman religion, Roman culture, and Roman attitudes throughout Achaia.

The Revival of Hellenism in Second-Century Corinth

The uniqueness of the Roman period in Corinth while Paul was there can be seen against the background of its Greek predecessor and also in comparison to the Hellenized Corinth of the second century onward. When Pausanias visited in 165 CE Corinth was at its peak politically, culturally, and commercially. Most of the buildings he describes did not exist in Paul's day, and there is a striking difference in "feel" between the early and later city. Corinth in 165 CE was bigger, more opulent, and much more Greek than a century earlier. By the time of Pausanias, the revival of Hellenism already had been going on for over 50 years. Nero (37–68) made an early failed attempt to revive Hellenism, but it was not until Hadrian (76–138) and his successors that Romans once again rediscovered, supported, promoted, and popularized all things Greek. In Corinth this process was naturally aided by the city's repopulation by Greeks and Greek-speaking immigrants from other parts of the empire. From the beginning of the second century official inscriptions increasingly are written in Greek, and by the third century what little Latin is still used is filled with grammatical and spelling errors, "indicating that its use was virtually forgotten."[32] As Dio Chrysostom (c. 80–150 CE) told the Corinthians, though he was a Roman, he had become as thoroughly Hellenized as they (Dio Chrysostom (Favorinus), *Corinthian Discourse,* xxxvii.26).[33]

A corresponding shift in religious emphasis accompanied the second-century revival of Hellenism, and Hadrian's reign marked a turning point in Roman religious attitudes. Now the mystical, magical, oracular, and irrational—in decline during Paul's era—find new life among even the educated classes.[34] This was a dramatic change from the sober virtue and piety of the Augustan Age. Plutarch (46–119) straddled these two periods and witnessed the change, thus making him an important source for this study. Writing in the 90s he could say that the numerous sites of oracles, which in years past had figured so prominently in Greek and Roman life, had dwindled to three: Delphi, Claros, and Didyma. He himself was a priest of Delphi, and in an essay written in dialogue style he defends the oracle against its generally perceived decline in a world increasingly insensitive, indifferent, skeptical, and even hostile to the presence and activity of the divine. But Plutarch lived to see his dialogue on decline become obsolete.[35] Delphi once again became a popular place of pilgrimage.[36]

The Roman influence on Paul's Corinth doesn't mean it was untouched by Greek culture. We can be sure that many in Paul's Corinth were of Greek background, spoke Greek, and had Hellenistic attitudes from the Eastern Roman Empire, where even among Romans the common language was Greek. In Rome itself the educated elite spoke Greek. And Paul, after all, wrote in Greek to the Christian communities in Corinth, in Rome, and throughout the empire. Even in Roman Corinth the Latin victory was not total.[37] But in St. Paul's day it is safe to conclude that the city placed primary stress on its Roman heritage, government, culture, religion, and values.

The Roman Revolution

To understand the driving force behind the Roman character of Paul's Corinth one must appreciate that it was still feeling the effects of what has been called the "Roman Revolution."[38] Corinth in the early 50s was an outpost of Roman civilization at a time when Rome was still carrying the banner of the Augustan revival of Roman culture, religion, and morals against an earlier invasion of Hellenistic influences. The religious piety of Corinth was still experiencing the effects of this upheaval.

For the roots of this cultural revolution we have to look at Rome in the years just before and after Julius Caesar's assassination in 44 BCE. Rome was plagued with political and military uncertainty, violence, and corruption, all leading to widespread gloom in the closing years of the Republic. It was commonly agreed that Rome was in decay—administrative, geographic, spiritual, and moral. When Octavian (who became Augustus) defeated Antony at Actium and took sole power in 31 BCE he immediately set to work cutting away the decay and resurrecting the glory of old Rome. He held a spiritual interpretation of the decline that was widely shared: Romans had rejected the traditional gods and values of Rome. They had imported foreign gods, especially from the Hellenistic world. Octavian believed that this foreign, Hellenistic, eastern influence on religion, philosophy, art, and mores had bathed Rome (most pointedly its leaders) in a soft lather of individualism, luxury, licentiousness, and religious neglect that was bringing Rome to the brink of ruin. And none epitomized this decadence more than Octavian's rival, Mark Antony, and his foreign consort, Cleopatra.[39]

In the minds of traditional Romans, Rome's political fortunes were historically linked to close observance of the religious rituals of Roman tradition. Quite apart from belief or behavior, what mattered most was the correct performance of the appropriate ritual. Livy cites the consul Quintus Marcius Philippus during the Macedonian campaign in 169 BCE saying, "The gods look kindly on the scrupulous observance of religious rites which have brought our country to its peak" (*History of Rome* XLIV, 1.11). The history of Rome was intimately connected to the gods, and the whole of Livy's account is a continuous record of successful and failed divination. Carelessness about the ritual requirements of the gods could have dire effects. "History to the Romans was the story of divine intervention in the affairs of men. . . . Roman gods were so intimately involved with human activities that neither could thrive without the co-operation of the other."[40]

This was as true on the personal level as it was for the state, as witnessed by the household shrines to the spiritual guardians of family and households: the *lares, penates,* and family *genii.* "Few Roman would take an important decision in their private affairs without first ascertaining the will of the god by some means of divination."[41] For the Romans, "all action is associated with and the result of divine spiritual agency."[42] Success was a sign of divine blessing, failure a sign of divine displeasure. But repeated and continuing failure was clear evidence to pious Romans that the traditions of religion that had been so successful in winning the cooperation of the gods in the past had been fundamentally neglected.

Religious revival was thus the basis for the Augustan reform that touched every aspect of life. Architecture, sculpture, household murals, images on coins, literature, and above all religion were harnessed in a massive public relations effort for "Roman values." Even written Greek was affected by the restoration of Roman values, as simpler Attic Greek forms replaced the florid and ornate "Asiatic" style of Greek popular in the East. This older style was now judged to be both aesthetically poorer and "an expression of moral decay": "The goal of [Augustus's] 'cultural program,' pursued with far-reaching and concentrated effort over the next twenty years, was nothing less than a complete moral revival. And it did in fact achieve a turnaround in public thinking. . . . Most importantly, through visual imagery a new mythology of Rome and, for the emperor, a new ritual of power was created."[43] The lascivious tastes of Hellenistic culture, so eagerly appropriated before, were now publicly—and often privately—abandoned in favor of what were regarded as the purer forms of Archaic and Classical Greece that better reflected the dignity of Augustan Rome.[44]

These images were used to convey the traditional Roman values exemplified by Augustus: bravery, clemency, justice, and piety.[45] Indeed Augustus claims this for himself in his autobiography, the *Res Gestae Divi Augusti* (The achievements of the deified Augustus):

> For this service on my part I was given the title of Augustus by decree of the Senate, and the doorposts of my house were covered with laurels by public act, and a civic crown was fixed above my door, and a golden shield was placed in the Curia Julia whose inscription testified that the Senate and the Roman people gave me this in recognition of my valour, my clemency, my justice, and my piety. After that time I took precedence of all in rank, but of power I possessed no more than those who were my colleagues in any magistracy.[46]

Thanks to Augustus, Roman values (the *mores maiorum*) were given new emphasis: simplicity and self-sufficiency, a strict upbringing and moral code, order and subservience within the family, diligence, self-sacrifice, and service to the community and state.[47] Under Hellenistic influence senators and other men of rank in the Roman Republic led double lives, maintaining a "Roman" mask in public affairs (*negotium*) and dropping the mask to live decadent "Greek" private lives at their country villas (*otium*). Now Augustus was calling them to live as whole men, as Romans. The importance of divine guidance in this revolution cannot be overemphasized, but as we shall see, this spiritual dimension was closely associated with action, virtue, and service rather than notions of mystical communion or ecstatic transport.

The Roman Imperial Cult in Corinth

The biggest change in the religious landscape of Corinth was not the Roman adaptations of Greek religion but the importation of the imperial cult:

> The archaeological evidence suggests that in the first century of the common era, the whole of downtown Corinth was gradually realigned architecturally to form a huge composite, splendid monument to the imperial family, with an altar to Julius Caesar in the centre, numerous imperial statues, and a huge temple dedicated to the genus, or family of the Julians. Anyone who visited Corinth in the mid to late first century would have confronted a breathtaking panorama in the centre of town testifying to the Victory of the Roman imperial rulers and the glorious arrival of salvation for the Roman people (among whom Corinthian citizens counted themselves, since Corinth was a Roman colony).[48]

The primary function of the imperial cult was to aid in "binding the empire together"[49] through the commonly accepted view that Roman power was the result of divine providence. The following inscription from Asia Minor is typical (Priene, 9 BCE): "Because providence has ordered our life in a divine way ... and since the emperor through his epiphany has exceeded the hopes of all former good news [*euangelia*], surpassing not only the benefactors who came before him, but also leaving no hope that anyone in the future will surpass him, and since the birthday of the god was the beginning of his good news [it may therefore be decreed that. . . .]"[50]

The imperial cult itself was largely modeled on other traditional religious practices. The regulations for the cult initiated in 14 CE by magistrates in Gytheon (near Sparta) to honor the late emperor Augustus and approved by the emperor Tiberius are one example, but probably fairly typical since Romans preferred uniformity in these matters. This was certainly true for colonies: "From even a cursory reading of Caesarian colonial charters, it is easy to sense that Roman inclination [favoring uniformity] and to infer some corresponding pressure from the centre to establish traditional Roman worship in traditional Roman forms wherever settlements were made."[51] The regulations appoint a six-day feast to be presided over by a priest and priestesses "in sacred garments." Images of the "god Augustus Caesar," Julia Augusta (mother of Tiberius), and Tiberius Augustus were to be placed on thrones in the theater, with incense burners and a sacrificial altar in front, a musical performance, and "prayers on behalf of our rulers' salvation." Each of the six days was to be dedicated to a different imperial commemoration and was to include athletic, musical, and theatrical competitions, followed by youth and other participants in white and wearing laurel wreaths in a grand procession from the temple of Asklepios and Hygeia. All were to proceed to the Kaisareon, the temple of the imperial cult. There the climax of the festival would take place with the sacrifice of a bull "for the well being of the rulers and the gods and the eternal continuation of their rule." The rites end with incense being offered by all public officials and table companies (social and kinship groupings called *syssitia* or *pheiditia*). The regulations also provide stiff penalties for embezzlement by any of the cult personnel and for noncompliance with regulations (for the latter: 2,000 drachmas, "payable to the gods," or about $40,000 to $50,000 at today's rate).[52]

The Roman Revolution and Divine Guidance

Keep in mind that Augustus was the adopted son of Julius Caesar, who was quickly proclaimed a god after his murder on March 15, 44 BCE. As the son of the deified Julius, the actions of Augustus were thus not merely human but those of the "Divi Filius," the Son of God. Augustus (then known as Octavian) saw a spectacular comet soon after the assassination—he reported that it was visible throughout the world for seven days—and this confirmed to him the apotheosis of his father. A haruspex (diviner of livers) named Vulcatius confirmed that the comet signaled a new age of happiness. Henceforth the star appeared not only on statues and coins of Julius Caesar but on those of Augustus as well. Augustus was able to use this incident as a powerful element in his political war precisely because of the "strong and widespread willingness to be influenced by celestial signs, an effective exploitation of this willingness, and a calculated association of public apparitions with eternal visual symbols."[53] The elevation of Julius Caesar into the ranks of the gods in the state cult, ratified by the Senate as early as 42 BCE, points to the heightened awareness of divine guidance that permeated the Roman world.

Looking for signs of divine guidance was part of the official routine of top Roman leadership, and Augustus's life abounded with signs of his divine election. It was standard, for example, to examine the livers of sacrificed sheep and cattle for signs of divine approval or displeasure. Thus the first time Augustus "took the auspices" as a general all the livers were turned inward, apparently a remarkable sign of good fortune. When he first became consul 12 vultures appeared, as they had to Romulus, the founder of ancient Rome. Dreams and omens—his own and others', including one of Cicero's—linked him to the sun and stars. But the conclusive sign came when he was still a teenager and the astrologer Theogenes knelt before him in homage to the glorious future he had seen for him in the stars. As the historian Suetonius writes, "From this moment he had such great faith in his own destiny that he made public his horoscope and later minted a silver coin with the Zodiac sign Capricorn, under which he was born."[54] He started to see himself as Apollo's protégé on earth and around 42 BCE began wearing Apollo's laurel wreath in public. He also took the sphinx as his seal, "symbol of the regnum Apollinis prophesied by the sybil" (Suetonius, *Augustus* 50). Symbols of Apollo, such as the tripod and the lyre, became shorthand symbols of Augustan piety and the revived Roman spirit. Reverence toward the gods (*pietas*) became the chief Roman value to be restored in the Roman Revolution,[55] as Octavian's choice of the title "Augustus" suggests.[56] He was to be the savior of Rome and of the world, but not on his own: he was being led at every step by divine guidance.

The renewal of *pietas* was especially connected to Augustus himself and the imperial cult: "We encounter evidence for the renewal of cults and temples everywhere. But outside Rome, from the very start, pietas was directed less at traditional divinities than at Augustus himself."[57] Wherever they occurred in the empire, the images that characterized the new *pietas* and its associated moral values were uniformly Roman.[58] As a western city and a Roman colony, Corinth naturally looked to Rome: statues of Augustus[59] as well as of his son Gaius or Lucius match Roman models exactly, as do other figures.[60]

Written inscriptions in Corinth support the conclusion that the social values of the Roman Revolution were central to early Roman Corinth, especially the importance placed on the duty of public service.[61] The best known inscription in this regard comes from a pavement stone near the theater: "Erastus pro aedilit [at]e s[ua] p[ecunia] stravit" (Erastus the aedile built this at his own expense).[62] This may or may not refer to "Erastus the city treasurer" mentioned in Romans 16:23, but in any case it is one of many such inscriptions in Corinth giving thanks for new buildings, pavements, building repairs, and statues, all of which attest to the "universal spirit of civic generosity, insistently pressed upon the wealthy of the community by their fellow citizens and by their own ambitions" in the world dominated by Rome.[63]

Corinth was a city with a communal ethic presupposing that positions of leadership are granted by the community—through election—as rewards for demonstrated service to the community as a whole. Indeed the Stoic view that service to others is the central vocation of a human being is essential to understanding Roman civic life in Corinth. Emperor Marcus Aurelius is typical of this Roman outlook: "What more do you want when you have done a man a service? Are you not content that you have done something conformable to your nature. . . . A man is formed by nature to acts of benevolence" (*Meditations* 9:42).[64] Fulfilling one's obligations of service is "what made men and women human and would lead to a life of piety, happiness and inner peace."[65]

It is important to underline this connection between piety and civic responsibility in order to appreciate that in Roman Corinth public service was directly connected to a divine imperative. As Dionysus of Halicarnassus wrote in 30 BCE, "To understand the success of the Romans, you must understand their piety."[66] While divination played a major role in both private and public life, the two were often connected. For example, individuals who had a dream or saw a sign that impinged upon the city or state were obliged by law to report this to the College of Augurs. "The Romans did not see themselves as independent individuals, as the Greeks did, but as part of a nexus of social relationships."[67]

This "nexus of social relationships" did not depend merely on the goodwill and piety of the wealthy and powerful; it was safeguarded, at least in part, by popular elections. Civil authorities were accountable not only to Rome but to

Fig. 1.4. Augustus at prayer, Corinth. Courtesy of HolyLandPhotos@comcast.net.

the local populace. "Even as late as the third century AD the Corinthian populace, rich and poor alike, still elected their magistrates. Although they could
not formulate the laws for their city, they retained the right to elect the officials
who would administer and interpret the laws among them. The magistrates were
accountable to the people as a whole, and they often had to make extravagant
promises (kept at considerable expense) to win election."[68]

It was understood that the emperor was at the heart of the empire's social
relationships. And as long as *he* was being divinely guided, the empire could rely
on an era of peace. One of the most enduring images of the Roman Revolution is
the tranquility exemplified by Augustus (Figure 1.4). Thus was born the ideology
of the Pax Romana. A century later Suetonius reported an anecdote that typifies
the image of pious Augustan peace: "His expression, whether in conversation
or when he was silent, was so calm and mild, that one of the leading men of the
Gallic provinces admitted to his countrymen that it had softened his heart, and
kept him from carrying out his design of pushing the emperor over a cliff, when
he had been allowed to approach him under the pretence of a conference, as he
was crossing the Alps" (*Lives of the Caesars* 2.79).

The face of Augustus—on statues, on coins—was everywhere one of tranquility, the embodiment of the Pax Romana. Tacitus writes, "There was the
rule of law for Roman citizens and decent treatment for provincials. . . . If a few
instances of force could be cited, it was to provide tranquility for the majority"
(*Annals* 1.25). Such peace was only an image, of course, and as such incomplete. Other aspects of the Augustan Age—gladiatorial contests and crucifixion
most infamously—reveal a much darker side. But whatever Rome's vices, it was
the virtues of the Roman Revolution that inspired the Corinth St. Paul knew
and loved.

2

The Archeology of Divine Guidance in Corinth

We may now more profitably look closely at what the archaeology of first-century Corinth reveals about the beliefs of its citizens concerning divine guidance, knowing that its temples and monuments were built with the music of the Augustan Age still very much in the air.

The Healing Temple of Asklepios

One of the first temples to be rebuilt by the Roman colonists soon after they arrived in 44 BCE was the Asklepeion, the healing shrine dedicated to Asklepios, the god of healing (Figure 2.1). Here, divine guidance was the central feature.

One of the three Greek inscriptions from this period (all the rest, 101, are in Latin) makes clear reference to a thanksgiving performed "according to divine command [*kat epitagēn*] dedicated to Asklepios." This inscription has been dated to the 50s CE and was found in the Asklepeion in May 1931 on a fragment of marble. It may have been erected in response to the perceived command of the god as a sign of gratitude for healing. The inscription does not say what inspired the donor, but perhaps he or she had a vision of the god in a dream. This would be perfectly consistent with the normal practice at such healing shrines throughout the Greco-Roman world. Or it may have been at the direction of a priest of Asklepios, another common way for the god's direction to be conveyed. In any case, the formula *kat epitagēn* is frequently found elsewhere in dedications to divinities.[1] Inscriptions of the form "I was commanded," referring to actions taken in response to sacred dreams, "are so frequently a boast as to be abbreviated in Latin inscriptions to VIDF: V(otum) I(ussu) D(ei) F(ecit). In Greek inscriptions, equivalents are, if anything, more easily found."[2]

Excavation of the Asklepeion show that it consisted of four sections: the temple proper, the *abaton* (a room for sleeping and receiving sacred dreams),[3] three dining rooms (each with 11 couches and seven tables and a hearth in the center), and an open courtyard surrounding a fountain. Nearby is a bathing area probably used as part of the purification process in the healing rites.

Divine Guidance. John A. Jillions, Oxford University Press (2020). © Oxford University Press.
DOI: 10.1093/oso/9780190055738.003.0001

Fig. 2.1. Statue of Asklepios, from Epidaurus. Courtesy of HolyLandPhotos@ comcast.net.

While there is not enough evidence in Corinth to give a detailed description of the healing rituals, the arrangement of the buildings is similar to other Asklepeia (like the much larger center at nearby Epidaurus), and the rites were most likely similar. The sanctuary would employ priests and attendants to conduct services and festivals and to carry out healing rites in the temple. The dining area could be used for purely social functions like celebrations of marriages and births, but it was located directly below the *abaton* and thus "inevitably conferred a religious character on the assembly."[4]

Divine guidance was central to healing in Asklepeia, and dreams figured prominently: "Patients could go themselves at any time to the Asklepeion or deputise others in their stead. The ritual was evidently very simple . . . consisting of sacrifices and purificatory bathing followed by spending the night in the *abaton*. While the patient slept the god would appear in a dream, either to cure him immediately or to prescribe treatment. The treatments were generally simple—drugs might be suggested, or a regimen of diet, bathing and exercise ordered."[5]

These two inscriptions (from Epidaurus) in gratitude for healing are typical. The second reveals a skeptic's change of heart:

Hagestratos: headache. He being oppressed by insomnia because of headache, when he was in the abaton, slept and saw a dream. The god seemed, after curing the pain in his head and standing him up naked, to teach him the attack used in the pancration [a martial art combining boxing and wrestling]. When the day came he went out well and not much later won the pancration at Nemea. (I.G. iv(2)1.122).[6]

Ambrosia from Athens, blind of one eye. She came as a suppliant to the god. Going around the shrine she mocked at some of the cures as incredible and impossible, of the lame and blind who become whole only by having a dream. But when she slept in the shrine of the god, standing over her, he seemed to say that he would cure her but that he would require her to give the temple a silver pig as memorial of her unbelief. Saying this, he cut open the diseased eye and poured in a drug. When day came she went away cured. (I.G. iv(2)1.121).[7]

Besides having a temple location, the worship of Asklepios and the goddess of health, Hygeia, was a feature of daily life through healing amulets, sealing rings, and statues in household shrines. One such sealing ring that may have belonged to a physician/priest in the temple of Asklepios (and now in the British Museum) shows a doctor doing an examination, while off to the side looking on is Asklepios leaning on his familiar serpent-entwined staff, indicating that the god was deemed to be present wherever healing took place and through whatever means.[8]

The piety at healing shrines may be seen in this hymn to Hygeia sung at the Epidaurus sanctuary and composed by Ariphron of Sicyon in the fourth century BCE. It was still being used in the third or fourth century CE:

> Hygeia, most revered of the gods among mankind,
> Would that I may dwell with you for the rest of my life!
> Be present and well-disposed to me, for if there is any delight in money
>   or in offspring
> Or in royal rule, equal to that of the gods among men, or in desires,
> That we hunt with hidden traps of Aphrodite,
>   Or if any other delight has been revealed to man from the gods,
> or any relief from pains,
> It is through you, blessed Hygeia, that they are all flourishing and are
>   brilliant in the Graces' speech.
> Apart from you no man counts as blessed.[9]

The Tomb of Diogenes

Paul might have walked by the tomb of Diogenes on many occasions. Diogenes the Cynic (412/404–323 BCE) died in Corinth in the fourth century BCE, but his tomb was still an honored site when Pausanias visited sometime in the mid-100s. Dio Chrysostom (c. 40–120 CE) says that Diogenes "camped out" in Corinth after abandoning Athens (*On Virtue*, in *Discourses* 8.5). The accuracy of Dio Chrysostom's depiction of Diogenes is less important to us than the evidence he sheds on the attitudes Diogenes inspired: simplicity, independence, and audacity. Holding up Diogenes as a Corinthian local hero, one who "risks his life against pleasure and hardship" (*Virtue* 8.26) and who railed most against the Sophists, "who wanted to be looked up to and thought they knew more than other men" (*Virtue* 6.21), says something about popular views among the self-made settlers who built the new city. And the fact that Diogenes left Athens to live in Corinth would have been a matter of local pride as well. However, many would have forgotten that Diogenes first came to Corinth to be "where fools were thickest" (*Virtue* 8.5).

As portrayed by Dio Chrysostom, Diogenes gives divine guidance none of the approval it receives elsewhere, since he regards simple virtue as incomparably more valuable than religious practices. Those who put their trust in looking for signs of divine guidance can't get away from the fact that the religious personnel at the temples and shrines, and they themselves, are all sinful human beings, says Diogenes. And this means that they don't have that perfect purity of spiritual insight that is the prerequisite for accurate discernment of divine guidance. Divination of the sort practiced in the Asklepeion is therefore useless. Even "Asclepius' sons, with all their healing power, nor prophetic seers nor priestly exorcists are of any use to them at all because of their excesses and wickedness" (*Diogenes*, in *Discourses* 6.25). Even worse, Diogenes observes, the search for divine guidance is rooted in fear. People are afraid of the gods and want to assure themselves that they are making no missteps that might bring down divine wrath. But for Diogenes, this is a blasphemous misrepresentation of God, who above all is kindly in his dealings with human beings. Even the punishment of Prometheus, who stole fire from the gods, is seen in this light: "The reason the myth says that Zeus punished Prometheus for his discovery and bestowal of fire was that herein lay the origin and beginning of man's softness and love of luxury; for Zeus surely did not hate men or grudge them any good thing" (*Diogenes* 6.25).

The most striking passage on divination comes in Dio Chrysostom's essay *On Servants*, where Diogenes is having an animated conversation about a runaway slave. Diogenes was on his way to Athens from Corinth. Meeting an acquaintance on the way he asks where he is going. The man replies, "I am on my way to Delphi, Diogenes, to make use of the oracle," but he adds that his plans have been upset by the escape of his slave. He's been forced to alter his plans and go instead to Corinth—armed with divine help from the oracle at Delphi—to look for the runaway. Diogenes then launches into a passionate attack on his friend's "using" the god: "And so you ridiculous fellow, are you attempting to make use of the god when you are incapable of using a slave? Or does the latter strike you as less difficult and dangerous than the former for those who are incapable of using things properly?" (*Servants,* in *Discourses* 10.1).

After long discussion Diogenes convinces his friend to abandon his pursuit and let his slave go free. But the friend is still puzzled and asks Diogenes, "Why do you object to my making use of the god?" (*Servants* 10.17). Diogenes replies that the very notion of "using the god" is absurd. Nothing can be used unless one knows how to use it. "To make the attempt without knowing is an extremely harmful thing. Or do you think that a man untrained in the use of horses could make use of them?" (*Servants* 10.17). A human being doesn't even know how to "use" himself, unless he knows himself. Yet no one really knows himself fully. "Is there anyone, then, who can make use of himself who does not know himself? . . . Have you ever heard of the inscription at Delphi, 'Know thyself'? . . . Is it not plain that the god gives this command to all, in the belief that they do not know themselves?" (*Servants* 10.22). When his companion admits that he does not know himself, Diogenes is exasperated: "And not knowing yourself, you do not know man; and not knowing man, you are unable to 'use' man; and yet, although you are unable to 'use' a man, you are attempting to 'use' a god, an attempt which we agree is altogether the greater and more difficult of the two" (*Servants* 10.22).

Diogenes concludes that all oracles are deceptive, not because the god is deceitful but because human beings are incapable of understanding the god. The language of the gods is so different from the language of human beings that "it naturally follows that the oracles are obscure and have already deceived many men. . . . But how about you? Have you no fear lest, when the god says one thing you may understand another?" (*Servants* 10.23, 24). Diogenes recounts disaster after disaster brought on by such misunderstanding of oracles and supposed signs of divine guidance. Yet none of these is to be blamed on the gods. "Do not imagine that Apollo ever ordered those that consult him to commit any dreadful or disgraceful act. It is as I said: although men are incapable of 'using' the god, they go ahead, try, and then blame him and not themselves" (*Servants* 10.27).

The message of Diogenes? Learn to know yourself and you will be free from the constraint of needing oracles. No imagined command from a god will help anyone do something he or she is incapable of doing. Even the strength for upright living is found only within, not through endless divine consultation.

You will not be able to live properly either, if you do not know how, even though you importune Apollo day after day and he gives you all his time. But if you are possessed of intelligence, you will know of yourself what you ought to do and how to go about it. . . . Aim first to know thyself; afterwards, having found wisdom, you will then, if it be your pleasure, consult the oracle. For, I am persuaded that you will have no need of consulting oracles if you have intelligence. (*Servants* 10.28)

Fortuna/Tyche

In what was probably the office of the *agonotheteion*, the powerful director of the Isthmian games, a mosaic has been uncovered depicting a victor holding a palm branch, wearing a leafy victory crown, and giving thanks to Fortuna (Tyche), the goddess of good fortune, or as we might say today, "Lady Luck."[10] The role of Fortuna in Corinth deserves particular attention in relation to divine guidance because, after Neptune and Venus, the most frequent depiction on Corinthian coins is Fortuna, attesting to her popularity.[11]

Evidence for devotion to Fortuna comes particularly from some fragments of sculpture beginning in the first century CE.[12] What do these fragments reveal about the cult of Fortuna, especially in relation to divine guidance? In one of the sculptures she is shown with a wheel, her identifying feature during this period. In the earlier Greek period the wheel was associated with Nemesis, when it symbolized "the seemingly accidental turns from prosperity to disaster."[13] But in the Roman period "Nemesis and Tyche share cults and iconography,"[14] and the wheel's symbolism is transformed: it is no longer a sign of arbitrariness but the instrument by which good luck is overturned when the recipient is ungrateful. Punished above all is *hubris*, arrogant pride.[15] In other words, luck is not blind but is closely linked with the practice of virtue; conversely, reversals of fortune are likely to be the result of arrogance.

Other attributes of Fortuna are the cornucopia, symbolizing "her power to bestow prosperity," and the oar, "to guide the lives of men."[16] An oar resting on a globe indicates that she guides not simply individual human destinies but the destiny of the cosmos as well. She is seen as a "motivating force in the universe" and an "ethical judge."[17]

Later Tyche/Fortuna becomes associated with the goddess Isis and her providential care, further demonstrating that good fortune is not blind but is the gift of the goddess who guides and responds with timely assistance.[18] It should be noted also that the cult of Fortuna was not limited to temples but was a frequent presence in household shrines. (An example of a typical home statuette of Tyche with her steering oar is found in the British Museum, Figure 2.2.)[19]

By the first century BCE the cult of Fortuna was widespread in the Roman world, where it was one of the few forms of public religious devotion in which

Fig. 2.2. Bronze statue of Tyche (with Isis attributes) holding horns of plenty and steering oars. British Museum 1955,1215.1. Courtesy of the Trustees of the British Museum.

slaves were allowed to participate.[20] Writing around 77 CE, Pliny the Elder confirms—or rather laments—the dominance of Fortuna: "Everywhere in the whole world at every hour by all men's voices Fortuna alone is invoked and named, alone accused, alone impeached, alone pondered, alone applauded, alone rebuked and visited with reproaches" (*Natural History* 2.5.22). He goes on to say that she is "deemed volatile and indeed by most men blind as well, wayward, inconstant, uncertain, fickle in her favors and favoring the unworthy. To her is debited all that is spent and credited all that is received, she alone fills both pages in the whole of mortal's accounts; and we are so much at the mercy of Fortuna, that Fortuna herself, by whom God is proved uncertain, takes the place of God."

Pliny attests here that for many, Fortuna retained the arbitrariness of the blind Greek goddess Tyche, with good and bad fortune completely independent of human virtue and vice. Instead of taking responsibility for the decisions of their daily lives the vast majority of people run to the gods for direction. Pliny detests this. He also finds preposterous the idea that God is interested in the petty details of one's daily life:

> That the Supreme being, whatever it be, pays heed to man's affairs is a ridiculous notion. Can we believe that it would be defiled by so gloomy and multifarious a duty? Can we doubt it? It is scarcely pertinent to determine which is more profitable for the human race, when some men pay no regard to the gods at all and the regard paid by others is of shameful nature: they serve as the lackeys of foreign ritual, and they carry gods on their fingers. . . . They do not decide on marriage or having a family [whether to keep or expose newborns] or indeed anything else except by the command of sacrifices. (*Natural History* 2.5.20)

All of this, in Pliny's view, comes from pernicious foreign influences. Romans would be better off as atheists rather than following such superstitions. But his observations reflect the later first-century world already distancing itself from the values of Augustan Romans, who never regarded Fortuna as blind. Pliny still has the traditional Roman sense that the divine presence justly rewards and punishes according to human behavior.[21] As the noted historian William Fowler wrote early in the 20th century:

> There is nothing to suggest that the virile and persistent Roman ever believed himself or his state to be at the mercy of mere chance. I do not think that he ever thought of his deities of family or state as capricious; they were always open to supplication, and were practically bound to give way to if approached by precisely the right method. His *virtus*, his manly independence never suffered from any sense of a capricious or irresistible power controlling him and his. . . . The better minds of Rome kept clear of any degrading doctrine of capricious chance with its corollaries of individual selfishness and laissez-faire.[22]

Earlier in the first century, at the time of Paul's visit to Corinth, the older Roman attitude would have carried particular weight. By the end of the first century the wave of Hellenism left followers of Pliny's traditional Roman outlook distinctly in the minority.

The Fountain of Glauce

Another relic of the Greek past that Paul's Corinthians would have associated with divine guidance was the Fountain of Glauce, the mythical queen of Corinth and the wife of the heroic Jason, whose exploits with the Argonauts won him fame. The fountain was not very prominent in the mid-50s of the first century, since at that time it would have been isolated in a quarry still being used for city reconstruction. But because of its deep connections to Corinth, the myth of Glauce would have been well known. A hundred years later it still played a strong role in local identity and imagination—at least among tourist guides— and Pausanias devotes a good deal of space to recounting the Homeric story and its association with Corinth. At this fountain and at other sites a line of three early mythical Corinthian kings figure prominently: Jason, Sisyphus, and Bellerophon.

In the story, Jason abandoned his lover, the sorceress Medea, after he fell in love with Glauce. In revenge the scorned Medea sent her children with a "gift" for Glauce, a beautiful dress secretly permeated with a fatal potion, and when Glauce put it on, the dress burst into flames. In desperation she threw herself into the fountain "in the belief that the water would be a cure for the drugs of Medea" (Pausanias, *Description of Greece* 2.3.6). But the fountain was of no help, and Glauce burned to death in torment. To avenge the murder of their queen the Corinthians immediately turned on Medea's children and stoned them. The dead children, however, reached from beyond the grave to exact retribution by placing a curse on Corinthian children: "As their death was violent and illegal the young babies of the Corinthians were destroyed by them until, at the command of the oracle, yearly sacrifices were established in their honour and a figure of Terror was set up" (*Description of Greece* 2.3.7).

Pausanias attests that the annual custom of offering sacrifices in honor of Medea's children was a response to the oracle's guidance. But he also adds, "The new settlers broke the custom of offering those sacrifices to the sons of Medea, nor do their children cut their hair for them or wear black clothes" (*Description of Greece* 2.3.7). This once again shows how the Roman colonists could dismiss an ancient local Greek tradition.[23]

Sisyphus

Antipater of Sidon (second century BCE) refers to Corinth as the "town of Sisyphus" (*Greek Anthology*, Vol. III, Book 9.151). Strabo mentions the remains of a "Sisypheion" (he wasn't sure if it was a temple or palace) on Acrocorinth, the mountain behind Corinth (*Geography* 8.6.21).[24] Since Pausanias does not mention it, most likely it was not rebuilt by the colonists and would have been in ruins during Paul's time in Corinth. But Sisyphus was still being mentioned when Pausanias visited. He was told that Sisyphus was supposedly buried some-where on the Isthmus, but no one knew where (*Description of Greece* 2.2.2). He may have seen the ruined Sisypheion, or it may have already disappeared under new construction, but whether he did or not makes little difference: Corinth was associated in the public mind with the myth of Sisyphus.

Everyone who heard or read Homer knew Sisyphus from Odysseus's description of his punishment in Hades. He was condemned to perpetually push a huge boulder to the top of a hill, only to have it roll back down as he neared the summit. "He would strain again and thrust it back, and the sweat flowed down from his limbs, and dust rose up from his head" (*Odyssey* 11.600). But the well-known myth had a particular Corinthian twist, associated with the spring of Peirene on Acrocorinth. Pausanias was told that Asopus, whose daughter had been raped by an unknown assailant, built the spring behind the temple of Aphrodite. Sisyphus told Asopus he knew the perpetrator but had been sworn to secrecy. He then bargained with Asopus and said he would divulge the name if Asopus built the spring. Asopus agreed, and when the spring was finished, Sisyphus told him that the rapist was Zeus himself. "And it is because of this," writes Pausanias, "that Sisyphus is punished in Hades—if anyone believes the story" (*Description of Greece* 2.5.1.) Stories about encounters with the divine continued to hold the interest of the popular mind, though not always without skepticism.

Bellerophon

Sisyphus's son was Bellerophon, another famous mythic figure associated with divine intervention in Corinth. His story too must have been very much alive in the public imagination during Paul's time in the city since the figure of Bellerophon with Pegasus is one of the most frequently encountered depictions on Corinthian coins and statues. He also had a sacred precinct near the shrine of Aphrodite Melainis ("the Dark One") on Acrocorinth.[25] "Fair Anteia [the wife of Proteus] lusted madly for Bellerophon, but could in no wise persuade wise Bellerophon since his mind was upright" (*Iliad* 6.162). Anteia took revenge by falsely telling her husband that Bellerophon had tried to seduce her (not unlike Potiphar's wife accusing Joseph in Genesis 39). Enraged, Proteus arranges secretly to send Bellerophon to his death, but the young man is "under the incomparable escort of the gods and is thus protected from harm" (*Iliad* 6.165–170). Likewise, Bellerophon was able to slay the hideous chimera "in obedience to the portents of the god" (*Iliad* 6.180–185) since he had consulted a seer and trusted what he had been told, that only by capturing the winged horse Pegasus would he be able to accomplish this task. His piety is rewarded by Athena, who bridles Pegasus and gives him to Bellerophon. As Pausanias reports, "Athena, they say, was the divinity who gave most help to Bellerophon, and she delivered to him Pegasus, having herself broken and bridled him" (*Description of Greece* 2.4.2).

Thus Athena too had a large statue and important shrine in Corinth and was known from this incident as Athena Chalinitis, "the Bridler."

It was said that Pegasus had uncovered the spring of Peirene when he struck his hoof on a rock. Since this spring continued throughout the Hellenistic and Roman times to be a dependable and powerful source of water for the city, it may be that the Bellerophon story came to mind regularly in the course of daily life. But perhaps with a bitter twist, for even Bellerophon "in his turn came to be hated by all the gods" (*Iliad* 6.200).

Dionysus

Pausanias records the existence in Corinth of two wooden images of Dionysus that were carved in response to an oracle, "as the Corinthians say" (*Description of Greece* 2.2.7). A certain man named Pentheus had climbed a tree to spy on the local women as they performed their reputedly lascivious Dionysian rites. When the voyeur was discovered, the women tore him to pieces for "treating Dionysus despitefully" (*Description of Greece* 2.2.7). Pausanias goes on to say, "The Pythian priestess commanded [the citizens] by an oracle to discover the tree and to worship it equally with the god. For this reason they have made these images from the tree" (*Description of Greece* 2.2.7). Roman relief bowls from second-century Corinth depict this story,[26] but whether or not the images existed in St. Paul's day is uncertain. Nevertheless the story had probably long been part of the mythological air that Corinthians breathed.

Corinth and the Oracle at Delphi

Delphi, the most famous ancient oracle site, is nestled on the side of Mount Parnassus, almost opposite Corinth inland from the northern coast of the Gulf of Corinth (Figure 2.3). We have testimony from Herodotus, Plutarch, and Pausanias of four occasions in ancient times when Corinthians sent official embassies to consult the oracle at Delphi, all before 146 BCE, and there were probably many more unrecorded occasions as well.[27] But studies of the Delphic oracle have confirmed that there was a sharp decline in formal, public consultations during the Roman period. From the time that Rome took control of Delphi in 190 BCE until 10 CE, only a single public oracle is recorded. "For the end of Greek independence was virtually the end of the Pythian Apollo's influence in public life."[28]

As we know from Strabo, this was part of a general pattern among the Romans, who preferred their own traditional modes of discovering the divine

Fig. 2.3. Temple of Apollo, Delphi, Mount Parnassus. Courtesy of
HolyLandPhotos@comcast.net.

will: "Among the ancients both divination in general and oracles were held in
greater honor, but now great neglect of them prevails, since the Romans are
satisfied with the oracles of Sibylla, and with Tyrrhenian prophecies obtained
by means of the entrails of animals, flight of birds, and omens from the sky"
(*Geography* 17.1.43).[29]

The Romans had once upon a time consulted at Delphi, but had "little use
for it in their later history."[30] Augustus's wife Livia once donated a golden letter
E for the façade. (The meaning of the cryptic *E* at Delphi was debated in the
ancient world. Plutarch wrote an essay on the subject, which will be discussed
later in this book.) Augustus once dedicated a weapon there in absentia. But
this was minimal patronage indeed. So when Nero visited in 66/67 he was by
far the "most eminent visitor in many generations." Yet even his visit was a
mixed blessing: he removed 500 bronze statues from Delphi and took them
back to Rome![31] The imperial revival of Delphi had to wait for Hadrian some
50 years later when he was emperor (117–138 CE), accepted the position of ar-
chon of Delphi, and appointed Plutarch, then procurator of Achaia, as priest of
Delphi.

In the mid-first century L. Iunnius Gallio, brother of Seneca and the proconsul of Achaia during St. Paul's first visit to Corinth (Acts 18:12–17), was involved in a short-lived attempt by Claudius to revive Delphi, or at least bolster its

population. We have part of a letter that Claudius wrote in 52 CE which mentions Gallio, the decline of Delphi, and Claudius's plan to repopulate it:

> Tiberius Claudius Caesar Augustus Germanicus . . . sends greetings to. . . . For long have I been well-disposed to the city of Delphi and solicitous for its prosperity, and I have always observed the cult of the Pythian Apollo. Now since it is said to be destitute of citizens, as my friend and proconsul L. Iunnius Gallio recently reported to me, and desiring that Delphi should regain its former splendour, I command you to invite well-born people also from other cities to come to Delphi as new inhabitants, and to accord them and their children all the privileges of the Delphians as being citizens on like and equal terms.[32]

Gallio's report should not be taken as a sign of his special interest in Delphi as a religious center. He was motivated by a desire to please the emperor, who was known to favor Greek culture (Suetonius, *Lives of the Caesars: Claudius*, 42). "Delphi was the traditional centre of the culture that the emperor admired so extravagantly, and Gallio was astute enough to recognize that evidence of his concern for that city would place him in the good graces of Claudius."[33] But Claudius's interest in the Pythian Apollo may reflect not simply love of things Greek but the Roman appropriation of Apollo. Indeed, as noted earlier, the Pythian tripod was a familiar symbol of Roman divine election.

It is also true that "between Plato who died in 347 BCE and Plutarch, born around 46 AD, no writer whose words are now extant goes beyond the externals and the formalities to express, with any force or conviction, the old faith in Apollo."[34] In other words, Delphi at the time of Paul was "no longer a vital spiritual centre."[35]

The lack of official consultations at Delphi, however, should not be allowed to mask continuing personal interest in oracles in first-century Corinth. Not only were private seers, soothsayers, astrologers, and fortunetellers active—to the chagrin of Cicero, Seneca, Dio Chrysostom, and Plutarch—but also traditional oracle sites were still quietly in operation serving private needs. Claros, Didyma, and Delphi had lost their big processions, fanfare, and public standing, but a continuous flow of people still came to each of these sites in search of personal divine guidance.

Plutarch's descriptions of the oracle confirm that a relatively tranquil spiritual climate prevailed at the site, in contrast to sensational views of Delphi, which imagined ecstatic frenzies:

> Modern scholarship has largely discounted any sensational explanation of [the oracle's] prophetic state, temporary or recurrent. . . . Moreover, her utterances, however agitated, were by no means incoherent ravings. The unfounded notion

that they were, and the corollary that the priest or prophet in attendance could and did make whatever he pleased of them and pass the imposture off upon the enquirer as the god's own response, originated with rationalists of the 18th and 19th centuries, who were prejudiced against all priestcraft. Their misunderstanding of Delphi has entered many textbooks on Greek history and religion but ought to be dispelled at last.[36]

Household Piety

Two inscriptions from Corinth are dedications to the *genius* of Augustus: GENIO SANCTISSIMO AUGUSTI.[37] While these refer to the public imperial cult, devotion to family *genii*, equivalent to the Greek *daimones*, was widespread as part of Roman household religion:[38]

> Roman household shrines of the imperial period found at Pompeii typically have a wall painting of the family genius accompanied by a snake, the symbol of the Greek *agathos daimon* [good daimon] or guardian of the house. The fact that Corinth was a colony of mixed Greek and Latin blood, together with the fact that the Roman genius tended to be conceived more and more like the Greek daimon in imperial times would make the belief in such spirits likely to be common to every household. The household daimon/genius would be the recipient of daily offerings at a shrine in wealthier homes or simply at the hearth in poorer ones.[39]

Each house also had a couch, the *lectus genialis*, dedicated to the *genii* of the family placed in the atrium facing the door.

The typical arrangement of the household shrine also includes an incense burner with a lampstand, statuettes of the family *lares* (the departed ancestors), *penates* (the household guardians), and other favorite gods and goddesses. Popular choices were Fortuna, the Ephesian Artemis (the Asiatic fertility goddess, distinct from the Greek goddess of same name; see Acts 19:27), and Silvanus (the god of uncultivated land who protected flocks and trees, especially favored in Campania and by slaves—and presumably their descendant freedmen). Mercury/Hermes was also popular as the messenger of the gods and guide to the souls of the dead. Among the Romans, Vesta played the part the Greeks assigned to Hestia, goddess of the hearth. Diodorus writes, "It is said that Hestia invented the establishment of houses, and because of this blessing she has been among almost all peoples installed in every house, receiving her share of worship and sacrifices" (*Library of History* V.68.1).[40] It must be said, however, that these family rites are not as extensively documented as public religion, probably because "it was so common as to be taken for granted."[41]

It is in this area of the personal and familial that we are most likely to see continuities between the Greek and Roman citizens of Corinth. The forms of devotion and the names may have changed, but each family was closely tied to its family gods as signs of divine presence in daily life. Plato had said, "When a person honors and respects the family relationship and the whole community of his kindred gods [*homognioi theoi*] which shares the same descent and blood, he would, correspondingly, enjoy the favor of the familial gods [*genethloioi theoi*], who will be well disposed toward his own begetting of children" (*Laws* V.729c).[42]

Knowing that the family religion was a fundamental aspect of social organization adds weight to the imperial cult as a means of expressing a deeply felt loyalty that glued Romans together as a family and extended some of the benefits of the Roman *familia* to subject peoples in return for appropriate veneration. But side by side with social and institutional religion, the guardian deities in each home "kept alive the sense of a close relation of Man and God at the very roots of social life, day by day, through good fortune and ill."[43] Here we have yet another "point of contact between the human and the divine"[44] and further confirmation that for people of Paul's day "the divine was present everywhere."[45] The stories recounted here were omnipresent in the lives of Corinthians and most likely exerted a powerful force in shaping, consciously and unconsciously, the attitudes of the population toward divine intervention and guidance in daily life.[46]

The next chapters in this section consider some of the poets, philosophers, and historians whose works shed further light on attitudes toward divine guidance that Paul might have encountered in Corinth.

3

The Literature of Divine Guidance

Homer, Virgil, and Horace

The archeology of first-century Corinth attests abundantly to the common public perception that God—or gods, daimons, *genii*, or other spiritual agents, like the *lares* and *penates*—were everywhere present, acknowledged, and consulted. As noted earlier, the healing temple dedicated to Asklepios—in which divine direction through dreams figured prominently—was one of the first buildings to be reconstructed by the new colonists in 44 BCE. But what were the various attitudes toward this phenomenon among those who went to these temples or sought direction from the gods in household shrines? And what of those who did not share in these rituals apart from obligatory social and civic requirements? It is difficult enough to dig up the remains of a first-century temple or shrine and substantiate its rituals and patronage. It is even more difficult to uncover the *attitudes* of those who were present, let alone those who chose to stay away. As we have seen, the external forms of religious worship may remain stable while being infused with new and unexpected meaning. There is also the possibility that participants may have had a range of personal attitudes toward the cult, which may or may not have conformed to the doctrine implied in the practice. We know, for example, that Cicero was an active participant in divination. He was a member of the College of Augurs and took his responsibility seriously. But we also know that he did not believe a word of it. For him, augury was a long-standing tradition of the Roman people and valuable only as such. Faith in Rome and its ancient cohesive traditions won Cicero's allegiance to the College of Augurs. Belief was irrelevant.

However, unless Cicero had told us his views it would have been almost impossible to determine his attitude based on his outward performance of his augural duties. We don't know what people really believe about what they are doing unless they tell us. What attitudes lie behind the practices of divination? Fear? Tradition? Social pressure? Or genuine devotion and belief? To what extent do personal attitudes conform to the meaning implied by the words and actions of the cult? For the first century, these questions can be answered only by what people tell us in the literary sources.

Unfortunately, outside St. Paul's letters, we have almost no literary sources for first-century Corinth. For any other picture of attitudes that may have been circulating in Corinth at that time we have to look to writers elsewhere.

Divine Guidance. John A. Jillions, Oxford University Press (2020). © Oxford University Press.
DOI: 10.1093/oso/9780190055738.001.0001

Supported by the archeological evidence, we might expect that as a major Roman colony the cosmopolitan city of Corinth would reflect the mixture of attitudes throughout the empire while leaning more heavily toward the Roman side of the Greco-Roman mix.

Some of our sources are indirectly related to Corinth in the first century. Diogenes, as depicted by Dio Chrysostom and discussed in the previous chapter, spent his final years in Corinth and died there. Cicero passed through Corinth in the late 70s BCE. Strabo (64/63 BCE–c. 21 CE) visited not long after it was colonized. Seneca addressed several essays to his brother Gallio, who was proconsul of Achaia and based in Corinth during Paul's first stay.

Given the strong connection between Rome and Corinth, we might expect that Roman authors would play a major role in reflecting, if not shaping, attitudes among educated Corinthians. The works of Virgil and Horace, often revered and memorized, would have had an essential place, but many Corinthians may have been familiar too with the poets Propertius, Ovid, and Lucan, the historian Livy, and the philosopher Lucretius, as well as the works of Cicero and Seneca. Even if individual authors were unknown to Corinthians, it is not unreasonable to assume that they reflect attitudes generally in circulation. But if Roman writers were of increasing influence especially after Augustus, Greek literature and philosophy also continued to be major forces.

All of this literature, both Greek and Roman, was of course initially produced by and for the educated elite. But Homer—and eventually Virgil—came to have an influence far beyond this privileged circle as bearers of popular mythology rather than as literature narrowly defined. Their writing reflects the mythology already in circulation, and in turn reinforced the continuing spread of that mythology and its reinterpretations. The stories were told and retold for generations and became models for coins, art, and architecture, which, as we have seen, were the mass media of the ancient world. Thus the works of Homer and Virgil influenced and reflected the attitudes of a much wider segment of society than merely the literati of the Greco-Roman Empire. Indeed they came to play an almost scriptural role and were used in popular attempts to discern the divine will: opening the *Iliad* or the *Aeneid* at random to discover divine direction became a common practice.

Also, we should not underestimate the sophistication of those who were not part of the elite. Formal education was quite widespread, as attested by papyrus records unearthed at archeological sites. It was common for cities to have a library, as did Corinth. The library at Ephesus contained 10,000 volumes, clear indication of its mass appeal. It was also common for people to employ tutors for the education of the household, including slaves. Education, as a sign of status, was hotly pursued.[1] The first century—especially in Corinth—was an age of rhetoric, and the consumers of rhetoric were not merely the educated elite but those like the citizens of Corinth who elected their local magistrates and participated in one or more of the many popular religious, philosophical, and social organizations in which rhetorical style played a major role in leadership.

This attention to rhetoric can be seen in the Christian community of Paul's day. Although it included few of the elite (1 Cor 1:26), the appeal of well-spoken "superlative apostles" who apparently far exceeded Paul's abilities could have been a divisive issue only because there were enough people in the congregation who could appreciate (or be seduced by) polished oratory and the well-turned phrase (see 2 Cor 10:10). Paul himself was no amateur here. Much recent study of the Pauline epistles has focused on their rhetorical features.[2]

If rhetoricians made extensive use of Homer and Virgil, they also promulgated the religious Stoicism that was the common currency of thought and intellectual underpinning of divination. Other philosophical streams were also in circulation—Epicureanism, for example—which were skeptical toward the mystical or suprarational, but these were far less popular. However, philosophical attitudes are imprecise, and the nuances of the originals were often lost or even completely misrepresented by followers, so we can't be too dogmatic in defining the philosophical trends of St. Paul's day. The hedonists Nero and Petronius both counted themselves Epicureans, but their writings and actions had little in common with the sober philosophy of Epicurus and his intellectual descendant Lucretius.

This brings us to a further point that needs underlining. The Greco-Roman mind had a vast living memory. The prominent writers and philosophers of the past were seen as contemporaries. One might agree or disagree with them, but their thought was alive and to be reckoned with. This was an important factor in creating the mix of ideas and attitudes in the first century. Cicero, for example, in rejecting divination engages in debate with the ancient Greek Stoics Chrysippus and Cleanthes, as well as with his own teacher Posidonius, because all of them had many contemporary adherents. This makes it necessary to look not simply at writers who are nearly contemporary with St. Paul but also earlier writers whose views were still very much in circulation.

Not only were "old" ideas still vigorously alive, but older was normally considered better. Hence Jewish and later Christian writers—Philo and Clement of Alexandria, for instance—argued on this basis for the superiority of Moses over Plato. This was not exceptional, for "throughout Hellenistic historiography, the idea of antiquity implies superiority: once a culture has been demonstrated to be the most ancient, it has also been demonstrated to be the source of all others."[3] This was a common assumption in Jewish, Egyptian, and Greek thought. The authority of Homer, as the earliest Greek literature, was therefore the most thoroughly entrenched in the public mind.

What follows cannot be more than a brief survey of the range of attitudes toward divine guidance found in a selection of writers and philosophers most prominent in the first-century Greco-Roman world. There are numerous literary studies on all the authors cited, as well as specialized studies on their religious views. But what is of interest here is the forest of attitudes on divine guidance that may have been circulating in a city like Corinth in the mid-first century.

Finally, the literary evidence demands as much caution in its use as the archeological evidence. The mere fact that in the first century CE a temple is dedicated to Venus or a reference made to Homer does not *necessarily* mean that Venus or Homer is being understood in precisely the same way as eight centuries earlier. The previous chapter demonstrated just how thoroughly the Roman Revolution reshaped the meaning of Greek monuments both archeological and literary. The religious and mythical images may have been long familiar, but they were systematically given new meaning. Through the Roman imperial cult they acquired a new immediacy that transcended their original meaning and gave them a new and dominant persona in the first century. So while we know that Homer's stories had been familiar for 800 years, we need to ask how they might have been heard anew in first-century Corinth.

Homer's *Iliad*

Homer's *Iliad* is the obvious place to begin exploring the literary evidence for attitudes toward divine guidance. Composed around the eighth century BCE, the *Iliad* is the earliest extant example of Greek literature and had enormous influence. Its frequent citation by later authors, its central place in classical education, and the honor that continued to be accorded it point to Homer's importance in molding the Greco-Roman worldview. Dio Chrysostom regards Homer as "a poet without peer" (*Homer and Socrates, Discourses* 55.6).[4] Plutarch calls Homer simply "the poet" (Table Talk 4, *Moralia*, Volume 8 667 F). Throughout the literary world of the first century Homer was the basic source of illustrations for all aspects of poetry, grammar, and rhetoric.[5]

To give an example of the influence Homer had in ancient Corinth itself, one can cite the story Plutarch tells about a boy captured in Mummius's sacking of the city in 146 BCE: "Best of all was the young Corinthian prisoner of war, when his city was destroyed, and Mummius was reviewing such freeborn boys as could read and write, ordered him to write down a line of verse, he wrote 'O thrice and four times happy Greeks who perished then' [Homer, *Odyssey* 5:306]. It is said that Mummius was affected to the point of tears and let all the boy's relations go free" (*Table-Talk 9, Moralia* Volume 9 737 A).

Plutarch recounts the incident with obvious delight. For all his Roman sympathy, as a Greek he could identify with the conquered people of Corinth (*Table-
Talk 9, Moralia* Volume 9 737 A).[6] The fact that this boy could cite these lines
appropriately is not fortuitous: memorizing Homer was basic to classical education.[7] As Bruce Winter has shown, Jews of the diaspora could also cite passages
of Homer naturally and approvingly. Philo, for example, says that "Homer [is]
the greatest and most reputed of poets" and that "[the Jews] give the title of
'the poet' to Homer in virtue of his pre-eminence." He has 20 direct quotations
from Homer, including a citation of chapter and verse from memory (*On the
Confusion of Tongues* 4, *On the Life of Abraham* 10).[8]

All of this clearly demonstrates the continuing influence of Homer before,
during, and after St. Paul's era.

From the very opening lines of the *Iliad* the pervasive presence of divine interaction with the characters is thrust upon the reader. The story begins 10 years
into the Greek siege of Troy, with King Agamemnon dishonoring the priest of
Apollo, Chryses, by capturing his beautiful daughter Chryseis and taking her
as his booty. The god takes revenge by sending a plague and inflaming the enmity between Agamemnon and the irreplaceable but arrogant war hero Achilles.
Immediately we are thrown into a world in which the gods are actively present
and in which divine guidance is always sought in decision-making.

Decisions are made through inspired thoughts sent by the gods. Whatever
happens, good or bad, is seen as sent by the gods. Thus when Achilles calls the
people together to consider their position after being defeated by the Trojans,
his first task is to determine the *divine* cause of their defeat. Even this act of
calling the assembly is the result not of careful deliberation or consultation but of
thoughts he perceived as divine guidance, "for in his mind did the goddess Hera
of the white arms put the thought, because she had pity on the Danaans [Greeks]
when she beheld them perishing" (*Iliad* I.55ff.).

Having assembled the people, and before planning any further action, Achilles
first urges them to consult someone who can discern the divine signs sent for
their direction: "But come, let us now inquire of some soothsayer or priest, yea,
or an interpreter of dreams—seeing that a dream too is of Zeus—who shall say
why Phoebus Apollo is so angry, whether he blame us by reason of some unper-
formed vow or sacrifice; if perchance he would accept the savour of lambs or
unblemished goats, and so would take away the pestilence from us" (*Iliad* I.60ff.).
Achilles assumes that defeat means the gods are in some way displeased, perhaps
because some vow or sacrifice has been left undone. He wants to remedy the situation but is unsure what to do until he can read the signs being sent. The augur
Kalchas then stands up to speak, since he knew "both things that were and that
should be and that had been before, and guided the ships of the Achaians to Ilion
[Troy] by his soothsaying that Phoebus Apollo bestowed on him" (*Iliad* I.69 ff.).

The ability to read the signs sent by the gods comes from Apollo, but this gift is not for all. Moreover those who claim the gift are to be tested by the results. So Kalchas can be called a "blameless seer" (*Iliad* I.92) only because he had been proven right in the past.

Homer then introduces a note of ambivalence into this clear picture of divine guidance. He begins to question attempts to mediate and interpret the divine presence, especially when the message is unpleasant. At the behest of Achilles, Kalchas urges Agamemnon to make peace with Apollo by making amends to Chryses, the offended Trojan priest, by returning his captured daughter, Chryseis. But Agamemnon is furious at this suggestion since he not only wanted to keep the woman as his own prize of battle but had fallen in love with her. "Yea, I prefer her before Clytemnestra my wedded wife" (*Iliad* I.113). So he turns on Kalchas and his gloomy prophesying: "Thou seer of evil, never yet hast thou told me the thing that is pleasant. Evil is ever the joy of thy heart to prophesy, but never yet didst thou tell any good matter nor bring it to pass" (*Iliad* I. 105ff.).

Nevertheless, for the good of his people King Agamemnon yields to Kalchas and to the assembly and agrees to give up the priest's daughter, for "rather would I see my folk whole than perishing" (*Iliad* I.117). But he also decides that he will no longer bother with Kalchas or any other doomsday prophet. He himself, without any intermediary, can listen just as well to the counsels of Zeus and find a happier message: "I have others by my side that shall do me honour, and above all Zeus, lord of counsel" (*Iliad* I.174–175). He now takes his own thoughts to be divinely inspired, and those thoughts tell him to avenge his loss of the beautiful Chryseis. So he demands that Achilles, who had instigated and supported Kalchas, hand over to Agamemnon *his* beloved captive bride, Briseis. The battle over individual interpretations of divine guidance is now set in motion.

Achilles gives in, but is broken-hearted, angry, and torn between a passion to kill Agamemnon and to restrain himself for the sake of the nation. After a period of indecision, Achilles feels divine sanction from the goddesses Hera and Athena to take action: "When grief came upon Peleus' son [Achilles], and his heart within his shaggy breast was divided in counsel, whether to draw his keen blade from his thigh and set the company aside and so slay Atreides [Agamemnon], or to assuage his anger and curb his soul . . . while yet he doubted thereof in heart and soul . . . Athena came to him from heaven, sent forth of the white-armed goddess Hera, whose heart loved both alike and had care for them" (*Iliad* I.188ff.). Achilles is tempted to attack Agamemnon, but Athena tells him to put away his sword and channel his anger through words instead: "With words indeed do thou taunt him" (*Iliad* I.211). Achilles answers, "Goddess, a man must observe the saying of you both, even though he be very angry in heart; for so is the better way. Whosoever obeys the gods, to him they gladly hearken" (*Iliad* I.216ff.). Note especially that while it is the goddess's direction that moves Achilles to a concrete decision, her intervention is not capricious but proceeds from genuine care for the two heroes. However, standing high above the intrigues of individual gods and goddesses is the overarching will of Zeus, who long ago determined that Agamemnon and Achilles would never make peace: "The counsel of Zeus wrought out its accomplishment from the day when first strife parted Atreides king of men and noble Achilles" (*Iliad* I.5–6).

From the very beginning Homer throws up questions about the potential for deception in divine guidance. King Agamemnon, though not lightly superstitious, trusts Zeus for guidance. And because Agamemnon is considered by the rest of the company to be especially sober in this regard, his decision to follow his personal guidance from Zeus and attack Troy is made all the more tragic, because Zeus deliberately deceives him. Zeus sends a "baneful Dream" (*Iliad* II.8) urging Agamemnon to order an assault and giving him false hope that he will capture the city that day: "For in truth he deemed that he should take the city of Priam [Troy] that very day, fool that he was, in that he knew not the plans that Zeus had in mind, who was willed to bring yet more grief and wailing on Trojans alike and Greeks throughout the course of the stubborn fights. Then woke he from sleep and the heavenly voice was in his ears" (*Iliad* II.37ff.).

Agamemnon shares his dream with the other leading warriors, including Nestor, king of Pylos, who, in spite of his usual caution about dreams and soothsaying, urges the rest of the company to accept the divine direction of Agamemnon's dream precisely because of Agamemnon's self-confidence: "My friends, captains and rulers of the Argives, had any other of the Achaians told us this dream we might deem it a false thing, and rather turn away from it; but now he has seen it who of all Achaians avows himself far greatest" (*Iliad* II.79ff.). Agamemnon is insistent that he knows the divine will. His infectious self-confidence in his ability to understand Zeus sweeps everyone else along and persuades them that he has indeed rightly discerned the mind of the god. Zeus's deception finds a willing partner in Agamemnon's pride; hubris thus becomes the cause of Agamemnon's defeat.

It must be repeated that this is not the place for a complete treatment of divine guidance in Homer. The purpose here is to simply show the theme's centrality. Even from this brief opening scene of the *Iliad* it should be apparent that divine guidance is at center stage and that Homer is provoking a host of questions: Are the "specialists"—the seers, augurs, and soothsayers –to be trusted? How is true divine guidance to be discerned from false? How is one to deal with competing claims to divine guidance? What is the role of the community in discerning the meaning of divine guidance? Do the gods deliberately deceive in order to accomplish their own purposes? Are dreams to be trusted as channels of divine guidance? Is the divine purpose ultimately one that cares for the human race or not? How confident can we be that we know the mind of God? But among all these questions there is one unquestioned assumption: the gods are intimately involved in human affairs and can make their interests known, whatever the ambiguities of that process.

Homer in the First Century

Returning now to the first century CE, we have to ask whether Homer's outlook of the eighth century BCE finds a home in St. Paul's Corinth. Through what filter of interpretation might a reader or listener have heard Homer in the first century? There is no doubt that there was a process of reinterpretation at work. It is very likely that the increasing influence of philosophical monotheism had a powerful impact on the rereading of Homer and all classical mythology. This process had been going on at least since Xenophanes of Colophon attacked Homeric theology in the late sixth or early fifth century BCE. "In ruthless criticism of Homer and Hesiod, [Xenophanes] denies that the gods resemble men in conduct, shape or understanding; there is a single, eternal self-sufficient Consciousness, which, without stirring, sways the universe through thought."[9] Others accepted the poetry and myths as metaphors, seeing them as expressing in poetic and story form deep truths about human beings and the universe they inhabit, governed by a single divine being equated with providence or fate. Following this line of thinking in the first century CE, Plutarch, for example, holds the commonplace Greco-Roman view that the many names for God merely correspond to different peoples and different divine powers, but that there is only *one* providence "which watches over them" (*Isis and Osiris*, 378).[10]

Philosophical monotheism became dominant in Hellenistic and first-century Greece and Asia Minor. Irina Levinskaya notes that "anonymous divinities with vague titles *osios* [venerable], *dikaios* [righteous] became widespread, which shows that an innovative movement in popular religion towards a less anthropomorphic and more abstract conception of the deity was in progress."[11]

Levinskaya stresses an important point: the trend to monotheism should not be misunderstood as excluding all other spiritual forces. Other gods, goddesses, daimons, and heroes were often understood to function as lesser spiritual beings or as the personifications of unseen forces ultimately attributed to one omnipotent and providential deity, such as Zeus. As the historian Fowler summarized early in the 20th century, "There was a tendency at once syncretistic and monotheistic, the old tendency to focus the manifestations of the Power at one point, and so to bring all its force to bear on the matter of interest to the worshipper."[12]

This trend toward reinterpretation into a monotheistic framework means that it is a mistake to give a literalist—and polytheistic— reading to all first-century references to the gods and goddesses of classical mythology.[13] The *New York*

Times columnist Nicholas Kristof made this error in a 2017 Christmas interview of Cardinal Tobin of Newark, arguing that denizens of the first century were much more credulous than sophisticated 21st-century folks: "Merry Christmas! Let me start with respectful skepticism. I revere Jesus' teachings, but I have trouble with the miracles—including, since this is Christmas, the virgin birth. In Jesus' time people believed that Athena was born from Zeus' head, so it seemed natural to accept a great man walking on water or multiplying loaves and fishes; in 2017, not so much. Can't we take the Sermon on the Mount but leave the supernatural?"[14] Many, if not most, in Paul's Greco-Roman world would have recoiled at a literal interpretation of the ancient myths without giving up on the mystical and miraculous. Although literalism and superstition persisted, it was precisely such misreading of God's true nature that impelled Cicero, Seneca, and Plutarch to rescue what they regarded as authentic piety from the clutches of superstition. But in this project of demythologizing, Plutarch—and other philosophers to a lesser degree—was especially concerned to not jettison all suprarational, miraculous, mystical experience and intuition. He believed that the rational and the mystical could be held together in balance. Indeed such a balance represented human wholeness, the human being connected to the universe seen and unseen.

Others, however, had little interest in Homer's theology, whatever interpretation might be given. Pausanias, for instance, had great affection for Homer out of interest in antiquity, literature, and religious history, but Homer's theological questions and nuances held very little interest for him personally. He had wanted to devote his life to Homeric scholarship, but circumstances forced him instead to become a physician and earn a living. So while his travelog has often been criticized for overemphasizing ancient religious sites and sometimes ignoring places of contemporary interest, this may have sprung less from personal piety than from his love of Homer and ancient mythology. He was interested precisely in the *ancient* sites and not the contemporary meaning of religion. In fact he gives only a few hints as to his own religious outlook. It's true that on several occasions Pausanias refuses to divulge religious secrets (Dionysian rites in Argos, the meaning of a statue at the temple of Hera in Mycenae; *Description of Greece* 2.7.5, 6), but this may have less to do with piety than with fear of reprisals from devotees.

Much more frequent are Pausanias's notes of skepticism as he reports the alleged mythical background of places, monuments, and events in his travelog: "so they say" and "if anyone believes the story" are regular refrains (e.g., *Description of Greece* 2.6.3, 7). Sometimes he blatantly contradicts the pious version of a received story. For example, of the town of Titane he writes, "The natives say that Titan . . . was the brother of Helios, and that after him the place got the name Titane. My own view is that he proved clever at observing the seasons of the year and the times when the sun increases and ripens the seeds and fruits, and for this reason was held to be the brother of Helios" (*Description of Greece* 2.24.1).

Generally he shows a surprising lack of warmth in his descriptions of things religious. This is quite in contrast to Plutarch, or to Homer himself. Underneath Pausanias's apparent coolness there is some anger toward God. In a rare burst of feeling, Pausanias laments the fate meted out to his two heroes, Homer and Demosthenes. The first ended his life as a blind beggar; the second suffered exile and violent death in old age. Their fates "have in my opinion, shown most plainly how spiteful the deity is" (*Description of Greece*, 2.33.3). Pausanias is admittedly a late source for this study, writing in the mid-second century, but he demonstrates that later generations could use Homer's work happily while not at all sharing in the religious or spiritual aspects of his worldview.

While being open to the possibility of new first-century interpretations of Homer's theology, we also need to ask what in Homer's view of divine guidance would still have been familiar and provoked a response of spiritual recognition. Surely one answer has to be the very assumption of divine presence and guidance so pervasively and vividly depicted in Homer: "The Homeric poems convey a sense of the relatively easy intimacy between gods and men—at least the men of heroic stature who dominate the *Iliad* and the *Odyssey*."[15] This would account for the continued hallowed use of Homer as a kind of sacred scripture in the Greco-Roman world. In this there is an impressive continuity over eight centuries. Religious skeptics like Pausanias were exceptions. Homer's conviction that God and other spiritual forces were present and active in the world remained essentially unchanged for the vast majority of people. God, or gods, or other forces—spirits, angels, daimons (evil, good, or both)—were continuously present and active and guiding (or misguiding) human beings. Few people questioned that the gods and their spiritual agents or adversaries were addressing them, observing them, influencing them, seeking their attention, their gratitude, and their offerings.

This popular view of divine presence was so pervasive that it was satirized famously in the *Satyricon* by the Roman courtier Petronius (27–66) during the reign of Nero: "The gods walk abroad so commonly in our streets that it is easier to meet a god than a man" (*Satyricon* 17). The question for most people was not about the *existence* of such forces but what one made of their existence and presence. How do I—although perhaps more often it was "we"—understand the signs sent by God or the gods? What is in store for me, my family, my country? Or if I have no sign, how do I induce Him, Her, or Them to give a sign that guides me in the decisions and dangers I face at home and in public life? These were the questions that drove people in all walks of life to their preferred form of divine guidance. First-century readers of the *Iliad* would recognize the story as ancient history, and they might reinterpret its theology in monotheistic terms, but for most of them Homer's understanding of divine presence and guidance was theirs as well.

Virgil

The *Aeneid* of Virgil (Publius Vergilius Maro, 70–19 BCE) became for Romans what Homer's writing was for Greeks: a sacred text and a pillar of education that was used to reinforce Roman identity and superiority. Virgil wrote his epic poem between 29 and 19 BCE (at the height of Augustus's power and the beginning of the Pax Romana) to trace the story of Aeneas, the mythical Trojan hero who settled in Italy and became the ancestor of the Romans, who saw themselves as displacing the Greeks as masters of the world stage. One of the earliest surviving fragments of Virgil, a piece of papyrus probably part of a student's copybook from first-century Egypt and now in the British Museum, repeats seven times a single line of this Trojan-Roman sentiment: "Non tibi Tyndaridis facies invisa Lacanae" (It is not the hated face of Spartan Helen; *Aeneid* 2.601).[16] Such was the *Aeneid*'s influence in the Roman Empire that it eventually displaced the *Iliad* as the sacred text of choice in looking at random passages for purposes of divining God's will.[17]

Virgil shares much of Homer's worldview on divine guidance. The *Aeneid* is replete with people who hear and respond to the gods. Knowing full well that his audience would be thoroughly familiar with "the Etruscan art" (divination), he can naturally refer in passing to an Etruscan who was "a medium between mankind and the gods, a master of divining from the entrails of sacrificed beasts, the stars in the sky, the songs of birds, the presage of lightning" (*Aeneid* 10.175–177).

One of the best examples of divine guidance in the epic is Aeneas's encounter with the Sybil of Apollo at the famous oracle site at Cumae, the Greek colony in Italy near Naples. ("Sibyl" derives from the Greek *sibylla*, meaning "prophetess.") Here Aeneas prays to Apollo to take away his ill luck and give him the kingdom promised long ago. (Apollo is addressed here by his forename, Phoebus— "bright," "pure"—which links him to the Titan Phoebe, his grandmother):

> Oh Phoebus . . . you were the guide I followed into so many seas, lapping
> great lands. . . .
> Let Troy's ill luck which has dogged us so far, follow no further. . . .
> And O most holy Sybil, foreseer of future things . . . grant—but I ask for
> the kingdom owed by my destiny—grant that we Trojans may settle in
> Latium, we and our wandering gods, the hard driven deities of Troy"
> (*Aeneid* 6.1).

Notice that Aeneas affirms that in all his exploits he followed the god's direction and now promises that when his kingdom is established, Apollo and the Sybil will be given special prominence.

Then I will found a temple of solid marble to Phoebus at Troy,
    appointing festival days in Phoebus' honour.
You too shall have your holy place in the realm to be,
Where I shall deposit the oracles, the mystic runes you utter

For my own people, ordaining a priesthood to your service, O gracious one.
(*Aeneid* 6:49ff.)

As we have seen, Rome under Augustus was virtually identified with Apollo and the fulfillment of prophecy: the oracle's incense tripod was one of Augustus's most widely used symbols. Augustus built a temple to Apollo on the Palatine Hill in the center of Rome to house the Sibylline books, which were to be consulted in times of national crisis by a special board of 15 priests. These books (not to be confused with the later Jewish or Christian Sibylline oracles) were a collection of ancient prophecies. According to Roman tradition, the Sibyl of Cumae had offered them for sale to the last king of Rome, Tarquinius Superbus, or Tarquin the Proud (died 495 BCE), before the establishment of the Roman Republic. The story goes that the Sibyl offered to sell the nine books to Tarquin but at what he regarded as an exorbitant price, so he refused. She then burned three of them and offered the remaining six at the same price. Once again he refused, whereupon she burned three more and offered the last three to him at the original price. Tarquin finally gave in, paid the full price, and had the books placed under guard in the temple of Jupiter on the Capitoline Hill in Rome.

It is against this background of the Augustan renewal and fulfillment of prophecy that Virgil's popularity must be understood. Through Aeneas Virgil gave Rome a mythical history of its own that builds upon Homer's mythical history of the Greeks. Aeneas was "the only one of the heroes who linked the mythology of Greece with the one great myth produced and valued by the Romans: the myth of Rome herself."[18] Rome's history moves in its divinely inspired destiny toward the golden age of Augustus and the Pax Romana. The *Aeneid* is thus a sort of New Testament to Homer's Old Testament, which pointed to a divine plan fulfilled in the founding of Rome. "For a Roman it was Rome which served as the focus for the reverence and interest which Greeks gave to their various myths and the relations which they revealed of humanity and the gods."[19]

Through Virgil, Homer is reread in the light of Rome's fulfillment of divine history. Augustus is "another Aeneas, another god-sent deliverer," who "establishes a reign of peace after decades of violence, immorality, confusion and despair."[20] The mythical power of Aeneas's story is transferred entirely to Augustus, who claimed descent from Aeneas and his mother, the goddess Aphrodite (Venus). As noted earlier, Augustus stressed his important divine-human family connections;

his Julian line came from the nobility of Alba Longa, a city older than Rome and traditionally founded by Iulus, the son of Aeneas.

Yet if the *Aeneid* had been merely a transparent piece of political propaganda it is unlikely that it would have endured and exerted the influence it did. Like Homer, Virgil suffuses his story with all the ambiguities of human and divine reality that make for profound literature. Virgil is fully aware of how slippery divine guidance can be. He is aware of the difficulties of knowing God's will and of accepting suffering and violence as part of that will. "Jupiter," he asks, "was it your will that nations destined to live in peace for ever, should clash so bitterly?" (*Aeneid* 12.508). Virgil knows that divination has built-in potential for deception. Thus he borrows Homer's image of the two portals of Hades, each exuding an inspiring vapor, one "an outlet for genuine apparitions," the other "for false dreams that impose upon us" (*Aeneid* 6.894, 896; compare *Odyssey* 19.562ff.).

Yet for all the ambiguity of divine guidance in Virgil as in Homer, we have the unquestioned assumption that the gods are intimately connected with the decisions and outcomes of history. This is no simplistic theodicy of good fortune, in which good comes to those who do good things, and bad to those who do bad things. On the contrary, Virgil emphasizes Aeneas's suffering and gives that suffering a saving role that makes possible the future glory of Rome.

A "tough love" form of divine guidance figures prominently in the *Aeneid*. The gods' direction is no gift of privileged information to smooth the way, but rather an opportunity for the hero to accept rigorous training and testing. For instance, Aeneas is ordered by the gods to leave the battlefront at Troy, to temporarily bracket his natural talents in order to serve a deeper, long-term purpose. But he instead wants to display his courage and support his compatriots, so he disobeys the gods and rushes off to fight. Only after repeated divine instructions, signs, and failures does he overcome his natural impulsiveness and learn to submit his will to the gods. As the Oxford scholar Jasper Griffin says, this makes Aeneas even more heroic than Achilles: "To the spontaneous courage and élan of the old-style hero is added the painful and onerous obligation to subject his will— even in his heroism—to the will of the gods."[21] This is hard for Aeneas to learn and harder to bear; hardest of all when, in obedience to the divine command, he must leave his broken-hearted lover, Dido. He explains his actions when he encounters her in the underworld:

> It was not of my own will, Dido I left your land.
> Heaven's commands, which now force me to traverse the shades,
> This sour and derelict region, this pit of darkness,
> Drove me imperiously from your side. (*Aeneid* 6.450ff.)

Aeneas is chosen by the gods to be the pivotal figure who will set in motion the great and glorious future history of Rome by uniting Troy and Italy: "From this blend of Italian and Trojan blood shall rise a people surpassing all men, nay, even the gods in godliness" (*Aeneid* 12.839). The ghost of his father, Anchises, prophesies Troy's revenge in the later Roman triumph over the great Greek cities, including Corinth:

> That one shall ride in triumph to the lofty Capitol,
> The conqueror of Corinth, renowned for the Greeks he has slain.
> That one shall wipe out Argos and Agamemnon's Mycenae,
> Destroying the heir of Aecus, the seed of warrior Achilles,
> Avenging his Trojan sires and the sacrilege done to Minerva. (*Aeneid*
>   6.836–840)

The fact that Aeneas is chosen by the gods and willingly embraces his vocation does not exempt him from suffering. On the contrary, the demands of his vocation *increase* his suffering. There is no reward for Aeneas, and he never sees the founding of the great city (not unlike the Jewish hero Moses, whom God did not permit to enter the Promised Land). More significant, Virgil ends the *Aeneid* with a note of tragic ambiguity about the hero's character as Aeneas takes vicious revenge on his fallen enemy. This is even worse than Homer's concluding portrayal of a grudging Achilles who finally gives way to the pitiful plea of the elderly Trojan king Priam begging for the dishonored corpse of his son Hector. Virgil leaves Aeneas with not even this shred of victor's dignity, and the hero is left imperfect and ugly. This underlines Virgil's central message about the interaction between the gods and Aeneas. In the *Aeneid* divine guidance is meant to fulfill the gods' purpose, not to vindicate Aeneas or make him happy. Indeed throughout the story, as Griffin points out, "Heaven makes it very clear that the happiness of Aeneas is not its concern."[22]

Horace

Alongside the works of Homer and Virgil, the poems of Horace (Quintus Horatius Flaccus, 65–8 BCE) also became favored texts—though less nearly sacred texts—in the conservative world shaped by Augustus, the Roman Revolution, and the Pax Romana.

In his younger days Horace himself was frustrated by this Roman taste for the old and traditional. He much preferred the Greek delight in creativity:

> If poems like wine improve with age, would somebody tell me
>   how old a page has to be before it acquires value?

> Take a writer who sank to his grave a century back—
> where should he be assigned? To the unapproachable classics
> or the worthless moderns?
> Suppose the Greeks had resented newness as much as we do,
> what would now be old? And what would the people have
> to read and thumb with enjoyment, each man to his taste?
>   (*Epistles* 2.1.34–38, 90–93)[23]

Horace may have seen himself as an innovator, but in religious terms he reflects the widely held religious Stoicism of the day (e.g., *Odes* 2.10, 2.11, 2.16, 3.2). Yet his philosophy does not share the entire outlook of Virgil and Homer on divine guidance. Horace accepts the presence and activity of the gods, but this is a much less pervasive theme for him, and his depiction of life is more independent of the gods. And he more persistently questions whether the gods actually care for human life: "Why make prayers to inattentive Jove?" (*Epode* 10.16); "Why pour your prayers into ears that are shut?" (*Epode* 17:52). He is all to aware of human suffering at the hands of divine arbitrariness: "Alas, how often he will weep at . . . the God's vacillations." (*Odes* 1.5.6).

In spite of his doubts, Horace's poetry often flows with a tone of genuine *pietas*. Consider this prayer to Mercury, for example:

> You bring in the dutiful souls
> to the mansions of joy, direct the tenuous throng
> with your golden wand, welcome alike to Gods
> above, below. (*Odes* 1.10.18–20)

Horace was the leading hymnographer of the imperial cult. In the following tribute he depicts Augustus as the divine incarnation sent by Jupiter to live among the Romans. He is revealed as their ever-present leader and the world's savior:

> To whom shall Jupiter assign the role
> of atonement? Come at length, we pray,
> prophetic Apollo, swathing in cloud your bright shoulder . . .
> be pleased to live among the Romans: and though
> our sins offend you, may no wind carry you away
> betimes: here rather may you enjoy great
> triumphs and the names of Father and Foremost
> nor tolerate Parthian raids while you are
> our Leader, Caesar. (*Odes* 1.2.29–51; see also *Centennial Hymn* 1.12)

Horace views his writing of poetry as the creative fruit of divine inspiration that emerges out of silence:

> I shun and keep removed the uninitiate crowd.
> I require silence: I am the Muses' priest
> and sing for virgins and boys
> songs never heard before. (*Odes* 3.1.1–7)

In an earlier verse Horace says, "The Muse has commanded me to speak" (*Odes* 2.12.12). Are these just formal nods to literary convention? Probably not, since elsewhere Horace admits to repenting of his earlier neglect of piety and his "ignorant wisdom." He says that he came to recognize God's supremacy and so returned to a life of genuine worship:

> A parsimonious and infrequent worshipper
> of the Gods, adept of an ignorant
> wisdom, I had gone astray, but now
> have gone about, am forced to resume
> the course I abandoned. . . .
> The God has the power
> to invert our zenith and nadir, raising obscurity,
> lessening fame: rapacious Fortune
> with shrill susurration removes his crown
> from one, yet gladly grants it to another. (*Odes* 1.34)

Horace considered divination's preoccupation with the future a distraction since human beings should be fully engaged with the present world. Divination is also a distraction from genuine *pietas* and devotion to God. In the following excerpts he reacts against "Babylonian calculations" and urges his friends to live in the present and be grateful. They should accept all that comes to them with equanimity, avoiding vain speculation and entrusting their unknown future to the care of the gods:

> Commit all else to the Gods . . .
> Avoid speculation
> about the future: count as credit the days
> chance deals; youth should not spurn
> the dance or sweet desire. (*Odes* 1.9.9–15)

> Do not inquire, we may not know, what end
> the Gods will give, Leuconoe, do not attempt

Babylonian calculations. The better course
is to bear whatever will be. . . .
Be wise, decant the wine, prune back
your long-term hopes. Life ebbs as I speak:
so seize each day, and grant the next no credit. (*Odes* 1.11)[24]

The soul content with the present
is not concerned with the future and tempers
dismay with an easy laugh. No
blessing is unmixed. (*Odes* 2.16.2–27)

Horace advocates the balanced, middle way of the sober Roman:

The proper course in life, Licinius,
is neither always to dare the deep, nor,
timidly chary of storms, to hug
the dangerous shore.

Who values most the middle way
avoids discreetly both the squalor
of the slum and a palace liable
to excite envy. (*Odes* 2.10.1–8)

His most famous poem, the *Centennial Hymn* commissioned by Augustus and written in praise of the Pax Romana, which was celebrated in 17 BCE, reflects his personal view of divine guidance and gives a clear picture of the official Roman attitude toward the divine. We see the pious, measured recognition of the Pax Romana as the fulfillment of the divine plan. Horace conveys the weight of responsibility imposed by Rome's divine election. Rome has been freed from wars and is full of rich harvests and fertile fields; civil strife is over; decency and propriety have returned. Thus delivered from violence and the fear of invaders, Romans are now free to order their lives as a wholesome family gathered under the gentle hand of an appropriate but not excessive piety that at all times, "on festal and working days," attends to its gods and divine heroes. Everything here is an image of tranquility and restraint, which is just how Augustus wanted it to appear.

And we, on festal and working days,
amid the gifts of cheerful Bacchus,
our wives and children about us,
having prayed to the Gods in due form,

> shall like our forefathers sing
> (to Lydian pipes) to heroes who died well,
> and Troy, and Anchises, and all
> the progeny of kindly Venus. (*Odes* 4.15.25–32)

Later, Christians also saw the peace and unity of the Roman Empire inaugurated by the Augustan Age as providential, though of course in very different terms than Horace expressed, and with Jesus now as savior of the world rather than Augustus. But they were not slow to pick up on the analogy that Augustus and the Pax Romana provided, as seen in this Byzantine hymn for the eve of Christmas, which is still sung in Orthodox Churches:

> When Augustus ruled alone upon the earth,
> the many kingdoms of men came to an end,
> and when You were made man of the pure virgin,
> the many gods of idolatry were destroyed.
> The cities of the world passed under one single rule,
> and the nations came to believe in one sovereign Godhead.
> The peoples were enrolled by the decree of Caesar,
> and we the faithful were enrolled in the name of the Godhead,
> when You, our God, were made man.
> Great is Your mercy, O Lord! Glory to You!

4

Other Roman Writers

Propertius, Ovid, Livy, Lucan, and Petronius

Having considered the attitudes to divine guidance found in the triumvirate of poets most influential in the first century—Homer, Virgil, and Horace—we turn now to other Roman writers who had varying degrees of popularity and influence. None of them was treated with the reverence accorded to these three great poets (though the histories of Livy were read more than the poems of Horace), but their writings do give some sense of the breadth of attitudes toward divine guidance at the time St. Paul was visiting Corinth.

Propertius

Divine guidance was not every Roman writer's preoccupation. The early poems of Propertius (c. 50/48 BCE–c. 2 CE) portray the gods as social formalities and literary props. Although he makes numerous references to the gods, it is hard to sense any genuine piety in his obsession with unfaithful "Cynthia," the subject of almost all his elegies.

There is also more than a touch of cynicism. Jove (Jupiter) is depicted as self-centered, spiteful, and deaf to prayer; he laughs at the distress of lovers. The god grants Propertius's petition and punishes Cynthia for her unfaithfulness only because Jove himself has suffered a "woman's treachery." (This too shows the god's hypocrisy, given his own reputation as a serial adulterer.)

> Not always does Jove calmly laugh at lovers' perjuries and turn a deaf ear to prayer. You have perceived the thunderclap run through all the sky, and the lightning bolt leap from its airy home. It is neither the Pleiades nor dark Orion that bring these things to pass; it is not for nothing that the wrath of the lightning falls. It is then that Jove is accustomed to punish faithless girls, since he also wept for a woman's treachery. (*Elegies* 2.1.45–49)[1]

Propertius has a jaundiced view of religious gatherings since they apparently provided Cynthia with the opportunities for her infidelity. The temples in Rome were social magnets and the "most frequent cause of all thy sins," he tells her.

Divine Guidance. John A. Jillions, Oxford University Press (2020). © Oxford University Press.
DOI: 10.1093/oso/9780190055738.001.0001

And so he urges her with some irony to leave Rome and go far away into the countryside, where such city-temple temptations won't distract her from true piety: "There will no games have power to corrupt you, no temples, most frequent cause of all your sins . . . there shall you bear a scanty offering of incense to some rural shrine" (*Elegies* 2.19.10ff.).

His apparent coolness toward religion makes Propertius's casual references to some of the standard forms of divination striking evidence for how deeply rooted such practices were in private as well as public life. In the following passages Propertius mentions astrology, dreams, omens, necromancy, casting lots, throwing dice, and the offering of incense and prayers at a household shrine:

> Yet do mortals inquire after the uncertain hour of death, and of the path by which your doom shall draw near, and in the unclouded heaven you seek by the art the Phoenicians found of old what star is good, what star is ill for man. (*Elegies* 2.27.1)

> The seer must gaze upon the path of heaven, on the road of truth that lies among the stars, and from the five zones seek assurance. (*Elegies* 4.1a.109)

> I wondered what omen the Muses had sent me as they stood before my couch in the red sunlight of dawn. They sent me a token that it was the birthday of my mistress. . . . Beloved, born under happy auguries, rise and pray to the gods who demand their due offering. . . . And pray that the beauty that is your might may endure always, and that you may be the queen of my heart forever. Then when you have appeased the wreathed altars with incense and their fire has flashed its blessing through all the house, give your thoughts to feasting. Let night speed mid the wine cup . . . and let your wanton words come fast and free. . . . Let us cast lots, let the fall of the dice reveal to us those whom the boy god [Cupid] lashes with heavy pinions. And then when the hours have been sped by many a goblet and Venus appoints those mysteries that wait on night, let us with all solemnity perform the anniversary's rite in our chamber, and thus complete the path of your natal day. (*Elegies* 3.10.1–32)

This next poem, a tribute to Augustus and his adoptive father, Julius Caesar, combines astrology with the budding imperial cult. The "Idalian star" refers to the comet that revealed Julius Caesar's apotheosis.

> My songs are spun for the glory of Caesar: while Caesar is the theme of the song, so Thou Jupiter, even Thou, rest from thy labors and give ear. (*Elegies* 4.6.12)

> O savior of the world, Augustus. (*Elegies* 4.6.37)

His sire Caesar gazed marveling from his Idalian star. I am a god, and your
victory gives proof that you are sprung from our blood.
(*Elegies* 4.6.56)

Propertius may have become more pious as time went on, perhaps because of
the general climate of the Augustan renewal or because of Cynthia's nearly fatal
illness. Seeing her cured after his fervent prayer, he urges her to render proper
thanks:

She has spurned the sanctity of the gods. . . . Wherefore if my prayer is granted
I bind myself with this solemn verse, to write: "The might of Jove has saved my
mistress." (*Elegies* 2.28.42)

Render Diana the dance you owe for an offering; and as is due, keep vigil in
honor of her who, once a heifer, is now a goddess, and on my behalf pay her ten
nights of worship. (*Elegies* 2.28A.59–60)

Cynthia dies sometime later, but Propertius senses that she has sent him a poetic message from beyond the grave encouraging his piety and urging him not to
reject the divine guidance that comes through dreams sent by the spirits of the
dead. In these verses Cerberus is the "hound of Hades," the vicious three-headed
dog preventing the dead from leaving the underworld; Lethe is the river in Hades
from which the ghosts of the dead drink to forget their mortal lives: "Nor spurn
the visions that come through holy portals; when dreams are holy they have the
weight of truth. By night we range in wandering flight; night frees the prisoned
shades, and Cerberus himself strays at will, the bar that chains him cast aside. At
dawn Hades' rule bids us return to the pools of Lethe: we are ferried across and
the mariner hands over his freight" (*Elegies* 4.4.87–91).

In another message from Cynthia's departed spirit—this one to her sons,
asking them to accept a potential stepmother—Propertius mentions the *lectus
genialis*, the symbolic couch in the atrium of each house that was dedicated to the
family genius: "Yet if another couch shall form the portals of our hall, and a wary
stepmother usurp my bed, my sons, praise and endure you father's spouse; your
virtues shall win her heart to yield" (*Elegies* 4.11.85ff.).

As he grows older Propertius joins the growing number of Roman intellectuals
lamenting the decline of Roman ways, especially Roman worship, as greed displaced piety. Even religion—especially astrology and divination—had become a
tool in service of profit:

But now the shrines lie neglected in deserted groves: piety is vanquished and
all men worship gold. Gold has banished faith, gold has made judgment to be

bought and sold, gold rules the law, and, law once gone, rules chastity as well. (*Elegies* 3.13.47–50)

Now have men turned the gods to profit and Jupiter is fooled by their gold; to profit they have turned the oft-scanned constellations of the slanting zodiac, the blessed star of Jove, the greedy star of Mars, the sign of Saturn that brings woe to one and all, the purport of the Fish and the fierce constellation of the Lion and Capricorn, bathed in the waters of the West. (*Elegies* 4.1a.81)

If Propertius in his early poems showed no interest in religion, he now views the decline of worship as a deep betrayal of Roman traditions and character and exhorts his fellow citizens to return to the old piety:

The Roman of today has nothing from his father except the name, nor would he believe that the she-wolf nurtured the blood from where he sprang. (*Elegies* 4.1.38)

You citizens, give me a fair omen, and from the right hand let some bird of augury sing me success. I will cry, "Troy you shall fall, and you Trojan Rome, shall arise anew!" and I will sing of all Rome's long perils by land and sea. Of holy rites and their days will I sing, and of the ancient names of places. This must be the goal toward which my foaming steed shall press. (*Elegies* 4.1.68ff.)

Coming to the end of his life, Propertius looks toward a renewed Roman tradition of piety, and images of divine guidance flow easily from his pen as he alludes to omens, augury, holy days, and rites.

Ovid

In lamenting the decline of Roman piety, Propertius would almost certainly have had in mind Ovid (P. Ovidius Naso, 43 BCE–16/17 CE) as one of the new generation of writers who exemplified Rome's moral decay. Ovid exerted tremendous influence on later poets, but his *Ars Amatoria* (The art of love), written in 2 CE, was one of the reasons Augustus banished him from Rome in 8 CE (although political factors also played a role). The *Ars Amatoria* was more social guide than sexual handbook, but even so Ovid from a young age became extremely popular as an erotic poet. And as such—in the eyes of Augustus—Ovid was having a pernicious influence on the aristocratic youth of Rome. For Augustus and like-minded citizens trying to regenerate Roman morals, "Ovid was the arch offender."[2]

Ovid may also have fallen afoul of the authorities for his open criticism of religious piety. He is blatantly cynical about the gods, divine guidance, and providence. In the *Metamorphoses*, his most famous work, he says that he prefers "simple truth" and detests religion, with its "rambling insincerities" (*Metamorphoses* 10.19–20).

The *Metamorphoses*, published about the same time as Ovid's exile in 8 CE, show that the gods are at best useless and at worst spiteful, vengeful, despisers of humanity and human love. For example, Orpheus invites the god Hymen to his wedding with his beloved, Eurydice, but the god is of little benefit, "for though he was certainly present, he did not bring good luck," and "the result of that sad wedding proved more terrible than such foreboding fates" (*Metamorphoses* 10.4–5). During the celebrations Eurydice went walking and dancing in a field with her bridesmaids, the naiads (spirits of the rivers). A snake hiding in the tall grass fatally bit her, so she died on her wedding day. When the disconsolate Orpheus goes looking for her in the underworld, he doubts that Pluto (Hades) and the gods know the meaning of that deep love motivating him to descend to death to look for his wife. He tries to explain this to Pluto, cynically alluding to Pluto's marriage with Proserpina (Persephone), knowing that the origin of that relationship is not in love but in Pluto's abduction, rape, and forced confinement of Proserpina in the underworld: "Love is a god well-known in the world above; whether he may be here too, I do not know, but I imagine he is familiar to you also, and, if there is any truth in the story of that rape long ago, then you yourselves were brought together by Love" (*Metamorphoses* 10.25–28).

Further on in the *Metamorphoses* Ovid retells the Greek myth of the beautiful Atalanta and her suitor Hippomenes. When she was born, Atalanta's father discarded her because he wanted a boy (a not uncommon practice in antiquity). Raised by a she-bear and protected by Diana (Artemis), the goddess of the hunt, Atalanta became a superb hunter and renowned athlete. And she swore that she would remain a virgin in honor of Artemis. Eventually she was reconciled with her father, who proposed to arrange a good marriage for her. She at first refused but then relented, on one condition: any suitor would have to beat her in a footrace. If he won, she would marry him. If he lost, he would be put to death. But Atalanta far exceeded the abilities of men, and many suitors died in the attempt to win her hand. Finally Hippomenes pleaded with Venus to help him, and the goddess gave him three magical golden apples to throw in front of Atalanta during the race. The apples were irresistible, and Atalanta slowed her pace as she bent down to pick up each apple. Hippomenes thus defeated her, and the two were married and were happy. As Ovid tells the story, when Atalanta first sees Hippomenes she is attracted to him and feels sorry for him. She assumes the gods must hate him simply because he is handsome. In spite they have encouraged him to run a race he will surely lose: "What god, hostile to a handsome face, wants to destroy this youth, and so induce him to seek my hand at the risk of his precious life?" Although Venus had been supporting Hippomenes, the goddess later turns on both of them for his insufficient gratitude. "Surely I deserved thanks and an offering of incense?" Venus fumes. "But the thoughtless man . . . expressed no gratitude to me, nor did he give me any such honour. My feelings suddenly changed to anger; indignant at being so scorned, I took good care to make an example of them, so that no one would despise me in future, and roused myself to punish them both" (*Metamorphoses* 10.681–685). As the couple pass by the shrine of Cybele, "the great Mother of the gods," Venus bewitches Hippomenes to be overcome right then and there with passion for his wife, taking her into a small room and making love in the temple precincts. The goddess Cybele, shocked by this blasphemous affront, turns the two into lions and yokes them to her chariot. Such is the gods' revenge for ingratitude and impiety.

But the impious are not the only victims of the gods. In telling the story of Alcyone, Ovid shows that the gods find reasons to punish the pious too. Alcyone's beloved husband, Ceyx, is on a dangerous sea voyage to consult an oracle, and Ovid describes her prayers and offerings for his safe return. But unbeknownst to her, he has already died at sea: "To all the gods she made dutiful offerings of incense, but first and foremost she worshipped in Juno's temple, visiting the altars of the goddess on behalf of the one who was no more, praying that her husband might be brought safely back to her, and that he might prefer no other woman to herself" (*Metamorphoses* 11.577–581). Juno responds to the prayer only out of irritation: "The goddess could not endure any further petitions for a man who was already dead" (*Metamorphoses* 11.584). She sends Morpheus, the god of dreams, to appear to Alcyone in the form of Ceyx and to tell her of his death. In despair, and after seeing his body wash up on shore, Alcyone commits suicide by throwing herself into the sea. Seeing their devotion to each other, the gods have a change of heart and transform the two lovers into "halcyon birds" (kingfishers).[3]

Ovid's disdain for popular superstition is seen in his retelling of the myth of Myrrha, who was obsessed with desire to commit incest with her father, King Cynaras. Myrrha tries to get her old nurse to help her with this scheme, but the nurse is scandalized at the thought and offers to find a magical cure for what must surely be madness. Then again, the nurse muses, Myrrha's perversion might simply be caused by the anger of the gods: "I am old but not useless. If it is some spasm of madness that has upset you, I know someone who can cure that, with charms and herbs: or if someone has laid a spell on you, you will be cleansed by magic ritual. Again, if the anger of the gods is distressing you, their anger can be appeased by offerings" (*Metamorphoses* 10.395–399).

Ovid's irony does not spare the ancient oracles. The oracle at Claros, for example, "comforts men in their distress" (*Metamorphoses* 11.412), but one of the main points of the *Metamorphoses* is that the gods themselves are the ones who devise and deliver distress in the first place.

Ovid's attitude toward the gods and divine guidance is summarized in his jaundiced advice in the *Ars Amatoria* to men who have religious qualms about breaking faith with a lover. He nods in the direction of traditional piety but in the end advises them not to worry: the gods don't really care. "It is good for us that there be gods, and that being so, let us suppose they really exist, let us carry on the old cults conscientiously. If we can fancy there are gods, let us at least believe them active and awake, not like those of Epicurus with their quietism and their slumber. No, let us keep faith and do right, imagining that they are not far from us. But if you make an exception and break faith with your girl, remember that they won't mind that!" (*Ars Amatoria* 1.631).[4]

Livy

Livy (Titus Livius, 59 BCE–17 CE or 64 BCE–12 CE) enjoyed great popularity and influence and was read by Romans more than any other Latin author except Virgil. He was Ovid's older contemporary, but their general outlook on life could not have been more different. First, Livy saw himself as a careful historian, not a florid poet. Second, he was a traditionalist. His monumental history of Rome begins with his famous and sober introduction, drawing the reader's attention to the lessons of history and the sad state of the present age: "Let him note how, with the gradual relaxation of discipline, morals first gave way, as it were, and sank lower and lower, and finally began the downward plunge which has brought us to the present time, when we can endure neither our vices nor their cure" (*History of Rome* 1.1.9).

Livy detested the "new" Rome of Ovid, with its immorality, its cynicism toward the most sacred traditions of Rome, its importation of foreign religions and Hellenistic excesses. He was an old-fashioned Roman who admired the ethical wholesomeness of Roman history, in which "righteousness and primitive simplicity so long resists the encroachments of wealth and luxury."[5] As we have seen, this was the widespread conservative view among upper-class Romans, so it is not surprising that Livy's success was "both immediate and lasting."[6]

Livy's *History* is consciously antipoetic in its approach to the gods and divine guidance. This does not mean he ignores divine interventions in history. Not at all: his history of Rome is full of portents, auspices, and accounts of divine activity. But he reports all this with skeptical reserve. From his perspective, faith in divine-human interaction belongs to the past, and from the start he puts some distance between himself and the mythical events he must report:

Such traditions as belong to the time before the city was founded, or rather was presently to be founded, and are rather adorned with poetic legends than based upon trustworthy historical proofs, I purpose neither to affirm nor to refute. It is the privilege of antiquity to mingle divine things with human, and so to add dignity to the beginnings of cities; and if any people ought to be allowed to consecrate their origins and refer them to a divine source, so great is the military glory of the Roman people, that when they profess that their Father and the Father of their Founder was none other than Mars, the nations of the earth may well submit to this also with as good grace as they submit to Rome's dominion. But to such legends as these, however they shall be regarded and judged, I shall, for my own part, attach no great importance. (*History of Rome* 1.1.6–8)

True to his word, Livy takes a less than credulous view of Rome's founding. His conservatism is combined with a refusal to leave untested even the most popular pious traditions. Take, for example, his comments on the paternity of Romulus and Remus, the legendary founders of Rome whose mother, Rhea Sylvia, a Vestal Virgin, claimed she was raped by Mars: "The Fates were resolved, as I suppose, upon the founding of this great city, and the beginning of the mightiest of empires, next after that of heaven. The Vestal was ravished, and having given birth to twin sons, named Mars as the father of her doubtful offspring, whether so actually, or because it seemed less wrong if a god were the author of her fault" (*History of Rome* 1.4.2).

Livy also has no trouble questioning the story of the she-wolf who cared for Romulus and Remus. "She-wolf," he says, was in fact a ribald name for Larentia, the shepherd's wife who found the children: "Some think that Larentia, having been free with her favours, had got the name 'she-wolf' among the shepherds, and that this gave rise to the marvellous story" (*History of Rome* 1.4.7). He cites numerous examples of divination, but these are often muffled with a questioning "they say" or some other hint that he is dubious.

As a critic of foreign religious influence Livy has to account for the tradition that Romulus himself established the Greek cult of Hercules at Rome. He underlines that this was the *only* foreign cult to be adopted, yet even so its purpose was to serve Roman destiny: "This was the only sacred observance, of all those of foreign origin, which Romulus then adopted, honouring even then the immortality won by worth to which his own destiny was leading" (*History of Rome* 1.7.15). Romulus, like Hercules, is divinely destined to a great vocation, but at the same time he is an active participant in making his future come to pass. There is no passivity in this understanding of destiny. Hercules wins his immortality "by worth," not by fate alone. This active participation in forming one's destiny is a characteristic Roman attitude toward events, in contrast to the passive fatalism Livy associated with Greek religion.

While Livy is skeptical about the legends he records, he also sees that divination and fate work hand in hand with human virtue. Wicked behavior, on the other hand, is likely to be followed eventually by predictable defeat and shame. This is one of the morals of book 1, most of which is taken up with the history of the Tarquin dictatorship, whose violence, intrigues, and self-serving betrayed Roman ideals. The last king, Lucius Tarquinius Superbus (who died in 495 BCE), like those before him, "seized the kingdom without the authorization of either Fathers or People" (*History of Rome*, Summary of Book 1, B). But the gods are not mocked. In a story that demonstrates once again the ambiguity of divine guidance, Livy shows what happened when the king's sons went to Delphi: "When his sons had gone to Delphi and were consulting the oracle as to which of them should be king in Rome, answer was made that he should reign who should first kiss his mother" (*History of Rome*, Summary of Book 1, B).

The Tarquin sons leave the oracle and agree to draw lots as to who should be first to kiss their mother upon returning home. The story now becomes more complicated. Brutus, a mentally disabled nephew of the Tarquin king, was accompanying them, and he immediately sensed a deeper interpretation. The Tarquins had murdered his brother and confiscated his property, and Brutus too would have been put to death to forestall any challenges to their rule, but they believed he was a harmless fool and posed no threat. Indeed he accompanied them "more as a butt than as a comrade" (*History of Rome* 1.56.9). But Brutus's apparent disability was an act to protect himself, since he had resolved "to find safety in contempt, where justice afforded no protection" (*History of Rome* 1.56.8). On overhearing the brothers discuss the oracle's words, Brutus concludes that there is another interpretation, but keeps this to himself. Arriving home, he pretends to stumble. Falling to the ground he "touched his lips to the Earth, evidently regarding her as the common mother of all mortals" (*History of Rome* 1.56.12). Later history proved Brutus right, says Livy, revealing him to be "the great soul which was to free the Roman People" (*History of Rome* 1.56.9): "The outcome sanctioned his act. For when Tarquinius Superbus had brought all men to hate him by the violence of his behaviour . . . Tarquinius was expelled, chiefly through the efforts of Brutus" (*History of Rome*, Summary of Book 1, B).

Livy's popularity, combined with his light skepticism, supports the claim that many Romans were not as fearfully superstitious and credulous as their religious practices might lead us to believe. Like Livy, they may have been at home with the *tradition* of divine guidance in life and history; they may also have insisted on maintaining traditional religious practices of divination. But this need not imply fervent belief in divine guidance. Their religious attitudes could be entirely separate from their religious practices. So Livy upholds faithfulness to tradition insofar as it promotes active virtue in service to Rome. He also acknowledges at times a divine providence that oversees history by vindicating the virtuous and casting down malefactors. But beyond that he has little instinct or patience for the mystical.

Lucan

Lucan (Marcus Annaeus Lucanus, 39–65 CE) was highly regarded by the Romans; some even gave him second place after Virgil.[7] Even so, neither this, nor the fact that he was the nephew of Seneca the Elder, could protect him from the madness of Nero, who was jealous of his popularity and swift rise. Nero banned public readings of Lucan's poetry and then, accusing him of treason, forced the 25-year-old to commit suicide. Although he was an extraordinarily prolific writer during his short life, the only full extant work is his 10-volume (and unfinished) epic poem recounting the war between Julius Caesar and Pompey, *Bellum Civile* (The civil war; also known as *Pharsalia*). Of the rest only fragments remain.

Although Lucan's poetic history discarded "the traditional apparatus of divine interventions,"[8] his attitude toward divine guidance is warmer than Livy's, seen most clearly in a long and moving passage on the decline of the oracle at Delphi (*The Civil War* 5). Here Lucan shows an exalted view of Delphi's holiness and accessibility while also accepting the immutability of fate: "This sacred shrine, which welcomes all men and is denied to none, nevertheless alone is free from the taint of human wickedness. There no sinful prayers are framed in stealthy whisper; for the god forbids mankind to pray for anything, and only proclaims the doom that none may change" (*The Civil War* 5.102–105).

Lucan accepts the common wisdom that sacred vapors inspire the priestess as she "breathes forth divine truth" (*The Civil War* 5.85). The god who dwells at Delphi is "ready to reveal himself to the nations, and patient of contact with mankind" (*The Civil War* 5.91). He is "a great and mighty God . . . whether he merely predicts the future or the future is itself determined by the fiat of his utterance" (*The Civil War* 5.93–94).

Like many others, Lucan laments the decline of Delphi. He blames it not on the gods but on "fearful kings" and the general sinfulness of the age: "The Delphian oracle became dumb when kings feared the future and stopped the mouths of the gods; and no divine gift is more sorely missed by our age" (*The Civil War* 5.102, 114–115). He asks, "Has the breath of inspiration failed?" (*The Civil War* 5.134). Is Delphi "dumb by the will of heaven?" Are the Sybilline books all that are really needed for "telling forth the hidden future" (*The Civil War* 5.140)?

Lucan sees a deeper reason for Apollo's apparent silence. Is it not that, "Apollo, accustomed to exclude the guilty from his shrine, finds none in our age for whose sake to unseal his lips?" (*The Civil War* 5.141–143). The sinfulness of the age makes true prophecy impossible, since there is no one left to faithfully hear and discern the messages from the gods.

Petronius

It would be difficult to find a Roman poet more viscerally contrary to Lucan and his sentiments on divine guidance than Petronius (d. 66 CE).[9] In antiquity Petronius was known to his contemporaries as little more than one of Nero's hedonistic courtiers. Tacitus mentions him in his *Annals* (16.17–20) but makes no mention of his literary work. But in the fragmentary *Satyricon* Petronius gives valuable insight into Roman Epicureanism, in terms of both sexual freedom and skepticism toward religion. He was writing in conscious opposition to the popular Stoicism of his contemporary, Seneca the Younger; *Satyricon* was written around 64 CE, soon after Seneca's fall from favor.[10]

The key passage to identify Petronius's Epicureanism is *Satyricon* 132. In an aside Petronius defends his depiction of Roman sexuality as honest and harmless, despite the criticism he expects to receive from pious guardians of public morality:

> The work you are now hearing no doubt provokes the usual strictures from the more censorious who believe that, in accordance with Stoic principles and literary theories, a work of art should be instructive and moral, not least in the narrowest sense of that term. Such critics will condemn this work, which is a reaction against our present modes of writing and old-fashioned Puritanism, and has its own literary and stylistic intentions. Its pure latinity has one end: to charm you, not instruct you. My subject is human behaviour and the narrative is realistic, although *honest* might be a better way of describing it. No one is unaware of the important place sex has in ordinary life. Does anyone take a moral stand against harmless and natural sexual enjoyment and comfort? As an Epicurean, I could even invoke philosophical principles in their defence and point to Epicurus' doctrines about its supreme importance.[11]

If Petronius is dismissive of Roman prudery, he is equally intent on ridiculing religion in all its manifestations. He targets especially the pious literary excesses of the poets. Throughout the book he mocks the flowery religious language of Homer and Virgil and the education system that revolves around them (and produced writers like Lucan).[12]

> I believe that college makes complete fools of our young men, because they see and hear nothing of ordinary life there. Yes, it is pirates standing with chains on the beach; yes, pirates writing edicts ordering sons to cut off their fathers' heads,

yes, oracles in time of pestilence demanding the blood of three virgins or more, honey-balls of phrases, every word and act besprinkled with poppy-seed and sesame. People who are fed on this diet can be no more sensible than people who live in the kitchen can smell good. (*Satyricon* 1, 2).

Later he upbraids his poet-friend Eumolpus for not speaking more straight-forwardly: "Tell me, cannot you get rid of your disease? You have been in my company less than two hours, and you have talked more often like a poet than like a man" (*Satyricon* 90).

On almost every page of the *Satyricon* reference is made to the superstitious beliefs of poets and populace. The ridicule is especially concentrated in Trimalchio, the wealthy and greedy ignoramus who struts about uttering pious stock phrases, completely self-absorbed and self-satisfied. Petronius mocks the pious murals in his hallway (*Satyricon* 29), his continuous talk of God's will and providence (*Satyricon* 48, 61, 78), his belief in astrology (*Satyricon* 35, 39), his superstitions (*Satyricon* 30, 64), his attention to the household gods (*Satyricon* 60), his credulity regarding the Sybil at Cumae (*Satyricon* 48), his pompous declamation on Fortune (*Satyricon* 55). Elsewhere Petronius satirizes divination in dreams (*Satyricon* 17), "immemorial mysteries" (*Satyricon* 17), charms (*Satyricon* 131), priestesses (*Satyricon* 134), divination by livers (*Satyricon* 137). Above all, he is revolted by the unfeeling indifference of the well-fed Trimalchio, who considers himself "blessed" but is deaf to the real needs of others.

In addition to the *Satyricon,* two of Petronius's poems are especially biting toward superstitious fears and pious greed, which he believes are the all-too-human origins of the gods, religious practice, and divination:

> It was fear first created gods in the world,
> when the lightning fell from high heaven. . . .
> The folly spread, and soon vain superstition bade the laborer
> yield to Ceres the harvest's chosen first fruits
> garland Bacchus with the fruitful vine-branch . . .
> and the man who wins his prayer or has betrayed the world for gold
> now strives greedily to create gods of his own. (*Poems* 3, in Petronius,
> Satyricon)

> It is not the shrines of the gods, nor the powers of the air,
> that send the dreams which mock the mind with flitting shadows;
> each man makes dreams for himself. (*Poems* 31, in *Satyricon*)

The scholar J. P. Sullivan may be right in concluding that Petronius's Epicureanism was merely a convenient label to dignify his own lifestyle of sensual pleasure. "Like most Roman Epicureans . . . he seems to have neglected the real spirit of the Master's cautious principles."[13] In fact the true Epicurean led a life of studied restraint. Whatever his motivations, Petronius's sustained attack on piety reveals him to be a careful observer who was genuinely dismayed by the results of Roman religion.

5

The Stoic Philosopher Posidonius

None of the writers considered thus far treated divine guidance in any systematic way. Some did raise probing questions, but for the most part divine guidance was simply a background assumption in their writing. But other Greek and Roman writers of influence in the first century BCE and CE did devote a great deal of thought and ink to the subject. The question of divine guidance—its possibility, meaning, methods, discernment, and deceptions—was vital to the vast majority of people, including some of the best minds. Even those who were skeptical or hostile could not ignore the subject but had to take such questions into consideration and frame their philosophical outlook around it. This alone is some indication of the currency of the issue.

Posidonius

If there was a philosophical orthodoxy in the first-century Roman Empire it was the religious Stoicism of the sort espoused most characteristically by Posidonius of Apamea (c. 135–c. 50/51 BCE). He and his predecessors—Zeno, Cleanthes, and Chrysippus—provided the theological foundation that supported the widespread acceptance divine guidance found in every class of Roman society.

None of Posidonius's works has survived, but his frequent citation by others is evidence of extensive influence. We have fragments of his historical and philosophical writing scattered throughout the works of Lucretius, Cicero, Manilius, Seneca, Pliny the Elder, and many others. Even when they cite Posidonius in order to disagree with him, they regard his position as the standard to debate.[1]

The extent of Posidonius's influence has been most extensively demonstrated in the work of I. G. Kidd, who has collected the fragments and commented on them. It is clear that the philosopher was keenly studied and often cited by ancient authors.[2] Not only was Posidonius "one of the most important and interesting figures of the first century B.C." and "the leading Stoic philosopher of his time," but "there is no doubt that he influenced a wide range of contemporary thinking and writing."[3]

Posidonius was emphatically Greek, although he lived in Rome, wrote a 52-volume history of Rome, and left a powerful influence on young Roman intellectuals of his day—Cicero, for one, who attended his school around 78 BCE.

Divine Guidance. John A. Jillions, Oxford University Press (2020). © Oxford University Press.
DOI: 10.1093/oso/9780190055738.001.0001

Posidonius first came to Rome from his native Rhodes to deliver a petition on be-half of the Rhodians; he stayed and became the leading philosopher of religious Stoicism. He wrote in Greek and by his own admission never mastered Latin while living in Rome. It is significant that while Cicero revered him as a teacher, it was precisely the Greek, mystical element of Posidonius's thought that drew Cicero's fiercest criticism.

Posidonius viewed divination as an essential component of religious Stoicism. He "gave explicit expression to the implication of the relationship between standard stoic philosophy and divination."[4] Cicero cites Posidonius as his au-thority for the view that "the mind of its own nature foresees inasmuch as it is imbued with kinship with the gods" (*Div.* 1.64). The notion of a human-divine kinship that makes it possible for human beings to know the divine mind was crucial for Posidonius. He believed that the human mind (the *nous*) is a daimon within us that is kin (*syngenis*) to the governing mind of the universe. Because of this kinship, the human mind can communicate with the divine mind.[5] This divine mind is so intimately involved in divination that the priests who prepare the sacrifices can even be guided to the specific animal to be sacrificed on a given occasion.

This is precisely the point at which Cicero enters the debate, arguing in dia-logue form with his brother, Quintus, that such beliefs are absurd:

> I am ashamed of Chrysippus, Antipater, and Posidonius who say exactly what you [Quintus] said: "The choice of the sacrificial victim is directed by the sen-tient and divine power which pervades the entire universe." But even more absurd is the other pronouncement of theirs which you adopted: "At the mo-ment of sacrifice a change in the entrails takes place; something is added or something is taken away; for all things are obedient to the divine will." Upon my word, no old woman is credulous enough now to believe such stuff! (*Div.* 2.35–36)[6]

In book 1 of Cicero's *On Divination* (*De divinatione*) Quintus had ear-lier presented the full philosophical basis for divination as outlined by Posidonius: "Wherefore it seems to me that we must do as Posidonius does and trace the vital principle of divination in its entirety to three sources: first to God . . . secondly to Fate; and lastly to Nature." Quintus says that Fate (the Greek *eimarmenē*) "is an orderly succession of causes in which cause is linked to cause and each cause of itself produces an effect. That is an immortal truth having its source in all eternity. Therefore nothing has happened which was not bound to happen, and likewise, nothing is going to happen which will not find in nature every efficient cause of its happening" (*Div.* 1.125–126).

According to Posidonius—as Cicero presents his thought—if one knew the causes of future events, one could predict the event. But this knowledge belongs only to a god, hence the need for divination: "Since such knowledge is possible only to a god, it is left to man to presage the future by means of certain signs which indicate what will follow them" (*Div.* 1.127). Diviners "may not discern the causes themselves, yet they discern the signs and tokens of those causes" (*Div.* 1.127).

The long history of such observations has evolved two types of divination, says Cicero. First, "that sort of divination, known as *artificial* [*imperatriva*], which is divination by means of entrails, lightnings, portents and celestial phenomena" (1.127). And second, *natural divination* (*oblativa*), with guidance through dreams, visions, and inspiration: "For as the souls of the gods, without the intervention of eyes and ears or tongue, understand each other and what each one thinks (hence men, even when they offer silent prayers and vows, have no doubt that the gods understand them), so the souls of men, when released by sleep from bodily chains, or when stirred by inspiration and delivered up to their own impulses, see things that they cannot see when mingled with the body" (*Div.* 1.129).

The whole universe is thus a connected, unified whole, according to Posidonius, and human beings—through their preexistent and immortal soul— have already experienced this wholeness prior to bring born into physical existence. And it is this preexisting unconscious knowledge that makes it possible for them to recognize and interpret divine signs: "Since all things have one and the same and that a common home, and since the human soul has always been and will always be, why then, should it not be able to understand what effect will follow any cause, and what sign will precede any event?" (*Div.* 1.131).

The central tenet of Posidonius's worldview is in the doctrine of "continual communion and mutual sympathy between the world of God and the world of man."[7] The daimon or genius implanted in every human soul is what links human beings to God and the universe. By following the inclinations of their daimon, human beings will be following the will of God and thus keeping in harmony with the universe. According to Posidonius, it is precisely this harmony between human and divine that is the definition of happiness. Conversely, when human beings choose to ignore the daimon within them and follow "the irrational, unhappy, godless element in the soul," the predictable result is disordered passion, disharmony, and unhappiness, as in this fragment cited by Galen (129–210 CE):

The cause of passions—the cause that is, of disharmony and of the unhappy life—is that men do not follow absolutely the *daimon* that is in them, which is akin to, and has a like nature with, the Power governing the whole cosmos, but turn aside after the lower animal principle, and let it run away with them. Those who fail to see this neither thereby set the cause of the passions in any better light, nor hold the right belief regarding happiness and concord. They do not perceive that the very first point in happiness is to be led in nothing by the irrational, unhappy, godless element in the soul.[8]

This doctrine of "cosmic sympathy" is the intellectual bedrock for divination: "Any event on earth, even a trivial one could reflect or foreshadow the intentions of the gods because the universe is a living organism, a whole, and what happens in one part might be caused by a happening in some distant part."[9]

"Cosmic sympathy" was also closely linked to astrology, which in the ancient world was not seen as separate from God. The stars were part of God's many forms of revelation, which, if one were sensitive to them, could give clear indication of his will.[10] Take, for example, this excerpt from an astrology handbook written by Marcus Manilius around 15 CE: "In this divine order do all things abide, following the guidance of the master. This good and all-controlling reason, then, derives to earthly beings from the signs of heaven; though the stars are remote at a far distance, he compels the recognition of their influences, in that they give to the peoples of the world their lives and destinies and to each his own character."[11]

To fully appreciate Posidonius we will need to look at Plato's thought, since this was fundamental in shaping Posidonius's outlook. However, since the historian Strabo claimed that Posidonius was an Aristotelian, we will also need to look at Aristotle's approach to divine guidance.

Posidonius and Plato

The notion of "cosmic sympathy" so prominent in Posidonius is closely linked to the construction of the soul in the thought of Plato (428/427–348/347 BCE), especially in the *Timaeus*.[12] In the first century BCE, "Platonism now (with Posidonius) began strongly to influence Stoicism. The *Timaeus* in particular came to be looked upon as Holy Writ, an inspired revelation of the nature of things."[13] Although none of the Posidonian fragments preserves a direct reference to Plato's teaching on divination, Posidonius's view is consistent with Plato's understanding of the individual soul as the human being's link to the rest of the universe.

Plato's understanding of the human soul—or rather souls, since there is both a mortal and an immortal soul—and its relation to the divine, immortal soul of the universe is exceedingly complex (*Tim.* 69C–71D). But it is important to look at this teaching in some detail in order to appreciate how a leading intellectual in the ancient world could understand divination as part of a broader worldview in which everything, both rational and suprarational, was linked. Struggling with the intricacies of Plato's speculation also helps explain why other intellectuals abandoned the mystical realm entirely, Plato's student Aristotle being the prime example.

In Plato's system God is the creator (*demiourgos*) of all things divine, including the immortal soul. But he places "his own engendered sons" in charge of creating all that is mortal, and this includes the mortal soul with its passions: "And they, imitating him, on receiving the immortal principle of soul, framed around it a mortal body, and gave all the body as its vehicle, and houses therein another form of soul, even the mortal form, which has within it passions both fearful and unavoidable" (*Tim.* 69C).

Plato's list of passions includes pleasure, pain, rashness, fear, anger, and hope (*Tim.* 69C–E). But these passions of the *mortal* soul had to be kept well away from the reason of the *immortal* soul. Thus the two souls are housed in different parts of the human body. The immortal soul is associated with the mind (*nous*), while the mortal soul is associated with the liver and internal organs.

> And blending these [passions] with irrational sensation and with all-daring lust, they thus compounded in necessary fashion the mortal kind of soul. Wherefore, since they scruple to pollute the divine, unless through absolute necessity, they planted the mortal kind apart therefrom in another chamber of the body, building an isthmus and boundary for the head and chest by setting between them the neck, to the end that they might remain apart. And within the chest—or "thorax" as it is called—they fashioned the mortal kind of soul. (*Tim.* 70A)

Even within the mortal soul there is a higher region that expresses natural virtues like courage. This region also enables the mortal soul to keep the passions in check when the rebellious body refuses to be ruled by the immortal soul's reason (*Tim.* 70A). The regions of the mortal soul that are "subject to appetites for food and drinks, and all other wants" (*Tim.* 70E) are found in the lower half of the body, below the ribs. The head, although it is "the most divine part and reigns over all the parts within us has difficulty ruling the passions of the body when they are not satisfied" (*Tim.* 44D). For this reason the creators of the universe (the *demiourgoi*) placed within the lower regions of the body a secondary organ of guidance, the liver. "And inasmuch as they [the *demiourgoi*] knew that [the body] would not understand reason, and that even if it did have some share in the perceptions of reasons, it would have no natural instinct to pay heed to any of them but would be bewitched [*psychagōgēsoito*] for the most part both day and night by images [*eidōla*] and phantasms, to guard against this God devised and constructed the form of the liver and placed it in that part's abode" (*Tim.* 71A–B).

Plato explains in detail how the physical condition of the liver is affected by thoughts that come from the ruling mind. Sometimes thoughts will bring "stern threats" that keep the body from acting on the passions. At other times, however, the mind sends gentle thoughts that bring serenity to the body, allowing it to be a channel for divination in dreams. At such times, "a breath of mildness from the intellect paints on the liver appearances of the opposite kind, and calms down its bitterness by refusing to move or touch the nature opposite itself. . . . It causes the part of the soul planted round the liver to be cheerful and serene, so that in the night it passes its time sensibly, being occupied in its slumbers with divination [*manteia*] seeing that in reason and intelligence it has no share" (*Tim.* 71D). Thus even while the rational part of the soul is shut down during sleep, the human being can still have access to truth through the mystical sense of divination:

> For they who constructed us, remembering the injunction of their Father, when he enjoined upon them to make the mortal kind as good as they possibly could, rectified the vile part of us by thus establishing therein the organ of divination, that it might in some degree lay hold on truth. And that God gave unto man's foolishness the gift of divination a sufficient token is this: no man achieves true and inspired divination when in his rational mind, but only when the power of his intelligence is fettered in sleep or when it is distraught by disease or by reason of some divine inspiration. (*Tim.* 71E)[14]

This is one of Plato's key insights. All human beings can "to some degree lay hold on truth" through their soul's organ of divination. But they have access to this only when they are in a mystical state when the rational faculties are shut down.

What, then, is the purpose of the *rational* state? Its function is to reflect on the raw material that has been given through the dreams, visions, and inspiration that come through the "divining and inspiring nature": "[It] belongs to a man when he is in his right mind to recollect and ponder both the things spoken in dream or waking vision by the divining and inspiring nature, and all the visionary forms that were seen, and by means of reasoning to discern about them all wherein they are significant and for whom they portend evil or good in the future, the past or the present" (*Tim.* 771E, 72A). In other words, rational and mystical faculties within the soul work together. Indeed correct evaluation of inspiration *requires* later reflection by a sound rational mind: "[It] is not the task of him who is still in this prophetic state to judge the apparitions and voices seen or uttered by himself; for it was well said of old that to do and to know one's own mind and oneself belongs only to him who is of sound mind" (*Tim.* 72A).

It is on this basis that Plato explains the tradition that oracles convey only divine messages, not their interpretations. The latter is left to the prophets: "Wherefore also it is customary to set the tribe of prophets to pass judgment upon these inspired divinations; and they indeed themselves are named 'diviners' by certain who are wholly ignorant of the truth that they are not diviners but interpreters of the mysterious voice and apparition, for whom the most fitting name would be 'prophets of things divined' [*prophētai manteuomenōn*]" (*Tim.* 72B).

Like the *Timaeus*, Plato's *Phaedrus* also regards the capacity for divination as one of the most natural and essential of the human senses. In this dialogue between Socrates and Phaedrus, Socrates says that he himself is a seer (though "not a very good one") and tells Phaedrus of the daimon that regularly counsels him:

> When I was about to cross the stream, the spirit [*to daimonion*] that usually comes to me came—it always holds me back from something I am about to do—and I thought I heard a voice from it which forbade my going away before clearing my conscience, as if I had committed some sin against the deity [*to theion*]. Now I am a seer [*mantis*], not a very good one, but as bad writers say, good enough for my own purposes; so now I understand my error. How prophetic [*mantikon*] the soul is my friend! For all along, while I was speaking my discourse, something troubled me, and "I was distressed," as Ibycus says, "lest I be buying honour among men by sinning against the gods." (*Phaedrus* 242CD)[15]

In the *Symposium*, Plato goes further and says that the daimons are the means of all human communication with the divine, and hence the spiritual person is someone who "has skill" in discerning their messages: "God with man does not mingle, but through this [daimon] is the means of all society and converse of men with gods and of gods with men, whether waking or asleep. Whosoever has skill in these affairs is a spiritual man [*daimonios anēr*] ...Many and multifarious are these spirits [*daimonoi*] and one of them is love" (*Symposium* 203A).

The importance Socrates gave to his own daimon and divine guidance was well known in the ancient world. One of his most famous students, the historian Xenophon (c. 430–354 BCE), points out that it was precisely Socrates's insistence that he received continual divine guidance from his own daimon that led to the criminal charge that he was "introducing new gods [*kaina daimonia*] which the city does not believe in" (*Memorabilia* I.2–5; DL II.40).[16]

Plutarch discusses in great detail the meaning of this daimon in *On the Daimon of Socrates* (*De genio Socratis*).[17] The setting is a conversation in which it is suggested by a certain Simias that Socrates's daimon was his ability to perceive the unspoken language of spiritual forces. The reference to "sappers" is to soldiers working underground to build tunnels. "For just as the sound of sappers' blows is detected by bronze shields, which re-echo it as it rises from the depths of the earth and strikes them, whereas through everything else it slips unnoticed; so the messages of *daimons* pass through all other men, but find an echo only in those whose character is untroubled and unruffled, the very men in fact we call holy and daimonic" (*Gen. Socr.* 589D).

Throughout the ancient world dreams are regarded as vehicles of divination, but here in Plutarch's dialogue Simias goes beyond this to argue that the person who is inwardly attuned to the divine presence is not limited to dreams. He or she receives divine guidance even when fully awake:

> In popular belief ... it is only in sleep that men receive inspiration from on high; and the notion that they are so influenced when awake and in full possession of their faculties is accounted strange and incredible. This is like supposing that a musician uses his lyre when the strings are slack, but does not touch or play it when it has been adjusted to a scale and attuned. This belief arises from ignorance of the cause of the insensibility: the inner lack of attunement and the confusion in the men themselves. (*Gen. Socr.* 589D)

This sensitivity to the spiritual world is precisely the "attunement" that Socrates possessed. How did he acquire it? Simias suggests that he learned from early childhood to trust his own inner direction because he was given so much freedom as a child. An oracle told his father to allow the boy "free play" while prayerfully entrusting him to the Muses and to "Zeus of the Marketplace" to guide and watch over him:

> From this [lack of inner attunement] my friend Socrates was free, as is shown by the oracle delivered to his father when Socrates was yet a boy. It bade him let the child do whatever came into his mind, and not do violence to his impulses or divert them, but allow them free play, taking no further trouble about him than to pray to Zeus Agoraeus [Zeus of the Marketplace] and the Muses, surely implying by this that he had a better guide of life in himself than a thousand teachers and attendants. (*Gen. Socr.* 589F)

The daimon of Socrates is just one of the aspects of divination Plato treats in *Phaedrus*. Elsewhere in this dialogue with Socrates skill for divination is linked with pleasing the gods by learning from them—most significant, learning from the gods how to love (*Phaedrus* 274B). Indeed for Socrates all philosophical discussion should be "directed towards love in singleness of heart" (*Phaedrus* 257B; compare 1 Cor 13). He concedes that love is an irrational madness (*Phaedrus* 244A) but upbraids the ancients for taking a negative view of madness. Yes, love is "madness," but it is beneficial and god-given. Socrates connects prophecy (*mantikē*) with madness (*mania*) but distinguishes between those forms of madness that spring from disease and those, like love, that are a "gift of the gods":

> For if it were a simple fact that insanity is an evil, the saying would be true, but in reality the greatest of blessings come to us through madness, when it is sent as a gift from the gods. For the prophetess at Delphi and the priestesses at Dodona when they have been mad have conferred many splendid benefits upon Greece both in private and public affairs, but few or none when they have been in their right minds; and if we should speak of the Sibyl and all the others who by prophetic inspiration have foretold many things to many persons and thereby made them fortunate afterwards, anyone can see that we should speak a long time. And it is worthwhile to adduce also the fact that those men of old who invented names thought that madness was neither shameful nor disgraceful; otherwise they would not have connected the very word *mania* with the noblest of arts, that which foretells the future, by calling it the *manic* art. No, they gave this name thinking that *mania*, when it comes by gift of the gods, is a noble thing, but nowadays people call prophecy the *mantic* art, tastelessly inserting a T in the word. (*Phaedrus* 244A–C)

Socrates tells Phaedrus that such divine madness is found not only at famous oracle sites like Delphi and Dodona, but anywhere there is worship and beauty. The madness of those who "take refuge in prayers and giving services to the gods" brings "a release from present ills." Likewise, without the divine madness of the Muses, no artist's technical skill alone can produce genuine beauty: "This takes hold upon the gentle and pure soul, arouses it and inspires it to songs and other poetry. . . . But he who without the divine madness comes to the doors of the Muses, confident that he will be a good poet by art [*ek technis*], meets with no success, and the poetry of the sane man vanishes into nothingness before that of the inspired madman. All these noble results of inspired madness I can mention and many more" (*Phaedrus* 245AB).

Socrates takes this further, telling Phaedrus that the greatest form of madness-as-beauty is love for the divine:

> This soul exhibits the greatest kind of madness, divine love, love of divine beauty in unfulfilled longing, who when he sees the beauty on earth, remembering the true beauty, feels his wings growing and longs to stretch them for an upward flight, but cannot do so, and like a bird, gazes upward and neglects the things below. . . . This of all inspirations, is the best and of the highest origin

to him who has it or who shares [*koinonounti*] in it, and that he who loves the beautiful, partaking in this madness is called a lover. (*Phaedrus* 249E)

The *mania* that comes from God is no cause for fear. It is far superior to cool human sanity alone, and brings inspiration, creativity, tranquility, and love. Plato distinguishes this god-given prophecy from engineered human attempts at divination such as astrology and augury, which reduce divination to a mechanical science: "The ancients, then, testify that in proportion as prophecy [*mantike*] is superior to augury, both in name and in fact, in the same proportion madness, which comes from god, is superior to sanity, which is of human origin" (*Phaedrus* 244D).

But how does one tell if some "sign" is divine? For Socrates, the criterion for evaluating such signs is truth. In the light of truth, even the most bizarre means of divine revelation may prove genuine. This gives him a new perspective on popular religion. "They used to say, my friend," Socrates tells Phaedrus, "that the words of the oak in the holy place of Zeus at Dodona were the first prophetic utterances. . . . The people of that time, not being so wise as you young folks, were content in their simplicity to hear an oak or a rock, provided it only spoke the truth; but to you perhaps, it makes a difference who the speaker is and where he comes from, for you do not consider only whether his words are true or not" (*Phaedrus* 275C).

The truth itself is perceived less by discursive reasoning than as "a vision" given in response to "following in the train of a god" (*Phaedrus* 250B). The soul becomes incarnate in a human body only when it loses its divine focus and stops following god. By turning away from the vision of god, the soul suffers the "loss of wings" and acquires a human body. Even then, however, the soul cannot erase the memory of what it has seen. Human life is thus "a collection of those things which our soul once beheld, when it journeyed with God and, lifting its vision above the things which we say now exists, rose up into real being."

> And therefore it is just that the mind of the philosopher only has wings, for he is always, so far as he is able, in communion through memory with those things the communion with which causes God to be divine. Now a man who employs such memories rightly is always being initiated into perfect mysteries and he alone becomes truly perfect; but since he separates himself from human interests and turns his attention toward the divine, he is rebuked by the vulgar, who consider him mad and do not know that he is inspired. (*Phaedrus* 249C–D)

Most have forgotten the divine realities they once saw, either because they had too brief a glimpse before they were born or because they turned to unrighteousness "through some evil communications" (*Phaedrus* 250A). On this point

Socrates has a complex theory of birth and rebirth that depends on which god one followed before birth. This is the god from whom they now "draw the waters of inspiration" within themselves: "When they seek eagerly within themselves to find the nature of their god, they are successful, because they have been compelled to keep their eyes fixed upon the god, and as they reach and grasp him by memory they are inspired and receive from him character and habits, so far as possible for a man to have [a] part in God" (*Phaedrus* 253A). As long as one is "uncorrupted" and in his first life, he lives "so far as he is able, honoring and imitating that god" (*Phaedrus* 252D).

In light of the divine fullness, all human thought and writing, no matter how exalted, is at best incomplete. And therefore no one but God can be called truly wise. "I think, Phaedrus, that the epithet 'wise' is too great and befits God alone; but the name 'philosopher,' that is, 'lover of wisdom' or something of the sort would be more fitting and modest" (*Phaedrus* 278D). But philosophy should not be confused with words and rhetorical skill. At the heart of philosophy are not mere written words but the *logos,* "written with intelligence in the soul of the learner which is able to defend itself and knows to whom it should speak, and before whom to keep silent . . . the living and breathing word of him who knows, not the written word which is justly called an image [*eidōlon*]" (*Phaedrus* 276A). It is the logos, the "word within himself" (*Phaedrus* 278B), to which one must pay closest attention, and then to the words of others that he recognizes as "descendants and brothers" of his own word. To any other words he need pay no attention (*Phaedrus* 278B).

All of this requires the most careful observation and cultivation of the inner world. But it also requires a finely tuned awareness of the outer world's impact on the inner life. Plato concludes *Phaedrus* with Socrates's famous prayer for inner and outer harmony: "O beloved Pan and all ye other gods of this place, grant me that I be made beautiful within, and that all external possessions be in harmony with my inner man" (*Phaedrus* 279C).

For all his awareness and experience of mystical reality, Socrates is also firmly planted in his experience of rational human reality and refuses to escape into the magical and mysterious. He has neither the inclination nor the patience to chase explanations for apparent miracles (*Phaedrus* 229C). Instead he puts all his effort into trying to fulfill the inscription at Delphi: "Know Thyself." "I am not yet able to, as the Delphic inscription has it, to know myself; so it seems to me ridiculous, when I do not yet know that, to investigate irrelevant things. And so I dismiss these matters and accepting the customary belief about them, as I was saying just now, I investigate not these things, but myself" (*Phaedrus* 230A).

Divine guidance and reason are thus closely bound together in Socrates's understanding of his life and mission, as presented by his student Plato. True divine guidance leads to insight about the self and one's vocation. Socrates's vocation as a philosopher begins with an oracle from Delphi. And on trial for his life in 399 BCE for continuing to speak and teach, he remains faithful to his god-appointed vocation: "The God gave me a station, as I believed and understood, with orders to spend my life in philosophy and in examining myself and others" (Plato, *Apol.* 28e).[18] "Men of Athens I respect and love you, but I shall obey the god rather than you, and while I live and am able to continue, I shall never give up philosophy or stop exhorting you and pointing out the truth to any one of you whom I may meet.... For know that the god commands me to do this, and I believe that no greater good ever came to pass in the city than my service to the god" (*Apol.* 29d, 30a).

Here in brief at his trial we have Socrates's signal contribution to Western thought: the attempt to show philosophy as a way of life that balances mystical experience with rational reflection, contemplation with action, external existence with inward being. As in his case, it is authentic life, but also costly.

Posidonius and Aristotle

The previous pages outlined the connections between Posidonius and Plato, but the Roman historian Strabo (64/63 BCE–c. 21 CE) knew Posidonius personally and did not consider him a Platonist. While Strabo himself was a Stoic (*Geography* 1.2.34; 7.3.4), he connected Posidonius more with Aristotle: "For in Posidonius there is much inquiry into causes and much imitating of Aristotle— precisely what our school avoids, on account of the obscurity of the causes" (*Geography* 2.3.8).[19] This was a minority view among ancient commentators, but since Strabo himself had once been an Aristotelian, his claim bears some investigation in relation to Posidonius's understanding of divine guidance.

Aristotle (384–322 BCE) joined Plato's Academy in Athens when he was 17 or 18 and remained there for over 20 years, leaving Athens only in 343 BCE after Plato died and Philip of Macedon invited Aristotle to tutor his son Alexander. If Plato looked at divination as a natural human aptitude that could be cultivated or lie fallow, Aristotle mostly avoided the issue entirely and turned his attention elsewhere, mainly to the visible world. In two very short essays, *Prophesying by Dreams* (*De divination per somnum*) and *Dreams* (*De somniis*), Aristotle stays clear of the theological speculations of his teacher Plato. As Dodds says approvingly, "His approach to the problem is coolly rational without being superficial, and he shows at times a brilliant insight. . . . He denies that any dreams are god sent (*theopempta*): if the gods wished to communicate knowledge to men, they would do so in the daytime, and they would choose the recipients more carefully." Unlike Plato, "he no longer talks of the soul's innate powers of divination, as he had in his romantic youth." In general, says Dodds, Aristotle's "whole approach to the problem is scientific, not religious."[20]

Yet Aristotle himself is less absolutely certain about this. On the one hand, he is skeptical about divination of the future or that human beings have an inborn memory of the future. In *Memory and Recollection* he says, "First, then, we must comprehend what sort of things are objects of memory; for mistakes are frequent on this point. It is impossible to remember the future, which is an object of conjecture or expectation (there might even be a science of expectation as some say there is of divination)" (1).[21] But even here he leaves open the possibility of divination, at least as a matter of debate. Elsewhere he is not entirely ready to dismiss as absurd the idea that divine guidance might come through dreams:

> As for prophecy [*mantikēs*] which takes place in sleep and is said to proceed from dreams, it is not an easy matter either to despise it or to believe in it. The fact that all, or at least many, suppose that dreams have a significance inclines one to believe the theory, as based on experience, nor is it incredible that on some subjects there should be divination in dreams; for it has some show of reason, and one might suppose the same of dreams as well. (*Prophesying by Dreams* 462b1–19)[22]

Aristotle is puzzled both by the apparent absence of a reasonable cause for such an explanation and because dreams come "to any chance person": "The fact that one can see no reasonable cause why it should be so, makes one distrust it; for apart from its improbability on other grounds, it is absurd to hold that it is God who sends such dreams, and yet that He sends them not to the best and wisest, but to any chance persons" (*Prophesying by Dreams* 462b.20–23). Nevertheless even these objections do not convince him that God cannot possibly be the source, particularly when the event foreseen occurs at some remote place apparently unrelated to the dreamer: "[If] we dismiss the theory of causation by God, none of the other causes seems probable; for it seems beyond our understanding to find any reason why anyone should foresee things occurring at the Pillars of Heracles or on the Borysthenes" (*Prophesying by Dreams* 462b.20–23).

The rest of Aristotle's short essay *Prophesying by Dreams* is limited to dealing with natural causes of dreams, though he is unwilling to dismiss dreams as having no significance whatsoever: "At any rate even accomplished physicians say that close attention should be paid to dreams; and it is natural for those to suppose so who are not skilled, but who are inquirers and lovers of truth" (*Prophesying by Dreams* 463a.6–8). However, Aristotle rejects the idea that dreams are actually sent by God (*theopempta*), other than in the most general sense that all nature is "divinely ordained" (*Prophesying by Dreams* 463b.12–14). He returns again to his biggest stumbling block: that the most common human beings have dreams. This in itself "shows that these are not sent by God" (*Prophesying by Dreams* 463b.15–16). If they happen to predict something correctly, this is mere chance, "for just as the saying goes, 'if you throw the dice often enough your luck will change'" (*Prophesying by Dreams* 463b.21).

But Aristotle remains perplexed about those dreams that seem to correctly predict major events and have no natural or coincidental explanation. He follows the conjecture of Democritus and suggests that these come from the "images and emanations" projected into the mind, in which case it is not surprising that ordinary men have such dreams, since they have less in their minds to obstruct impressions coming from outside! But Aristotle again resists the notion that God might be the origin of a dream, adding the argument that if God wished to communicate he would send messages by day and to more discerning recipients: "If it were God who sent them they would appear by day also, and to the wise" (*Prophesying by Dreams* 464a.22). Though not answering satisfactorily his own question, Aristotle was much more at home with the scientifically provable, and in his voluminous writings he rarely refers to divination, dreams, oracles, etc. He avoids speculation by skirting entirely both the perplexities of mystical experience and the ambiguities of the inner world to concentrate on the certainties of the here and now.

Returning to Posidonius, it is clear that at least in his approach to divination he owes much more to Plato than to Aristotle. Strabo himself, however, despite his avowed Stoicism, remained closely tied to Aristotle. He included divination among all those religious superstitions that had a role in maintaining social order among the uneducated but should have no place in the life of a philosopher for whom virtue, reason, and simple belief in providence as the First Cause were the pillars of genuine reverence: "For in dealing with a crowd of women, at least, or in any promiscuous mob, a philosopher cannot influence them by reason or exhort them to reverence, piety, and faith; nay, there is need of religious fear also, and this cannot be aroused without myths and marvels. For thunderbolts, aegis, trident, torches, snakes, thyrsus, lances—arms of the gods—are myths, and so is the entire ancient theology" (Strabo, *Geography* 1.2.8).

Unlike Aristotle and Strabo, Posidonius was unwilling to distance himself from popular piety. To him everything in the world was capable of speaking of God and conveying divine messages of the most specific sort. Everything in the spiritual and eternal realm was connected with the material and temporal realm. This view had important practical implications for him. It meant that the divine world and the world of history were one. This in turn meant that actions taken in this world have eternal ramifications and significance, so that civic duty and religious duty were deeply bound together. This outlook was especially congenial to Roman aspirations, so it is not surprising that Posidonius gave so much attention to Rome's recent history, writing a 52-volume account (no longer extant) that covered the period from 146 BCE "probably to the mid-80's and possibly unfinished."[23]

Posidonius gave a philosophical rationale to those—the majority—who believed in divination, divine intervention, divine guidance. But there were other Roman writers who were deeply disturbed by these superstitions and rejected both their practice and their philosophical underpinnings. To these opposition voices, beginning with Lucretius, we turn next.

6

Roman Philosophers

Lucretius, Cicero, Seneca, Pliny

Lucretius and the Epicureans

Epicureans traced their outlook on life to the fourth-century BCE Greek mate-
rialist philosopher Epicurus (341–270 BCE), whose philosophy took shape in
reaction to the mystical dimensions of Plato and the Stoics. Epicurus didn't believe in any form of divine intervention or in divining the future. He saw these
as superstitions that ensnared the credulous and kept them from enjoying the
pleasure of the present, which for Epicurus is the very aim of life. But he didn't
mean this in a hedonistic sense. True pleasure is a state of tranquility derived
from gaining knowledge of oneself and of the world, avoiding excess, and following a balanced, modest way of life that rises above conventional ideas of both
pleasure and pain.

Lucretius (Titus Lucretius Carus, c. 99–55 BCE) was the most influential
Roman Epicurean. His only known work, *De rerum natura* (On the nature
of the universe) is a long poem written with missionary zeal dedicated to the
overthrow of popular superstition. In Lucretius's view of reality there is no
spiritual world, and intelligent society should have no place for providence,
divine intervention, Fate, immortality of the soul, divination, and religious
rituals. Everything human beings need to know is found in Nature and
comes through the physical senses alone. Lucretius "found Nature blind,
soulless and purposeless, but with a breathtaking beauty and majesty that
could dispense with any personal attributes."[1] For him, "true piety lies . . . in
the power to contemplate the universe with a quiet mind" (*De rerum natura*
5.1200).

According to Lucretius, all religion was an invention of the ancients that kept
human beings enslaved to superstitions by playing on their anxieties, desires,
fears, and ignorance. People of the past "took refuge in handing over everything
to the gods and making everything dependent on their capricious whims."

> Poor humanity, to saddle the gods with such responsibilities and throw in a
> vindictive temper! What griefs they hatched then for themselves, what festering
> sores for us, what tears for our posterity! This is not piety, this oft-repeated show

Divine Guidance. John A. Jillions, Oxford University Press (2020). © Oxford University Press.
DOI: 10.1093/oso/9780190055738.001.0001

of bowing a veiled head before a graven image; this bustling to every altar; this kow-towing and prostration on the ground with palms outspread before the shrines of the gods; this deluging of altars with the blood of beasts; this heaping of vow upon vow. True piety lies rather in the power to contemplate the universe with a quiet mind. (*De rerum natura* 5.1190ff.)

Nothing has produced so much human misery as religion, says Lucretius. But he warns his reader (the work is addressed to Memmius, a Roman statesman, Epicurean, and patron of Lucretius) that superstition is an extremely powerful force that is difficult for even the most convinced Epicurean to resist:

> You yourself, if you surrender your judgment at any time to the blood-curdling declamations of the prophets, will want to desert our ranks. Only think what phantoms they can conjure up to overthrow the tenor of your life and wreck your happiness with fear. And not without cause. For if men saw that a term was set to their troubles, they would find strength in some way to withstand the hocus-pocus and the intimidations of the prophets. As it is they have no power of resistance, because they are haunted by the fear of eternal punishment after death. (*De rerum natura* 1.96ff.)

For Lucretius nothing could be worse than the ignorance fostered by the Delphic oracle. Even the Greek philosophers with whom he disagrees "have certainly made many excellent and divine discoveries and uttered oracles from the inner sanctuary of their hearts with more sanctity and far surer reason than those the Delphic prophetess pronounces, drugged by the laurel fumes from Apollo's tripod" (*De rerum natura* 1.737ff.; repeated in 5.112).

Given his attitude toward the gods, it is perhaps surprising that Lucretius begins *De rerum natura* with a prayer to Venus:

> Mother of Rome, delight of Gods and men,
> Dear Venus . . .
> 'tis thou alone
> Guidest the Cosmos, and without thee naught
> Is risen to reach the shining shores of light,
> Nor aught of joyful or of lovely born,
> Thee do I crave co-partner in that verse
> Which I presume on Nature to compose . . .
> Wherefore indeed, Divine one, give my words
> Immortal charm. . . . Pour from those lips soft syllables to win
> Peace for the Romans, glorious Lady, peace! (*De rerum natura*, 1.1–40)

Lest this be taken as anything more than Roman poetic convention, Lucretius quickly moves on to praising Epicurus for delivering humanity from superstition, diagnosing its causes and cure (*De rerum natura* 1.62–79, 80–145). The first of Lucretius's propositions is that "nothing can ever be created by divine power out of nothing." This is the key to his argument for abandoning superstition. "The dread and darkness of the mind" can be dispelled only

> by an understanding of the outward form and inner workings of nature. . . . The reason why all mortals are so gripped by fear is that they see all sorts of things happening on earth and in the sky with no discernible cause, and these they attribute to the will of a god. Accordingly, when we have seen that nothing can be created out of nothing, we shall have a clearer picture of the path ahead, the problem of how things are created and occasioned without the aid of the gods. (*De rerum natura* 1.146ff.; see also 5.1161–1240)

The world is perfectly capable of regulating itself without divine assistance: "Nature is free and uncontrolled by proud masters and runs herself without the aid of gods" (*De rerum natura* 2.1090; see also 2.167–183, 2.1090-1104, 6:45ff.). Nature's independence is the example human beings should follow, for in imitating nature people would live by "the evidence of their own senses," not by imagined divine direction (*De rerum natura* 5.1130). Trusting their own senses and experience will also protect them from dependence on human guides and "savoring life through another's mouth" (*De rerum natura* 5.1130).

At the root of all superstitious fears, argues Lucretius, is the fear of death. Even among people who philosophize dispassionately, fear of death lurks deep in their hearts:

> I know that men often speak of sickness or of shameful life as more to be dreaded than the terrors of hell. . . . But all this talk is based more on desire to show off rather than on actual proof, as you may infer from their conduct. These same men, though they be exiled from home, banished far from the sight of their fellows, soiled with some filthy crime, a prey to every torment, still cling to life. Whenever they come in their tribulation, they make propitiatory sacrifices, slaughter black cattle and dispatch offerings to the Departed Spirits. The heavier their afflictions, the more devoutly they turn their minds to superstition. Look at a man in the midst of doubt and danger, and you will learn in his hour of adversity what he really is. (*De rerum natura* 3.35ff.)

Lucretius believes that death is not an enemy to be feared but a blessing to be welcomed, because it brings peace. The poets' descriptions of hell are merely symbolic of *earthly* sufferings (*De rerum natura* 3.830–1023). True happiness lies in cheerfully accepting death as the universal fate of all, rather than perpetually seeking to run away from it. Only such serene acceptance frees human beings from the chains of superstition, anxiety, alienation, and their frantic search for other sources of happiness:

> Men feel plainly enough within their minds a heavy burden, whose weight depresses them. If only they perceived with equal clearness the causes of the depression, the origin of this lump of evil within their breasts, they would not lead such a life as we now see all too commonly—no one knowing what he really wants and everyone for ever trying to get away from where he is, as though mere locomotion could throw off the load. . . . So long as the object of our craving is unattained, it seems more precious than anything besides. Once it is ours we crave for something else. So an unquenchable thirst for life keeps us always on the gasp. (*De rerum natura* 3.1040ff.)

Thus freed from fear of death, one may enjoy life to the full. But here Lucretius makes a sharp distinction between the tranquil enjoyment of nature's pleasures and the riotous, frenetic satisfaction of cravings. Such passions merely demonstrate that people are still anxiously grasping at life and that fear of death still has a hold on them.

In Lucretius's discussion of sensual pleasure in book 4 of *De rerum natura*, he says almost nothing about wine, women, and song; indeed most of his argument is about the natural "penalties" of passion. Lovers' passions are "storm-tossed" and violent "because their pleasure is not pure." Lovers are "goaded by an undying impulse to hurt the thing, whatever it may be, that gives rise to these budding shoots of madness" (*De rerum natura* 4.1078ff.). Faced with such sexual temptations, celibacy is much the better course of life, says Lucretius. "Do not think that by avoiding grand passions you are missing the delights of Venus. Rather, you are reaping such profits as carry with them no penalty." Such *rational* restraint—as opposed to superstitious restraint—will keep "life's best years [from being] squandered in sloth and debauchery" (*De rerum natura* 4.1138).

De rerum natura was published posthumously, a few months after Lucretius's death in 55 BCE, and his poetry was highly praised. Cicero's brother, Quintus, wrote him a letter with a favorable review, and we have Cicero's response of February 10, 54 BCE: "The poems of Lucretius are just as you write—with frequent flashes of genius, and yet exceedingly artistic" (*The Letters to His Brother* 2.11.5). But he says no more. Lucretius's uncompromising philosophy had few genuine adherents, even among fellow skeptics like Cicero. Many might be willing to suspend belief in divination, but few were willing to give up entirely on tradition, religion, or a sense of divine purpose. Others might call themselves Epicureans but have little in common with the ascetic teaching of Lucretius himself: "Under the Roman Empire there were many avowed Epicureans; but they were interested in the Master's tolerant and easy-going morality rather than its scientific and philosophic foundations."[2]

Cicero

If Lucretius had only limited philosophical success in the ancient world, the same cannot be said of Cicero (Marcus Tullius Cicero, 106–43 BCE). He had a major influence on Roman attitudes toward divination with his *De divinatione* (On divination), completed in 45 BCE.[3] The following year, devastated by the death of his only daughter, Tullia, at age 26, a month after the birth of her second child, Cicero wrote *De fato* (On fate). Both of these were meant as concluding volumes to his earlier series, *De natura deorum* (On the nature of the gods).[4]

De divinatione (like the other two works in the series) is a model of academic even-handedness. Cicero presents as fairly as he can the arguments for and against divination, and he respects the skill of writers who have defended it:

> While most of my war of words has been with these men, it is not because I hold them in special contempt, but on the contrary, it is because they seem to me to defend their own views with the greatest acuteness and skill. Moreover, it is characteristic of the Academy to put forward no conclusions of its own, but to approve those which appear to approach nearest the truth; to compare arguments; to draw forth all that may be said on behalf of any opinion; and without asserting any authority of its own, to leave the judgment of the inquirer wholly free. (*Div.* 2.70.150)

None of this apparent academic objectivity, however, masks Cicero's deeper mission. He is firmly on the side of the skeptics and fully convinced that the debate over superstition in all its forms is no mere intellectual exercise. Like Lucretius he believes that superstition is the source of terrible fears and needless anxieties. The superstitious are always seeing some sort of "sign"—from stars and planets, flights of birds, lightning, dreams, chance sayings. They are driven mad by this multitude of incomprehensible messages and are forced to run to oracles and soothsayers and temples to keep themselves and their families from divine peril. "And since necessarily some of these signs are nearly always being given, no one who believes in them can ever remain in a tranquil state of mind" (*Div.* 2.72.149). Ridding people of this scourge is a public service:

> Speaking frankly, superstition, which is widespread among the nations, has taken advantage of human weakness to cast its spell over the mind of almost

every man. This same view was stated in my treatise *On the Nature of the Gods*; and to prove the correctness of that view has been the chief aim of the present discussion. For I thought that I should be rendering a great service both to myself and to my countrymen if I could tear this superstition up by the roots. (*Div.* 2.72.148; see also 2.5.16)

Cicero has no doubt that divination is widely—and wildly—popular, even among ancient and modern philosophers who, in his opinion, should know better. But the mere popularity of divination is no proof of its truth: "As if there were anything so absolutely common as want of sense" (*Div.* 2.39.81). No, in spite of its popularity, Cicero concludes after exhaustive analysis that divination "is compounded of a little error, a little superstition, and a good deal of fraud" (*Div.* 2.39.83).

In analyzing divination Cicero was not setting up a straw man. In dialogue form book 1 presents divination in its best light, as defended by his brother Quintus. And even Quintus can reject the shams of marketplace divination. He tells Cicero:

I do not recognize fortune tellers, or those who prophesy for money, or necromancers, or mediums. . . . In fine I say, I do not care a fig for Marsian augurs, village mountebanks, astrologers who haunt the Circus grounds, or Isis-seers, or dream interpreters—for they are not diviners, either by knowledge or skill, but superstitious quacks, averse to work, or mad, or ruled by want, directing others how to go, and yet what road to take they do not know themselves. (*Div.* 1.58.132)

Laying all these aside, Quintus still defends the central Stoic contention, that the gods care for human beings, and therefore they "often advise and forewarn" (*Div.* 1.58.132). Thus he approves of "divination which is not trivial and is free from falsehood and trickery" (*Div.* 1. 58.132). Above all, this means that Quintus accepts the "natural divination" of dreams and prophecy.

This is not enough for Cicero. In his view Quintus and Romans like him have been seduced by Greek philosophy, and one of the key aims of *De divinatione* is to counteract this pernicious foreign influence with solid Roman thought. He hopes that all his books "[will] redound to the fame and glory of the Roman people to be made independent of the Greek writers in the study of philosophy" (*Div.* 2.2.5). The best he can say about Quintus's position is that "[he] illustrated [his] arguments with many incidents taken from Roman sources" (*Div.* 2.3.8).

Both sides in this debate accept the assumption that when they use the word "divination" they are speaking about the prediction of future events. Divination is a power "by which the future is foreseen" (*Div.* 2.48.100; see also 1.1.1, 2.49.101,

2.51.105, 2.52.107). The purpose of divination is "to know in advance the dispo-sition of the gods towards men, the manner in which that disposition is shown and by what means the gods may be propitiated and their threatened ills averted" (*Div.* 2.63.130, quoting the Greek Stoic philosopher Chrysippus, 279–206 BCE). In defining divination Cicero equates the Latin *divinatio* with the Greek *mantikē* and characteristically sees even this difference in terminology as evidence of Roman superiority: "Just as we Romans have done many other things better than the Greeks, so have we excelled them in giving to this most extraordinary gift a name which we have derived from *divi*, a word meaning 'gods,' whereas ac-cording to Plato's interpretation they have derived it from madness [*mantikē, mania*], meaning frenzy" (*Div.* 1.1.1).

Cicero has zero taste for the confusing and ambiguous nature of divination. If the gods wanted to communicate, then surely they would do so straightfor-wardly and simply: "What is the need of a method which, instead of being di-rect, is so circuitous and roundabout that we have to employ men to interpret our dreams? And if it is true that God consults for our advantage he would say 'do this,' 'don't do that' and would give us visions when we are awake rather than when we are asleep" (*Div.* 2.61.127; see also 2.64.131). Nor is there any comfort if a few dreams prove true from time to time. How is one to distin-guish the true from the false? "As a rule we do not believe a liar even when he tells the truth" (*Div.* 2.71.146).

Cicero gives the decline of the Delphic Oracle as evidence that the pre-sent generation is less credulous than their ancestors: "The main question is this: Why are the Delphic oracles . . . not uttered at the present time and have not been for a long time? And why are they regarded with the utmost con-tempt?" (*Div.* 2.57.117). He goes on to dismiss the defensive argument that the vapors that inspired the priestess no longer operate. This is too conven-ient: "When did the virtue disappear? Was it after men began to be less cred-ulous?" (*Div.* 2.57.117). He cites Demosthenes, who accused the priestess of being a political tool:

By the way, Demosthenes, who lived nearly three hundred years ago, used to say even then that the Pythian priestess "philippised," in other words, that she was Philip's ally [King Philip of Macedon]. By this expression he meant to infer that she had been bribed by Philip. Hence we may conclude that in other instances the Delphic oracles were not entirely free of guile. But for some inexplicable cause, those superstitious and half-cracked philosophers of yours would rather appear absurd than anything else in the world. You Stoics, instead of rejecting these incredible tales, prefer to believe that a power had gradually faded into nothingness, whereas if it ever had existed it certainly would be eternal. (*Div.* 2.57.119)

Cicero's argument seeks to undermine divination at the level of its two deepest philosophical assumptions: (1) that there is "cosmic sympathy" and (2) that the future is predetermined (*Div.* 2.1, 2.51). But since both of these assumptions "are the subject of doubt and discussion," they cannot be used as the logical foundation to build a case for divination (*Div.* 2.1.104).

First, "cosmic sympathy" is an untenable idea, argues Cicero. While he accepts the link between natural causes and effects, he ridicules other "sympathetic" connections: "What natural bond of union is there between dreams, on the one hand, and treasure, legacies, public office, victory . . . on the other?" (*Div.* 2.69.142).

Second, the future is not predetermined, so he rejects fatalism: "It is not certain what the future will be" (*Div.* 2.1.106). He agrees that everything happens through a cause, but sometimes mere chance is the cause and there is no "plan" (*Div.* 2.11.28). It may be called fate, but what occurs is neither predetermined nor planned. Thus Cicero rejects those who argue that passive acceptance of all that occurs is the best course in life:

> For they argue as follows: "If it is fated for you to recover from this illness, you will recover, whether you call a doctor or do not; similarly, if it is fated for you not to recover from this illness, you will not recover whether you call in a doctor or do not; and either your recovery or your non-recovery is fated; therefore there is no point in calling in a doctor." This mode of reasoning is rightly called "idle" and indolent, because the same train of reasoning will lead to the entire abolition of action from life. (*Div.* 2.11.28–29)

Cicero admits that external circumstances influence human beings, but our free will remains. In contrast, fatalism takes away freedom of assent and action:

> If all things take place by fate, all things take place with an antecedent cause; and if desire is caused, those things which follow desire also are caused; therefore assent is caused. But if the cause of desire is not situated within us, even desire itself is also not in our power; and if this is so, those things which are caused by desire also do not rest with us. It follows therefore that neither assent nor action is in our power. (*On Fate* 17.40)

If "neither assent nor action is in our power," then "there is no justice in either praise or blame, either honors or punishments" (*On Fate* 17.40). Cicero sees this as contrary both to reason and to human experience, and on this basis too fatalism must be rejected (see also *Div.* 2.7–10). No, our minds are our own. Our thoughts are under our own control and free of external compulsion: "No external cause need be sought to explain the voluntary movements of the mind; for voluntary motion possesses the intrinsic property of being in our power and of obeying us, and its obedience is uncaused, for its nature is itself the cause of this" (*On Fate* 11.25).

Surprisingly, Cicero's critique of divination doesn't mean that he would follow Lucretius and do away with religion entirely: "I want it distinctly understood that the destruction of superstition does not mean the destruction of religion" (*Div.* 2.72.148). Indeed it is a duty to "extend the influence of religion" as well as to "weed out every root of superstition" (*Div.* 2.72.149). But he clearly distinguishes true religion from the superstitions he has been debunking.

True religion for Cicero has two powerful unifying forces that call for his allegiance: nature and tradition. First, Cicero links religion to the beauty and order of the physical world: "The celestial order and the beauty of the universe compel me to confess that there is some excellent and eternal Being who deserves the respect and homage of men" (*Div.* 2.71.148). He says his opponents are rash for basing their belief in the gods on such flimsy grounds as divination. Although divination is false, "we must hold on to the gods": "Observe how rashly they commit themselves to the proposition, 'if there is no divination, there are no gods.' I say 'rashly,' for it is yet evident that divination has been destroyed and yet we must hold on to the gods" (*Div.* 2.17.41).

Elsewhere Cicero speaks of the "surpassing excellence in all things" of the "immortal gods" (*Div.* 2.63.129). Yet far from enhancing the gods, divination *demeans* them. Take dreams, for example. Are we to imagine, he asks, that the gods flit about "and when they find someone snoring, they throw at him dark and twisted visions, which scare him from his sleep and which he carries in the morning to a dream expert to unravel? . . . Which is more consonant with philosophy: to explain these apparitions by the superstitious theories of fortune-telling hags, or by an explanation based on natural causes?" (*Div.* 2.63.129).

Despite his sustained philosophical attack on divination, for Cicero faithfulness to Roman tradition is a powerful reason to preserve its religion, including some aspects of divination: "For I consider it the part of wisdom to preserve the institutions of our forefathers by retaining their sacred rites and ceremonies" (*Div.* 2.72.148). But while the religious forms remains the same, and thus link Romans past and present, the meaning attributed to the rites has been utterly changed. Cicero accepts the forms but rejects belief. Having refuted divination with intellectual force and passion, he finds no conflict in fulfilling his duties as a dedicated member of the College of Augurs, which was entrusted with interpreting the Sibylline books and other divine signs affecting the empire. As far as he is concerned, the maintenance of such offices is an essential aspect of Roman culture and public service. The office of augur is now about tradition, culture, and "political expediency," not belief in divination: "For my part . . . I think that, although in the beginning augural law was established from a belief in divination, yet later it was maintained and preserved from considerations of political expediency" (*Div.* 2.35.75). He concedes that his stance may appear hypocritical, or at least inconsistent. But this should not present a problem for a modern Roman citizen who no longer accepts the many "erroneous views" of the ancients and can distinguish between belief and practice:

> "To argue against auspices is a hard thing," you say, "for an augur to do." Yes, for a Marsian [Athenian], perhaps; but very easy for a Roman. For we Roman augurs are not the sort who foretell the future by observing the flight of birds and other signs. And yet, I admit that Romulus, who founded the city by the direction of auspices, believed that augury was an art useful in seeing things to come—for the ancients had erroneous views on many subjects. But we see that the art has undergone a change, due to experience, education, or the long lapse of time. However, out of respect for the opinion of the masses and because of the great service to the State we maintain the augural practices, discipline, religious rites and laws, as well as the authority of the augural college. (*Div.* 2.33.70)

Cicero is thus quite comfortable divorcing theology from practice. Religion as practiced by Cicero has nothing to do with inner convictions or philosophy of life. On that score, he says, the best course to follow for happiness is a life of simple virtue, not the intricate puerilities of divination. In one of his last works, *De officiis* (On duties), he refers approvingly to Panaetius, a Greek admirer of the Roman spirit who rejected divination with its passive submission to Fortune. Like Cicero, he championed as true religion the use of reason and human free will for the benefit of self and others.[5] Divination exploited anxieties and fears while promoting false hopes. It encouraged people to be preoccupied with their private spiritual traumas and consumed with vain speculation about their personal futures. Most significant, belief in divination diverted attention away from the flesh-and-blood challenges of visible reality. Quoting Democritus, Cicero too lamented, "No one regards the things before his feet, but views with care the regions of the sky" (*Div.* 2.13.30). The old Roman values of public virtue and service to the community were dying out, and superstition was to blame. Yet unlike Lucretius, with his scorched earth policy toward religious faith, Cicero had a much surer hand on the pulse of his age. He "recognized the difficulty which educated men faced in his own time, viz., the decline of confidence in the traditional gods and in divine providence, i.e., the divine rule of the world, and at the same time a half-conscious longing for a rational and defensible belief in divine purpose."[6]

Seneca

Seneca (Lucius Annaeus Seneca, 4 BCE–65 CE) was the most eminent statesman and intellectual of St. Paul's day. Indeed, for the historian Tacitus (c. 56–c. 118 CE) Seneca is one of the few heroes in the sordid history of Nero's Rome (see Tacitus, *Annals* 13.2, 14.51ff., 15.60ff.). The second son of the famous rhetorician of the same name, Seneca the Elder (L. Annaeus Seneca, 55 BCE–c. 37/41 CE), Seneca the Younger was a prolific and enormously influential writer. He tutored the young Nero and was then co-regent of Nero's empire eight years, 54–62 CE, with Sextus Afranius Burrus (1–62 CE).[7] Later historians regarded those first five years, "the quintennium," as one of the best periods of the Pax Romana. Seneca's fortunes changed when Nero as emperor became increasingly depraved. Nero most likely had Burrus poisoned in 62, and three years later Seneca was viciously maligned and forced to commit suicide. As mentioned earlier, Seneca's nephew, the poet Lucan, also fell out of favor with Nero and was also forced to put an end to his own life the same year.

Seneca's older brother Gallio was proconsul of Achaia in 52 CE, when Paul was brought before his tribunal in Corinth (Acts 18:12–17). At least two sets of Seneca's essays were addressed to Gallio: the three books of *On Anger* (*De ira*), written in the early 40s, and *On the Happy Life* (*De vita beata*), written in 58–59 CE. Nero forced Gallio to commit suicide a year after he did the same to Seneca and Lucan.

The early Christian church had such a high regard for Seneca, who was almost an exact contemporary of St. Paul, that it was widely believed Seneca and Paul corresponded extensively. This supposed correspondence was well known and long viewed as authentic, according to Jerome.[8] The apocryphal *Passion of Paul* (fourth century CE) says that Seneca frequently corresponded with Paul, admired him, and read his letters to Nero. And no less an authority than Augustine quotes approvingly Seneca's arguments against pagan religion (*City of God* 6.10–11).

Seneca has no patience for most of the religious life percolating around Rome. Like Cicero 80 years earlier, he viewed superstition as a travesty of true worship. But he is more uncompromising than Cicero. Seneca is unwilling to concede that maintaining Roman tradition justifies practices that dishonor God. Roman tradition is no excuse for religion that misrepresents the true nature of God. And unlike Cicero, Seneca refuses to divorce theology from practice. True worship must spring from a correct understanding of God's nature. To reform the religious attitudes of Rome, one must begin with good theology, otherwise no genuine reformation will take root:

Precepts are commonly given as to how the gods should be worshipped. But let us forbid lamps to be lighted on the Sabbath, since the gods do not need light, neither do men take pleasure in soot. Let us forbid men from offering morning salutation and to throng the doors of temples; mortal ambitions are attracted at such ceremonies, but God is worshipped by those who truly know him. Let us forbid bringing towels and flesh-scrapers to Jupiter, and proffering mirrors to Juno; for god seeks no servants. Of course not; he himself does service to mankind, everywhere and to all he is at hand to help. (*Epistles* 95.47)[9]

For Seneca, the fundamental fact of theology is God's goodness. Only when this begins to be appreciated can a person be freed from slavery to religious practices based on fear of the gods as brutal and vindictive:

Although a man hears what limit he should observe in sacrifice, and how far he should recoil from burdensome superstitions, he will never make sufficient progress until he has conceived a right idea of god, regarding him as one who possesses all things, and allots all things, and bestows them without price. And what reason have the gods for doing deeds of kindness? It is their nature. One who thinks that they are unwilling to do harm, is wrong; they *cannot* do harm. They cannot receive or inflict injury; for doing harm is in the same category as suffering harm. The universal nature, all-glorious and beautiful, has rendered incapable of inflicting ill those whom it has removed from the danger of ill. (*Moral Letters* 95.47–48)[10]

Seneca deals directly with divine guidance in several of his works, the most important of which is *On Providence* (*De providentia*), written in 41 or 42 CE or perhaps later, and included among his *Moral Essays*.[11] Here Seneca begins by asserting God's goodness and his care for all; indeed the main theme throughout the essay is that God "is at hand to help." Seneca puts his trust in this beneficent providence, and in all circumstances, pleasant and unpleasant, searches for the benefit to be found, arguing that this is the best route to happiness and tranquility. Most people would rather worship Bona Fortuna, he says, but this leaves them generally unhappy since good fortune occurs so rarely (*De prov.* 1.1).

There is a close friendship—even kinship and likeness—between the gods and those who are good. But this does not translate into ease of life. On the contrary, it is precisely this human-divine kinship that demands God's strict attention to disciplined training of his children: "Friendship do I say? Nay, rather there is a tie of relationship and a likeness [*similitudo*], since in truth, a good man differs from God in the element of time only; he is God's pupil, his imitator, and true offspring, whom his all-glorious parent, being no mild task-master of virtues, rears, as strict fathers do, with much severity" (*De prov.* 1.5).

Seneca's essay was originally a response to a question put to him by his friend Lucilius. Why, if providence rules the world, do so many evil misfortunes befall good people? Seneca, however, rejects the premise that misfortune is evil (*De prov.* 4.7). The very fact that someone is good demands that he or she be given the best training and testing. This is the function of all of those so-called evils. He compares them to harsh surgical and medical treatments, or the demanding regimens prescribed to only the most promising athletes (*De prov.* 2.6). Only in this way can providence shape people of strong character (*De prov.* 3.2). But there is no elitism here, since everyone at some point in his or her life will be trained and tested in this way. Lest those who have not experienced these trials feel less "promising" and less loved, Seneca assures them that they too will have their turn: "In like manner God hardens, reviews, and disciplines those whom he approves, whom he loves. Those however whom he seems to favor, whom he seems to spare, he is really keeping soft against ills to come. For you are wrong if you suppose that anyone is exempt from ill" (*De prov.* 4.7). Suffering is a sign of worthiness, a gift for which one should offer grateful thanks: "God has deemed us worthy instruments of his purpose to discover how much human nature can endure" (*De prov.* 4.8). "Why then is it strange if God tries noble spirits with severity? No proof of virtue is ever mild. If we are lashed and torn by Fortune, let us bear it; it is not cruelty but a struggle, and the oftener we engage in it the stronger we shall be. . . . We should offer ourselves to Fortune in order that, struggling with her, we may be hardened by her. Gradually she will make us a match for herself" (*De prov.* 4.12).

Scorn poverty, scorn pain, scorn death, urges Seneca. Scorn even Fortuna, for God says, "I have given her no weapon with which she may strike your soul" (*De prov.* 6.6). The greatest afflictions belong to the best of human beings, so it is an honor to receive them (*De prov.* 4.8). Misfortune is thus the primary means of divine guidance. By welcoming afflictions the well-trained human being may even "outstrip God": "He is exempt from enduring evil, while you are superior to it" (*De prov.* 1.6).

For Seneca, this line of reasoning eliminates one of the basic premises of divination: that the future needs to be known in order that the gods might be propitiated and misfortune averted. But if misfortunes are actually to be welcomed, why seek to avoid them? Why be anxious about the future? Accept all that comes as a gift from the bounty of divine providence. Contrary to popular belief, says Seneca, one should be wary of so-called good fortune. What causes most damage to one's soul and character is not perpetual misfortune but its opposite: constant *good* fortune. "While all excesses are hurtful, the most dangerous is unlimited good fortune. It excites the brain, it evokes vain fancies in the mind, and clouds in deep fog the boundary between falsehood and truth" (*De prov.* 4.10).

Seneca's understanding of divine providence is closely related to his views on fate and happiness. God is good and cares for all human beings, but the entire universe—God included—is bound by a predetermined fate which is controlled by the moon, planets, and stars: "On even the slightest motion of these hang the fortunes of nations, and the greatest and smallest happenings are shaped to accord with the progress of a kindly or unkindly star" (*To Marcia on Consolation* [De Consolatione ad Marciam], *Moral Essays 2*, 18.3).

This sounds very much like Posidonius's "cosmic sympathy." But for Seneca, unlike Posidonius, this cosmic interconnection of all events does not imply that divination is worthwhile. On the contrary, trying to divine the future or appease Fortuna only breeds anxiety, fear, and superstition. He views divination as "the depth of servitude" (*De prov.* 15.4) and says, "The whole domain of Fortune I despise" (*De prov.* 25.5).

Seneca accepts that the universe is a finely tuned harmony ultimately governed by fate, but this doesn't mean one has to take a passive approach to life. However, he recognizes that there is a limited field in which to make decisions, since for most human beings the external aspects of their lives are *not* under their control. (Hence Seneca views suicide as the supreme divine gift of self-determination. It is ironic, then, that he was *forced* to take his own life.)

The one area in which a person has complete freedom of action is his or her inner life of attitudes and reactions. Therefore even a predetermined divine plan imposed from outside cannot restrict one's freedom. Seneca willingly and actively cooperates with the plan set down by God; he does not merely throw up his hands in passive submission: "I am under no compulsion, I suffer nothing against my will, and I am not God's slave but his follower, and the more so, indeed because I know that everything proceeds according to a law that is fixed and enacted for all time" (*De prov.* 5.7).

Seneca needs no divination because he seeks no escape from the future. He faces the future unafraid, greets whatever fate the future brings with open arms. His cooperation, however, has no effect whatsoever on his fate. Cooperation merely allows his inner being to remain free, unconstrained, and tranquil. Whatever decisions he makes are ultimately the decision he was meant to make, since everything happens as it must:

> Fate guides us, and it was settled at the first hour of our birth what length of time remains for each. Cause is linked with cause, and all public and private issues are directed by a long sequence of events. Therefore everything should be endured with fortitude, since things do not, as we suppose, simply happen—they all come. (*De prov.* 5.7)

> What then is the part of a good man? To offer himself to Fate. It is a great consolation that it is together with the universe that we are swept along; whatever it is that has been ordained us so to live, so to die, by the same necessity it binds

also the gods. One unchangeable course bears along the affairs of men and gods alike. Although the great creator and ruler of the universe himself wrote the decrees of Fate, yet he follows them. He obeys forever, he decreed but once. (*De prov.* 5.8)

Seneca's fabulous wealth—the result of his close association with Nero—inevitably drew scorn from critics of his philosophy. He was criticized for having too much power (though Tacitus reports that Seneca offered to resign and withdraw to a life of study; *Annals* 14.53). He was accused of being a hypocrite, since his luxurious lifestyle and power clashed dramatically with his austere Stoic preaching. Not least among his critics was his older brother Gallio, to whom Seneca dedicated a blistering essay in response, *De vita beata*, written when he had already retired from Rome after Nero turned against him (Tacitus, *Annals,* 14.51).

Seneca admits that he isn't perfect, but this shouldn't be surprising, since he is still on a spiritual journey. At least he knows he's on the right path, since he has had a taste of innocent suffering: "I have already had the good fortune to win the displeasure of the wicked, which is proof enough of my uprightness" (*De vita beata* 24.5). But then he turns the tables on Gallio and goes on the offensive. He accuses Gallio of being unwilling to learn about this path to genuine happiness. He is too superstitious, too addicted to pleasure, too obtuse to see his own miserable condition. And he is too critical of others to see his own faults: "Have you the leisure to search out others' evils and pass judgment upon anybody? . . . You look at the pimples of others when you yourself are covered with a mass of sores" (*De vita beata* 27.4). Seneca adopts Socrates's defense against his critics: their judgments about him are just as false as their judgments about God: "I put up with your babblings even as Jupiter Greatest and Best puts up with the silly fancies of poets [who depict the gods as unjust, cruel, adulterers, ravishers, parricides and usurpers]. . . . All that they have accomplished is that men are relieved of shame at doing wrong if they believe the gods are such" (*De vita beata* 26.7).

Guidance is one of the main themes of *De vita beata*. Everyone wants "happiness," but what is it? How does one get it? There are so many competing answers crying out in the bazaars of pleasure, religion, and ideas that most human beings are in a permanent state of confusion trying to find a reliable path. Therefore the first step toward leading a happy life is to find an experienced guide:

So long as we wander aimlessly, having no guide, and following only the noise and discordant cries of those who call us in different directions, life will be consumed in making mistakes—life that is brief even if we should strive day and night for sound wisdom. Let us therefore decide both upon the goal and upon the way, and not fail to find some experienced guide who has explored the region towards which we are advancing; for conditions on this journey are different from those most travel. On most journeys some well-recognized road and inquiries made of the inhabitants of the region prevent you from going astray; but on this one all the best beaten and the most frequented paths are the most deceptive. (*De vita beata* 1.1–2)

Where can such a guide be found? Certainly not by following the crowd. Seneca warns that the crowd is the surest guide where *not* to go; imitation should never take precedence over reason. "It is the example of other people that is our undoing; let us merely separate ourselves from the crowd, and we shall be made whole" (*De vita beata* 1.5).

Our own instincts and judgments are a much surer guide: "So long as each one of us is more willing to trust another than to judge for himself, we never show any judgment in the matter of living, but always a blind trust, and a mistake that has been passed down from hand to hand finally involves us and works our destruction" (*De vita beata* 1.4). Seneca cites Socrates, who refused to change his life merely to suit the opinions of others: "Upon nothing, says Socrates, or any other who has like authority, am I more strongly resolved than not to change my course of life to suit your opinion" (*De vita beata* 26.5).

Seneca defines happiness as "life in harmony with its own nature" (*De vita beata* 3.4; also 8.1–2). The way of nature is God's way, and thus nature is the surest guide to happiness. And since we ourselves are of nature, we must take ourselves as guide. To follow and obey God means to follow natural virtue (*De vita beata* 4.6), which for Seneca begins with tranquility in the face of all external events. Happiness is the fruit of being "superior to pleasure, superior to pain" (*De vita beata* 4.4) and "indifferent to Fortune" (*De vita beata* 4.5). "The happy man therefore is one who has right judgment; the happy man is content with his present lot, no matter what it is, and is reconciled to his circumstances; the happy man is he who allows reason to fix the value of every condition of existence" (*De vita beata* 6.2). The person who obeys God in this way is both happy and truly free, because he is the tranquil master of all that is under his control. Thus Seneca paradoxically equates obedience with freedom: "To obey God is freedom" (*De vita beata* 15.7).

God himself, as the source of nature, is the ultimate example of the one who is guided from within.

For God also, the all-embracing world and the ruler of the universe, reaches forth into outward things, yet, withdrawing from all sides returns unto himself. And our mind should do the same; when, having followed the senses that serve it, it has through them reached to things without, let it be master both of them and of itself. In this way will be born an energy that is united, a power that is at harmony with itself, and that dependable reason which is not divided against itself, nor uncertain either in its opinions, or its perceptions, or its convictions; and this reason, when it has regulated itself, and established harmony between all its parts, and, so to speak, is in tune, has attained the highest good. (*De vita beata* 8.6)

Nature is guide, and nature is also the motivation for doing good to others, not under compulsion but freely, as we recognize the connections we have to each other: "Nature bids me to do good to all mankind—whether slaves or freemen, freeborn or freedmen, whether the laws gave them freedom or a grant in the presence of a friend—what difference does it make? Wherever there is a human being there is the opportunity for a kindness" (*De vita beata* 24.3).

In contrast to this philosophy, says Seneca, popular religion undermines such virtue by promoting superstitious self-preoccupation, fear, listening to priests and oracles, and going to temples and shrines for countless rituals. All of this is a distraction from noticing and serving the needs of others. Instead of obsessing about religious oracles, it is much better to seek opportunities for doing good by listening to the inner "oracle" of virtue: "It is far more necessary that you lay this command upon yourself, in order that, whenever utterance is delivered from that oracle [virtue] you may listen with attentive ear and hushed voice" (*De vita beata* 26.7).

While firmly rejecting traditional forms of divine guidance, Seneca is a profoundly moral and spiritual man, aware of the divine presence in the world and in people whose lives are made holy by their tranquility and service to others. In a letter to his friend Lucillius not long before Seneca's death, he urges him to look at the beauties of the natural world if he wants evidence of God: "They will persuade you of the presence of the deity" and "strike into your soul some inkling of the divine." But even more convincing proof of God is the holy person, whose peace demonstrates the presence of a divine power: "Someone never alarmed by dangers, never affected by cravings, happy in adversity, calm in the midst of storm, viewing mankind from a higher level and the gods from their own . . . Into that body there has descended a divine power."[12]

In speaking of the holy person, Seneca may well have had in mind the example of his admired friend, the Cynic Demetrius, of whom he spoke in his essay *On Providence*:

Here is another spirited utterance which, I remember, I heard that most valiant man, Demetrius, make: "Immortal gods," said he, "I have this one complaint to make against you, that you did not earlier make known your will to me; for I should have reached the sooner that condition in which, after being summoned, I now am. Do you wish to take my children? it was for you that

I fathered them. Do you wish to take some member of my body? take it. No great thing am I offering you, very soon I shall leave the whole. Do you wish to take my life? why not? I shall make no protest against your taking back what you once gave. With my free consent you shall have whatever you ask of me. What then is my trouble? I should have preferred to offer than to relinquish. What was the need to take by force? You might have had it as a free gift. Yet even now you will not take it by force, because nothing can be wrenched away from a man unless he withholds it." (*De providentia* 5.5–6).

Perhaps Demetrius best summarizes that resilience, tranquility, and inner freedom—even in the face of an uncertain divine will—to which Seneca himself aspired.

Pliny the Elder

Like the other Roman philosophers we've surveyed so far, Pliny the Elder (Gaius Plinius Secundus, 23–79 CE) has little good to say about divination or perceptions of divine guidance, all of which he viewed as superstition. But religious and philosophical questions are far from his main interests. His talents as a writer and orator were noted early in his life; he served as a navy and army commander, held high political offices (including several postings as a provincial procurator), and was a friend of Emperor Vespasian (9–79 CE). His encyclopedic *Naturalis Historia* (Natural history) runs 37 volumes covering mainly subjects in science and engineering—botany, zoology, astronomy, geology, mineralogy and mining, agriculture—but also the history of art. And he includes as well the subject of religion, although he admits to being cautious in this area because of the varied feelings such controversial discussions arouse in his readers. He also recognizes that religion might appear to be out of place in a natural history, but he is willing to express his strong views on god, fate, and divination since these topics "have already been widely disseminated because of the unceasing enquiry into the nature of God" (*Nat.* 2.27).

Pliny sees divination as a natural human temptation: "Our mind is always on the lookout for something big, something adequate to move a god, or rather impose our will on his divinity" (*Nat.* 28.4.228). He admits that even Emperor Augustus followed common superstitious practices:

After a serious accident in his carriage, [Augustus] is said always, as soon as he was seated, to have been in the habit of repeating three times a formula or prayer for a safe journey, a thing we know that most people do today. (*Nat.* 28.6.30)

We certainly still have formulas to charm away hail, various diseases and burns, some actually tested by experience, but I am very shy of quoting them, because of the widely differing feelings they arouse. Wherefore everyone must form his own opinion about these matters as he pleases. (*Nat.* 28.6.30)[13]

In book 2 Pliny gives his own view at some length. He says that the universe is itself "divine" (*numen; Nat.* 2.1), but it is "at once the work of nature and nature herself" (*Nat.* 2.2). Within nature, the sun is the ruling principle: "Taking into account all that he effects, we must believe him to be the soul, or more precisely the mind of the whole world, the supreme ruling principle and divinity [*numen*] of nature. . . . He is glorious and pre-eminent, all-seeing and even all-hearing" (*Nat.* 2.13).

The sun may be "the supreme ruling principle," but this does not mean it is God in any personal sense. For Pliny, the very existence of a God is a debatable subject, but the idea of "gods" in the plural is just foolish: "Whoever God is—provided there is a God—and in whatever region he is, he consists wholly of sense, sight and hearing, wholly of soul, wholly of mind, wholly of himself. To believe in gods without number . . . is even a greater height of folly" (*Nat.* 2.14). The many gods of religious traditions are merely human constructs: "Frail, toiling mortality, remembering its own weakness, has divided such deities into groups, so as to worship in sections, each the deity he is most in need of" (*Nat.* 2.15). He dismisses all the mythical stories of gods as the "fancies of children" (*Nat.* 2.17).

As noted in an earlier chapter, Pliny also rejects one of the basic tenets of divination: that a supreme being is interested in human events. Such a belief is just human self-importance (*Nat.* 2.25). "That this Supreme Being, whatever it is, pays heed to man's affairs is a ridiculous notion. Can we believe that it would not be defiled by so gloomy and multifarious a duty? Can we doubt it?" (*Nat.* 2.20).

Pliny is scandalized by the popularity of religion and the superstitions it breeds, much of it imported from the Greek and Oriental East. How can any of this be of benefit to society? At least atheism does not promote degrading practices that promote fear and servility:

It is scarcely pertinent to determine which is more profitable for the human race, when some men pay no regard to the gods at all and the regard paid by others is of a shameful nature: they serve as the lackeys of foreign ritual, and they carry gods on their fingers [engraved on rings] . . . they subject themselves to awful tyrannies, so as to find no repose even in sleep; they do not decide on marriage or having a family [whether to rear or to expose the children born to them] or indeed anything else except by the command of sacrifices. (*Nat.* 2.20–21)

Pliny also dismisses the cult of Fortuna, which had invaded every corner of Roman life: "Chance herself, by whom God is proved uncertain, takes the place of God" (*Nat.* 2.23). But if Fortune does not rule the universe, neither does some predetermined cosmic Fate. Pliny rejects fatalism and every type of divination it spawns, especially astrology:

> Another set of people banishes Fortune also, and attributes events to its star and to the laws of birth, holding that for all men that ever are to be God's decree has been enacted once for all, while for the rest of time leisure has been vouchsafed to Him. This belief begins to take root, and the learned and unlearned mob alike go marching towards it at the double: witness the warnings drawn from lightning, the forecasts made by oracles, the prophecies of augurs and even inconsiderable trifles—a sneeze, a stumble—counted as omens. (*Nat.* 2.5.22–25)

Who or what is God, then, for Pliny? Certainly not an omniscient and omnipotent personal supreme being. Pliny shows such a God to be powerless in many instances. He can't make mortals immortal. He can't change the past. He can't "cause twice ten not to be twenty." And above all, he can't commit suicide, which for human beings is "the supreme boon that he has bestowed on man among all the penalties of life" (*Nat.* 2.5.27).

Pliny's God is simple virtue, "mortal aiding mortal." As a devoted Roman pragmatist he especially despises the intricacies of Greek writing and theology. Rome is at the heart of Pliny's thought, and he is deeply offended by the spread of foreign books that lead people astray into useless speculations, away from the true God of virtue. He even ridicules the florid titles of Greek books: "When you get inside them, good heavens, what a void you will find between the covers!" Romans, in contrast, not only "use more serious titles" (*Nat.* Preface, 24); they have a vast "appetite for all things useful and good" (*Nat.* 2.25.4).

Not surprisingly, Pliny finds this God of virtue best revealed in Rome's past and present leaders, most notably his friend and patron, Emperor Vespasian: "God is mortal aiding mortal; and this is the road to eternal glory: by this road went our Roman chieftains, by this road now proceeds with heavenward step, escorted by his children, the greatest ruler of all time, His Majesty Vespasian, coming to the succour of an exhausted world. To enroll such men among the deities is the most ancient method of paying them gratitude for their benefactions" (*Nat.* 2.5.19). To call the emperor a god is thus a traditional sign of gratitude for his selfless service to Rome.

In emphasizing public service Pliny takes Livy to task for writing the history of Rome merely for his own pleasure and fame: "For assuredly he ought to have composed his history for the glory of the world-conquering nation and of the Roman name, not for his own; it would have been a greater merit to have persevered from love of the work, not for the sake of his own peace of mind, and to have rendered this service to the Roman nation and not to himself" (*Nat.* Preface, 16).

In summary, Pliny is not interested in theology. For him, the only guidance that counts is whatever leads a person privately and publicly to the selfless service of others.

7

Plutarch

Greco-Roman Bridge between Rational and Mystical

In Plutarch (L. Mestrius Plutarchus of Chaeronia, c. 45–c. 120 CE) we see a writer who straddles the first and second centuries, Greece and Rome, the rational and the mystical. He combines the sober realism of the Roman philosophers with the equally real awareness of divine guidance found in Homer, Virgil, and Posidonius. Like Cicero, Plutarch was critical of popular superstition while also formally involved in the religious cult, in his case as a priest of Delphi, responsible for overseeing the site and interpreting the sayings of the oracle (Figure 7.1). But unlike Cicero, he carried out his role not only out of duty to Rome but out of a deep conviction that God was present and guiding.

It might be argued that as a late first-century writer, a Greek living near Delphi and serving as one of its priests in a period of Roman Hellenism, Plutarch may not reflect the general spirit of Corinth in Paul's day. Indeed the very flavor of some of his essays reflects the Greek mystical preoccupations of a later age: *Isis and Osiris, The "E" at Delphi, The Oracles at Delphi No Longer Given in Verse, The Obsolescence of Oracles, The Daimon of Socrates.*

Yet it is reasonable to assume that some in first-century Corinth (and I would argue Paul, chief among them) would have shared Plutarch's desire to hold rational and mystical together in a unified worldview. Plutarch's outlook might have been especially amenable to people who were unwilling to accept either of two extremes: abandoning notions of personal divine guidance entirely, or giving in to wholesale superstition. In this way, "Plutarch is a crossroads of hardly reconciled teachings; this makes him, with his few claims to originality, a good witness to the perplexities of his age."[1]

Born in Greece not far from Delphi and educated in Athens, Plutarch then spent many years in Rome as a Platonic philosopher and teacher. "He made and retained a large acquaintance with the prominent Romans of his day, and was familiar with the questions which most occupied the minds of men at the political centre of the world."[2] He was proudly Greek and lived in Rome under Trajan and Hadrian, at a time when interest in things Greek was especially high. And like Posidonius he admits that he never felt completely at home in Latin.

At the same time Plutarch took a highly sympathetic view of Roman culture and institutions. He lived in Greece for the last 30 years of his life, where

Divine Guidance. John A. Jillions, Oxford University Press (2020). © Oxford University Press.
DOI: 10.1093/oso/9780190055738.001.0001

Fig. 7.1. Pythian priestess sitting on tripod in the Temple of Apollo at Delphi. Print, 1889. Source: iStock.com/2U_09.

he continued to be an influential figure in government circles and an active exponent of partnership between Greece and Rome. This makes him a uniquely valuable source for the first-century Mediterranean world that was both Greek and Roman.

Despite his Greek roots, Plutarch's *Lives* attests to his genuine appreciation for what was best in Roman culture. He was most attracted by the Roman emphasis on virtue, service, and action in the public domain. The very purpose of writing parallel accounts of Greek and Roman heroes was an attempt to remind a Greek audience that they too had historical figures who exemplified balanced lives of reason, piety, and public service. This was especially uplifting at a time when the Greeks, under long Roman occupation, had lost their confidence for decisive action.

Plutarch's writings on the religious and philosophical issues associated with divine guidance—providence, fate, divination—are "rightly regarded by recent scholarship as the most significant part of his many sided activity."[3] Among his vast collection of works are a number that deal directly with divine guidance, including many no longer extant, such as *On the Art of Prophecy* (*Peri Mantikēs*). This is in addition to the many positive references to the phenomenon in other essays (e.g., *Theseus and Romulus* 1.5, 3.1, 3.2; *Lycurgus and Numa*, 1.1). Plutarch attests to the widespread popularity of all forms of divination. But he regards much of this as superstitious trash; as such, it is more pernicious than atheism. This is the central argument of his essay *On Superstition* (from the Latin translation, *De superstitione*; the original Greek is *Peri Deisidaimonias*, "On fear of daimons"), in which he compares atheism and superstition. The latter, he says, has nothing in common with true piety (*eusebeia*):

> Ignorance and blindness in regard to the gods divides itself into two streams, of which one produces in hardened characters, as it were in stubborn soils, atheism, and the other in tender characters, as in moist soils, produces superstition. Every false judgment, and especially concerning these matters, is a mischievous thing; but where emotion also enters, it is most mischievous. For every emotion is likely to be a delusion that rankles; and just as dislocations of the joints accompanied by lacerations are hardest to deal with, so also is it with derangement of the soul accompanied by emotion. (*Superstition* 164E–F)

Fear and false reasoning are the keys to understanding both atheism and superstition, and both lead to wrong conclusions about God. While atheism leads falsely to *no* fear of God, superstition produces *false* fear: "The atheist apparently is unmoved regarding the Divinity, whereas the superstitious man is moved as he ought not to be. . . . For in the one man ignorance engenders disbelief in the One who can help him, and in the other it bestows the added idea that he causes injury, whence it follows that atheism is falsified reason, and superstition an emotion engendered from false reason" (*Superstition* 165C). The superstitious fear that God might arbitrarily attack and injure is "of all kinds of fear the most impotent and helpless" because it drives a person to see potential harm in everything: "He who fears the gods fears all things" (*Superstition* 165D). Even sleep, with its dreams and nightmares, provides no respite from these superstitious terrors: "When later, such persons arise from their beds, they do not condemn nor ridicule these things, nor realize that not one of the things that agitated them was really true, but, trying to escape the shadow of a delusion . . . during their waking hours they delude and waste and agitate themselves, putting themselves into the hands of conjurors and impostors" (*Superstition* 166A).

Plutarch goes on to list other superstitious practices reputed to be helpful, but none of these can free a person from irrational fear, based as it is on a false understanding of the divine. For the fearfully superstitious there is no escape:

> As for the man who fears the rule of the gods as sullen and inexorable despotism, where can he remove himself, where can he flee, what country can he find without gods, or what sea? Into what part of the universe shall you steal away and hide yourself, poor wretch, and believe that you have escaped God?

There is a law even for the slaves who have given up all hope of freedom, that they may demand a sale, and thus exchange their present master for one more mild. But superstition grants no such exchange; and to find a god whom he shall not fear is impossible for him who fears the gods of his fathers and his kin, who shudders at his saviors, and trembles with terror at those gentle gods from whom we ask wealth, welfare, peace, concord and success in our best efforts in speech and action. (*Superstition* 166E)

Even the temples of the gods, which provide safe haven to runaway slaves and criminals, are for the superstitious person "the very things that most inspire a shuddering fear and dread" (*Superstition* 166E), and "they approach the halls or temples of the gods as they would approach bears' dens or snakes' holes or the haunts of monsters of the deep" (*Superstition* 169E). This cowering dread only proves "how foolish are the words of Pythagoras who said that we reach our best when we draw near to the gods" (*Superstition* 169E). Even the prospect of death cannot bring relief, since there is the prospect of "undying evils and tortures, making fear endure longer than life" (*Superstition* 166F).

Superstitious fear cripples every aspect of life: "Thus unhappy superstition, by its excess of caution in trying to avoid everything suggestive of dread, unwittingly subjects itself to *every* sort of dread" (*Superstition* 167A). In unpleasant circumstances the superstitious person is quick to blame the gods either for their vindictiveness or for meting out a punishment he abjectly deserves. He "lays the responsibility for everything upon God, and says from that source a heaven-sent stream of mischief has come upon him with full force . . . that he's hateful to the gods, that he's being punished by the gods and that the penalty he pays and all that he is undergoing are deserved because of his own conduct. . . . [All troubles] are classed as 'afflictions of God' or 'attacks of an evil spirit'" (*Superstition* 168A).

Superstitious fear has yet another dire effect. By attributing causes to unseen powers greater than himself—often arbitrary and malicious—the superstitious person has no incentive to take practical action to remedy a bad situation:

He has no heart to relieve the situation or undo its effects, or to find some remedy for it or to take a strong stand against it, lest he seem to fight against God and to rebel at his punishment; but when he is ill the physician is ejected from the house, and when he is in grief the door is shut on the philosopher who would advise and comfort him. "Oh Sir," he says, "leave me to pay my penalty, impious wretch that I am, accursed and hateful to the gods and all the heavenly host." (*Superstition* 168C; see also 168E–F)

The superstitious person becomes despondent and helpless, submitting passively to all adversities as though they are being thrown at him by the gods for some fault known or unknown. This apparently pious behavior is in marked contrast to the rest of human beings, "who desperately fight against misfortunes and force their way through difficulties, contriving for themselves means to escape and avert things undesired" (*Superstition* 168C). The atheist in similar trials looks instead for the immediate causes of his problems—other people, unavoidable circumstances, his own error—and either takes action and "tries to procure for himself means of help and comfort," or, if nothing can be done, simply "throws up his hands and rails against chance and the general and inevitable confusion of life" (*Superstition* 168A).

His many years of experience as a priest in Delphi made Plutarch an extremely perceptive observer of religious behavior, and he was not fooled by piety. He notes that the superstitious devote themselves to religion and fawn over their idols but are likely to be self-righteous and judgmental; they are contemptuous of the apparent impiety of philosophers who distance themselves from this sort of religion. Yet it is the philosophers who are closer to the truth, for they "try to prove that the majesty of God is associated with goodness, magnanimity, kindliness and solicitude" (*Superstition* 167E).

If the superstitious attribute harshness to the gods, says Plutarch, in their hearts they must secretly hate the gods. Their religious devotion is thus a thinly veiled attempt to appease a hated and unpredictable master:

> They assume that the gods are rash, faithless, fickle, vengeful, cruel, and easily offended; and as a result, the superstitious man is bound to hate and fear the gods. Why not, since he thinks that the worst of his ills are due to them, and will be due to them in the future? As he hates and fears the gods, he is an enemy to them. And yet, though he dreads them, he worships them and sacrifices to them and besieges their shrines. (*Superstition* 170E)

These devotees are like slaves serving a dreaded overlord of whom they are terrified; while to his face they feign devotion, in their hearts they hate him. The superstitious person is enslaved to a belief he actually despises: "The atheist thinks there are no gods; the superstitious man wishes there were none, but believes in them against his will, for he is afraid not to believe. . . . The superstitious man by preference would be an atheist, but is too weak to hold the opinion about the gods that he wishes to hold" (*Superstition* 170F). It is such beliefs and behaviors of the superstitious that are responsible in large part for producing atheists, who recoil at such disturbing excesses: "The ridiculous actions and emotions of superstition, its words and gestures, magic charms and spells, rushing about and beating drums, impure purifications and polluted sanctifications, barbarous and outlandish penances and mortifications at the shrines—all these give occasion to some to say that it were better there should be no gods at all than gods who accept with pleasure such forms of worship, and are so overbearing, so petty, and so easily offended" (*Superstition* 171B).

The superstitious have thus completely misrepresented the gods and true piety. They take the "gods' kindliness to be frightful, their fatherly solicitude to be despotic, their loving care to be injurious, their slowness to anger to be savage and brutal" (*Superstition* 167D). This is vastly more unholy, says Plutarch, than the atheist's denial of God:

> Why for my part, I should prefer that men should say about me that I have never been born at all, and there is no Plutarch, rather than that they should say "Plutarch is an inconstant fickle person, quick-tempered, vindictive over little accidents, pained at trifles. If you invite him to dinner and leave him out or if you haven't the time and don't go to call on him, or fail to speak to him when you see him, he will set his teeth into your body and bite it through, or he will get hold of your little child and beat him to death, or he will turn the beast that he owns into your crops and spoil your harvest." (*Superstition* 170A)

So far, there is much in Plutarch that is similar to the biting critique of Lucretius, Cicero, Seneca, and Pliny. But Plutarch is unwilling to settle either for atheism or for a civilized deism in which God in any personal sense is comfortably absent while nature and virtue and human responsibility reign supreme. So if Plutarch rejects superstition, he also parts company with these other Roman philosophers. He refuses to give up his experience that God is present, active, and knowable. Superstition is worse than atheism, yet it remains a profound tragedy to have no awareness of God in any personal sense. It is "a great misfortune for the soul . . . for it is as if the soul had suffered the extinction of the brightest and most dominant of its many eyes, the conception of God" (*Superstition* 167B). Avoiding superstition is laudable, but rushing to the opposite extreme is not the answer. The path of true piety (*eusebeia*) is found between these two (*Superstition* 171F).

In Plutarch's view, God cares for the humblest concerns of the individual as much as for the great affairs of state and universe. Plutarch advocates a balanced outlook that integrates reason and personal responsibility on the one hand, with providential divine presence and guidance on the other. This was the kind of co-operative divine-human balance he found, for example, in Homer's Ajax: "As he was about to engage in single combat with Hector, he bade the Greeks pray to the gods for him, and then, while they were praying, donned his armor" (*Superstition* 169C).[4]

We can see this cooperative divine-human synergy in Plutarch's *On the Obsolescence of Oracles*, probably written not long before his election as priest of Delphi around 90 CE. (He was one of two permanent priests responsible for overseeing the site and interpreting the sayings of the oracle, the Pythian priestess.)

As discussed in chapter 1, the decline of Delphi was a well-known phenom-enon, commented on by others in the first century, but Plutarch devotes several essays to Delphi and shows it to be very much alive, albeit more simply and pri-vately than in its heyday. The first point he makes is that oracles have not ceased; only the number of oracular sites has declined owing to a smaller population. He denies that the source of inspiration has dried up, though he also rejects the idea that it was some divine vapor or *daimonoi*, "guardian spirits" (*Obsolescence* 418D). But he admits that many believed there has been a decline, and that "now a great drought in prophecy has overspread the land" (*Obsolescense* 411F). Why, then, has the inspiration apparently evaporated, asks one of Plutarch's friends in a fictional conversation, since such divine guidance would seem to be more necessary than ever in these trying times? Plutarch recounts popular arguments about the decline of the oracles: "People assume one of two things: either that the prophetic priestess does not come near to the region in which is the godhead, or else that the spirit [*pneumatos*] has been completely quenched and her powers have forsaken her" (*The Oracles at Delphi No Longer Given in Verse*, 402C).

Didymus, another participant in this fictional conversation, adds that popular approaches to oracles are irreverent and unworthy of God, so it is not surprising that the oracles have ceased:

> [The oracles] are constantly being occupied with shameful and impious questions which people propound to the god, some of whom try to make a test of him as though his wisdom were an affectation, while others put questions about treasures or inheritance or unlawful marriages; so Pythagoras is proved to be utterly wrong when he says that men are at their best when they approach the gods. Thus those maladies and emotions of the soul which it would be good to disclaim and conceal in the presence of an older man, they bring naked and exposed before the God. (*Obsolescence* 413B)[5]

Didymus's opinion that the gods have no concern for the day-to-day burdens of individuals provokes an indignant reaction. Heracleon jumps up and grabs Didymus by the cloak. Plutarch steps between them but defends Heracleon's pas-sionate conviction that Didymus has spoken rash blasphemy. God indeed cares for all human beings in even their most mundane concerns:

> Cease provoking the God,. . . for he is of good and mild disposition, And towards mortal men he hath been judged the most gentle, as Pindar says. And whether he be the sun or the lord and father of the sun and of all that lies be-yond our vision, it is not likely that he should deny his utterance to people of the present day because of their unworthiness, when he is responsible for their birth and nurture and their existence and power to think; nor is it likely without

that Providence, like a benign helpful mother, who does everything for us and watches over us, should cherish animosity in the matter of prophesy only, and take away that from us after having given it to us at the beginning, as if the number of wicked men included among a larger population were not larger at that earlier time when the oracles were established in many places in the inhabited world. (*Obsolescence* 413D)

God's most precious gift in caring for human beings, says Plutarch, is prophetic communication. This he would never take away. A smaller population means fewer oracles are needed, but oracles as such have never ceased: "Today there is one priestess and we do not complain, for she meets every need. There is no reason therefore to blame the god; the exercise of the prophetic art which continues at the present day is sufficient for all, and sends away all with their desires fulfilled" (*Obsolescence* 414B–C).

Similarly, to explain the sign *E* displayed at the entrance to Delphi, one of the suggestions Plutarch puts forward is that it signifies in Greek *Ei*, meaning "if." In other words, people approach the oracle to ask *if* they will succeed, *if* they will do this or that. And since Apollo welcomes inquiries from anybody, nothing attached to the *if* is outside his concern (*On the E at Delphi* 356C).

If the oracle is still operating, then what is the source of its continued inspiration? Plutarch rejects the "vapor" theory as hardly befitting the many blessings received: "When I take into account the number of benefactions to the Greeks for which this oracle has been responsible, both in wars and in the family of cities, in cases of pestilence and failure of crops, I think it is a dreadful thing to assign its discovery and origin not to God and Providence but to chance and accident" (*Obsolescence* 435D–E). Nevertheless prophecy is imperfect in this world: "The power comes from the gods and demigods, but for all that, it is not unfailing nor imperishable nor ageless, lasting into that infinite time by which all things between earth and moon become wearied out, according to our reasoning" (*Obsolescence* 438D).

In another essay Plutarch sees no need to believe that the god is the direct author of the oracle's verses, but sees divine inspiration and the prophetess acting together in synergy: "Let us not believe the god has composed [the verse] but that he supplied the origin of the incitement, and the prophetic priestesses are moved each in accordance with her natural faculties.... He [the god] puts into her mind only the visions, and creates a light in her soul in regard to the future; for inspiration is precisely this" (*Oracles No Longer Given in Verse* 397C). Heracleon argues that it is the demigods or guardian gods (*daimonoi*) that speak and not the gods themselves "since the gods ought properly to be freed of earthly concerns" (*Obsolescence* 418E). This leads to a discussion on the nature of daimons. Could there be *evil* daimons?

Other Greco-Roman writers rarely treat the subject of evil guidance. But Plutarch considers that guidance toward evil—what might called antiguidance—must come from some other spiritual source besides God, perhaps from a daimon. The "commingling" of good and evil in this life is the common human experience that has led him to this conclusion. But he is unwilling to ascribe evil purposes to God. In *Isis and Osiris* he leans toward the view that there are two opposing forces in the universe:

> [Inasmuch] as Nature brings, in this life of ours, many experiences in which both evil and good are co-mingled . . . it has come about as the result of two opposed principles and two antagonistic forces, one of which guides us along a straight course to the right, while the other turns us aside and backward. . . . The great majority of the wisest men hold this opinion: they believe that there are two gods, rivals as it were, the one the artificer of good and the other of evil. There are also those who call the better one a god and the other a daemon, as for example, Zoroaster the Sage. (*Isis and Osiris* 369)

Plutarch goes on to show how the idea of two opposing forces, as sources of guidance and antiguidance, are expressed in various religions and philosophies. He emphasizes that these forces are not of equal strength, "but the predominance rests with the better. Yet it is impossible for the bad to be completely eradicated, since it is innate, in large amount, in the body and likewise in the Universe, and is always fighting hard against the better" (*Isis and Osiris* 371).

All human beings, not just oracles and diviners, have at least some degree of innate power to perceive the future and to prophesy, even if dimly. But this gift belongs especially to the purest souls and is most clearly manifested in dreams and at death. The soul's divining power,

> oftentimes discloses its flower and radiance in dreams, and in some in the hour of death when the body becomes cleansed of all impurities and attains a temperament adapted to this end, a temperament through which the reasoning and thinking faculty of the souls is relaxed and released from their present state as they range amidst the irrational and imaginative realms of the future. It is not true as Euripides says, that "the best of seers is he that guesses well"; no, the best of seers is the intelligent man, following the guidance of that in his soul which possesses sense and which, with the help of reasonable probability, leads him on the way [*kath' odon*]. (*Obsolescense* 432C–D)

The human soul in its present state is an imperfect reflection of its divine pattern, so while it can apprehend divine guidance because it has a like nature to God, it does so imperfectly as a result of all the "alien" elements it now contains:

The soul is created to be the instrument of God, and the virtue of an instrument is to conform as exactly as possible to the purpose of the agent that employs it by using all the powers which Nature has bestowed upon it, and to produce, presented in itself, the purpose of the very design; but to present this, not in the form in which it was existent in its creator [*demiourgon*], uncontaminated [*katharon*], unaffected [*apathēs*] and faultless [*anamartiton*] but combined with much that is alien to this. (*Oracles No Longer Given in Verse* 404C)

Balance is Plutarch's interest. He says that the "earliest theological writers and poets" focused on Zeus as the ultimate cause: "Zeus the beginning, Zeus in the midst, and from Zeus comes all being" (*Oracles No Longer Given in Verse* 436D). This approach was flawed, in that it did not recognize secondary causes. But later philosophers went to the other erroneous extreme. "The younger generation that followed them" overstressed the natural causes of events: "Hence the reasoning of both parties is deficient in what is essential to it, since the one ignores or omits the intermediary and the agent, the other the source and the means" (*Oracles No Longer Given in Verse* 436E).

Plutarch is no mere rationalist, but like Plato, he sees reason working together with divine guidance. The very ambiguity of divine communication *demands* the use of reason to unravel its meaning and application. Nor does he look for divine guidance on every issue that arises. Indeed, because most oracles are ambiguous, only those questions that cannot be solved by reason might benefit from an oracular response. Rightly understood, the oracle does not promote unhealthy spiritual dependence. On the contrary, the oracle's ambiguity leads to greater personal responsibility and reliance on the power of reason. This is part of Apollo's purpose in giving oracles: he uses the natural human inclination to seek divine guidance in order to direct human beings back to their reason. This is what prompts, for example, the curiosity to discover the meaning of the *E* at Delphi:

It seems that our beloved Apollo finds a remedy and a solution for the problems connected with our daily life by the oracular responses which he gives those who consult him; but problems connected with the power of reason, it seems that he himself launches and propounds to him who is by nature inclined to love of knowledge, thus creating in the souls a craving that leads toward the truth, as is clear in many other ways, but in particular the dedication of the E. (*The E at Delphi* 385A)

"Inquiry is the beginning of philosophy, and wonder and uncertainty the beginning of inquiry"; thus reasonable mysteries are instigated by the god in order to stimulate and invite people to "investigate, to read, to talk about them" (*The E at Delphi* 385B).

Plutarch concludes that the *E* posted at the entrance to the oracle's precincts at Delphi means "Thou art" (*Ei*). This is ultimately the only appropriate response to the other famous inscription at the entrance to Delphi, the god's injunction "Know Thyself." In seeing this notice everyone who comes to seek advice receives a "word" from God even before they make known their personal request:

> For the god addresses each of us as we approach him with the words "Know thyself," as a form of welcome, which certainly is in nowise of less import than "Hail" [*chaire*] and we in turn reply to him, "Thou art" [*ei*] as rendering unto him a form of address which is truthful, free from deception, and the only one befitting him alone, the assertion of Being. (*The E at Delphi* 392A)

> [This is] an utterance addressed in awe and reverence to god as existent through all eternity, while the other ["Know Thyself"] is a reminder to mortal man of his own nature and the weaknesses that beset him. (*The E at Delphi* 394C)

Plutarch's method of combining reason and divine guidance is seen especially in *The Oracles in Delphi No Longer Given in Verse*. The loss of poetic oracles is not to be lamented, he says, because the simplicity of prose is suited to the present age. This is just what is needed for a generation accustomed to excess and luxury, which has lost its ability to discern the truth: "The fact is . . . that we are ailing both in ears and eyes, accustomed as we are, through luxury and soft living, to believe and declare that the pleasant things are fair and lovely. Before long we shall be finding fault with the prophetic priestess because she does not speak in purer tones than Glauce" (*The Oracles in Delphi No Longer Given in Verse* 397B).

Plutarch cites various prose oracles and goes on to show that the change in form has less to do with a change in the god than with a change in the kinds of people who come to Delphi and the sort of requests they bring. God does not so much tell or conceal as *indicate* his purposes:

> He employs the prophetic priestess for men's ears just as the sun employs the moon for men's eyes. For he makes known and reveals his own thoughts, but he makes them known through the associated medium of a mortal body and a soul that is unable to keep quiet, or, as it yields itself to the One that moves it, to remain itself unmoved and tranquil, but, as though tossed amid billows and enmeshed in the stirrings and emotions within itself, it makes itself more and more restless. (*The Oracles in Delphi No Longer Given in Verse* 404E).

To make the divine message clearer, the means of communication must change as human beings change. Changes in human habits and aptitudes account for the changes in the mode of revelation from embellished verse to simple prose, in order that the truth God is communicating may be seen more clearly: "So as language also underwent a change and cut off its finery, history descended from its vehicle of versification and went on foot in prose, whereby the truth was mostly sifted from the fabulous" (*The Oracles in Delphi No Longer Given in Verse* 406E).

> Philosophy welcomed clearness and teachability in preference to creating amazement and pursued its investigations through the medium of everyday language. The god put an end to having his prophetic priestess call her own citizens "fire blazers," the Spartans "snake devourers," men "mountain roamers" and rivers "mountain engorgers." When he had taken away from the oracles epic versifications, strange words, circumlocutions and vagueness, he had thus made them ready to talk to their consultants as the laws talk to the states, or as kings meet with common people, or as pupils listen to teachers, since he adapted the language to what was intelligible and convincing. (*The Oracles in Delphi No Longer Given in Verse* 406F)

Plutarch's long conclusion to this essay is a beautiful defense of this trend toward simplification. He notes the growing public suspicion of metaphors, obscurity, and esoteric manipulation by wandering charlatans: "tricksters, mountebanks and false prophets" (*The Oracles in Delphi No Longer Given in Verse* 407C). Also, the settled conditions of the Pax Romana meant that personal, simpler, day-to-day requests, not the public petitions of city-states, were being made known to God, and therefore simpler answers were also more appropriate (*The Oracles in Delphi No Longer Given in Verse* 408C).

Plutarch says that some complain about this new simplicity, as if it detracts from the fame and long tradition of the hallowed place (*The Oracles in Delphi No Longer Given in Verse* 408D–E). But this is an immature response since it confuses changeable expressions with the god himself and unchanging truth:

> Such an attitude of mind is altogether puerile and silly. It is a fact that children take more delight and satisfaction in seeing rainbows, haloes and comets than seeing moon and sun; so these persons yearn for the riddles, allegories, and metaphors which are but reflections of the prophetic art when it acts upon a human imagination. And if they cannot ascertain to their satisfaction the reason for the change, they go away, after pronouncing judgment against the god, but not against us or against themselves for being unable by reasoning to attain to a comprehension of the god's purpose. (*The Oracles in Delphi No Longer Given in Verse* 409C–D)

Assessing Plutarch

By education and temperament Plutarch appreciated reason and the philosophical search for truth. Truth was for him the single criterion by which everything—including religious experience—was to be tested. So he rejected those gross forms of popular religion, superstition, and divination incompatible with his conception of the truth about God. Yet, as I have shown, he retained a profound sense of divine presence and guidance in human affairs.

By the time Plutarch was at the end of his life, in 120 CE, his writing reflected a world far removed from some of the basic assumptions about civic engagement in his own parallel lives of the Greeks and Romans or in Paul's Roman Corinth. The Roman Empire was in full control and opportunities were fewer. The days of free Athenian citizens were long past, and now a Roman bureaucrat could decide one's fate. Consider Plutarch's letter to a young Greek to discourage him from considering a civil service career in the Roman Empire:

> [When] entering upon any office whatsoever, you must not only call to mind those considerations of which Pericles reminded himself when he assumed the cloak of a general: "Take care, Pericles, you are ruling free men, you are ruling Greeks, Athenian citizens," but you must also say to yourself, "You who rule are a subject, ruling a State controlled by proconsuls, the agents of Caesar . . . and not have great pride and confidence in your crown, since you see the senatorial shoes of the proconsul just above your head." . . .
>
> The statesmen will instruct his people both individually and collectively and will call attention to the weak condition of Greek affairs, in which it is best for wise men to accept one advantage—a life of harmony and quiet—since fortune has left us no prize open for competition. For what dominion, what glory is there for those who are victorious? What sort of power is it which a small edict of a proconsul may annul or transfer to another man and which, even if it last, has nothing in it seriously worthwhile? (*Praecepta gerendae reipublica* 813D–F, 824 E–F)[6]

Plutarch's advice to lay low and have minimal expectations is made all the more tragic knowing how active a life he led and advocated earlier. But as he looks back, aware perhaps of the paltry results, frustrations, and humiliations, he now recommends acceptance of the status quo. This was probably very good practical advice at the time. But it was in sharp contrast to the older Roman ideals he advocated in the *Lives*. We are again in *Graecia capta*, where Greeks are no longer free, where their actions can be of only limited range and limited influence under the Roman occupation. Even among Romans the private realm of home and family was gradually becoming the only castle over which a man could exercise his freedom. The world of the second-century citizen was now largely determined by forces beyond his control. No wonder, then, that there was a growing sense of helplessness that would have consequences for religious life as well.

Plutarch's emphasis on the private role of the oracle at Delphi also signals a departure from the ideals of Augustus demonstrated in Corinth, where religion was meant to be social, public, and useful. Private religion—exemplified by the diviners and charlatans of the marketplaces—was seen as a threat both to society and to genuine piety. One of the chief threats presented by this new private religion was its encouragement of passivity, personal spiritual self-preoccupations, and the opting out of practical responsibilities both private and public.

This threat was not new. Theophrastus in the fourth century BCE had similarly disparaged the superstitious man's dreamy refusal to act, even in response to divine guidance: "If a mouse gnaws into his bag of barley meal, he goes to the soothsayer to ask what he should do; and if his response is that he should give it to the leatherworker to fix, he pays no attention to the advice, but goes off to make propitiatory sacrifices" (*Character Sketches*, 16).[7]

By the second century CE this was the norm. The historian Charles Dodd writes that the outlook on the world as an unreal and unimportant drama became typical in the later empire: "To identify oneself with such a world, to take it seriously as a place to live and labour in, must have demanded more courage than the average man possessed: better that it is an illusion or a bad joke, and avoid heartbreak."[8] Reality was not to be engaged so much as endured; it was the raw material for one's private practice of self-discipline, devotions, and cultivation of inner freedom, not for public engagement and public service.

One final observation: for all the attractiveness of Plutarch's balance of rational and mystical, there is still something missing and unsatisfying. His gods are caring, they give guidance, they deal with external conditions beyond human control and work together with them and with nature, but they do not themselves enter human struggles. They look on from a distance, willing to help but not touched enough by human life and suffering to share in it themselves. Zeus orders all, oversees all, but he does so "from above." Like Castor and Pollux, who come to the aid of men who are laboring in a storm, the gods may help, and they may rescue, but they are not "sailing on the ships and sharing in the danger."

> Soothing the oncoming raging sea,
> Taming the swift-driving blasts of the winds
> Not however, sailing on the ships and sharing in the danger, but
> appearing above and rescuing. (*The Sign of Socrates* 426C)

Conclusions: Greco-Roman Attitudes toward Divine Guidance

The Roman Empire, contrary to popular misconception, was not especially decadent. This, as Peter Brown says, was a "romantic fantasy." Instead it was "an Empire whose tone had long been set by somber and careful persons" who viewed the world "with inflexible certainty."[9] There was paramount emphasis on orderly behavior and traditional virtues, especially *pietas*, loyalty, service.

The sober and rational philosophical presentations of men like Lucretius, Cicero, Seneca, and Pliny, while differing on various theological and practical issues, were united in their disdain for divine guidance understood in any personal sense, whether it was through dreams, oracles, prophecy, astrology or any other of the many forms of divination popular in Rome. To these men, the notion of divine guidance—even in its most intellectually attractive forms, as presented by Greek apologists like Posidonius and Plutarch—was an embarrassment and an affront to nature, to reason, to virtue, to Roman virility. Certainly there had been Greeks who resisted divination as much as any of these Romans: Aristotle, Epicurus, Diogenes, and others. But given the Roman polemic we have seen throughout these authors in favor of Roman attitudes, Roman character, and Roman tradition and against the inroads of Greek influence, it is hard to resist the conclusion that there was a deep element of linguistic, cultural, and political antipathy in the Roman philosophical rejection of the Greek mystical tradition.

But they were in the minority. For most Romans, a rational worldview did not exclude the mystical. The poet, holding his libation bowl as a symbol of divine guidance, stood much higher in the public mind than the philosopher, and "with few exceptions the masses were more receptive to religion than to philosophy."[10] Robin Lane Fox summarizes well the spirit of the age: "Through myth and Homeric poetry, the visits of the gods continued to draw on a deep reserve of potential experience, which poets and artists could exploit but which most people did not exclude from life's possibilities."[11] There was a great deal of texture in this picture. As we have seen, attitudes toward divine guidance in the first-century Roman Empire were extremely diverse, ranging from hostility to indifference, cautious receptivity, and wild credulity. Certainly the Corinth Paul knew would have had a similar mix. Most strikingly, however, from the perspective of a modern Western world in which sacred and secular, rational and mystical have been banished to separate corners of life, the authors surveyed here reveal a world that experienced and reflected deeply upon the realities, ambiguities, and temptations of divine guidance.

PART II

JEWISH ATTITUDES
TOWARD DIVINE GUIDANCE

8

The Jewish Community

If Jews had questions about how or even whether God's guidance was still being given through prophecy, there was no question about adopting pagan divination practices from the surrounding Greco-Roman world. The Torah was uncompromising on this taboo:

> [9] When you come into the land that the Lord your God is giving you, you must not learn to imitate the abhorrent practices of those nations. [10] No one shall be found among you who makes a son or daughter pass through fire, or who practices divination, or is a soothsayer, or an augur, or a sorcerer, [11] or one who casts spells, or who consults ghosts or spirits, or who seeks oracles from the dead. [12] For whoever does these things is abhorrent to the Lord; it is because of such abhorrent practices that the Lord your God is driving them out before you. [13] You must remain completely loyal to the Lord your God. [14] Although these nations that you are about to dispossess do give heed to soothsayers and diviners, as for you, the Lord your God does not permit you to do so.(Deut 18:9–14)[1]

And yet condemnation of pagan divination did not mean that Jews excluded divine guidance, understood in their own terms. On the contrary, this very passage from the Torah, which forbids adopting pagan practices, continues with Moses describing how prophetic divine guidance is to function in the Jewish community after his departure:

> [15] The Lord your God will raise up for you a prophet like me from among your own people; you shall heed such a prophet. [16] This is what you requested of the Lord your God at Horeb on the day of the assembly when you said: "If I hear the voice of the Lord my God any more, or ever again see this great fire, I will die." [17] Then the Lord replied to me: "They are right in what they have said. [18] I will raise up for them a prophet like you from among their own people; I will put my words in the mouth of the prophet, who shall speak to them everything that I command. [19] Anyone who does not heed the words that the prophet shall speak in my name, I myself will hold accountable. [20] But any prophet who speaks in the name of other gods, or who presumes to speak in my name a word that I have not commanded the prophet to speak—that prophet shall die."

Divine Guidance. John A. Jillions, Oxford University Press (2020). © Oxford University Press.
DOI: 10.1093/oso/9780190055738.001.0001

[21]You may say to yourself, "How can we recognize a word that the Lord has not spoken?" [22]If a prophet speaks in the name of the Lord but the thing does not take place or prove true, it is a word that the Lord has not spoken. The prophet has spoken it presumptuously; do not be frightened by it. (Deut 18:15–22)

Here too we see questions raised about divine guidance and how to discern true from false.

Paul was rooted in Judaism, and the Corinthian Christian community included both Jews and Gentiles, so no picture of the attitudes in Corinth toward divine guidance would be complete without including views of the first-century Jewish community. In this chapter I begin by reviewing what is known about Judaism in Corinth, followed by consideration of the general characteristics of Judaism in this period, and then a survey of what contemporary first-century Jewish sources say about divine guidance. I draw on material from Philo, Josephus, the Dead Sea Scrolls, rabbinic literature, and other material from what is called the "intertestamental period," i.e., between the shaping of the Hebrew Bible (Old Testament) and the New Testament. As will be seen, the formation of both testaments was quite fluid, and this very open-endedness to the biblical canon bears on how divine guidance was understood within the community's continuing life and not simply enshrined in a book.

It is also crucial to remember that the first-century Jewish and Christian worlds were at home in a larger body of scripture than was defined by the later Hebrew canon and the Protestant Reformation: "The early church received the Holy Scriptures from early Judaism at a time when both the relative status of the Hebrew-Aramaic and the Greek Bible text, and the third part of the Old Testament canon [wisdom literature apart from Psalms], were still open questions."[2]

The fluidity of the sacred text is a key piece of evidence that the living God and His community—rather than the text alone—were seen as the ultimate authorities for divine guidance within Judaism. The text by itself could often present a variety of attitudes and practices that required community discernment as to their subsequent application. The Hebrew Bible brings together a variety of strands from different periods—within books and between books—in what has been called the "anthological habit," meaning "the tendency of gathering together discrete, sometimes conflicting retellings of stories or traditions (e.g., the two versions of the creation of woman, or analogous lists of unrelated commandments and miscellaneous laws), and preserving them side by side as though there were no difference, conflict, or ambiguity between them."[3]

The Jewish community that gathered these books did not look upon them as having a life independent of the community's inspired guidance. The compilers and readers were not unaware of the contradictions and differences within the books, but their juxtaposition presented no stumbling block. I argue (1) that the question of divine guidance was at the center of Jewish thought and was rarely isolated from the total life of the community with its written and oral Torah, and (2) that there was a range of attitudes toward divine guidance, testifying to the remarkable flexibility of Judaism in the first century. As we have seen, the Greco-Roman world also had a variety of attitudes toward divine guidance, but these were often in competition. The Jewish community was able to preserve a similar variety but within one religious community united by faith in the God of Israel.

The Jewish Community in Corinth

Paul was a zealous and well-trained Jewish teacher who belonged to the school of the Pharisees (2 Cor 11:22; Gal. 1:13–14; Phil 3:5–6; cf. Acts 22:3). Even after his encounter with the risen Jesus Christ on the road to Damascus (Acts 9:1–22) Judaism remained his natural milieu. His views and subsequent theological battles continued to be filtered through his formation in Judaism, whatever new Christian key he acquired for understanding his ancestral faith. We see this illustrated in his 18-month stay in Corinth, from 49 to 51. His first contact there was with the Jewish couple Aquila and Priscilla (Acts 18:2), and his first preaching was in the synagogue, where every Sabbath he "persuaded Jews as well as Greeks" (Acts 18:4). A prominent Jew was among his first converts: Crispus, the ruler of the synagogue. Crispus's successor Sosthenes may have followed him as a convert later (Acts 18:17; 1 Cor 1:1). Paul also attracted Jewish sympathizers among the Gentiles, like Titius Justus, "a worshipper of God" (Acts 18:7).[4]

Despite suffering the aftershocks of periodic Roman persecution, such as the expulsion of Jews from Rome in 49 (or possibly 41),[5] the Jewish community in Corinth was publicly engaged, passionate, and bold, as we can see from its response to Paul's preaching. There, as often elsewhere, Paul's words provoked sharp division within the Jewish community at all levels. Some followed him, while others opposed and reviled him (Acts 18:6ff.). Paul had no qualms about being provocative or offending if necessary. When opinion turned against him at the Corinthian synagogue, for example, instead of quietly moving across town he settled in next door, at the home of Titius Justus (Acts 18:7). The Jews of Corinth in turn had no hesitation going public with their anger toward Paul and his sympathizer Sosthenes. They took their case directly to the highest Roman authority in town, the proconsul Gallio (Seneca's brother). And failing to convince him, they immediately took justice into their own hands and gave Sosthenes a beating right in front of Gallio (Acts 18:17).[6]

Scholars have long recognized the diversity and local character of Judaism in the first-century Greco-Roman world, often speaking of "Judaisms" in the plural.

But for Corinth the first-century evidence is very meager. The archeological evidence is nonexistent: not a single Jewish find has been dated to the first century.[7] Jewish literary sources for first-century Corinth—other than Acts and Paul's letters—are little better. Philo mentions the Jewish population of Corinth as part of the wide and influential dispersion of Jews throughout the Roman Empire. He calls them "Jewish colonies" that have Jerusalem as their capitol (*On the Embassy to Gaius*, 281–282; see also 214).[8]

This lack of Jewish evidence is not unique to Corinth. It is true generally throughout the Jewish diaspora that "as regards the first century CE and the period immediately preceding it, we can only piece together fragments of information."[9] However, given the influential role of Corinth as a major Roman colony and the capital of Achaia at this time, "it seems highly likely that this city was the most important Jewish city in Greece, south of Macedon."[10] Beyond this there are serious limits to the certainty with which we can describe Jewish thinking and life specific to Corinth. But two facts make it possible to draw a general view from elsewhere in the diaspora: (1) Corinthian links with Rome and (2) the essential unity within diaspora Judaism around the centrality of the Torah. In addition, a cosmopolitan community like Corinth attracted Jewish residents and visitors from throughout the Roman Empire (and further afield) and so would reflect a wide range of Jewish attitudes. This makes evidence from around the Jewish diaspora particularly relevant.

Corinth and Rome

Given the powerful Roman influence throughout Corinthian institutions and culture, it is likely that Rome's Jewish community would also have a major influence on Judaism in Corinth, especially with the arrival of expelled Italian Jews like Priscilla and Aquila (Acts 18:2). Paul wrote his letter to the Romans while living in Corinth, and his long list of greetings (Romans 16) to Christians in Rome (most of them Jews) is evidence of just such personal connections between the capital and the colony.

A well-organized Jewish community would not have been exceptional in a Roman city like Corinth, which had numerous religious and social associations.[11] The Jewish community in Rome was flourishing at the time of Augustus, and most likely this had been true at least since the 50s of the first century BCE.[12] Jewish life in Rome was vibrant and varied and engaged men, women, and children. The synagogues, of which there were a number in Rome, were only part of this organized community. There were also Jewish employer associations, guilds, schools, hospitality societies, and cemetery organizations. Close links with Judea were maintained through personal letters, correspondence with the Sanhedrin,

pilgrimages, as well as hospitality to Jewish visitors from throughout the diaspora.[13] It is very possible something similar was transplanted by Roman Jews to
the colony at Corinth and later taken as a model for the multifaceted life of the
Christian church there.

The history of the Jews in Rome would have had ripple effects in Corinth as
well, for good and ill. Roman Jews had benefited from Julius Caesar's benevolence. While outlawing all *collegia* other than those founded in ancient times, he
made a deliberate exception for the Jewish associations.[14] Hence the historian
Suetonius said the Jews of Rome more than any other national group mourned
the death of Caesar when he was assassinated in March 44 BCE.[15] Caesar's tolerant policy continued under Augustus, although he himself "had little sympathy for the Jewish religion."[16]

Tiberius abandoned Caesar's policy and gave free rein to his antipathy for all
things foreign, including Judaism. He expelled the Jews from Rome in 19 CE as
part of a general plan to "curb the influence the Egyptian and Jewish creeds were
gaining among the higher circles of Roman society, and to preserve the purity of
the native religion."[17]

Claudius reversed all these measures, but only temporarily, restricting the
Jews' right to assembly in 41 CE and expelling them in 49 CE as punishment
for—as Suetonius remarks in a significant and much quoted phrase—"constantly
making disturbances at the instigation of Chrestus" (Suetonius, *Claudius* 25).[18]
That the Jews were on the Roman agenda, at least periodically, is evidence of
their high profile in Rome.

The Torah as Center of Divine Guidance

Despite many local variations, there is evidence to be found throughout the diaspora of a remarkable degree of common Jewish faith. Josephus contrasts this
with the surrounding Greco-Roman world's fractured philosophical and religious values:

> Among us alone will be heard no contradictory statements about God, such
> as are common among other nations, not only on the lips of ordinary individ-
> uals under the impulse of some passing mood, but even boldly proclaimed by
> philosophers; some putting forward crushing arguments against the very exist-
> ence of God, others depriving him of his providential care for mankind. Among
> us alone will be seen no difference in the conduct of our lives. With us all act

alike, all profess the same doctrine about God, one which is in harmony with our Law and affirms that all things are under his eye. Even our womenfolk and dependants would tell you that piety must be the motive of all our occupations in life. (*Against Apion* 2.179–181)

Josephus may have been exaggerating somewhat, but he wasn't far off. The identity of Jews, whatever their differences, was centered on the Torah. While "Torah" usually refers to the first five books of Moses in the Hebrew Bible (the Pentateuch), it can also be used to encompass the whole of Jewish learning, written and oral. "The most striking characteristic of the Jewish people in the period of the Second Temple was the observance of the Law of the one God, as revealed in the written Torah and the oral tradition."[19]

Jewish identity at this time is thus fundamentally connected to the Jewish understanding of divine guidance as the weaving together of written and oral Torah. This connection between written and oral divine guidance is encountered repeatedly in Jewish literature of the period. Here is its classical formulation in the Mishnah, the written collection of oral law: "Moses received Torah at Sinai and handed it on to Joshua, Joshua to elders, and elders to prophets. And prophets handed it on to the men of the great assembly. They said three things: 'Be prudent in Judgment, raise up many disciples, make a fence around the Torah.'"[20] The oral law was the community's protective "fence around the Torah." Written law apart from oral law was inconceivable for most Jews of the first century, since the oral law clarified the essential practical implications of written law. In other words, to understand and learn how to apply the written law, one had to look to the oral law.[21] This simultaneous faithfulness to written and oral Torah is crucial for understanding Jewish attitudes toward divine guidance.

Jewish groups that did not hold this view of the Law had little influence in the diaspora.[22] This is quite remarkable given the dominance of Greco-Roman culture and its potential for diluting traditional practice. On the other hand, that very threat may have been a catalyst for Jewish unity: "It is clear from the sources that all the circles which departed from the spirit and practice of Jewish observance remained isolated. . . . All the literary sources, as also the inscriptions, give us to understand that the religious sentiment of Judaism and the practice of the Jewish law dominated the whole world of the Jewish diaspora. . . . Though the Jews of the diaspora were apparently part and parcel of Hellenistic culture and society, they regarded themselves essentially as Hebrews living abroad."[23]

How the oral law developed bears significantly on our question of divine guidance. Faithful Jews understood that God gave to Moses on Mount Sinai not only the written Law but also the nucleus of the oral law, and this included how scripture was to be read and understood. The rest of the oral law was a constantly growing body of decisions that adapted to the changing situations, needs, and questions of the community over time. This view of written and oral law has important ramifications for the understanding of divine guidance since it locates the source of guidance both in the divinely revealed written word *and* in the oral word as it developed through the community's history of interpretation and application. The human decision-making that resulted in the oral law of the community became itself a form of binding divine guidance. Quite apart from written revelation, this record of human decisions was authoritative in itself, as recognized and sanctioned by the community as the people of God.[24] Indeed, to see the oral law as dependent upon the written law is to misunderstand the relationship between the two. According to the Jewish scholar Hyam Maccoby:

> Scholars outside the Jewish milieu have often derided the tortuous arguments by which the rabbis allegedly derived laws from Scripture. But this is to misunderstand the process. The rabbis, on the whole, did not operate a bizarre system of exegesis in order to produce new laws, though they sometimes produced bizarre arguments in order to add scriptural support to laws they already knew to be valid. In fact (a point generally overlooked), the more bizarre the argument, the more likely that the law in question was regarded as unquestionable by reason of its antiquity, and therefore required scriptural derivation by hook or by crook.[25]

At the same time, on occasion over the centuries the community, through its collective reflection, considered some reform of the written code to be absolutely necessary. This superseded the written Law, not by changing it but by reinterpreting it. As Maccoby says, "There are *some* examples of rabbis using the exegetical apparatus to create changes in the law, but this is almost always in cases when some urgent *reform* was felt to be necessary." He then gives the example of Rabbi J. ben Zakkai's abolition of the trial by ordeal, sanctioned by the Bible, for a woman suspected of adultery, requiring here to drink a "water of bitterness" that—if she were guilty—would cause her "thigh to fall away and her body to swell" (see Numbers 5:16–28).[26]

While the written Torah remains the "perfect Word of God," the purpose of the oral Torah was to "fill in the gaps."[27] This process was inevitably fallible since it depended upon the human decision-makers who, regardless of their wisdom, were conditioned by their time and place. Nor was explicit divine guidance normally part of the process of deciding the oral law. On the contrary, rabbinic tradition expressly forbids the formulation of community law on the basis of supposed divine revelations:

> The chief characteristic of the Oral Torah (apart from its Sinaitic nucleus) in point of authority, in contrast with the written Torah, was thus its *fallibility*. This

derived from the fallible status of its enactors and decision-makers; for it was considered that the Torah itself had given religious authorities of each successive age a power of decision or of enactment (within certain limits), which did not depend on the possession of inspiration ("the holy spirit," *ruah ha-qodes*), but was simply inherent in the office of sage or judge. This meant that in principle, the enactment or decisions of the authorities of one generation could be reversed by the authorities of some succeeding generation, if they felt that there was good reason: for example, if the special circumstances leading to an enactment had ceased to hold, or even if the earlier authorities had made a mistake in their interpretation of the written Torah, or of the traditions of the oral Torah.[28]

The notion of fallibility and caution about personal revelations is obviously a key factor in Jewish attitudes toward divine guidance, and more about this will be discussed further.

In first-century Corinth, the application of the law may have had its own particularities, since there was a degree of flexibility in the law that would make local variations possible and acceptable: "Individuals, families or associations could apply their own measure of rigour, or stress one particular commandment, or take on works of supererogation. These differences, which could be found all over society, from Pharisees to *am-ha-aretz* [uneducated Jews], did not always stem from differences of biblical exegesis or tradition. They were the spontaneous outcome of religious vitality on the lookout for new ways of expressing itself."[29] This fluid aspect of the law is reflected in the fact that it was still *oral* law in the period that concerns us.[30] It remained oral for at least two reasons: first, its complexity required that it be learned under personal supervision of a teacher who knew the student and could convey the nuances of the law,[31] and second, to keep the decision-makers responsive and fresh in the face of new needs.[32]

Synagogue and Scripture

The flexibility of the oral law can be seen in the synagogue's liturgical tradition.[33] The first-century synagogue was an all-encompassing Jewish community center for public assemblies, court, study, dining hall, and lodging for travelers. Within Palestine these, rather than worship, were the synagogue's primary functions.[34]

In the diaspora, however, the synagogue was often known as a *proseuchē*, meaning "prayer" in Greek, indicating that public prayer was central to the diaspora synagogue (though public prayer did not *require* a building; see, e.g., Acts 16:13, where communal prayers take place by a river just outside Philippi). Here too evidence for the precise form and content of prayers is very poor, although an order of public synagogue prayers certainly existed before 70 CE.[35] Prayers were in the form of a standard pattern of blessings, but these could be freely adapted and supplemented by the officiant with sayings and verses from the Bible.[36] In the first-century diaspora public prayer was probably limited to Sabbath and feast day services, which were attended—without segregation—by men, women, and children.[37]

Lay leadership was a unique feature of synagogue worship that distinguished it both from worship at the Jerusalem Temple and from Greco-Roman rites. Various members of the congregation were chosen each week to lead the prayers, read the scriptures (in Hebrew and Greek), and comment on the readings or issues of the day. A sage might be invited to speak, but anyone could offer a comment.[38]

Reading and explication of the scriptures were at the center of synagogue worship, a point that is repeatedly underlined in the sources as its most distinctive feature in comparison with the surrounding Gentile world: "For Jewish authors the unique feature of synagogue worship was not the recitation of prayers, hymns, or psalms—activities no less familiar in pagan religious settings [as ritual processions, sacrifices, and odes]—but rather the public reading and expounding of the Holy Scriptures. Thus, no matter what the context in which these sources refer to the synagogue, their authors tended to focus on its unique feature."[39]

A portion of the Torah was read, probably from a fixed calendar of readings—there was more flexibility in choice of reading from the prophets—or from the reading for a feast day. (For the period before 70 CE the only certain festal reading we know is Esther, for the feast of Purim.) Live translation of the Torah was given verse by verse, after the reading in Hebrew by someone who had memorized the passage (though indelicate passages like Gen 35:22 were left untranslated).[40] The prophets were treated more freely and translated in blocks of three verses.

Translation served two important purposes beyond the simple need to make the text accessible to the uneducated, women, children, and—notably—any Gentiles who might be present. First, translation acted as an initial commentary in light of oral tradition, since the translation was not meant to be a literal rendering. As the Babylonian Talmud prescribes, "R. Judah says: 'Anyone who translates a (biblical) verse literally is a liar, and anyone who adds to it is a blasphemer and a curser.'"[41] Second, translation placed the listener in the position of hearing the word through a mediator, just as their ancestors had done when they first heard the Word of God through Moses: "The gift of Scripture was being made anew, as it were, when it was read, and so had to come indirectly."[42]

Scripture study was also a regular feature in the informal settings of club dinners and homes.[43] Maccoby emphasizes that scriptural literacy formed the basis of the oral tradition and was centered on exposition of the Bible in synagogue, house of study, and house of judgment (bet din). But the rationale for so much study and discussion was the "unfinished quality of the Oral Torah." This arose from the sense of the "inexhaustibility of the Bible, the conviction that discussion of it could never be brought to completion because each new generation was able to discover new insights or to apply it in previously unforeseen ways."[44]

It should be clear at this point that the Torah itself, and the Bible more broadly, is the best primary source for Jewish attitudes toward divine guidance, since this was the common source acknowledged, read, and studied by all. This was a period in which interpretation of the text became widely regarded as a new form of prophecy; more will be said about this later. Jewish approaches to scriptural text and interpretation are therefore of prime importance in relation to divine guidance.[45]

The Septuagint

Paul usually quotes the Septuagint, the Jewish pre-Christian Greek translation of the Hebrew Bible.[46] This was hardly unusual either in the synagogues of Palestine or especially in the diaspora, where the use of Greek was widespread: "The mere fact of the prevalence of the Greek *koine* [its common spoken form] over Hebrew and/or Aramaic is a valuable indication of the receptivity of the Jews of the Diaspora to teaching in this language, a fact that agrees well with their profound respect for the Septuagint and the wide diffusion of the Philonic and New Testament literature, written in Greek."[47]

The Septuagint is abbreviated conventionally as LXX, signifying "the seventy," referring to the 72 translators who traditionally were responsible for what came to be regarded as a miraculous translation from Hebrew to Greek. First-century Jews had great respect for the LXX, and we have much evidence for the widespread use and profound influence of this Greek translation as it circulated side by side with the Hebrew scriptures. It played a unifying role, especially in the diaspora, although it was used throughout Palestine as well. Josephus praises the Septuagint in his prologue to *Jewish Antiquities* (1.10–12); Philo repeats the story of its miraculous translation (*On the Life of Moses* 2.25ff.) and uses the LXX throughout his voluminous writings.[48] He also reports that Alexandrian Jews regarded the LXX and Hebrew Bible "with admiration and respect like two sisters, or rather, as one and the same work" (*Moses* 2.40).[49]

The Septuagint's stature may be seen from the popular account of its translation in the *Letter of Aristeas* (variously dated between 200 BCE and 33 CE). According to this tradition, Demetrius of Phalerum, the chief librarian of the Royal Library at Alexandria—one of the seven wonders of the ancient world—advised King Ptolemy of Egypt that the Hebrew Bible would be an essential addition to the collection. He recommended that the Jewish High Priest Eleazar be commissioned to gather translators from among the many learned Jews who had been taken into Egypt as slaves. The king accepted this plan, gave an order liberating these scholars, paid off their owners, and with Demetrius as supervisor appointed Eleazar to take charge of the project. Eleazar then appointed 72 translator-scholars, six for each of the 12 tribes of Israel, and they set to work:[50]

[121] The High priest [Eleazar] selected men of the finest character and the highest culture, such as one would expect from their noble parentage. They were men who had not only acquired proficiency in Jewish literature, but had studied most [122] carefully that of the Greeks as well. They were specially qualified therefore for serving on embassies and they undertook this duty whenever it was necessary. They possessed a great facility for conferences and the discussion of problems connected with the law. They espoused the middle course—and this is always the best course to pursue. They abjured the rough and uncouth manner, but they were altogether above pride and never assumed an air of superiority over others, and in conversation they were ready to listen and give an appropriate answer to every question. And all of them carefully observed this rule and were anxious above everything else to excel each other in [123] its observance and they were all of them worthy of their leader and of his virtue. And one could observe how they loved Eleazar by their unwillingness to be torn away from him and how he loved them.

In 72 days, the same number of days as translators, these worthy men completed their work, and the finished product so perfectly reflected the sacred Hebrew text that the Jewish community agreed that not a word of the translation should be altered. The finished text was read to the king as well, who was amazed that such a profound book had not been translated sooner. More than that, "he was greatly astonished at the spirit of the lawgiver."

[308] When the work was completed, Demetrius collected together the Jewish population in the place where the translation had been made, and read it over to all, in the presence of the translators, who met with a great reception also from the people, because of the great benefits which they had [309] conferred upon them. They bestowed warm praise upon Demetrius, too, and urged him to have the whole law transcribed and present a copy to their leaders. [310] After the books had been read, the priests and the elders of the translators and the Jewish community and the leaders of the people stood up and said, that since so excellent and sacred and accurate a translation had been made, it was only right that it should remain as it was and no [311] alteration should be made in it. And when the whole company expressed their approval, they bade them pronounce a curse in accordance with their custom upon any one who should make any alteration either by adding anything or changing in any way whatever any of

the words which had been written or making any omission. This was a very wise precaution to ensure that the book might be preserved for all the future time unchanged. [312] When the matter was reported to the king, he rejoiced greatly, for he felt that the design which he had formed had been safely carried out. The whole book was read over to him and he was greatly astonished at the spirit of the lawgiver.

The use of the LXX is not a side issue in relation to divine guidance. The role of the community in accepting the LXX, and more broadly in shaping the canon itself, is closely linked to how oral law and divine guidance were understood in Judaism. Paul, like many first-century educated Jews, is at ease in both the LXX and the Hebrew Bible. Yet the numerous differences between the LXX and the Hebrew Bible are well known and are still the subject of much analysis and debate.[51] It is also clear that other Greek and Hebrew versions were in circulation and quoted or adapted (sometimes quite freely) by Jewish and New Testament writers. That these versions circulated with virtually equal authority is remarkable testimony to Judaism's ability to live with a degree of fluidity that depended much more on trust in the community than on the *ipsissima verba* of the original biblical text alone, assuming that could even be established.

This attitude toward scriptural authority has obvious implications for the question of divine guidance, because in contrast to many Protestant Christians, the Jews gave much more importance to the community's evolving interpretation than to the biblical text. "This does not mean that the written law was relinquished or ignored. In theory all authority flows from the word of the written scripture, but only in the way interpreted by the rabbis or 'sages.'"[52]

The Apocrypha

The books of the Hebrew Bible were translated into Greek over a period of many decades, and therefore not all of them were technically part of the miraculous LXX. Later books, written originally in Greek rather than Hebrew, came into circulation and were included in the broad scope of what was considered "scripture." In addition, the Jewish community's outlook on the Septuagint soured during the first-century debates with early Christians, who used the LXX as their primary biblical text. As a result, other Greek translations came into existence (the versions of Theodotion, Aquila of Sinope, and Symmachus), and the approach to canonicity tightened markedly. Late Jewish works from the Hellenistic period (Tobit, Sirach, and others) had circulated widely and were popular in first-century Jewish communities. These books were alluded to in the New Testament and reflect the range of approaches to divine guidance found elsewhere in the Old Testament. But they were excluded from the Jewish canon in the second century as Jews and Christians parted ways. The Reformation removed these books from the Bible as well (and labeled them "Apocrypha"), but they remain part of the Christian biblical canon in Catholic and Orthodox Bibles, with a few minor variations (the last three, in italics, appear only in Orthodox Bibles):[53]

The First Book of Esdras
The Second Book of Esdras
Tobit
Judith
The Additions to the Book of Esther
The Wisdom of Solomon
Ecclesiasticus, or the Wisdom of Jesus the Son of Sirach
Baruch
The Letter of Jeremiah
The Prayer of Azariah and the Song of the Three Young Men
Susanna
Bel and the Dragon
The Prayer of Manasseh
The First Book of Maccabees
The Second Book of Maccabees
The Third Book of Maccabees
The Fourth Book of Maccabees
Psalm 151

Although this is not the place for a full discussion of these books, they are important because they reflect popular Jewish attitudes in the first century. So I will look at three stories that give the most textured picture of divine guidance: Tobit, Judith, and Susanna.

Tobit (200–180 BCE)

Tobit was one of the most widely read books among Jews of St. Paul's day, as attested by the many varying editions in circulation.[54] The complicated plot can be boiled down to this: after a long journey from Nineveh, blind Tobit's son Tobias is given the opportunity to marry Sarah, the daughter of Raguel. But Sarah is beset with a terrible demon, Asmodeus, who has brought about the death of her previous seven husbands on their wedding night. So Tobias faces a terrible risk. With the help of the angel Raphael (also known as Azarias), he prepares a potion that defeats the demon and later cures his father's blindness. He and Sarah return to Nineveh with Raguel, and they all live in peace to a ripe old age.

The story features guidance by God or his angels (and the "antiguidance" of demons) through thoughts, visions, dreams, and voices. All of this is in marked contrast to other Jewish wisdom literature that emphasizes that divine guidance is received primarily through the keeping of the Torah commandments, as taught by sages and parents. Yet even in Tobit mystical experience never displaces the Torah and rational thought. Tobit exhorts Tobias to keep the law, to focus especially on traditional Jewish good works (4:1–21, 12:6–12, 14:9), and to "seek advice from every wise man" (4:18). Tobias accepts the traditional teaching and agrees to all that his father commands (5:1).

Yet Tobit is also conscious of God's direction in daily decisions and urges his son to nurture this lively awareness within himself: "Bless the Lord on every occasion; ask him that your ways may be made straight and that all your paths and plans may prosper. For none of the nations has understanding; but the Lord himself gives all good things, and according to his will he humbles whomever he wishes" (4:19).

While God's blessing is to be sought, there is freedom in making choices as long as Tobias is choosing a path that is "pleasing in His sight" (5:21). The only stipulation is that he "refuse to sin or to transgress the commandments" (4:5). Beyond this there is no need to wait for divine inspiration before taking action, since practical choices are normally made without God's specific guidance.

Divine guidance in Tobit comes in *response* to the initiative already taken and to help fulfill the human plan. Thus an angel is sent to guide and guard Tobias on his journey, open up unexpected opportunities, and show him how to overcome obstacles. Divine guidance also gives Tobias a scheme to defeat the demon Asmodeus (5:4ff.). Carrying out the plan is a divine-human cooperative effort, as the angel's name, Azarias (God helps), signifies. God indeed helps, but He does not work alone. Tobit believes in this divine-human synergy and trusts that his son will be safe because "a good angel will go with him" (5:21).

Even the antidemon remedy in the story is not simply a magical potion independent of faith in the God of Israel (6:16). After bringing Tobias and Sarah together, the angel gives the couple a potent incense to ward off the demon Asmodeus. But first the angel instructs the newlyweds on prayer: "And when you approach her, rise up, both of you, and cry out to the merciful God, and he will save you and have mercy on you. Do not be afraid, for she was destined for you from eternity. You will save her, and she will go with you, and I suppose that you will have children by her" (6:17). Raguel too believes that Tobias will have God's guidance: "The merciful God will guide you for the best" (7:12).

For all its awareness of human freedom and human agency, the book of Tobit has a clear understanding that God's guidance is the key factor in their success. God is the one who ultimately brings all the players together for the happy outcome of this story. There is a continual interchange of man, God, demons, and divine messengers, but it is God's hand that is dominant in these events, as seen in the thanksgiving prayers of Raguel (8:15), Tobias (11:1), and Tobit (11:14). The protagonists are aware of God's presence even while making plans freely, asking for His help, and recognizing it when it comes (e.g., 12:3). The angel directs the couple to make known to others how God has worked among them in these events (12:20): "So they confessed the great and wonderful works of God, and acknowledged that the angel of the Lord had appeared to them" (12: 22).

This connection between the angel and the Lord is significant in light of Greco-Roman views, which saw daimons as spiritual forces independent of the divine will. Raphael expresses this contrast most explicitly: "For I did not come to you as a favor on my part, but by the will of our God" (12:18). The angel and the human stand on the same level: both are under the one God who is sovereign over all (13:2), who afflicts sinners (13:5), and who turns to those who turn to Him with their whole heart (13:6). The gods and daimons of the Gentiles, represented as idols, will in the new age be overthrown as the Gentiles turn to "fear the Lord God in truth and will bury their idols" (13:6).

The book of Tobit balances the mystical with the rational. While God's guidance is at the root of the spiritual worldview represented here, the appearance of angels is not regarded as a normal occurrence. The events described here were understood to be unique. Once the story was over, the participants "saw [the angel] no more" (12:21). Also, while the guidance was at times—and for some of the participants—very clear and direct, there were other moments when it was not. So while Tobias's journey is prolonged, Tobit and his wife at home are in complete darkness as to the outcome. For Tobit this is true literally and figuratively, since he was blind for eight years (14:2). Tobit is distressed by this absence of clear guidance but puts a brave face on it and tells his wife, Edna, that ultimately everything will be fine (though his distress is evidence that he's not entirely certain about that; 10:3). For her part Edna is not at all persuaded; she abandons all hope of ever seeing her son alive again (10:7). Thus the period of uncertainty is one of deep darkness for both of them. Throughout the story Tobit and his family trust that all events are guided by God, but in the end they know this for certain only because on this one occasion the angel reveals himself to them (12:15). The message to be drawn is that angels guide in many ways, but they are rarely seen, and they never answer all one's questions.

Judith

The popularity of Judith, like Tobit, is evidenced by its many recensions.[55] Yet unlike Tobit, this book is "untouched by the aura of the marvelous" and its theme could be "God helps those who help themselves."[56] But it would be a mistake to read this as the absence of divine guidance. Judith is fully convinced that her actions are done in cooperation with the Lord.

Judith is more parable and folktale than factual history, but the story line is as follows. The Jews are under attack, besieged by the Assyrian general Holofernes. As the deadline for the final assault approaches, the Jews are becoming more and more hopeless. The beautiful and pious widow Judith is distressed that the priest Uzziah and the elders appear helpless. In the face of this impending calamity all they do is pray, which is well and good, but the situation demands practical action. With the blessing of the elders and the community Judith concocts a daring secret plan, and with the help of her loyal maid goes into the enemy camp, ingratiates herself with Holofernes, and deceives him into believing that she is willing to give him information about the Jews. Thinking he might seduce this fascinating woman, Holofornes invites her to his tent for food and wine. Instead he falls asleep in a drunken stupor. Judith cuts off his head, stuffs it in a bag, and returns to the besieged city. Seeing their general's head displayed from the city walls, the Assyrians flee and the Jews are saved.

The main message of the book is to underline Judith's human initiative and rational decision-making, which are in sharp contrast to the paralyzed and demoralized community and its leaders. They can do no better than ask God to deliver them—by a certain deadline, no less—from their plight. Although there is admirable cooperation between the leaders and people, with no hint that the leaders view themselves as autocratic guides, in this case their democratic sentiments are dangerous. Uzziah and the leaders are shown to be abdicating their responsibility for guiding the community by submitting too readily to the people's fatalism and their demands for capitulation to Holofernes (7:23ff.). Under these conditions, when no divine help appears by the appointed deadline, it is not surprising that "they were greatly depressed in the city" (7:32).

Judith rebukes the leaders for "putting the Lord Almighty to the test" (8:13). She rejects the pagan assumption that God can be forced to act either by threats or special pleading (8:11–16). The Jews are to wait for God's deliverance and ask for His help (8:17), but this is no excuse for passivity. On the contrary, they must take initiative and do their part, and if God so desires He will help. But they can't just wait for divine guidance. As Judith forcefully reminds the leaders, the lives of the people "depend on *us*" (8:24).

Meanwhile Uzziah's focus remains exclusively fixed on prayer, which in this case is not a virtue but dereliction of duty. He and the rulers are incapable of taking any practical initiative to address the city's dire situation. They ask for Judith's prayers, but they think nothing more can be done (8:31). Judith, however, has a practical plan, which the leaders bless without even hearing it (8:32–34). She is known to the leaders to be godly and to act with integrity (in spite of her criticism of their leadership) and is therefore trusted to act for the good of the community (8:35, 10:8). Uzziah recognizes that Judith's wisdom and her heart's right disposition toward God and the Torah make her prayer acceptable (8:29–31). Far from being a mere activist, Judith is shown to have "scrupulous devotion" to the Mosaic Law, even going beyond its requirements (8:6, 8:16, 12:7, 12:9, 13:20).[57]

Judith's plan is completely her own, even kept secret from the leaders in view of their faintheartedness (8:34). But this should not be interpreted as individualism. Carrying out the plan is a cooperative work (13:4–5, 14–17, 16:6). She asks God to "direct her way" and to show her the concrete opportunities that will enable her to carry out her plan (12:8). She has the blessing of the community to act (even though they don't know precisely what she has in mind), she has their prayers, and she seeks the Lord's cooperation (13:12, 15, 17, 16:1ff.). She also understands that her initiative is God's answer to the *community's* prayer and fasting (4:1–15, 6:19).

The book makes clear that the initiative for saving the people comes from Judith. But she needs God's help and the people's prayers to make the plan work. Her prayer in chapter 9 is a model of synergy between God, herself, and the community. It reflects the three essential aspects of the operation: her plan, God's help, and the community's prayer. Indeed Judith's appearance with a plan is God's answer to the people's prayers:

"Behold now, the Assyrians are increased in their might; they are exalted, with their horses and riders; they glory in the strength of their foot soldiers; they trust in shield and spear, in bow and sling, and know not that thou art the Lord who crushest wars; the Lord is thy name. [8]Break their strength by thy might, and bring down their power in thy anger; for they intend to defile thy sanctuary, and to pollute the tabernacle where thy glorious name rests, and to cast down the horn of thy altar with the sword. [9]Behold their pride, and send thy wrath upon their heads; give to me, a widow, the strength to do what I plan. [10]By the deceit of my lips strike down the slave with the prince and the prince with his servant; crush their arrogance by the hand of a woman.

[11]"For thy power depends not upon numbers, nor thy might upon men of strength; for thou art God of the lowly, helper of the oppressed, upholder of the weak, protector of the forlorn, savior of those without hope. [12]Hear, O hear me, God of my father, God of the inheritance of Israel, Lord of heaven and earth, Creator of the waters, King of all thy creation, hear my prayer! [13]Make my

deceitful words to be their wound and stripe, for they have planned cruel things against thy covenant, and against thy consecrated house, and against the top of Zion, and against the house possessed by thy children. [14]And cause thy whole nation and every tribe to know and understand that thou art God, the God of all power and might, and that there is no other who protects the people of Israel but thou alone!" (Judith 9:7–14)

Note that Judith's prayer takes place "at the very time when that evening's incense was being offered in the house of God in Jerusalem" (9:1). Although the story underlines the bold initiative taken by one person in response to an obvious need, Judith is no egomaniac convinced of her power to save the people. Her prayer is humbly addressed to "the God of the lowly, helper of the oppressed, upholder of the weak" (9:11). Her strength is in God. But she asks God's help to accomplish *her* plan. Notably she asks God to prosper her deceit! (See 9:10, 13.) Later, in her dialogue with the wicked Holofernes, she will use his credulity in divination to trap him, by convincing him that she has been sent by God (11:16), that she will be told by God what sins Israel is committing (11:17), and that she has "mystical foreknowledge" (11:19, 12:4).

Judith's initiative sits side by side with the conviction that the results are ultimately God's will (9:5–6). But the conviction that God's will rules over all does not prevent her from taking bold action to address an intolerable situation.

Susanna

Susanna is included in the Greek version of the book of Daniel (Dan. 13:1–65, although the position in the various manuscripts is not consistent). It was most likely composed around 100 BCE within the Jewish community in Babylon, but in what original language is still debated: Hebrew, Aramaic, or Greek.[58] It is a remarkable story that shows how all the elements of divine guidance are intertwined and work together in Jewish tradition. Yet one of its main themes is caution and discernment, since even the most trusted institutions of Jewish tradition can be tools of deception.

The beautiful and righteous Susanna refuses the lecherous advances of two respected Jewish sages who spy her bathing. In revenge they publicly accuse her of adultery. She is condemned by the court and led away to execution. The young prophet Daniel hears a word from the Lord declaring her innocent. The crowd stops the legal process to listen to Daniel, who then uncovers the lies of the elders.

The story begins with the same devotion to the Law that characterizes the rest of Daniel. Susanna's parents "were righteous, and had taught their daughter according to the Law of Moses" (verse 3). Her father, Joakim, was an elder to whom others would come for counsel, presumably because of his deep knowledge of the Law. This points to the high regard given to sages. Yet the thrust of the story is that even this trusted institution of the elders is imperfect apart from ultimate trust in the ever-present God of Israel, who guides His people in unexpected ways. The community is called to constant awareness of His presence among them and to be prepared to see God's guidance outside the normal channels even of His own institutions. The elders, in particular, are called to remember that while they sit in God's seat giving judgment, God Himself is not absent. The Lord will ultimately vindicate the innocent and punish the wicked.

The people trusted the two elders' corrupt judgment of Susanna precisely "because they were elders of the people and judges" (41). The "guidance" by the elders is deceitful because it has been deliberately twisted by their own passions (9; cf. 56): "They perverted their minds and turned away their eyes from looking at Heaven or remembering righteous judgments." Susanna, in contrast, "looked upward toward heaven for her heart trusted in the Lord" (35). Thus correct judgments are to be based not only on learned knowledge of the law but on living according to the commandments and "looking at Heaven," i.e., attentiveness to God's presence and remembering that He is the ultimate judge.

How God acts in the book of Susanna is most instructive for appreciating the interplay of human and divine, individual and communal, hierarchical and popular, rational and mystical in the Jewish tradition of discerning divine guidance.

1. The court of elders is assumed to have rendered a true judgment in condemning Susanna (41).
2. Susanna prays for vindication against her false accusers (42–43).
3. Through God's inspiration Daniel perceives that Susanna is innocent: "God aroused the holy spirit of a young lad named Daniel" (45), and "he cried with a loud voice, 'I am innocent of the blood of this woman'" (46). His disavowal of the decision also shows that the community as a whole took responsibility for the judgment rendered by the elders.
4. The people accept Daniel's rebuke ("are you such fools"; 48), admitting the possibility that he has been divinely inspired and that the two elders "have borne false witness" (48–49). They allow Daniel to speak his mind even though they have already come to an agreed judgment.
5. The people bring Daniel to the attention of the wider body of elders, who then take responsibility for investigating the matter further, acknowledging that God may have spoken to Daniel directly. They tell him, "Sit among us and inform us, for God has given you that right" (50).
6. Daniel does not rest on his assertion of special divine insight but proceeds to test the two lying elders, so that the case may be proven rationally and fairly. He separates the two men for questioning, demonstrates their lie, and

so proves the case (51–59). Thus the idea that Susanna is innocent has been divinely inspired, but its proof is demonstrated rationally.

7. The whole assembly confirms the decision with thanksgiving, recognizing God's hand acting through Daniel to vindicate Susanna's innocence. They "loudly blessed God, who saves those who hope in him" (60).

8. Finally, the community acts on this series of divine and human insights by following the prescriptions of the Law and putting the false accusers to death (62; cf. Deut 19:16–21).

The story of Susanna is thus an instructive and practical synthesis, showing in concrete circumstances how Jews of the intertestamental period viewed the weaving together of human and divine in a single decision-making process.

9

Philo

Philo of Alexandria (c. 15 BCE–50 CE) is "the most important representative of Hellenistic Judaism."[1] As a contemporary of St. Paul his thought is especially relevant to our study. Although there is continuing debate about how well he represents mainstream Jewish thought in the first century—and whether he was too thoroughly Hellenized—there is no question that Philo saw himself as solidly representative of Judaism. He says that it is precisely *because* he is Jewish that he is able to find truth in Greek philosophy. As a Jew whose life and thought are shaped by the revealed law of the one God, he can recognize all other manifestations of divine truth. This alone enables him to distinguish true and false within the tangled strands of Greek philosophy.[2] For Philo there can be no essential division between philosophy, with its focus on natural revelation, and scriptural revelation, since truth is one and has its source in God. But priority in interpreting the facts of nature belongs to Moses. "Moses was for Philo *the* wise man (*pansofos*), exceeding in age and wisdom even the Seven Wise Men of the Greeks who flourished as the pillars of civilization in the seventh and sixth centuries BC."[3]

If the philosophers were looking ultimately to deepen their understanding of nature, Philo saw Moses as the key to unlocking the mystery of nature. Moses encapsulates the meaning (*logos*) of Nature in the Law, since the Lawgiver is the one God who created nature. Those who follow Moses and the Law are at the same time therefore capable of understanding nature. God Himself is thus *the* great teacher, while Moses is the interpreter of God and the instructor of humanity.[4]

Scriptural exegesis is therefore the basis for most of Philo's voluminous writings. Exegesis is also his key for evaluating the philosophical movements of his day, and in this he was remarkably creative. Bruce Winter notes that Philo "was part of a pioneering attempt to bring together the Old Testament and philosophy, that is, he sought to exegete the Old Testament in light of those philosophical traditions which he perceived as being most closely allied to it."[5]

In this project Philo is not satisfied with scriptural generalities. In true rabbinic fashion he explores apparently minor points, so convinced is he of the value of ruminating upon every portion of the scriptures: "I hold that such matters are like condiments set as seasoning to the Holy Scriptures, for the edification of its readers, and that inquirers are not to be held guilty of any far-fetched

Divine Guidance. John A. Jillions, Oxford University Press (2020). © Oxford University Press.
DOI: 10.1093/oso/9780190055738.001.0001

hair-splitting, but on the contrary of dereliction if they fail to inquire" (*On Dreams*, 2.301).[6]

Philo understands scriptural study and exegesis to be incomprehensible apart from communion with God, who illumines the reader. Therefore Philo experienced scriptural translation, exegesis, and interpretation as inspired tasks driven by divine guidance. It was this inner meaning that Philo as a biblical interpreter hoped to convey, something that transcends the literal: "There is a higher thought than these. I heard it from a voice in my own soul, which often times is God-possessed, and then divines where it does not know. This thought I will record in words if I can" (*On the Cherubim* 27).[7]

Thus allegiance to the text of scripture is intertwined with a remarkable freedom of allegorical interpretation. Philo relies less on the repeated wisdom of past sages and more on the direct insight given through immediate divine illumination. But in following this method he doesn't see himself as unique. Scripture study and interpretation influenced by divine guidance was especially evident among the Theraputae, a Jewish quasi-monastic community Philo describes in *On the Contemplative Life*. He speaks about the consecrated room (*monastērion*) where "they are initiated into the mysteries of the sanctified life," which means primarily inspired scriptural study that leads to a deepening of their spiritual life:

They take nothing into it, either drink or food or any other of the things necessary for the body, but laws and oracles delivered through the mouth of prophets, and psalms [*ymnous*] and the other things [*ta alla*, probably meaning "the other books" of the OT; *On the Contemplative Life* 25] which fosters and perfects knowledge and piety. They keep the memory of God alive and never forget it, so that even in their dreams the picture is nothing else but loveliness of divine excellences and powers. Indeed many when asleep and dreaming give utterance to their holy philosophy. . . .

Twice every day they pray, at dawn and at eventide; at sunrise they pray for a fine bright day, fine and bright in the true sense of the heavenly daylight which they pray may fill their minds. At sunset they ask that the soul may be wholly relieved from the press of the senses and the objects of sense and sitting where she is consistory and council chamber to herself pursue the quest of truth. . . .

The interval between early morning and evening is spent entirely in spiritual exercise [*askēsis*]. They read the Holy Scriptures and seek wisdom from their ancestral philosophy by taking it as an allegory, since they think that the words of the literal text are symbols of something whose hidden nature is revealed by studying the underlying meaning. (*On the Contemplative Life* 25–28)

At the weekly festal gathering the one presiding expounds the scriptures very carefully and with attention to being understood by all: "The exposition of the sacred scriptures treats the inner meaning conveyed in allegory. For to these people the whole law book seems to resemble a living creature with the literal ordinances for its body and for its soul the invisible mind laid up in its wording. . . . Then the President [*proedros*] rises and sings a hymn composed as an address to God, either a new one of his own composition or an old one by poets of an earlier day" (*On the Contemplative Life* 78–80).

Their method of allegorizing—or better, spiritual interpretation—has its roots not in individualistic free association but in a creative tradition "from men of old" that blesses the composition of new hymns and psalms: "They have also writings of men of old, the founders of their way of thinking, who left many memorials of the form used in allegorical interpretation and these they take as a kind of archetype and imitate the method in which this principle is carried out. And so they do not confine themselves to contemplation but also compose hymns and psalms [*asmata kai ymnous*] to God in all sorts of metres and melodies which they write down with the rhythms necessarily made more solemn" (*On the Contemplative Life* 29).

The culmination of divine guidance in the community of the Theraputae comes in the celebration of the sacred vigil (*pannychida*) following the expounding of scriptures and the festal supper. Hymns, sung by choirs of men and women—sometimes antiphonally, sometimes together—play a central role. The image of order and harmony in the carefully written and executed music is combined with the evident freedom that fills the inspired form as all are directed toward communion with God, the source of all illumination:

Lovely are the thoughts, lovely the words and worthy of reverence the choristers, and the end and aim of thoughts, words and choristers alike is piety [*eusebeia*]. Thus they continue till dawn, drunk with this drunkenness in which there is no shame, then not with heavy heads or drowsy eyes but more alert and more wakeful than when they came to the banquet, they stand with their faces and whole body turned to the east and when they see the sun rising they stretch their hands up to heaven and pray for bright days and knowledge of the truth and the power of keen sighted thinking. And after the prayers they depart each to his private sanctuary once more to ply the trade and till the field of their wonted philosophy. (*On the Contemplative Life* 88–89)

Philo is profoundly aware that God is at work in all human events, not just in scripture (*On Providence* 2.72). His historical writing "is permeated with faith in divine providence, and in particular with the divine concern for the fate of the Jews, as well as with the ultimate victory of justice, the enemies of the Jews coming to learn that in the end God saves the Jews."[8] But He cares for *all* as a father: "In the same way God too, the Father of reasonable intelligence, has indeed all who are endowed with reason under his care but takes thought also for those who live a misspent life, thereby giving them time for reformation and also keeping within the bounds of his merciful nature, which has for its attendant virtue and loving kindness [*philanthropia*] well fitted to keep watch as sentry around God's world" (*On Providence* 2.6). Philo views this very thought as coming from God: "Here is one thought. Receive it, O Soul, and ponder it awhile as a trust committed to thee by Him" (*On Providence* 2.7).

In addition to inspired thoughts while awake, dreams while asleep are forms of divine guidance. Although Philo takes his starting point from scriptural accounts of dreams, he clearly believes that divine guidance through dreams is a present reality and devotes a three-volume study to this subject. (Only the last two volumes have survived.) These are usually cited simply as *On Dreams,* but the full title is significant: *That Dreams Are Sent by God* (*Peri tou theopemptous einai tous oneirous*).

The Hebrew scriptures are replete with God-inspired dreams, and Philo is not the first Jewish writer to reflect on this. Job, for example, saw dreams as one means of God's communication (especially warnings), which human beings may or may not perceive or understand:

> For God speaks in one way,
> and in two, though man does not perceive it.
> In a dream, in a vision of the night,
> when deep sleep falls upon men,
> while they slumber on their beds,
> then he opens the ears of men,
> and terrifies them with warnings,
> that he may turn man aside from his deed,
> and cut off pride from man. (Job 33:14–17)

Philo discusses two types of inspired dreams: those God sends directly and those "in which our own mind, moving out of itself together with the mind of the universe, seems to be possessed and God-inspired [*theophoreisthai*], and so capable of receiving some foretaste and foreknowledge of things to come" (*On Dreams* 1.1–2).

For all his openness to the divine, Philo was "no stargazer."[9] Reasoned reflection, deliberate and diligent study of nature, philosophers, and especially scripture are central to his thought and practice. The "soul's eyes" must "strain" to contemplate "as far as human reason can do so." This connection between reason and revelation can be clearly seen in his discussion on discernment of good: "If indeed you would strain the soul's eyes to contemplate the providence of God as far as human reason can do so, you will gain a clearer vision of the true good and laugh to scorn what here are reckoned as goods which hitherto had your admiration" (*On Providence* 2.10–11). At the same time, these very fruits of human reason are a gift of divine revelation, since for Philo no insight into truth can be separated from God, who gives insight as "the food without which we cannot live": "Then awestruck at that divine revelation, so good and so excellent, you will surely recognize that none of the things mentioned above ranks of itself in the sight of God as good; for mines of silver and gold are the most worthless portion of the earth, utterly and absolutely inferior to that which is given up to the production of fruit. For there is no likeness between abundance of money, and the food without which we cannot live" (*On Providence* 2.11).

Philo advocates the full use of reason, but he sees it working well *only* in conjunction with God's revelation. Without revelation, human reason alone—which is easily distorted by delusions, passions, and vices—is utterly fallible in its judgments:

For in the first place the judgments of men and God are not alike. For we inquire into what is manifest but He penetrates noiselessly into the recesses of the soul, sees our thoughts as though in bright sunlight, and stripping off the wrappings in which they are enveloped, inspects our motives in their naked reality and at once distinguishes the counterfeit from the genuine. Let us never prefer then our own tribunal to that of God and assert that it is more infallible and wiser in counsel, for that religion forbids [or "is unholy," *ou gar osion*]. Ours has many pitfalls, the delusions of the senses, the malignancy of the passions and most formidable of all the hostility of the vices; while in His there is nothing that can deceive, only justice and truth, and everything that is judged according to these standards brings praise to the judge and cannot but be settled aright. (*On Providence* 2.35–36)

God can bring consolation and restoration to our reason in times of passion, confusion, and darkness, but only if we are willing to receive his illumination. If God's light is ignored, it will disappear, leaving us to our own self-chosen darkness (*On Dreams* 1.114). Even so, Philo trusts God to guide even when the soul is lazy or weak: "[Even] if we do close the eye of our soul and either will not take the trouble or have not the power to regain our sight, do thou thyself, O Sacred Guide, be our prompter [*ypechei*] and preside over our steps and never tire of anointing our eyes, until conducting us to the hidden light of hallowed words thou display to us the fast-locked loveliness invisible to the uninitiate" (*On Dreams* 1.165).[10]

Not only does God help the weak, says Philo, but having a sense of one's weakness is itself a *prerequisite* for perceiving God's presence and guidance:

> For so long as mind and sense-perception imagine that they get a firm grasp, mind of the objects of mind and sense of the objects of sense, and thus move aloft in the sky, the divine word is far away. But when each of them acknowledges its weakness, and going through a kind of setting passes out of sight, right reason is forward to meet and greet at once the practicing soul [*asketikēs psychēs*], whose willing champion he is when it despairs of itself and waits for him who invisibly comes from without to its succour. (*On Dreams* 1.118)

While Philo has a very broad view of the scope of divine revelation, in *On the Life of Moses* he also describes three distinct types of direct divine guidance: (1) guidance that comes directly from God through a prophet as interpreter; (2) guidance to the prophet through "question and answer"; and (3) guidance that is "spoken by Moses in his own person, when possessed by God and carried out of himself":

> The first kind are absolutely and entirely signs of the divine excellence, graciousness and beneficence, by which he incites all men to noble conduct, and particularly the nation of his worshippers, for whom he opens the road which leads to happiness. In the second kind we have combination and partnership: the prophet asks questions of God about matters on which he has been seeking knowledge, and God replies and instructs him. The third kind are assigned to the lawgiver himself: God has given him of His own power of foreknowledge and by this he will reveal future events. (*Moses* 2.189–190)

For Philo, the stories of divine guidance in the lives of Abraham, the Patriarchs, and Moses are not of mere antiquarian interest; they are examples of what is still possible in the present. They are to be regarded less as heroic tales of old—and as such unique and unrepeatable—than as the prototypes of what was made accessible to everyone through the Law.[11]

Philo begins his discussion of the Law by recounting the lives of the Patriarchs Abraham, Isaac, and Jacob, who exemplified the Law even before it was revealed to Moses. They thus also demonstrate that what the Law requires is not exotic or onerous but is consistent with nature and embedded in the human soul:

> These are such men as lived good and blameless lives, whose virtues stand permanently recorded in the most holy scriptures, not merely to sound their

praises but for the instruction of the reader and as inducement to him to aspire to the same; for in these men we have laws endowed with life and reason, and Moses extolled them for two reasons. First he wished to show that the enacted ordinances are not inconsistent with nature; and secondly that those who wish to live in accordance with the laws as they stand have no difficult task, seeing that the first generations before any at all of the particular statutes was set in writing followed the unwritten law with perfect ease, so that one might properly say that the enacted laws are nothing else than memorials of the life of the ancients, preserving to a later generation their actual words and deeds. For they were not scholars or pupils of others, nor did they learn under teachers what was right to say or do: they listened to no voice or instruction but their own: they gladly accepted conformity with nature, holding that nature itself was, as indeed it is, the most venerable of statutes, and thus their whole life was one of happy obedience to law. Thy committed no guilty action of their own free will or purpose, and where chance led them wrong they besought God's mercy and propitiated Him with prayers and supplications, and thus secured a perfect life guided aright in both fields, both in their premeditated actions and in such as were not of freely-willed purpose. (*On Abraham* 5–6)

Regarding the inner sense that perceives God's direction and guidance, Philo says Abraham was "[eager] to follow God and to be obedient to His commands; understanding by commands not only those conveyed in speech and writing but also those made manifest by nature with clearer signs, and apprehended by the sense which is the most truthful of all and superior to hearing, on which no certain reliance can be placed" (*On Abraham* 6).

Philo applied Abraham's experience directly to his own daily life as a thinker and writer, in which periods of darkness mixed with sudden inspiration:

I feel no shame in recording my own experience, a thing I know from its having happened to me a thousand times. On some occasions, after making up my mind to follow the usual course of writing on philosophical tenets, and knowing definitely the substance of what I was to set down, I have found my understanding incapable of giving birth to a single idea, and have given it up without accomplishing anything, reviling my understanding for its self-conceit, and filled with amazement at the might of Him who is, to Whom is given the opening and closing of the soul-wombs. On other occasions, I have approached my work empty and suddenly become full, the ideas falling in a shower from above and being sown invisibly, so that under the influence of the Divine possession I have been filled with corybantic frenzy and have been unconscious of anything, place, person present, myself, words spoken, lines written. For I obtained language, ideas, an enjoyment of light, keenest vision, pellucid distinctness of objects, such as might be received through the eyes as the result of clearest showing. (*Migration of Abraham* 33–35)

Migration is a key theme in Philo, for whom this means much more than the limited historical events that led Abraham from Ur to Canaan. Migration is fundamentally the story of every soul being led through a divine-human synergy toward creativity, illumination, and communion with God—a fitting summary of Philo's understanding of divine guidance in the Greco-Roman world he sought to bridge with his Jewish experience.

10

Josephus

Titus Flavius Josephus (37–100 CE), the Jewish Roman scholar, historian, general, and advisor to Vespasian and Titus, was born Joseph ben Mattathias in Jerusalem of a wealthy priestly family on his father's side and the royal Hasmonean family on his mother's side. He was marked out for leadership at a young age and by his 20s had already been sent to Nero to negotiate the release of 12 imprisoned priests. Later he was appointed military governor of Galilee. But he was a Jewish patriot, so when it came to choosing sides in the First Roman-Jewish War he initially and successfully fought the Roman occupation in Galilee. The Romans eventually brutally defeated his troops, and thousands of Jewish soldiers were put to death. According to his own account, he escaped with about 40 others, hid in a cave, and agreed to commit mass suicide rather than surrender. They drew lots and killed each other, one by one. When Josephus and one other were left they changed their minds, surrendered, and defected to the Roman forces led by Vespasian and his son Titus in 67. After two years in prison, he was released and continued to serve the Roman forces. In the siege of Jerusalem in 70 he was appointed to negotiate with the Jewish defenders before the city was razed and the Temple destroyed. Josephus became a Roman citizen and was in Titus's entourage when he returned to Rome triumphantly in 71, bringing with him the plunder of Jerusalem and its Temple.

Like Philo, Josephus views direct divine guidance as not only possible but also normal. In his *Life*, for example, he recounts several such incidents that occurred to him personally. In 66–67 he was leading the Jewish forces against Rome in Galilee; he describes the distress he felt when he received a letter from his father telling him about a rumored secret plot by some of his troops to kill him. His father pleaded with him to abandon his soldiers and Galilee, but Josephus felt torn between his fear and the Jewish forces' need for leadership:

> That night I beheld a marvelous vision in my dreams. I retired to my couch, grieved and distraught by the tidings of the letter, when I thought that there stood by me one who said: "Cease, man, from thy sorrow of heart, let go all fear. That which grieves thee now will promote thee to greatness and felicity in all things. Not in these present trials only, but in many besides, will fortune attend thee. Fret not thyself then. Remember that thou must even battle with the

Divine Guidance. John A. Jillions, Oxford University Press (2020). © Oxford University Press.
DOI: 10.1093/oso/9780190055738.001.0001

Romans." Cheered by this dream vision I arose, ready to descend into the plain. (*Life* 208–209)[1]

Divine guidance thus decisively strengthened Josephus's resolve to stay the course with his troops against Rome. A sense of divine guidance also saved his life after the Roman forces under Vespasian defeated his troops in 67. After he turned himself in and was put in prison, he heard that he would be sent to Nero, whose madness and cruelty were creating havoc in Rome. Josephus asked for a private interview with Vespasian and his son Titus in order to share with them a prophetic message from God. In his *Jewish War* he recounts what he told them:

> "You imagine, Vespasian, that in the person of Josephus you have taken a mere captive; but I come as a messenger of greater destinies. Had I not been sent on this errand by God, I knew the laws of the Jews and how it becomes a general to die. To Nero do you send me? Why then? . . . *You* will be Caesar Vespasian, you will be emperor, you and your son here. . . . For myself, I ask to be punished by stricter custody, if I have dared to trifle with the words of God." To this speech Vespasian, at the moment, seemed to attach little credit, supposing it to be a trick of Josephus to save his life. Gradually, however, he was led to believe it, for God was already rousing in him thoughts of empire and by other tokens foreshadowing the throne. (*Jewish War* 3.400–404)

Two years later Josephus was freed when it became clear that his prediction was coming true. (Vespasian became emperor in July 69.) Josephus also reports his correct prediction of the fall of Jotapata and his own capture (*Jewish War* 3.406–407). This prediction was investigated by Vespasian and helped confirm his view that Josephus was a prophet.

However, while Josephus is unwilling to dismiss dreams and special revelations, they in fact play only a minor role in his view of divine guidance. As with Philo, the leading role belongs to Moses. He is "our legislator . . . who proved himself the people's best guide and counselor; and after framing a code to embrace the whole conduct of their life induced them to accept it, and secured, on the firmest footing, its observance for all time" (*Against Apion* 2.156). Josephus is devoted to the Jewish scriptures far above any private revelation or philosophy: "For our people do not favor persons who have mastered the speech of many nations, or who adorn their style with smoothness of diction. . . . But they give credit for wisdom to those alone who have an exact knowledge of the law and who are capable of interpreting the meaning of the Holy Scriptures" (*Jewish Antiquities* 13.288).[2]

We have given practical proof of our reverence for our own scriptures. For although such long ages have now passed, no one has ventured either to add, or to remove, or to alter a syllable; and it is an instinct with every Jew, from the day of his birth, to regard them as the decrees of God, to abide by them, and if need be, cheerfully to die for them. Time and again ere now the sight has been witnessed of prisoners enduring tortures and death in every form in the theatres, rather than utter a single word against the laws and allied documents. (*Against Apion* 1.42–43)

Josephus argues that Greek philosophy, being younger than the Jewish Law, unknowingly imitated the more ancient Law of Moses: "Plato followed the example of our legislator [Moses]. He prescribed as the primary duty of the citizens a study of their laws, which they must all learn word for word by heart" (*Against Apion* 2.257). He points out, "Our earliest imitators were the Greek philosophers, who, though ostensibly following the laws of their own countries, yet in their conduct and philosophy were Moses' disciples, holding similar views about God, and advocating simple life and friendly communion [*koinonia*] between man and man" (*Against Apion* 2.282).

While Josephus upholds the centrality of scripture, he does not believe it is a substitute for God's guidance in the present. God remains with His people and continues to guide them through both the Law and its continuing communal interpretation. God's very election of the Jewish people was proof that He is the ultimate guide of His people. Moses founded a theocracy and thus placed "all sovereignty and authority in the hands of God":

To Him he persuaded all to look, as the author of all blessings, both those which are common to all mankind, and those which they had won for themselves by prayer in the crises of their history. He convinced them that no single action, no secret thought, could be hid from Him. He represented him as One, uncreated and immutable to all eternity, in beauty surpassing mortal thought, made known to us by His power, although the nature of his real being surpasses knowledge. (*Against Apion* 2.167)

Josephus goes on to say, "Religion governs all our actions and occupations and speech; none of these things did our lawgiver leave unexamined or indeterminate" (*Against Apion* 2.171).

In common with most Jews at the time, Josephus's view of scripture is much broader than the text alone. Louis Feldman (1926–2017), the leading contemporary Josephus scholar, draws attention to scripture as the heart of Josephus's argument but says his claim to be faithful to scripture has "occasioned much amazement, since he has modified the Bible, sometimes drastically, on almost every page."[3] What Josephus meant by his faithfulness to scripture "is of great importance, since it involves the issue of how much liberty one was permitted in interpreting the Bible during this period."[4]

Feldman says that Josephus includes in "scriptures" the Jewish tradition generally, implying the existence of an early written form of biblical interpretation (*midrashim*) for which we now have early evidence in the Dead Sea Scrolls, and thus predating Josephus by a full century. "Moreover, there would seem to be precedent for modifying the sacred LXX text which Josephus cites. . . . Even the rabbis in obvious praise, refer to the miraculous way in which the translation was accomplished, despite the fact that deliberate changes were made in the process of translation."[5] This means that the biblical text *and* the communally sanctioned history of its interpretation are *together* understood as "scripture."

Divergent First-Century Jewish Views of Divine Providence

If Josephus viewed Judaism as united in its devotion to the Law, he also recognized important differences among Jews of his day. He reports that one of the issues that divided the three major Jewish groups of the first century—Pharisees, Sadducees, and Essenes—was their attitude toward divine providence. Or put another way, they differed in how they saw the relative balance between God's will and human freedom:[6]

> The sect of the Essenes declares that Fate [Divine Providence, *eimarmenē*] is the mistress of all things, and that nothing befalls man unless it is in accordance with her decree. (*Antiquities* 13.172)[7]

> The Sadducees do away with fate altogether, and remove God beyond, not merely the commission, but the very sight of evil. They maintain that man has the free choice of good or evil, and that it rests with each man's will whether he follows the one or the other. (*Jewish War* 2.8.14)

> The Pharisees attribute everything to fate and to God; they hold that to act rightly or otherwise rests, indeed, for the most part with men, but that in each action fate cooperates. (*Jewish War* 2.8.14)

Josephus favors the Pharisee view of synergy between God and human beings. As he says, "It was God's good pleasure that there should be a fusion and that the will of man with his virtue and vice should be admitted to the council-chamber of fate" (*Antiquities* 18.13). This, he reports, is also the majority opinion among

Jews, since the Pharisees are "the most accurate interpreters of the laws, and hold the position of the leading sect" (*Jewish War* 2.8.14).

According to Josephus, the Pharisees were content to live with the paradox of two apparently incompatible assertions. On the one hand, God is sovereign in human life and history; on the other, human beings have free will and will be judged on the basis of their freely chosen decisions. As Ephraim Urbach comments, the Pharisees "did not retreat from contradiction, for their aim was not to find a smooth philosophical solution, but to activate all man's powers—both the potency inherent in the consciousness of freedom and the will to do good and that which flamed from the feeling of the nullity of man and his complete dependence on Divine Providence, for their religious thought was directed, in equal measure, towards God and towards the world and society."[8]

Josephus and Philo

Josephus and Philo were both well trained in contemporary philosophy, so perhaps their ready acceptance of divine guidance is not surprising, given its widespread currency in the Greco-Roman world. But they are both also expressing distinctly Jewish ideas that had no clear parallel in the Greco-Roman world.

How faithful were they as interpreters of first-century Judaism? Josephus himself testifies that "Philo was held in the highest honor" in the Jewish community at Alexandria.[9] As for his own stance vis-à-vis the surrounding world, Josephus saw common ground with many Greek philosophers, but not with Greek religion. In *Against Apion* and in *Antiquities of the Jews* he clearly identified himself with mainstream Judaism. What's more, says Feldman, "Josephus had so many enemies that he had to be careful not to give occasions for a charge of heresy."[10]

We have no reason to believe that their respective Jewish communities saw either Philo or Josephus as betrayers of Jewish teaching. So we may safely conclude at the very least that their views on divine guidance were representative of an important strand within first-century Judaism.[11]

11

The Dead Sea Scrolls, Pseudepigrapha, and Expansions of Scripture

The Dead Sea Scrolls

In 1947 a large number of ancient scrolls was discovered in a cave not far from the western shore of the Dead Sea in the area known as Khirbet Qumran, normally cited simply as Qumran (*khirbet* is Arabic for "ruin on a hill" and is found in many place names throughout the Middle East). Written on leather and papyrus variously in Hebrew, Greek, and Aramaic, these were a monumental find that opened up our understanding of Jewish religion and life in the intertestamental period, revealing archeological layers of communities from 700 BCE to 135 CE. Since that time many more discoveries in other caves nearby (11 in total) and in the Judean desert beyond the Dead Sea have been found, and collectively these documents are referred to as the Dead Sea Scrolls. Two of the most celebrated scrolls are known as "The Community Rule" (1QS) and "The Damascus Document" (CD).

The community at Qumran that produced the scrolls was founded in the second century BCE and exemplifies the Essenes described by Josephus. While this is not the place for an overview of the rich material about the community, what can be said about their approach to divine guidance is that it was firmly rooted in the Jewish scriptures.[1] God's direction in Qumran comes above all through "what was commanded by means of the hand of Moses and his servants the prophets" (1QS 1.2). As David Instone-Brewer notes, the Qumran community viewed themselves as "the true Israel" who "'dig the Law' to find hidden truth (CD 8.3; 1QS 7.12), and the community attempted to meditate on the Law day and night, by dividing the night into shifts and taking it in turns to expound Scripture (1QS 6.6.)."[2]

Although faithfulness to the biblical text was important, the Qumran community members (also known as "covenanters") were not literalists. Like Philo and Josephus, they understood inspired exegesis to be essential for understanding the scriptural message in the present, and "new knowledge was constantly expected to be revealed to members of the community who would then share that knowledge with others (1 QS 6.9)."[3] That said, Qumran's understanding of divine guidance through inspired exegesis is quite sober and remains closely tied to careful study

Divine Guidance. John A. Jillions, Oxford University Press (2020). © Oxford University Press.
DOI: 10.1093/oso/9780190055738.001.0001

of the biblical text, with their Teacher of Righteousness—the Founder—as the authoritative instructor: "It must be underlined that in Qumran we have no dreams, visions, voices or similar apocalyptic revelatory fictions: the new revelation is discovered in the old scriptural text itself, and the main work of the covenanters is studying the sacred text, copying it, reading it, interpreting it and being ready for its final fulfillment. The Founder is primarily the teacher, the instructor."[4]

But once again the Bible does not stand alone. Readers of the sacred scriptures who stubbornly reject the community's insight will suffer not only deception but defilement: "Defiled, defiled shall he be all the days he spurns the decrees of God, without allowing himself to be taught by the Community of his counsel" (1QS 3.6). According to this teaching, human beings outside the safety of the Qumran community were subject to chaotic good and evil influences coming in from all sides, seen and unseen, and personified as the Angel of Light and the Angel of Darkness (1QS 3.18ff). In order to escape this spiritual warfare between good and evil, people were invited to become part of the community and "acquiesce to the authority of the sons of Zadok, the priests who safeguard the covenant and to the authority of the multitude of the men of the community, those who persevere steadfastly in the Covenant" (1QS 5.1–3).

Under the authority of these priests, decisions "in every affair" regarding law, property, and judgment were to made by lot. Special revelations were not excluded, but they were to be shared with and correctly discerned by the council of elders (1QS 8.11ff.). The Teacher of Righteousness was the final authority. He was the overseer of "the sons of Zadok" and was thus responsible for discerning the correct path according to the intellect and spirit of each person under his charge (1QS 9.16ff.).

If Qumran were to have a motto for its approach, it might be called "divine guidance through submission." Through obedience to the community, its elders, and the Teacher of Righteousness, members of Qumran would thus find not only insight and security but spiritual freedom.

Jewish Pseudepigrapha and Expansions of Scripture

Many other Jewish writings, which like the Qumran texts did not find their way into the scriptures, circulated in first-century Palestine and in the Jewish diaspora. These give more evidence for the range of views on divine guidance within Judaism of the period. Among these are the pseudepigrapha, writings from about 200 BCE onward. These were composed under the pseudonym of a biblical patriarch or prophet or some other famous figure.

An extensive collection of such pseudepigrapha has come down to us, and the following are often cited as examples of the genre from this period: 1 Enoch, the

Book of Jubilees, the Testament of Moses, the Letter of Aristeas (cited earlier in discussing the origin of the Septuagint translation), the Psalms of Solomon, and the Sibylline Oracles (ranging from the second century BCE and edited between 50 BCE and 70 CE).[5]

These examples are but a tiny selection of the vast body of literature—epics, philosophical treatises, scriptural expansions, psalms, odes, hymns—produced by Jews in this period, all of which were understood at the time as creative works rooted in the Jewish scriptures and inspired by the God of Israel. Although regarded now as spurious and outside the canonical Jewish scriptures, a number of these texts were widely read and regarded as spiritually profitable. Some, like the Prayer of Manasseh, also found their way into Jewish and Christian liturgical life. A few pseudepigrapha of high standing among Jews were later included in various Christian versions of the Old Testament: the Prayer of Manasseh, 2 Esdras, 3–4 Maccabees, and Enoch. The fact that this literature exists and was widely circulated confirms the view that Judaism in the first century combined the ideal of faithfulness to the Torah with a lively sense of divine guidance—and the possibility of demonic antiguidance—both in daily life and in the process of biblical interpretation.[6]

We will look briefly at a selection from some of these better-known texts to put together a picture of how they handle questions of divine guidance.

The Prayer of Manasseh

God's sovereignty, His transcendence, and the coming apocalypse are frequent themes in the pseudepigrapha, but these texts also continued to affirm God's nearness and guidance. According to James Charlesworth, "Apocalypses that stressed the grandeur and transcendence of God were customarily interspersed with hymns that celebrated God's nearness, and prayers that were perceived as heard and answered."[7] The Prayer of Manasseh (pre-70 CE) is a moving example of this.

> O Lord, according to your great goodness
> you have promised repentance and forgiveness
> to those who have sinned against you,
> and in the multitude of your mercies
> you have appointed repentance for sinners,
> so that they may be saved. . . .
> [13]I earnestly implore you,
> forgive me, O Lord, forgive me!
> Do not destroy me with my transgressions!

Do not be angry with me for ever or store up evil for me;
do not condemn me to the depths of the earth.
For you, O Lord, are the God of those who repent,
[14]and in me you will manifest your goodness;
for, unworthy as I am, you will save me according to your
great mercy,
[15]and I will praise you continually all the days of my life.
For all the host of heaven sings your praise,
and yours is the glory for ever. Amen.[8]

Although the Prayer of Manasseh is grounded in the communal experience of Israel and is "constructed in accord with the best liturgical forms,"[9] it is also profoundly individual and personal.[10]

Notably, the prayer is an expansion of 2 Chronicles 33:10–13, a short passage in the canonical scriptures that describes Manasseh's refusal to listen to God, followed by his change of heart and subsequent prayer. But the Chronicles account is itself a complete rewriting of the history found in 2 Kings 21, in which Manasseh is depicted as unredeemable. Indeed the author of 2 Kings underlines this later when he says Manasseh "filled Jerusalem with innocent blood, and *the Lord would not pardon*" (2 Kings 24:4). But the author of Chronicles, and the subsequent Jewish tradition reflected here, took the view that no one, not even Manasseh, is beyond the reach of redemption.

[10]The Lord spoke to Manas'seh and to his people, but they gave no heed. [11]Therefore the Lord brought upon them the commanders of the army of the king of Assyria, who took Manas'seh with hooks and bound him with fetters of bronze and brought him to Babylon. [12]And when he was in distress he entreated the favor of the Lord his God and humbled himself greatly before the God of his fathers. [13]*He prayed to him, and God received his entreaty and heard his supplication and brought him again to Jerusalem into his kingdom. Then Manas'seh knew that the Lord was God.*

The Prayer of Manasseh is a creative expansion of this last verse and illustrates the distinguishing features of this vast and varied pseudepigraphical literature: its anchor in the canonical scriptures.[11] This emphasis on the Bible produces not a narrow biblical literalism but a flowering of expansions like the Prayer of Manasseh that embellish, reinterpret, and even rewrite portions of the scriptures, confirming once again the remarkable freedom found in at least some segments of first-century Judaism.

Jubilees

The Book of Jubilees contains many such expansions of scripture. For instance, the following passage beautifully embellishes the very brief account of Abram's momentous call in Genesis 12:1–3. Here is the original biblical text:

> [1]Now the Lord said to Abram, "Go from your country and your kindred and your father's house to the land that I will show you. [2]I will make of you a great nation, and I will bless you, and make your name great, so that you will be a blessing. [3]I will bless those who bless you, and the one who curses you I will curse; and in you all the families of the earth shall be blessed."

This comes suddenly in Genesis, with no warning or context. Jubilees is written to fill in this gap and show how God's intervention is in fact his *response* to Abram's humble request for guidance.

> And in the sixth week, in its fifth year, Abram sat up during the night on the first of the seventh month, so that he might observe the stars from evening until daybreak so that he might see what the nature of the year would be with respect to rain. And he was sitting alone and making observations; and a word came into his heart, saying, "All of the signs of the stars and the signs of the sun and the moon are all in the hand of the LORD. Why am I seeking?

> > "If he desires, he will make it rain morning and evening,
> > and if he desires he will not send it down;
> > and everything is in his hand."

> And he prayed on that night, saying:

> > "My God, the Most High God, you alone are God to me.
> > And you created everything,
> > and everything which is was the work of your hands,
> > and you and your kingdom I have chosen.
> > Save me from the hands of evil spirits
> > which rule over the thought of the heart of man,
> > and do not let them lead me astray from following you,
> >   O my God;
> > but establish me and my seed forever,
> > and let us not go astray henceforth and forever."

And he said, "shall I return unto Ur of the Chaldees who seek my face so that I should return to them? Or shall I dwell here in this place? Make the straight path prosper before you in the hand of your servant that he might serve. And do not let me walk in the error of my heart, O my God."

And he finished talking and praying and behold, the word of the Lord was sent to him by my hand [an angel of the presence], saying, "Come forth from your land and from your kin." (Jubilees 12.16–22)

God's guidance here is given through an angel, and not, as in the biblical text, directly. This incident, as expanded here, does not simply satisfy literary curiosity; it also has a theological point. It represents Abram's conversion from an astrological spirituality aimed at control of the future (divination by the stars) to one based on trust in the Lord, regardless of what the future might hold.

The Sibylline Oracles

The Sibylline Oracles (as distinct from the Roman Sibylline books) offer yet another view of Jewish attitudes toward divine guidance in the pseudepigrapha. As J. J. Collins notes in his translation, the Oracles are theologically important "less in their actual content than in the phenomenon which they represent—the attribution of inspired Jewish and Christian oracles to the pagan Sibyl."[12] While the Sibyl was identified as the daughter or daughter-in-law of Noah, "the oracles represented a remarkable attempt to find a mode of expression common to Jews (or Christians) and gentiles. As such the Jewish Sibylline oracles originated in the apologetic literature of Hellenistic Judaism. The willingness to incorporate material from pagan oracles shows a significant readiness to build on the common human basis of Jews and gentiles. At least the earliest oracles in Sibylline Oracle 3 express a very positive attitude to their gentile neighbors."[13]

But it would be a mistake to read too much universalism into this Jewish work. While expressed in the language of pagan oracles, these writings are repeatedly critical of pagan idolatry, divination, and immorality. They call on the Gentile world to acknowledge the one God "who is sole ruler ineffable, who lives in the sky, self-begotten, invisible, who himself sees all things" (Sibylline Oracles 3.11–12). These are not merely Jewish sentiments but were shared by many Gentiles, as we have seen in the review of Greco-Roman attitudes toward divine guidance. The Sibyl emphasizes that the Jews—unlike superstitious Gentiles—reject the divination practices so prevalent everywhere else. And these practices are not harmless. They come from demonic forces that encourage greed, individualism, neglect of virtue and of service, and spread confusion about what is true or false. Jews, in contrast, are concerned with "good counsel and noble works" and thus reject pagan divination practices that "have taught errors" and led to "many evils."

> They [the Jews] are always concerned with good counsel and noble works
> for they do not worry about the cyclic course of the sun
> or the moon or monstrous things under the earth
> nor the depth of the grim sea, Oceanus,
> nor portents of sneezes, nor birds of augurers,
> nor seers, nor sorcerers, nor soothsayers,
> nor the deceits of foolish words of ventriloquists.
> Neither do they practice the astrological predictions of the Chaldeans
> nor astronomy. For all these things are erroneous,
> such as foolish men inquire into day by day,
> exercising themselves at a profitless task.
> And indeed they have taught errors to shameful men
> from which many evils come upon mortals on earth
> so that they are misled as to good ways and righteous deeds. (Sibylline
>   Oracles 3:218–233)

The Jewish author of the Sibylline Oracles here takes direct aim at pagan divination, which overemphasized personal, individual spirituality at the expense of reason and public virtue. In fighting the fearmongering of pagan religion, Jews stressed their attractive monotheism but also the divine gift of rational decision-making, common service, virtue, and holy transcendence. As we have seen, thoughtful Greek and Roman observers often shared the Jewish critique of pagan religion, and the Sibyl builds on this by describing the virtuous lifestyle of the Jews, who followed the divine Law and were thus constantly preoccupied with mutual care and social justice:

> But they care for righteousness and virtue
> and not love of money, which begets innumerable evils
> for mortal men, war and limitless famine.
> They have just measurements in fields and cities
> and they do not carry out robberies at night against each other
> nor drive off herds of oxen, sheep, or goats,
> nor does neighbor move the boundaries of neighbor,
> nor does a very rich man grieve a lesser man
> nor oppress widows in any respect, but rather helps them,
> always going to their aid with corn, wine and oil.

Always a prosperous man among the people gives a share
of the harvest to those who have nothing, but are poor,
fulfilling the word of the great God, the hymn of the Law,
for the Heavenly One gave the earth in common to all. . . .
. . . [And when Moses] came leading his people, which God led from Egypt to
    the mountain, Sinai, God also gave forth
the Law from heaven, having written down all just ordinances on two tablets
    and enjoined them to perform it.
And if anyone should disobey he would pay the penalty of the Law, whether at
    human hands
or escaping men; he would utterly be destroyed in all justice.
[For the heavenly one gave the earth in common to all
and fidelity, and excellent reason in their breast]. (Sibylline Oracles 3.220–260)

Like the other examples in this chapter, this passage demonstrates again the centrality first-century Jews gave to keeping the Torah, which they regarded as God's fundamental divine guidance, through which every other form of guidance was to be evaluated. But writings like the Sibylline Oracles took this further and argued that the Jewish Law was also universal and compatible with the natural laws of virtue and reason that philosophers revered and that the Creator had implanted in every human heart.

3 Maccabees

As a final example of Jewish pseudepigrapha, consider 3 Maccabees, written sometime in the first century BCE and which, like the Prayer of Manasseh, was incorporated into the scriptures of the Christian East. The name of the book is misleading since the setting of 3 Maccabees is not the Maccabean revolt in Jerusalem against Antiochus Epiphanes (175–164 BCE) but the earlier revolt of Alexandrian Jews against Ptolemy IV Philopator (221–203 BCE), which began when he returned to Egypt after being miraculously prevented from entering the temple at Jerusalem and so defiling its sacred precincts.

In revenge for this humiliation Philopator ordered all the Jews in Alexandria to be rounded up and brought to the hippodrome. Those who refused to give up their faith would be put to death by a herd of 500 maddened elephants that had been deliberately intoxicated on Philopator's orders. The Jewish elders failed to get him to relent, but various miraculous interventions—notably the elder Eleazar's fervent prayer—thwarted the evil plan. As a result, Philopator had a dramatic change of heart, held a banquet for the Jews, permitted their return to Jerusalem, and issued a decree putting to death all Jewish apostates.

3 Maccabees was probably written to strengthen Jews of the first century BCE who were periodically under threat from the Romans, but regardless of the book's historical authenticity ("most of the material is legendary"),[14] it is valuable for its portrayal of the religious attitudes of at least a segment of the Jewish community. A close reading of the story yields a number of key points about divine guidance and decision-making.

1. The Jews need no extraordinary divine guidance before they react to Philopator's wickedness. "The bolder of the citizens" (3 Macc 1:22) take immediate action to resist him. This decisive attitude is also shown by most of the Alexandrian Jews, who "acted firmly with a courageous spirit and did not depart from their religion" while remaining "resolutely hopeful of obtaining help" (3 Macc 2:32).

2. Hierarchical and communal are intertwined in the decisions taken. The elders are caught in the middle, trying to convince Philopator not to carry out his plan, while also restraining the Jewish hotheads who want to react immediately. Meanwhile the rest of the Jewish community comes together to pray with fervor. Then the distressed crowd rushes to the scene, making a "continuous, vehement, and concerted cry" that results in an "immense uproar" (3 Macc 1:28). The people share a sense of full responsibility before God and each other for the welfare of the community and don't leave the leaders alone. After failing to change Philopator's angry decision, the elders join the crowd "to call upon Him who has all power to defend them in the present trouble and not to overlook this unlawful and haughty deed" (3 Macc 1:27). Up to that point the efforts of the elders to negotiate a settlement had continued side by side with the community's prayer to God. Now the elders recognize that they can do no more, and as a last resort they ask God to deliver them. They need no divine guidance to tell them that they must not back down. Indeed "all at that time preferred death to the profanation of the place" (3 Macc 1:29).

The prayer remains hierarchical and communal: the priest prays on behalf of all the people, "facing the sanctuary, bending his knees and extending his hands with calm dignity" (3 Macc 2:1). The same pattern—hierarchical yet communal—is seen in Eleazar's culminating prayer, when all hope seems to be lost:

[13]And let the Gentiles cower today in fear of your invincible might, O honored One, who have power to save the nation of Jacob. [14]The whole throng of infants and their parents entreat you with tears. [15]Let it be shown to all the Gentiles that you are with us, O Lord, and have not turned your face from us; but just as you

have said, "Not even when they were in the land of their enemies did I neglect them," so accomplish it, O Lord. (3 Macc 6:13–15)

Eleazar and the people trust in God to give them help for an obvious need, and their focus is neither guidance nor even self-protection but deliverance for the sake of the Lord's own name.

This is an admirable bonding of the leaders and the people. But there is also an ugly side here to community solidarity: those who apostatize are seen as enemies who destroy the community from within. At a minimum they must be rejected from "common fellowship and mutual help (*euchrestia*)" (3 Macc 2:33), and when that is not enough, 3 Maccabees also authorizes a violent purge (3 Macc 7:10–15).

3. Deliverance is ascribed solely to God's gracious gift and not to the valiant efforts of the troops. Everything that happens is ultimately under God's direction. He is the sovereign God, "who oversees all things, the first Father [*propator*] of all, holy among the holy ones" (3 Macc 2:21). Defeat too is ascribed to God, but as punishment for sins in order to bring the nation to repentance. Even the fact that Philopator's scribes ran out of pens and paper and were thus prevented from completing a census of the Jews is seen as an act of God's "invincible providence" (3 Macc 4:17–21; see also 5:11–13; 28–35). God's sovereign guidance can overturn events in a moment; not to be aware of this is plain foolishness (3 Macc 3:11).

4. Perceptions and feelings of God's guidance may be seriously wrong. Philopator interprets the absence of resistance to his initial entry of the temple as a divine sign that he was meant to enter the inner sanctuary (3 Macc 1:13). One of the Jews rebukes him for reading signs in this way (3 Macc 1:14–15), but he insists on pushing forward, to the horror of the gathered priests and populace (3 Macc 1:16ff.). Similarly, Philopator's feelings of joy on occupying the temple are no guarantee of true divine guidance. On the contrary, his feelings on this occasion are a sign of his total deception.

"The king was greatly and continually filled with joy, organizing feasts in honor of all his idols, with a mind alienated from truth and with a profane mouth, praising speechless things that are not able even to communicate or to come to one's help, and uttering improper words against the supreme God" (3 Macc 4:16).[15] Joy here is not a sign of divine guidance. On the other hand, Philopator's later derangement is ascribed to God as the means by which the people were saved (3 Macc 5:30). Likewise, when God reveals himself to the enemies of the Jews, what they experience is "confusion and terror": "[The Lord] revealed his holy face and opened the heavenly gates, from which two glorious angels of fearful aspect descended, visible to all but the Jews. They opposed the forces of the enemy and filled them with confusion and terror" (3 Macc 6:18–19).

* * *

As we have seen repeatedly, despite the diversity that scholars have rightly noted within intertestamental Judaism, the scriptures were the unifying force. But reliance on the scriptures did not mean dependence on its texts alone for inspiration and direction. As compositions like the Prayer of Manasseh, the Sibylline Oracles, and 3 Maccabees illustrate, Jews in many and various ways continued to experience and express the personal divine guidance of the God of Israel.[16]

12

Rabbinic Sources

The first and second centuries saw the flowering of classical Jewish teaching as expounded by the great rabbinic sages, the Tannaim, and their immediate precursors (most famously Hillel and Shammai). They were closely associated with the Pharisees as upholders of Jewish tradition against perceived compromises with Roman ways. Yohanan ben Zakai (first century CE) thus opposed the Sadducees; Hillel's great-grandson Shimon ben Gamaliel (c. 10 BCE–70 CE)—referenced very favorably in Acts as a voice of reason and as Paul's teacher (Acts 5:34-40, 22:3)—opposed the appointment of Josephus as military governor of Galilee.

In Jewish tradition the era of these rabbis is known as the Tannaitic period and roughly covers the years 10–220. Their teachings form the basis of the Mishnah, the collection of the earliest rabbinic oral law that is the core of the Talmud. These teachings were almost exclusively oral until the third century, and it was not until much later that they were compiled and edited into what became two versions of the Talmud (the Jerusalem Talmud c. 450, and the Babylonian Talmud, c. 600).

These late dates mean that the rabbinic documents, though claiming antiquity, must be used with caution when considering what views circulated in the first century. Most scholars agree that pre-70 rabbinic material can be used with a fair degree of certainty that it was faithfully transmitted.[1] Later rabbinic material is also valuable where it confirms a pattern of thought seen in earlier sources (such as in Philo or Josephus). Hyam Maccoby's conclusion reflects the general consensus: "On the whole then, the strong likelihood is that the rabbinic literature is, as its creators claimed, the culmination of a long process of oral Torah."[2] Nevertheless, as we have seen with Philo, Josephus, the Dead Sea Scrolls, and other Jewish writings outside the Bible, the oral Torah included diverse strands of thought about divine guidance, so we should remain cautious about reading back into the first century the later dominance of rabbinic Judaism.

This should not lead us to believe that this rabbinic stream, represented by Pharisees in the first century, was just one among many, all equally influential. Josephus reports that the Pharisees were clearly the leading voice. This may represent his own prejudice, of course (though the leading Pharisee of his day, Gamaliel, opposed him), but we have no reason to doubt the truth of his statement, especially given the New Testament support for this view.

Divine Guidance. John A. Jillions, Oxford University Press (2020). © Oxford University Press.
DOI: 10.1093/oso/9780190055738.001.0001

How the rabbis approached scripture is significant for their view of divine guidance. They may have been concerned with the literal sense of scripture in all its details, but this was not to be equated with historicism. What interested the rabbis most was the present spiritual meaning of these ancient texts. According to Jacob Neusner, "People wrote to tell the truth about what happens every day, which is to say, the Torah and what it tells about what God is and what humanity should strive to become: 'in our image, after our likeness,' as portrayed in the Torah, written and oral, of Sinai."[3]

The rabbis were preoccupied above all with hearing God's voice through the scriptures, and then responding. But if their focus was divine guidance through the scriptures, it was also true that God's voice could be heard in other ways as well. Indeed the theme of the "heavenly voice" (the Bat Kol) was a topic the rabbis discussed at length.[4]

The Heavenly Voice

The Bat Kol was a less intimate sign of God's presence than the Shekinah (the indwelling or settling divine presence), which in some rabbinic traditions did not rest on the second Temple as it had on the first .[5] Still, the Hebrew scriptures frequently mention hearing the voice of God. In Deuteronomy 4:12 Moses says, "The Lord spoke to you out of the midst of the fire; you heard the sound of words, but saw no form; there was only a voice." Elijah famously heard the Lord as a "still small voice" (1 Kings 19:11–13).

There are scores of other examples throughout the scriptures of God's voice being heard, but the rabbis said that this voice was in reality the Bat Kol (בַּת קוֹל), the "daughter of a voice," since it was impossible to hear God himself speaking. This was a supernatural voice sometimes compared with that of a dove,[6] although in many places in scripture it was more like the roaring of a lion (Jeremiah 25:30; Joel 3:16–17; Amos 1:2) or ground-shaking thunder (Psalm 29; Job 37:1–5).

There were also debates as to what language this voice spoke. One sage decided for Aramaic, but this was unpopular since the rabbis were generally intent on restoring Hebrew as the Jewish lingua franca. Others said the Bat Kol could be heard in any number of languages, since its purpose was to be generally understood.[7]

A number of rabbinic stories circulated about the Bat Kol. For example, there was this anecdote about the sages Rabbi Eliezer and Rabbi Akiba. When the latter's prayer was answered, but not the former's, the rabbis "began to utter suspicion against R. Eliezer. However, a heavenly voice came forth and proclaimed: 'R. Akiba is not greater than R. Eliezer, but the one is of a forbearing disposition, while the other is not.'"[8] And this: Abba Tahnah had stopped to help a sick man lying by the road, but as a result he was late returning home for the Sabbath and was struck with a guilty conscience, wondering if he had done the right thing. "Then a heavenly voice called out and said, 'Go, eat thy bread with joy, and drink thy wine with a merry heart, for God has accepted thy deeds: thy reward will be allotted to thee'" (Ecclesiastes 9:7).[9] Note that the voice responds with a verse from the scriptures.

> The Talmud has this general instruction on the permissibility of following a heavenly voice.
>
> Rabbi Johanan interpreted Isaiah 30:21 ("And thine ears shall hear a word behind thee") to mean that "one may make use of a Heavenly Voice" in the sense of divining the future and drawing inferences from a voice heard by chance. And he acted according to this rule. On one occasion, overhearing the voice of a lad reading a verse during lessons—"And Samuel died"—R. Johanan and Resh Laqish concluded that the Amora [scholar] Samuel in Babylonia had died, and so cancelled their intended journey to Babylonia to visit him. R. Eleazar expounds this incident to mean "we may follow the instruction of a Heavenly Voice."[10]

The pagan world also looked for and responded to signs like a voice heard by chance, but here we see a similar phenomenon in the Jewish milieu, where in this period it was sometimes associated with anticipating the Messiah. As a contemporary rabbinic commentary on the New Testament says, "Authenticating signs were commonplace . . . among Jews from the days of Moses (see Exod 4:1ff.). In the Talmudic literature the Rabbis speculated about authenticating signs in connection with the coming of the Messiah."[11]

"The Law Is Not in Heaven"

Despite all the foregoing, the "heavenly voice" did not play a major role in rabbinic thought. Miracles in general held a subsidiary place: "Hillel declared that the process by which man gets his daily bread is a greater miracle than the cleaving of the Red Sea." [12] The rabbis were grateful for the biblical miracles, but these were heroic events of the past performed by God for earlier generations worthy of such spectacular events .[13] The present generation was unworthy, but even so, "faith without miracles is superior to faith based on them."[14]

This was neither skepticism nor generational humility. The rabbis believed that the Law, together with its communal mode of interpretation and application, had already been given to Moses and Israel on Sinai. Paying too much attention to heavenly voices and miracles was a distraction that could lead to evading earthly responsibilities, including the duty of individually and collectively expending effort in studying, teaching, weighing arguments, and considering solutions to practical problems of the day.

The following story illustrates this point. Rabbi Eliezer was engaged in an argument concerning the interpretation of a particular point of law:

> After using all possible arguments to substantiate his opinion, but still unable to convince the rabbis, he turned to performing miracles, none of which impressed them, including a voice from heaven that asked them, "what have you against R. Eliezer? The Halakah is always with him [his view is always right]." Then R. Joshua got up and said, "It is not in heaven" (Deut 30:12). What did he mean by this? R. Jeremiah said, "The Law was given from Sinai. We pay no attention to a heavenly voice. For already from Sinai the Law said, 'By a majority you are to decide'" (Exod 23:2 as homiletically interpreted). R. Nathan met Elijah and asked him what God did in that hour. Elijah replied, "He laughed and said, 'My children have conquered me.'"[15]

The principle "the law is not in heaven" became a pillar of rabbinic legal practice. As Aaron Schreiber explains in *Jewish Law and Decision-Making*, "This was a reflection of the symbiosis that exists in Jewish law between the perspective that the law is transcendental and yet mundane. [The rabbis] clearly felt that it was God's will that humans should decide the law according to their own wisdom, rather than follow the dictate of 'heaven' which admittedly reflected abstract 'truth.'"[16]

The rabbis upheld "the right of those who shape the Oral Torah to make mistakes," says Hyam Maccoby. This is a vital point. They sanctified "the human process of reaching truth, or provisional truth, by an effort of reasoning and discussion, and banned divine perfection from the right to regulate human life. When they read 'the law is not in heaven' (Deut 30:12) they took it to mean that while the Torah, in its written form, was given *from* Heaven, its practical implementation, the Oral Torah, was on earth and must partake of earthly imperfection."[17]

Schreiber says that the rabbis insisted on human decision-making precisely because human beings are familiar with the changing circumstances in which laws must be applied:

> The Talmud always refers to the Prophet Elijah, rather than Moses the lawgiver, as the one who will solve all the legal problems remaining unanswered by the time of the coming of the Messiah, although Moses would also be resurrected by that time. . . . Only a personage like Elijah could fulfill this function, since according to the Talmudic interpretations of the scriptures, he never dies but

continues to mingle among men in human form. He is therefore familiar with circumstances as they change throughout time and recognizes the consequent need to change the law. Moses, who had died and was resurrected at a much later time, would be unaware of the changed circumstances of men.[18]

Yet even Elijah's prophetic voice must bend to that of the religious court, the *beth din*: "A prophet is not permitted from now on to introduce anything new" and "Even if Elijah were to come . . . he would not be listened to."[19] In other words, even a prophet cannot overturn the precedents established over time by the Jewish courts.

In the rabbinic view the scriptures give only general guidelines. This is "in order that wise men of every generation should be able to apply them to new events."[20] This emphasis on the human court is also found in the rabbinic rule that in order to prevent false or mistaken claims to divine guidance, "a prophet may not decide questions of law on the basis of divine revelation, nor can he overrule decisions by human decision-makers."[21] Even God binds Himself to the decisions of the human court: "When the heavenly angels gather before the Holy One, Blessed be he, to ask, 'When is Rosh Hashannah; When is Yom Kippur?' [when, according to the Talmudic tradition, human destinies for the coming year are to be decided], the Holy One, Blessed be He, says to them, 'Do you ask *me*? You and I will both go together to the earthly *beth din* [the court].' "[22]

This approach to balancing human and divine initiative had profound implications for Jewish life. The Jews looked at action within the world as their right and responsibility as "co-creators": "The Talmudic conception that man was granted exclusive control over law has an elevated place in the Talmudic conception of religion and the cosmos. It implies that man can, and should, create new law. This places man (created in the 'image of God') alongside God as a co-creator of the world, in view of the vital importance of law in the Talmudic metaphysical view."[23]

It is through the Torah, oral and written, that all spiritual experience is to be processed and evaluated. The centrality of the Law as divine guide in first-century Judaism must therefore be kept in mind when considering rabbinic statements on divine guidance through the "heavenly voice." As Maccoby says, rabbinic Judaism is characterized by its "fundamental rationalism and this-worldly emphasis."[24] While mysticism and saintliness

form part of the rabbinical conspectus, they are always kept firmly on the periphery, a fact that should be borne in mind when considering aspects of rabbinical literature that seem to invite comparison with religions, say, of centrally mystical orientation. . . .

To study the *halakah* [the Jewish tradition of religious laws] and thus work towards the kind of society envisaged by the *halakah* is, to the rabbis, to pursue the specifically human task, and also the task especially entrusted to the Jews who understood themselves as deputed by God to lead humanity, not in the acquisition of spiritual or artistic gifts of an unusual kind, but in the development of a just and kindly community life as the essential basis without which the cultivation of special gifts is mere selfishness.[25]

The rabbis were restrained in their approach to divine guidance. They refused to be immediately bowled over by the miraculous. Yet even among the rabbis, "despite all the divergences of opinion, the essential premise that miracles are possible cannot be doubted; to believe in miracles is to believe in a Living, Omnipotent God."[26] It is this conviction that the rabbis, for all their sobriety and attention to communal tradition and legal precedent, refused to jettison.

Divine Guidance in an Age of Silent Prophets

It was a commonplace among Jews of the first century that they were living in an era when "the prophets ceased to appear among them" (1 Macc 9:27; also 4:46, 14:41). But how this was understood varied greatly. "The plain fact is that some Jews of the period under discussion maintained these beliefs in prophetic silence and a quenched spirit, whereas others not only opposed them, but indeed believed themselves endowed with the spirit and the prophetic gift."[27]

The waters become even muddier when we consider that a shift in definition of prophecy was under way. The absence of classical prophets did not necessarily mean the absence of divine guidance. Josephus speaks of the "failure of the exact succession of the prophets" (*Against Apion* 1.41), but as we have seen, he clearly believes God is still speaking. Hillel, one of the most famous sages (c. 110 BCE–10 CE), thought that the Holy Spirit had departed from individuals but now rested instead on the community as a whole.[28]

Yet even Hillel's communal emphasis does not exclude the activity of the Spirit among individuals: "It once happened that when the Sages entered the house of Guryo in Jericho, they heard a Heavenly Voice say, 'there is a man here who is worthy of the holy spirit, but his generation is not worthy of it,' and they all looked at Hillel." [29] Hillel was not alone, for "he had eighty disciples, thirty of whom were worthy that the Divine Presence should rest upon them." [30]

Urbach reads this as indicating a fundamental change in the Jewish understanding of prophecy. In the Bible the giving of the Spirit to a prophet is entirely in the sovereign will of God and is quite independent of personal worth. According to the sages, however, "a man is vouchsafed the Holy Spirit by virtue of his fitness and the qualities of character and virtues that he has acquired, and even these are insufficient and he requires certain objective, external conditions."[31] Prophecy thus evolved into a "mystic experience" based on acquisition of wisdom through study and observance of the Torah. "Since the destruction of the Temple prophecy was taken away from the prophets and given to the Sages."[32] Urbach notes similar statements from the influential medieval rabbi known as Rashi (Rabbi Shlomo Yitzhaki, 1040–1105), who distinguishes "the prophecy of the prophets, which consists of visions and revelations" from "the prophecy of the sages, which is vouchsafed through wisdom."[33]

Prophetic foretelling of the future continued among the sages. Gamaliel "divined by the holy Spirit," and Rabbi Simeon ben Yohai "saw by means of the holy Spirit."[34] But prophecy in this sense was not limited to sages, for according to Rabbi Johanan, "since the day that the Temple was destroyed, prophecy was taken away from prophets and given to idiots and children."[35]

Rereading the Bible through Divine Guidance

As we have seen, most forms of intertestamental Judaism allowed for the continuing presence of the Spirit and divine guidance. But "the greatest and most genuine manifestation of the prophetic spirit . . . was the inspired activity of Bible rereading."[36] In other words, the most prevalent form of divine guidance was in the reading, expansion, and reinterpretation of the scriptures. This is important point for two reasons: (1) it shows how closely Jews connected divine guidance with Holy Scripture (more broadly defined than it came to be later), and (2) it demonstrates that the text was not viewed in isolation from God's inspiration within the living interpretative community.

In Qumran, for example, the Teacher of Righteousness was not merely a parrot of Torah. He was to be a creative instructor who used the inspiration he received through his own spirit. This creative element in Torah reflection is found not only in Qumran but also throughout Jewish sources from this period. We see it in Josephus and Philo, the Septuagint and other translations, the Targumim (Aramaic commentaries), in scribal glosses, in the pseudepigrapha and intertestamental literature, and in rabbinic texts. All of these reflect a creative process that recasts the meaning of earlier texts in light of later experience and doctrine. "Later beliefs concerning the covenant, the law, God's word, the messiah, the national destinies, the angels (satan), resurrection, immortality and the future life, were inserted in the biblical text when the earlier tradition came to be reedited."[37]

This method of reinterpretation is already found within the scriptures themselves, as Michael Fishbane's exhaustive review of the Hebrew Bible has shown.[38] Rereading spilled over into the formation of new oral law as rules in the Pentateuch required further unpacking and reworking by later generations. This method of legal growth was the foundation for the *halakhah*, the system of Jewish law. The process of rereading allowed Jews to keep the Bible's words alive and fresh, just as the righteous are like flourishing palm trees that "still bring forth fruit in old age, they are ever full of sap and green" (Psalm 92:14).[39]

Nowhere was this rereading spiritually more important than in biblical books that dealt with time-limited kings, nations, and events. The Yale biblical scholar Brevard Childs proved that the rereading of historical prophecies in an *eschatological* perspective—in light of the eschaton, God's final victory in the age to come—allowed otherwise dead events to be included in the canon of scripture. Childs gives the example of the book of Nahum. Prophesying sometime around 626–612 BCE, Nahum joyfully predicts the destruction of the violent Assyrian Empire that had oppressed the region for centuries. And indeed the Assyrians and their capital at Nineveh were overthrown in 612 BCE. But Nahum's rejoicing is premature. He did not foresee the rise of Babylon just over the horizon, bringing even worse destruction. How did later readers understand Nahum in this new context? Hadn't Nahum predicted that God would bring an *end* to the violence and "restore the majesty of Jacob as the majesty of Israel" (Nahum 2:2)? Hadn't he said they would "behold on the mountains, the feet of him who brings good tidings, who proclaims peace! . . . For never again shall the wicked come against you, he is utterly cut off" (Nahum 1:15).

Childs advances the method of "canonical criticism," looking at how each book is seen as part of the larger whole of the emerging biblical canon. Rereading allows the historical text to remain in the canon alongside the new eschatological interpretation that looked beyond the confines of history: "[The] original prophecies were placed within an interpretative framework which provided a theological appropriation of Nahum's original message. This shaping did not require a dehistoricizing of the time-conditioned oracles. Indeed, they remained virtually untouched in their particularity, but a new role was assigned the oracles. They now functioned as a dramatic illustration of the final, eschatological triumph of God over all his adversaries. From this testimony within scripture each generation of suffering Israel derived its hope."[40] The very formation of the canon reveals an interpretative framework in which the historical limitations of individual books are transcended through inspired rereading. Obscure events of the past and apparent failures of past prophecy (like Nahum's) are given deeper meaning as part of a theological whole within the community of faith.[41] This process paved the way for an age of Messianic expectancy that looked through the window of the text to the coming of a Savior.

* * *

Alfred Guillaume pointed out long ago that divine guidance was viewed as normal and expected among Jews and their neighbors; its *absence* was exceptional. Indeed the absence of divine guidance was cause for lament, since "inspiration should not be viewed as an extraordinary intrusion of the divine into the human personality, but a divine response to human submission and co-operation."[42]

I will argue in the following chapter that this outlook on divine guidance in Judaism is in large measure shared by Paul. The antinomies we have seen in Jewish approaches to divine guidance and decision-making—direct/indirect, miraculous/mundane, spirit/letter, individual/communal, freedom/submission, certain/unpredictable, rational/supernatural—all reflect the mystery God's guidance that Paul will pick up and reorient in bringing to Corinth the message of the crucified Messiah.

PART III
PAUL

13

Neither Jew nor Greek

1 Corinthians, Paul's Primer on Divine Guidance

As I have shown in the previous chapters, divine guidance was a lively topic of discussion in the Greco-Roman and Jewish worlds. Among both Gentiles and Jews there was a remarkably broad and highly textured range of attitudes on issues related to God's perceived role in guiding personal and public life.

Paul's early Christian community in Corinth was drawn from both these worlds, but his own thoughts on the subject, while firmly rooted in Jewish tradition, explicitly chart a new and distinctive approach to divine guidance based ultimately on his new calling revealed in Christ. This new key for making decisions is perhaps best summarized by this verse from 1 Corinthians: "For I decided to know nothing among you except Jesus Christ and him crucified" (1 Cor 2:2; Figure 13.1 shows part of the path Jesus is traditionally believed to have taken on the way to his crucifixion).

Before launching into this section of the book a word of explanation is needed since the chapter departs significantly from the previous chapters both in form and content. The earlier parts of the book were primarily a broad survey of what we know about attitudes toward divine guidance in the Greek, Roman, and Jewish worlds that would have impacted Corinth in Paul's day. In this chapter I look in detail at Paul's argument as it is woven throughout 1 Corinthians, moving section by section through the letter.

This is necessary for several reasons. First, while there are many excellent detailed commentaries on 1 Corinthians—and this is not another one—this is the first study to propose that the theme of divine guidance is in fact central to Paul and can be found in virtually every part of his writing, and 1 Corinthians is a prime example. Second, if we want a picture of early Christian approaches to divine guidance alongside Greco-Roman and Jewish views, then Paul's Corinth is the obvious place to explore in depth, since we know more about this first-century city and its Christian community than any other. Third, through Paul's Corinthian correspondence we are given a glimpse into early Christianity at a formative period. Fourth, and more important, this slice of history has been given permanent value because of its inclusion in the New Testament, and thus it continues to help shape Christian thought, practice, and debate 2,000 years later.

Divine Guidance. John A. Jillions, Oxford University Press (2020). © Oxford University Press.
DOI: 10.1093/oso/9780190055738.001.0001

Fig. 13.1. Via Dolorosa, Jerusalem Old City. Source: iStock.com/alexsi.

Paul's Language of Divine Guidance

The first arresting observation is that the phrase "divine guidance" never occurs in Paul's letters. The noun "guidance" (*odēgia*) doesn't occur either. In fact the term is found nowhere in the Bible. Paul also steers clear of the verb "to guide" (*odēgeō*), although it is quite common in the Septuagint (the ancient Greek translation of the Hebrew Bible), especially in Psalms. The related noun "guide" (*odēgos*) appears only once in Paul's letters, when he uses it in an ironic sense, in his letter to Jewish Christians in Rome asking them sarcastically "if [they] are sure that [they] are a guide to the blind, a light to those who are in darkness" (Rom 2:19). Elsewhere in the New Testament the word "guide" is invariably linked negatively to the leaders and teachers who are "blind guides" (Matt 15:4, 23:16, 23:24; Luke 6:39). In Acts the word is applied to Judas, who became a "guide" to those who arrested Jesus (Acts 1:16). Paul also uses the related word *paidagōgos* pejoratively—they were slaves tasked with being child-minders—to contrast with his own role of spiritual father: "For though you have countless guides [*paidagōgous*] in Christ, you do not have many fathers" (1 Cor 4:15). Such guides, or what we might call life coaches, abounded in Corinth. Recent studies have shown how widespread, through all levels of society, was the demand for personal guides/trainers/coaches in rhetoric and philosophy.[1] Perhaps this was a sign of Corinthian prosperity, but this need for guides—and the resulting competition among guides and their disciples—was one of the chief sources of tension that mired the Corinthian church in its infamous factionalism (1 Cor 1:10ff.).[2]

Paul avoids *odēgeō*, but on two occasions he does use the synonym *agō* (to lead).[3] In Romans and Galatians it is the leading of the Spirit that *defines* Christians and distinguishes them from those who are under the written law: "For all who are led [*agontai*] by the Spirit of God are sons of God" (Rom 8:14); "If you are led [*agesthe*] by the Spirit you are not under the law" (Gal 5:18; see also Rom 7:6, 2 Cor 3:6).[4] This corresponds to the use of the word in John 10, where it comes in reference to hearing and being led by the Good Shepherd's voice (John 10:3, 10:16).

If Paul does not use familiar guidance language, I believe this is largely in order to preserve the Jewish understanding that guidance ultimately comes from God alone, whatever form the mediation of His guidance might take. Paul's first-century world was characterized by allegiance to human guides of all kinds. Rhetors, philosophers, priests, rabbis, astrologers, and a host of others took advantage of the public's desire for sure and sound guidance. It was this bull market for divine direction (and fear of getting it wrong) that led to the perennial superstitions that repelled Lucretius, Seneca, Cicero, Plutarch, and others. Contemporary Judaism, on the other hand, while conscious of God's direct guidance, was overwhelmingly focused on the Law and its protective communal tradition, written and oral, as the fundamental divine guide to life.

Through the Cross to the Spirit

For Paul, Christ's appearance, crucifixion, resurrection, and sending of the Spirit changed everything, including how divine guidance was to be understood. Here was where Paul parted company with those Jews who did not recognize Jesus as Messiah. Christ displaced the Law as the center of divine guidance. As James Dunn says, "For Paul a believer's conduct is now determined not primarily by a written code, but by the immediate direction of the Spirit" (Rom 7:6; 2 Cor 3:6). Indeed, access to the Spirit becomes *the* distinguishing feature of the messianic age in which Paul found himself.[5]

However, this view needs to be balanced with Paul's understanding of how the Spirit's direction is heard through the community's life. Here he remained firmly anchored in the Jewish concepts of community and tradition that helped guard against deception.

The Spirit decisively shapes divine guidance in Paul's thought, but he begins with the Cross. This is a crucial point. As shared faith in the Torah was the anchor for Judaism, so faith in the Crucified Christ who fulfils the Torah is the anchor for Paul's Gospel. The besetting temptation among Corinthian Christians was to bypass the Cross on their way to the Spirit or to look elsewhere than the Crucified God for their divine guidance. To the extent this deviation took hold among Paul's Corinthians, they found themselves (1) splintered into factions, (2) squabbling over authority and who was the best guide to follow, and (3) pursuing a disembodied spirituality in which Christ's historical and material incarnation, death, and resurrection had little influence.

By the time Paul was writing 2 Corinthians, 18 months later, the consequences of their excessive dependence on the guidance of others had become all too apparent as the majority fell under the sway of so-called super-apostles (2 Cor 10–13). Paul's letters to the Corinthians are an extended attempt to rebuild the confidence of the majority in the Spirit's guidance founded on the Cross. He aims to correct their individualistic spirituality, awaken their sense of responsibility for the community, and break their excessive dependence on the human authorities who held them in thrall.

In spite of Paul's reticence to use guidance language, a close reading of his Corinthian letters shows that guidance by the Holy Spirit is basic to his view of Christian life. This does not mean that the Spirit acts only by immediate direction to individuals. Paul firmly upholds the hierarchical, scriptural, liturgical, and communal modes of divine guidance inherited from Jewish experience. These correct the potential deceptions and delusions of individual claims. He clearly views his own apostolic authority as divinely given and worthy of acceptance by others: "Now, even if I boast a little too much of our authority, which the Lord gave for building you up and not for tearing you down, I will not be ashamed of it" (2 Cor 10:8). He likewise urges the Corinthians to submit themselves to men like Stephanas, longtime converts who had proven themselves worthy of trust through Christian service (1 Cor 16:15). But these checks and balances are never allowed to eclipse the mystery of the Holy Spirit's immediate, direct, and unpredictable guidance to individuals and communities.

1 Corinthians can be read as Paul's primer on divine guidance. Basic principles are outlined in 1 Cor 1–4, and the rest of the letter applies these principles in the varied practical situations Paul addresses in 1 Cor 5–16. What follows highlights the divine guidance theme that runs through the epistle, following this map of its content.

I. First principles of divine guidance, 1:1–4:21
    I.1 God calls, 1:1–3
        I.1.1 God calls Paul
        I.1.2 God calls the apostles
        I.1.3 God calls the Corinthians

I. First Principles of Divine Guidance, 1:1–4:21

I.1 God Calls, 1:1–3

I.1.1 God Calls Paul

Divine guidance in 1 Corinthians begins with the first words of the epistle: "Paul, called by the will of God to be an apostle of Christ Jesus" (1 Cor 1:1). Paul repeatedly begins his letters with a reminder of the divine origin of his apostolic ministry (Rom 1:1; 2 Cor 1:1; Gal 1:1; Eph 1:1; Col 1:1).

Although Paul alludes to his call elsewhere by way of reminder (1 Cor 15:8), only in his letter to the Galatians does he write at length about what happened to him (Gal 1:11–2:10). And even then he omits most of the details, focusing on how he discerned that this was indeed God's personal intervention in his life. I cite the passage in full because the experience is so central to Paul's life and work:

[11]For I want you to know, brothers and sisters, that the gospel that was proclaimed by me is not of human origin; [12]for I did not receive it from a human source, nor was I taught it, but I received it through a revelation of Jesus Christ.

[13]You have heard, no doubt, of my earlier life in Judaism. I was violently persecuting the church of God and was trying to destroy it. [14]I advanced in Judaism beyond many among my people of the same age, for I was far more zealous for the traditions of my ancestors. [15]But when God, who had set me apart before I was born and called me through his grace, was pleased [16]to reveal his Son to me, so that I might proclaim him among the Gentiles, I did not confer with any human being, [17]nor did I go up to Jerusalem to those who were already apostles before me, but I went away at once into Arabia, and afterwards I returned to Damascus.

[18]Then after three years I did go up to Jerusalem to visit Cephas and stayed with him fifteen days; [19]but I did not see any other apostle except James the Lord's brother. [20]In what I am writing to you, before God, I do not lie! [21]Then I went into the regions of Syria and Cilicia, [22]and I was still unknown by sight to the churches of Judea that are in Christ; [23]they only heard it said, "The one who formerly was persecuting us is now proclaiming the faith he once tried to destroy." [24]And they glorified God because of me.

[2:1]Then after fourteen years I went up again to Jerusalem with Barnabas, taking Titus along with me. [2]I went up in response to a revelation. Then I laid before them (though only in a private meeting with the acknowledged leaders) the gospel that I proclaim among the Gentiles, in order to make sure that I was not running, or had not run, in vain. [3]But even Titus, who was with me, was not compelled to be circumcised, though he was a Greek. [4]But because of false believers secretly brought in, who slipped in to spy on the freedom we have in Christ Jesus, so that they might enslave us—[5]we did not submit to them even for a moment, so that the truth of the gospel might always remain with you. [6]And from those who were supposed to be acknowledged leaders (what they actually were makes no difference to me; God shows no partiality)—those leaders contributed nothing to me. [7]On the contrary, when they saw that I had been entrusted with the gospel for the uncircumcised, just as Peter had been entrusted with the gospel for the circumcised [8](for he who worked through Peter making him an apostle to the circumcised also worked through me in sending me to the Gentiles), [9]and when James and Cephas and John, who were acknowledged pillars, recognized the grace that had been given to me, they gave to Barnabas and me the right hand of fellowship, agreeing that we should go to the Gentiles and they to the circumcised. [10]They asked only one thing, that we remember the poor, which was actually what I was eager to do. (Gal 1:11–2:10)

Paul experienced his call from God as (1) a dramatic breaking in to his life as a zealous and violent defender of Jewish orthodoxy, (2) God's direct guidance to him personally, and (3) confirmed by the other leading apostles. Paul also makes it very clear that his own conviction of God's immediate guidance was by far more significant than what others thought about it (Gal 1:1, 1:11). He stresses that he was chosen by God "from my mother's womb," that he received direct revelation, that he did not confer with "flesh and blood," and that he went alone into Arabia before returning to Damascus (Gal 1:15–17). Not until three years later did he visit Jerusalem to see the apostles, and only then to see the leaders Peter and James (Gal 1:18–19). Seventeen years went by before he sought the confirmation of the whole apostolic body in Jerusalem. And even that decision to travel to Jerusalem was itself motivated by direct divine guidance: "I went up by revelation [*kata apocalypsin*] and I laid before them (but privately before those who were of repute) the gospel which I preach among the Gentiles, lest somehow I should be running or had run in vain" (Gal 2:2).

While submitting his gospel to those "who were of repute" Paul continues to insist that the leading apostles added nothing to the gospel revealed to him directly: "And from those who were reputed to be something (what they were makes no difference to me; God shows no partiality)—those, I say, who were of repute added nothing to me" (Gal 2:6). This verges on being downright rude. However, Paul does not minimize the role of the other apostles in order to magnify his own importance. On the contrary, he later tells the Corinthians, "I am the least of the apostles, unfit to be called an apostle, because I persecuted the church of God" (1 Cor 15:9). But his humility rides alongside his firm insistence that his apostleship comes from a direct encounter with the risen Jesus.

For Paul, this is not just about his own personal divine revelation; it is also about the role of prophetic voices challenging the leadership. Far from deferentially kowtowing before the leading apostles, he even rebukes Peter publicly for his hypocrisy at Antioch, when Peter had backed away from mixing with Gentiles for fear of criticism from the "circumcision party" (Gal 2:11–14). Paul is boldly stating that no respect of persons—even of the leading apostles—displaces the prophetic word that comes through personal and direct divine guidance.

We know that after his Damascus Road experience Paul was baptized and became part of the Christian community and thus demonstrated his acceptance of the church and its emerging tradition. Throughout his ministry he acknowledged the role of tradition, hierarchy, and community in divine guidance. (See his discussion later on the Lord's Supper, for example: 1 Cor 11.) Paul is a firm upholder of doing everything "decently and in order" (1 Cor 14:40), "For God is not a God of confusion but of peace" (1 Cor 14:33). But at the same time he refuses to set aside confidence in the calling he received directly from God and the day-to-day communion and guidance that is his experience of life in Christ. No matter how disruptive that might be.

I.1.2 God Calls the Apostles

Paul is intent on preserving the authority of direct divine guidance that is accessible to all. And yet he asserts with equal force that divine guidance to the church comes through the ministry of the apostles. In 1 Cor 1:1 he merely hints at this, leaving the explanation of what it means to be an apostle for later in the letter (1 Cor 3–4, 9). In those later chapters it becomes clear that apostles are to be considered "servants of Christ and stewards of the mysteries of God" (1 Cor 4:1). They are "servants through whom you believed" (1 Cor 3:5) and "God's fellow workers" (1 Cor 3:9). Paul can say that he became father to the Corinthians and urges them to imitate him (1 Cor 4:16). He emphasizes his role as a channel of divine guidance, not for his own benefit but to serve the Corinthians by giving them a living example to observe and follow, as good fathers do. Indeed the context of 4:16 is surrounded with qualifiers that point away from Paul to Christ and the Gospel.

It is this conviction that God is calling all and is accessible to all that Paul underscores from the beginning. It is true that God speaks through the apostles, but the apostles are still human beings. The main problem in Corinth is that the people have confused these men with Christ. As John Chrysostom paraphrases, "*Christ* is your teacher, how then can you register the names of men as patrons of your doctrine?" (*Homilies on 1 Corinthians*, 2:7).

Even the grace and peace that Paul sends to the congregation is not from himself but "from God our Father and the Lord Jesus Christ" (1 Cor 1:3). This is Paul's common adaptation of the typical Greco-Roman opening for letters, "Grace to you and peace." The Old Testament records many blessings pronounced by patriarchs, parents, prophets, kings, and priests. Blessings were not understood as mere wishful thinking for God to act in some beneficial manner. They were powerful and prophetic pronouncements of divine presence and action, mediated by the one offering the blessing. Hence Esau's dismay over the blessing Jacob stole from their father, Isaac (see Gen 27–28). Jacob's ill-gotten blessing, no matter how it was deceitfully obtained, was still an authoritative word from God with binding effect. However mediated, it is the Lord Himself who is present to give the blessing, as God instructed Moses about priestly blessings:

> Speak to Aaron and his sons, saying, "Thus you shall bless the Israelites: You shall say to them,
>
> The *Lord* bless you and keep you;
>
> the *Lord* make his face to shine upon you, and be gracious to you." (Num 6:24–26)

Paul's expression—"Grace to you and peace from God our Father and the Lord Jesus Christ"—can be read not simply as a conventional greeting but as a daring statement of divine guidance, claiming as it does that Paul himself is conveying *God's* blessings of grace and peace.

Paul's phrase may also have been a liturgical formula.[6] He is deeply conscious of the divine guidance that comes through the liturgical experience of the community. This is an underappreciated aspect of his thought to which we will return repeatedly. But whatever the origin of this particular phrase, Paul emphasizes the direct grace of God at work in the lives of his hearers while at the same time affirming his apostolic authority to convey—and not merely request—God's grace and peace (see Rom 1:7; 2 Cor 1:2; Gal 1:3; Eph 1:2, 6:23; Phil 1:2; Col 1:2; 2 Thess 1:2; Phlm 1:3).

I.1.3 God Calls the Corinthians

While Paul writes with assurance about his divinely appointed ministry and expects his authority to be followed (no less than rabbis accepted responsibility for giving direction), he is also very careful not to equate his every opinion with divine guidance. Later in the epistle he will make a clear distinction between the word he has from the Lord and his own word. Paul refuses to make himself the sole channel of divine guidance for the Corinthians. He is confident that God Himself is illuminating the lives of everyone in the Corinthian church and calling each to a specific vocation (see 1 Cor 2:7ff.). They are all "sanctified in Christ Jesus," they are all "called to be saints" (1 Cor 1:2; 1:24). It is *God* who sanctifies them and gives them grace (1:4), who enriches them in speech and knowledge (1: 5), with every gift (1:6), and who sustains them to the end (1:8).

The words "sanctified [*ēgiasmenois*] in Christ Jesus" (1 Cor 1:2) may well be a technical phrase for baptism[7] and rooted in the Jewish liturgical view of sanctification as consecration for divine service. In this context, divine guidance is mediated by the liturgical act of baptism, which initiates the believer into the community of Christ (see 1 Cor 6:11).[8] But this is more than a ritual act. Some prior personal experience of direct divine guidance led each believer to the point of desiring baptism (keeping in mind that adult baptism was then the norm). Their response to *God's call* brought them to Christ, to the church, and to each other in an experience of divine guidance shared "by all those who call upon the name of our Lord Jesus Christ in every place" (1 Cor 1:2). This rings an egalitarian note to contrast with the elitist tendencies in Corinth. Christ is the Lord shared by all who call on his name, wherever they are. The mystery of God's guidance leading diverse people to baptism is recognized and shared by all who have entered into communion with Christ and His Body through baptism. For this reason Paul can keep referring them back to their initial experience as a reminder of their vocation (1 Cor 1:15, 6:11; 2 Cor 1:22; Rom 6).

For Paul, being "sanctified" is associated with receiving the Holy Spirit, especially at baptism, although not exclusively. The point of baptism is for believers to die with Christ to their old ways and to rise with Him to a new manner of living inspired by the Holy Spirit. This receiving of the Spirit is central to Paul and to the church's tradition that he inherited even at this early stage. In the gospels the ultimate aim of Christ's appearance is to baptize with the Holy Spirit, as John the Baptist says (Matt 3:11; Mark 1:8; Luke 3:7; John 1:33). In Acts the outpouring of the Holy Spirit on Pentecost is the culmination of the Gospel promise (Acts 2:1–21).

"In Christ Jesus" and similar phrases ("in the Lord," "in Christ") are used some 165 times in the epistles and have a rich set of meanings that point to the intimate connection between Christ, the Christian, and the community of the church. Indeed "in Christ" can be understood as synonymous with "in the body of Christ."[9] This ecclesial dimension of the spiritual life is underscored because Paul is facing currents in Corinth that would atomize the Christian experience. He focuses simultaneously on the direct divine guidance that comes to each believer and on the communal aspect of guidance; God's call to the individual believer is rarely unmediated, but most often comes *through* church life and its faithful.

This is entirely in keeping with Paul's Jewish experience. The community's witness through reading (or chanting) of scripture, preaching, singing, and liturgical life are catalysts for individuals to hear God's call again and again—or for the first time. Paul recognizes the powerful effect this communal liturgical life can have on outsiders, for good or ill, and he will return to this repeatedly in his letters. In the best case, liturgical life for Paul functions as prophecy, by stirring participants to more vibrant life in Christ. While later Christian history in various places excluded the unbaptized from the Eucharistic liturgy, Paul welcomes them. He assumes that unbelievers are present at gatherings of the church and that their experience of inspired worship could be decisive in bringing them to faith: "[24]But if all prophesy, an unbeliever or outsider who enters is reproved by all and called to account by all. [25]After the secrets of the unbeliever's heart are disclosed, that person will bow down before God and worship him, declaring, 'God is really among you'" (1 Cor 14:24–25). The phrase "called saints" (or "called to be saints," *klētois agiois*) is associated with the Sabbath assembly in the Septuagint, thus linking divine calling both with communal election and communal liturgical experience.[10] The use of the term "brother" (*adelphos*, 1:1), the reference to Sosthenes, and the mention of believers elsewhere (1:3) underline Paul's personal and communal understanding of God's call.

The Corinthians saw and heard Paul's preaching, but they recognized this as *God* calling them into communion with Christ in the church (1 Cor 1:9). God's call, Paul's preaching, the witness of others, and liturgical experience are thus intimately intertwined in the process of divine guidance that led each person to "the church of God which is in Corinth" (1 Cor 1:2).

I.2 Divine Guidance through Spiritual Gifts, 1:4–9

Paul has already indicated that divine guidance is not the exclusive province of the apostles. Every believer has been called directly by the Lord. Now, rather than emphasize his own apostolic authority as a channel of God's guidance, he magnifies the abundance of the Corinthians' gifts. Going further he tells them that among themselves they have *all* the gifts (1:7), especially gifts of speech and knowledge (1:4–5). His focus on *their* gifts is particularly significant in light of how the Corinthians were challenging his authority and boasting of their spiritual experiences. Rather than placing himself at the center of all divine guidance on their behalf, Paul acknowledges and rejoices in the outpouring of God's grace upon them. So while the exercise of their gifts has presented problems, he still wants to assure them that they do indeed have direct guidance from God. He thus seeks to strengthen their dependence not on himself, but on God in Christ. It is *His* appearance they are all awaiting (1:7–8).

Once again, however, Paul reminds them of the ecclesial dimension. It is by being "in Christ" that they received their spiritual gifts in the first place (1:4). Their divine guidance is not independent of the Body that Paul links so closely with the phrase *en Christō*.

The apostle's authority does not negate the direct divine guidance given to individuals in the community. Nor do their gifts undermine his apostolic authority. As will become clear later in the letter, all the gifts are to be used to bring the church members together into one body as they serve in the Lord's name. Their spiritual gifts are confirmation that Paul's preaching of the gospel has been received (1:6). Thus the *indirect* divine guidance that came to the Corinthians through Paul's preaching is confirmed by their *direct* experience of the Spirit's gifts.

After putting their spiritual gifts on a pedestal, Paul then immediately downgrades the importance of those gifts. If the Corinthians do indeed have genuine spiritual gifts directly from God, then these serve only a temporary purpose as they await the ultimate revelation, the day of the Lord's appearance and judgment (1:7–8; see also 1 Cor 13; Rom 2:16, 14:10; 2 Cor 5:10). This is his first warning to them that all divine gifts will be judged on the basis of what the recipients have done with them for the benefit of others.

Paul ends his introductory comments by summarizing his main point. The Corinthians have been directly called by God, but not for individualistic purposes, however spiritual. They have been grafted "into the fellowship [*koinonia*] of his Son, Jesus Christ our Lord" (1 Cor 1:9). This fellowship should be understood with all the deeply ecclesial, liturgical, eucharistic, and social connotations the term *koinonia* carries for Paul, and which he develops throughout the Corinthian letters (1 Cor 10:16, 18, 20; 2 Cor 6:14, 8:4).[11]

I.3 The Crucified Christ as Guide, 1:10–2:5

Factions, Baptism, and the Cross

> [11]For it has been reported to me by Chloe's people that there are quarrels among you, my brothers and sisters. [12]What I mean is that each of you says, "I belong to Paul," or "I belong to Apollos," or "I belong to Cephas," or "I belong to Christ." [13]Has Christ been divided? Was Paul crucified for you? Or were you baptized in the name of Paul? (1 Cor 1:11–13)

As the letter unfolds it becomes increasingly apparent that the Corinthians are obsessed with what they considered advanced forms of divine guidance through esoteric knowledge, wisdom, revelations, and exalted spiritual experiences (e.g., 1 Cor 8:1, 10, 11; 12–14).[12] Paul immediately brings them back to mundane reality by telling them of his own, very earthly form of guidance: the grapevine of news from his own local contacts in Corinth, "Chloe's people" (1:11). "For it has been reported [*edēlōthē*] to me by Chloe's people that there is quarreling among you, my brethren." Perhaps Paul uses *edēlōthē* here with a touch of irony, since in the Septuagint forms of this verb were used almost exclusively of *divine* revelations (e.g., Ps 50:8; Isa 42:9; Dan 2:28, 29, 7:16).[13] The reports he's heard reveal some very worldly divisions (1:11ff.), immorality (5:1ff.), litigation (6:1–8), disorderly conduct at the Lord's supper (11:18ff.), and denial of future resurrection (15:12ff.). These were decidedly unspiritual aspects of their community life that the Corinthians themselves had left out of their high-minded correspondence with Paul on matters of the Spirit (7:1ff., 7:25ff., 8:1ff., 12:1ff.).

Choose Your Guide: The Cross or Human Wisdom?
Paul is faced with divisions caused by misplaced zeal for the guidance of particular teachers. They have turned Paul, Apollos, Cephas, and even Christ Himself into just another excuse for partisan bickering (1:10–12). Paul reminds the Corinthians that all guidance must now be completely reevaluated in the full light of Christ who was crucified for them and into whose name they chose to be

baptized in the Body of Christ. "Is Christ divided? Was Paul crucified for you? Or were you baptized in the name of Paul?" (1 Cor 1:13; see also Rom 6:3).

By linking Christ's crucifixion and the Corinthians' baptism Paul clearly implies that they knew what they were getting into. At baptism they accepted Christ's death on their behalf. They died to themselves. From that moment they willingly identified their life and all their future decisions with the crucified Lord. *Who* baptized them is unimportant. No one should identify with any teacher more than they do with Christ (1:14–16). But the aim of their baptism was not merely to follow Christ as individuals. They were baptized into His Body—the Church—and made "members of one another," as Paul will later expound at length (see 11:12–31).

Paul's own vocation, he tells them, has been shaped by Christ's direction and is closely linked to the Cross: "For Christ did not send me to baptize but to preach the gospel, and not with eloquent wisdom, lest the cross of Christ be emptied of its power" (1:17; see also 3:5). His understanding of this mission had evolved over time, and he initially included the ministry of baptizing new converts as one of his tasks. Only later did he give this up as peripheral to his true vocation (1:14–17; see also 9:16). For Paul everything comes back to the example of the Crucified Christ, even the halting method of his preaching, which is "not with eloquent wisdom." Some reject him and his message as either foolishness or "a stumbling block," but others see in his words and his weakness "the power of God" (1:18, 24).

Three Forms of Guidance: Signs, Wisdom, and Christ Crucified

> [20]Where is the one who is wise? Where is the scribe? Where is the debater of this age? Has not God made foolish the wisdom of the world? [21]For since, in the wisdom of God, the world did not know God through wisdom, God decided, through the foolishness of our proclamation, to save those who believe. [22]For Jews demand signs and Greeks desire wisdom, [23]but we proclaim Christ crucified, a stumbling block to Jews and foolishness to Gentiles, [24]but to those who are the called, both Jews and Greeks, Christ the power of God and the wisdom of God. [25]For God's foolishness is wiser than human wisdom, and God's weakness is stronger than human strength. (1 Cor 1:20–25)

Paul contrasts three forms of guidance in 1:20–25: Jewish signs, Greek wisdom, and the preaching of Christ crucified. Most commentators understand "signs" as indications concerning the identity of the Messiah.[14] Together with Greek wisdom this represents what might be called the *managed* approach to discerning God's intervention. The human being is in control of evaluating events, looking to find God behaving in expected and predictable ways based on past experience.[15] This desire to control is the essence of human wisdom, both Jewish and Greek, and Paul contrasts this with the wisdom of the Cross. The divine guidance that comes from the Cross is the utterly unexpected, unpredictable, disconcerting, and distressing appearance of a crucified Messiah. As John Chrysostom comments, the Cross is contrary to all known signs (*Homilies on 1 Corinthians*, 4.5).

The problem for Paul is not simply the widespread search for signs but the popular assumption that God's blessing must be associated with a "good" sign. In this way of thinking it is impossible, even scandalous to imagine that a "bad" sign—crucifixion—might represent a blessing. The Cross thus introduces a radically counterintuitive form of wisdom not "of this age or of the rulers of this age, who are doomed to pass away" (1 Cor 2:6). As the most horrific of signs, the Cross overturns the most basic assumption about divine guidance held by most people in both the Greek and Jewish worlds.

God Is the Seeker

Paul reverses the standard philosophical approach to God, in which God is the passive object, while human beings are the active subjects who can choose to seek and follow—or not. For Paul, *God* is the active seeker and *He* does the choosing (1:26–29). Paul emphasizes this here by the repeated use of words that stress God's initiative in calling the Corinthians and electing them (*klētois* in 1:24; *klēsin* in 1:26; *exelexato* is used three times in 1:27–28). And he tells them that God turns the election process upside down. He doesn't choose the powerful; he chooses the weak. God chooses people whom the world discards as foolish, low, despised nothings (*ta mē onta*, "things that are not," 1:28). And he does this "so that no human being might boast in the presence of God" (1:29). In other words, God tends to choose those who have some sense already that they are lost, broken, fearful, anxious, incomplete, wanting, or in distress (1:26–31). Thus, in Paul's upside-down recalculation, to be vulnerable in this way and to admit weakness, need, foolishness, to humbly allow oneself to be the object sought and not the seeker is to demonstrate one's election. Paradoxically this humility releases the believer for the freedom of life in Christ, where the Cross is no longer a sign of weakness; now it is a sign of "the power of God and the wisdom of God" (1:24).

Divine guidance through the Cross has everything to do with Paul's view of salvation as God's initiative. Only such an unexpected and shameful sign could overcome the intractable human pride that is the barrier to shared life in communion with God (1:29). Paul understands the relationship between God and the world not in terms of human beings searching for truth or for God. Instead it is God who is searching for and calling out to broken human beings in need of forgiveness and healing through the Cross. The Corinthians' initial willingness to admit weakness at the time of their call (1:26–27) is the very reason they now have access to the wisdom and power of God.

But something had changed, and Paul is asking them what happened. Had the Corinthians become ashamed of their weakness? Were they again being swayed by the wisdom of this world? Paul urges them to go back to their weakness to recover the power of their divine election.

Divine Guidance through Paul's Weakness

> ¹When I came to you, brothers and sisters, I did not come proclaiming the mystery of God to you in lofty words or wisdom. ²For I decided to know nothing among you except Jesus Christ, and him crucified. ³And I came to you in weakness and in fear and in much trembling. ⁴My speech and my proclamation were not with plausible words of wisdom, but with a demonstration of the Spirit and of power, ⁵so that your faith might rest not on human wisdom but on the power of God. (1 Cor 2:1–5)

Paul does not proclaim the mystery or testimony of God by rhetorical excellence but through words and behavior that have passed through the filter of the *Crucified* Christ. Significantly he does not choose to focus on the transfigured, resurrected, or glorified Christ. He allows his own weakness to be a visible demonstration of the saving Cross of Christ. This is the form of divine guidance that Paul stresses: the paradoxical but powerful word of God that is heard and displayed through the living witness of a weak human being.

The divine guidance that comes to the Corinthians as a demonstration of the Spirit's power comes mainly through Paul's weakness, fear, and trembling (2:3). What all people saw and heard was a weak human being, but in that earthen vessel some also heard the voice of God.

The importance Paul attributes to this personal demonstration of the Cross means that he does not view God as acting *primarily* through direct, immediate divine guidance. God's guidance for Paul is not be confused with mystical inner sensations cut off from the realities of flesh-and-blood humanity. God guides most especially through weak human messengers who, like Paul, bring the living word of the Cross. Indeed the message of the Cross can be fully manifested *only* in this way. Divine guidance for Paul is thus firmly bound with what one sees in another human being. Only such "weak" testimony can match the message of the Cross and have any power to save (1:21).

Excursus: Divine Guidance through Scripture

Already in the first two chapters of 1 Corinthians Paul quotes and alludes to the Hebrew scriptures a number of times, so this is a good place to consider his approach toward scripture in the process of divine guidance. Even a cursory reading of his letters shows Paul's deep roots in the scriptural approach of Judaism.[16] In 1 Corinthians alone he directly quotes the scriptures 17 times and alludes to it almost 100 times.

Paul's connection with the scriptures needs to be underlined because it points to his formation in mainline Jewish tradition. With only rare exceptions, his quotations and allusions come from the canonical books of the Bible. A rough review of these yield the following results.[17] Of some 454 quotations and allusions, 95% (424) come from the Torah, the later Prophets, Psalms, and Proverbs; 85% (389) come from just seven books: Isaiah (80), Psalms (75), Genesis (58), Deuteronomy (49), Exodus (39), Jeremiah (27), and Proverbs (20). In 1 Corinthians the Torah, Psalms, and Prophets account for 16 out of 17 quotations (94%) and 85 out of 93 allusions (91%).

It appears that Paul makes no reference *at all* to a long list of books in the Hebrew Bible: Judges, Obadiah, Zephaniah, Haggai, Ruth, Song of Songs, Esther. Other deutero-canonical books are alluded to but never quoted: Wisdom (8), Sirach (6), 4 Maccabees (1), Baruch (1).[18] This clearly shows that Paul was drinking from a very traditional fountain of Jewish scriptural guidance.[19]

But it would be a mistake to read Paul's devotion to the scriptures through the "sola scriptura" debates of the Reformation. His use of scripture cannot be separated from the Jewish tradition of scriptural reading and rereading. As David Bentley Hart notes in his new translation of the New Testament, Paul's "interpretive habits are rarely literalist."[20] As in Judaism, the guidance he receives from the scriptures is closely tied to the community of faith, which paradoxically stands at once both over and under the judgments of scripture. For Paul, however, the guiding faith is Christ, and the community is the church. These are what give him his new interpretative key. Instead of reading, interpreting, and applying the scriptures via the community's life in the Torah, Paul now looks at scripture in the light of Christ, which for him is inseparable from life in the Christian community. This Christocentric communal approach to the Scriptures draws a line between Christ and all that comes before. *Everything* that the Hebrew scriptures presents as images of divine and human is to be reevaluated by the coming of the One who is the *perfect* image of God and the human person. This is Paul's hermeneutic method.

Thus anything in the Bible that is incompatible with the new revelation in Christ is to be reinterpreted or set aside.[21]

For Paul, the Bible is not a stand-alone form of divine guidance. On the contrary, he uses scripture to undermine the scribal approach that uses the text of scripture as the basis of its wisdom (1 Cor 1:20; see also 2 Cor 3:6). Note as well that the biblical passages he brings to the Corinthians have already passed through a process of communal selection, interpretation, and application. This, as C. H. Dodd pointed out long ago, shows that for Paul and the early church the scriptures were not aids for individualistic divine guidance but were already closely connected to a communal tradition of scriptural use in the fledgling church.[22]

1.4 All Are Taught by God: From the Cross to Spirit, 2:6–16

Paul frequently writes in the first-person plural, and this brief section is a prime example:

- "We speak God's wisdom"
- "We have the Spirit that is from God"
- "We speak in words taught by God"
- "We have the mind of Christ"

But who, exactly, is this "we"? Scholars haven't reached a consensus. Is Paul using an editorial "we"?[23] Is he referring to himself and his fellow preachers[24] or to all mature Christians[25]? Is he simply reporting the argument of "the spiritual" (*pneumatikoi*) who are the "we" of this passage?[26] Or is he referring to all believers?[27] While there is no definitive answer, I am inclined to accept the last suggestion as most plausible. The Corinthians would have readily seen themselves as mature, perfected (*teleioi*), spiritual leaders (*pneumatikoi*) who were "perfectly docile to the indwelling Spirit."[28] Up to this point in the letter they might have had heard Paul using "we" to include themselves. They would have been quite pleased to affirm the special status they shared with him and agreed that "we have the mind of Christ" (2:16). Indeed their spiritual pride is what Paul is counting on, since this makes 3:1 the stinging rebuke he intends it to be: "And so, brothers and sisters, I could not speak to you as spiritual people, but rather as people of the flesh, as infants in Christ."

In addition, as noted earlier, Paul has already been emphasizing the Corinthians' election and the abundance of their spiritual gifts (1:1–9). If they had not already been taught directly by the Spirit (2:13), then Paul's word of the Cross would have been utter foolishness to them (2:14). But in fact, he says, they *have* received his word and demonstrated the Spirit's life in their midst. In other letters too Paul is clear that God directly teaches the Christian community. This is explicit in 1 Thess 4:9: "You yourselves have been taught by God [*theodidaktoi*]." Paul tells the Philippians that they should strive to have the same mind, "and if you think differently about anything, this too God will reveal to you" (Phil 3:15). According to Paul Tarazi, the fact that Christians are now *theodidaktoi* is the eschatological fulfillment of Jeremiah 31:33: "[This] is the covenant that I will make with the house of Israel after those days, says the Lord: I will put my law within them, and I will write it on their hearts; and I will be their God, and they shall be my people."[29]

The notion of being directly taught by God is clear in other parts of the New Testament as well (e.g., Acts 19:1–8; Heb 8:11, 10:16). In the Johannine writings, direct teaching by God through the Holy Spirit is a central theme (e.g., John 6:45, 16:13; 1 Jn 2:27). But God's direct teaching, as we have seen, is not only a Christian experience. It is found throughout the Hebrew Bible (e.g., Ps 25:4–5, 8–9, 12, 32:8, 71:17, 86:11, 119 passim; Isa 28:26, 30:20, 42:16, 54:13; Joel 2:28).[30]

Paul ended the previous section by reminding the Corinthians that they had witnessed the Spirit's power working through Paul's weakness, fear, and trembling (2:3). He tells them that he made a conscious decision to close the door on being a disciple of Greek or Jewish wisdom and to follow the Cross instead: "For I decided to know nothing among you except Jesus Christ and him crucified" (2:2). The Cross has become Paul's divine guidance. Rather than project a powerful image of himself based on command of language and human wisdom (whether Greek or Jewish), he deliberately decided to allow the weaknesses in his own life to be the vehicle for his message of the Cross.

The Corinthians know that they had first experienced God's guidance through Paul's weakness and imperfect rhetoric. As Paul reminded them earlier, "I came to you in weakness and in fear and in much trembling. My speech and my proclamation were not with plausible words of wisdom" (2:3–4). He goes on to recall that their faith, built on this "weak" foundation, has given them access through the Spirit to a much deeper wisdom than is possible with mere human wisdom (2:5–7). Through this new revelation they know "what God has prepared for those who love Him" (2:9–10). The direct teaching of the Spirit through the weak presence of Paul paradoxically empowered them to discern what is of God (2:12). This is what it means to "have the mind of Christ." To everyone else these "spiritual things" remain inaccessible foolishness (2:12–16).

Paul is not saying that the Corinthians are *un*spiritual, or merely a bundle of thoughts and emotions, *psychikos* (2:14). But they remain sadly immature and haven't lived up to their potential. This is because their manner of living is incompatible with the way of Christ and thus prevents the Spirit from bearing fruit in their lives. The truth is that they are not the mature, perfected, sanctified, spiritual people they think themselves to be. On the contrary, they are behaving as "fleshly people," *sarkinois* (3:1).

Paul's schema of focusing first on the Cross and then on the Spirit may well fit the Corinthians' own experience of becoming Christians and members of the church via baptism. The Cross and the Spirit are the two poles of baptism (or what developed later as baptism-chrismation (or baptism-confirmation). Identifying with the Cross and death of Christ is the gateway to the grace of the Spirit which enables the believer to walk in newness of life (see Rom 6:4; Gal 3:1–2, 3:27). If baptism is indeed the background to this passage, then this is yet another instance of the close link between divine guidance and liturgical experience in Paul's thought.

Excursus on Paul's Use of Scripture: 1 Cor 2:9–10 and Isaiah 64:4

Paul includes in 1 Cor 2:9 a quotation from Isaiah, but difficulties over the source of the quotation again raise questions about how he viewed scripture in his overall approach to divine guidance.

Consider Paul's text beside the translation of the Hebrew text and of the ancient Septuagint Greek:

But, as it is written,
"What no eye has
seen, nor ear heard,
  nor the human heart conceived,
what God has prepared for those who love him"—
[10]these things God has revealed to us through the Spirit. (1 Cor 2:9–10)

From ages past no one has heard,
  no ear has perceived,
no eye has seen any God besides you,
    who works for those who wait for him. (Isaiah 64:4)

From ages past we have not heard,
nor have our eyes seen any God besides you,
and your works,
which you will do to those who wait for mercy. (LXX Isaiah [Esaias] 64:4 NETS)

Paul's citation of Isaiah 64:4 is not exact. Is it part quotation and part commentary?[31] Is it an amalgamation of Old Testament texts already in circulation in apocalyptic Judaism prior to Paul?[32] Does it come from the Apocalypse of Elijah, as Origen thought?[33] Or is it a free adaptation from memory to suit the occasion? Each of these possibilities suggests that in keeping with biblical interpretation in first-century Judaism, Paul's purposes govern the selection, interpretation, and application of texts.

What makes this even more intriguing is the larger context of LXX Isaiah 64:4. A few verses earlier, Isaiah 63:13–14 speaks about God's direct guidance of his people at the Exodus:

> He led [ēgagen] them through the deep
> like a horse through a wilderness, and they did not become weary, and
>   like cattle through a plain.
> A spirit came down from the Lord and guided [ōdēgēsen] them.
> Thus you led [ēgages] your people,
> to make for yourself a glorious name. (LXX Isa 63:13–14 NETS)

Paul surely would have had this in mind as he made the case for God Himself being the ultimate guide to his people, then and now.

I.5 Divine Guidance and Community Responsibility, 3:1–23

Paul now returns to the unpleasant infighting over teachers first described in 1 Cor 1:10–17. The issue is not the teachers themselves, but the *absolutizing* of a teacher's authority. This is what led to jealousy and strife among their disciples (3:3–4). Some Corinthians have accepted too wholeheartedly the notion that God is speaking through these teachers. By overemphasizing the role of apostles and teachers they have underemphasized the personal and direct voice of God. Others see themselves as standing above the fray and claim to rely exclusively on Christ alone as their teacher, as if they don't need human teachers or the community at all. If the first group of factionalists is too dependent on their teachers, the second group is too proudly independent. The latter are spiritual individualists who don't recognize the diverse gifts God distributes throughout the Body, and Paul will address this serious flaw more fully in chapters 12–14.

But here Paul deals with the first group, those who have glued themselves with unhealthy dependence on the apostles Paul, Cephas, and Apollos. Apostolic teaching and ministry are right and good, but Paul insists that the divine guidance that comes through this inspired teaching is never meant to replace personal and direct communion with God. He is at pains—though unsuccessfully, as it turns out—to deflate their overblown view of teachers because it is just this sort of excessive deference that will pave the way for the false apostles of 2 Cor 10–13. These "super-apostles" will take advantage of the Corinthians' servility to make slaves of them under the guise of spirituality (2 Cor 11:4, 20).

Paul is not interested in being a guru to the Corinthians. The apostles are merely servants: "What then is Apollos? What is Paul? Servants through whom you believed, as the Lord assigned to each" (1 Cor 3:5). He stresses yet again that his particular vocation came through God's guidance. Even the manner of his service has been "according to the grace of God given to me" (3:10; see also 15:8–11). Divine guidance does not empty human initiative and effort of value, and Paul can be so bold as to call himself and Apollos "co-workers [synergoi] of God" (3:9). But the apostles have a particular and limited function in the life of God's church in Corinth. They can't function alone; they need all the other members of the Body, and together all of them will be held accountable for how they have used their gifts for the building up of the church (3:10–17; see 1 Cor 12, where Paul develops this thought much more).

Paul is urging the Corinthians to see God's guidance as poured out on the community as a whole, and not just on select apostles and teachers. The Corinthians must recognize that *they* are God's temple and will be held personally responsible for its holiness and integrity: "Do you not know that you are God's temple and that God's Spirit dwells in you? If anyone destroys God's temple, God will destroy that person. For God's temple is holy, and you are that temple" (3:16–17). Paul underlines the outpouring of grace on *all* of them. But he goes on immediately to give them a warning about self-deception. Anyone who thinks he is wise should "become a fool that he may become wise" (3:18). At the same time, this warning encourages the majority to distance themselves from would-be leaders who base their claims on human wisdom, power, and privilege rather than on the weakness of Christ and the Cross. To be taken in by such appearances is to be deluded (*exapatatō*, 3:18).

Paul does not develop this idea of deception any further here, but by 2 Corinthians he lays out very clearly his view that Satan is the ultimate source of such deception (2 Cor 2:11, 11:14).[34] For Paul, the test for unmasking deception is the example of Christ's self-emptying love on the Cross. Is the one who claims insight or authority living by the Cross, in service to others for Christ's sake (2 Cor 11–12)? Or is he serving his own interests? John Chrysostom puts this test very simply: false apostles sacrifice your interests to theirs; true apostles sacrifice their interests to yours (*Homilies on 1 Corinthians*, 24.2).

Paul quotes Job 5:13 (1 Cor 3:19–20), and when read in context this strengthens his argument that it is the lowly, the mourning, and the poor whom the Lord lifts up rather than the crafty and powerful:

> [He] sets on high those who are lowly,
>> and those who mourn are lifted to safety.
> ¹²He frustrates the devices of the crafty,
>> so that their hands achieve no success.
> ¹³He takes the wise in their own craftiness;
>> and the schemes of the wily are brought to a quick end.
> ¹⁴They meet with darkness in the daytime,
>> and grope at noonday as in the night.
> ¹⁵But he saves the needy from the sword of their mouth,
>> from the hand of the mighty.
> ¹⁶So the poor have hope,
>> and injustice shuts its mouth. (Job 5:11–16)

If any of the Corinthian flock remained secretly or publicly ashamed of their weakness in matters of human wisdom, then Paul once again gives a boost to their corporate dignity and takes down the "wise":

> "The Lord knows the thoughts of the wise,
>> that they are futile." [Ps 93:11 LXX]

> So let no one boast about human leaders. For all things are yours, whether Paul or Apollos or Cephas or the world or life or death or the present or the future— all belong to you, and you belong to Christ, and Christ belongs to God. (1 Cor 3:20–22)

In other words, wisdom is overrated; it's nothing in comparison with all they have received in Christ. Even the apostles are part of this abundant inheritance given to them for their upbuilding.

One additional note concerning Paul's quotation of the Septuagint Psalm 93:11. The original Greek text of the psalm reads, "The Lord knows the thoughts of human beings [*anthrōpon*], that they are futile." Paul has deliberately substituted "the wise" (*sophōn*) for "human beings" (*anthrōpon*), demonstrating yet again his unapologetic adaptation of scripture to suit his argument.

I.6 Divine Guidance through the Apostolic Ministry, 4:1–21

As we have seen, some in Corinth were giving excessive deference to the apostles, and Paul countered this by putting apostolic service in humble perspective as just one of God's many gifts of guidance to the church. But now Paul writes to correct the opposite extreme, the faction that dismissed the apostles as rather pointless.

As they would say, "*We* are followers of Christ." And they take that as giving them the right to judge Paul, Cephas, Apollos, and all the apostles.

Paul doesn't want to be misunderstood. When he says that the apostles are merely "servants"—or more accurately, "slaves"—he does not mean they have no authority or are subservient to the Corinthians. This had become an issue because some in the community felt it was their right to compare Paul and Apollos—using the criteria of human wisdom—and to judge for one or the other, thus creating the factionalism Paul describes. This congregationalist attitude led to much deeper disruption later with the arrival of the "super-apostles" of 2 Cor 10–13. Many in the congregation at that time decided to throw their vote to the newcomers rather than to Paul, as they felt it was their right to choose. But then inexplicably the Corinthians went to the other extreme and practically sold themselves into slavery to these authoritarian leaders: "For you gladly put up with fools, being wise yourselves! For you put up with it when someone makes slaves of you, or devours you, or takes advantage of you, or exalts himself, or gives you a slap in the face" (2 Cor 11:19–20). The Corinthians accepted these "super-apostles" who take their money, their freedom, and their honor, and who then throw abuse at them on top of that. But that was two years later. Now, in this earlier stage of their discontent, Paul gives his first response to the Corinthian antihierarchical rumblings against him. He tells them that the apostles are first *Christ's* servants, not theirs (4:1). And *Christ*—not the Corinthians—will be the judge of how faithful Paul and everyone else has been to the vocation they have received (4:2–5). He dismisses human evaluations, theirs and his, as incomplete and imperfect. It is the Lord who will judge everyone according to the hidden motivations of the heart.

"Nothing beyond What Is Written"

This verse, "that you may learn through us the meaning of the saying, 'Nothing beyond what is written'" (4:6), is a puzzle to commentators. Some scholars conclude that its original meaning is "beyond recovery,"[35] "unintelligible,"[36] and "probably beyond our ability to pick up."[37] Others regard it as a quotation referring to the scriptures cited earlier in Paul's letter.[38] Some interpret the phrase more generally to be Paul's exhortation to live according to the scriptures.[39]

One interpretation of 4:6 that must be excluded, however, is the view that Paul means by this phrase to tie the Corinthians to the "letter" of scripture, a position that he explicitly rejects in 2 Corinthians: "Such is the confidence that we have through Christ toward God. Not that we are competent of ourselves to claim anything as coming from us; our competence is from God, who has made us competent to be ministers of a new covenant, not of letter but of spirit; for the letter kills, but the Spirit gives life" (2 Cor 3:4–6).

That said, it must also be reiterated that one of the striking features of Paul's reasoning is how closely tied it is to the words of scripture. In 1 Corinthians he refers to the scriptures as "what is written" a dozen times (*gegraptai* 9 times; *gegrammenos* 1 time; *kata tas graphas*, "according to the scriptures," 2 times), normally using these terms to introduce a biblical quotation central to his argument. His high regard for scripture is thoroughly Jewish, but he is also addressing one of the key pastoral issues of the predominantly Gentile community in Corinth. The "spiritual" party (the *pneumatikoi*) was focused on the esoteric delights of spirituality, knowledge, revelations, and speaking in tongues. They relished their spiritual freedom from the law, but this had degenerated into a selfish individualism that was pulling the community apart. Paul thus had good reason to anchor them to "what is written."

Paul's exhortation is reminiscent of Deuteronomy 29:29: "The secret things belong to the Lord our God; but the things that are revealed belong to us and to our children for ever, that we may do all the words of this law." Paul's Gospel of Christ had opened to Jews and Gentiles a new freedom apart from law, but this was never meant to be a spirituality entirely cut off from God's past revelation in the Scriptures. Yes, Paul says later, scripture's ritual rules may have been set aside, but God's commandments are still in force. "Circumcision is nothing, and uncircumcision is nothing; but obeying the commandments of God is everything" (1 Cor 7:19). Of course, the next question would be "Which commandments?" The answer to that comes as the letter unfolds, and most succinctly in 1 Cor 13.[40]

Awareness of Divine Guidance Prevents Boasting

Paul's main point is that God's guidance is a gift, so no one has cause to boast. But boasting is exactly what the Corinthians have been doing. With sharp irony he rebukes their sense of spiritual superiority (4:8). They think they too could be apostles? They want that honor? He reminds them that God's guidance to the apostles has been anything but comfortable. The truth is exactly the opposite: the apostles are branded with disrespect, physical distress, and shame: "For I think that God has exhibited us apostles as last of all, like men sentenced to death; because we have become a spectacle to the world, to angels and to men" (4:9).

If the Corinthians see spirituality as a way to inner ease and outward status, Paul immediately disabuses them of this conceit. He lets them know the realities of being an apostle: hunger, thirst, ridicule, threats, no permanent home, hard physical labor, persecution, and dishonor (4:9–13). The reality of apostolic service is to be at the bottom of the world's scale of honor: "We have become, and are now, as the refuse of the world, the offscouring of all things" (4:13). He accepts all of this as God's guidance.

Divine Guidance through Paul's Example

Given his attack on Corinthian boasting, we might expect Paul to minimize his own role with them. But instead of humbly effacing himself and telling the Corinthians to look elsewhere for their guidance, he does the opposite. He tells them to look directly at him if they want to see an example of what it means to be a follower of the Crucified Christ. Paul uses himself as a living demonstration of a weak human being living by faith in the Cross of Christ. They have more than enough spiritual guides competing for their attention and approval (4:15). In contrast, Paul has taken on the sacrificial role of a true father whose children learn from his openly exposed way of life, for good or ill.

The Corinthians aren't his patients, clients, or customers. Nor is he just a *paidagōgos,* the household slave who takes children back and forth to school as their guardian. The term *paidagōgos* also had the connotation of hovering annoyance. (Plutarch says that the Roman general Fabius Maximus, c. 280–203 BCE, was known disparagingly as the *paidagōgos* of Hannibal because he always followed at his heels rather than attack directly during the Second Punic War, 218–201.)[41]

In contrast to these impersonal guides, Paul is inextricably their *father* in Christ. He is committed to their welfare, growth, and freedom as his own children. Similarly in 1 Thessalonians, his earliest extant letter, he uses the image of a tender nurse "caring for her own children." This passage brings together Paul's example as both father and mother:

> [We] were gentle among you, like a nurse tenderly caring for her own children. [8]So deeply do we care for you that we are determined to share with you not only the gospel of God but also our own selves, because you have become very dear to us. [9]You remember our labor and toil, brothers and sisters; we worked night and day, so that we might not burden any of you while we proclaimed to you the gospel of God. [10]You are witnesses, and God also, how pure, upright, and blameless our conduct was toward you believers. [11]As you know, we dealt with each one of you like a father with his children, [12]urging and encouraging you and pleading that you lead a life worthy of God, who calls you into his own kingdom and glory. (1 Thess 2:6–11)

Paul here combines humility and boldness—traits commonly opposed to each other—to tell the Corinthians that they should look at him and imitate him as he imitates Christ (1 Cor 4:16, 11:1). Example and imitation is a constant theme in his letters, where his readers are exhorted to imitate him, the apostles, and other churches (1 Thess 1:6, 4:1; Phil 3:17, 4:9; 2 Thess 3:7; 2 Tim 3:10). In 1 Thessalonians, writing with Silvanus and Timothy he says, "[You] became imitators of us and of the Lord, for in spite of persecution you received the word with joy inspired by the Holy Spirit" (1 Thess 1:6). The Thessalonians imitated the apostles. They endured persecutions and thus also "became imitators of the churches of God in Christ Jesus that are in Judea" (1 Thess 2:14). Then in turn the Thessalonians themselves "became an example to all the believers in Macedonia and in Achaia" (1 Thess 1:7).

Paul in effect is telling the Corinthians, "You've seen me, you know me; you know how I cared for you, how I poured out my life for you. I'm not just teaching you words from a book." To underline this message he sent Timothy as a reminder of his ways: "Therefore I sent to you Timothy, my beloved and faithful child in the Lord, to remind you of my ways in Christ, as I teach them everywhere in every church" (4:17). Paul's primary guidance to the Corinthians is his preaching of Christ and the Cross, made real by his own example of imperfect but sacrificial love empowered by the Holy Spirit.

He ends this section of his letter by recapping the two sides of God's guidance, both divine and human. All plans are ultimately subject to God's will: "I will come to you soon, if the Lord wills, and I will find out not the talk of these arrogant people but their power" (4:19). He repeats his claim that God gave him this vocation to act with fatherly authority among the Corinthians. If necessary, he will come to them "with a rod" (4:21). But Paul doesn't isolate his authority from the community's guidance to *him*. Their response ("What do you wish?") will determine how and in what spirit he will use his authority (4:21).

II. Divine Guidance in Practice, 5:1–16:24

Paul's letter thus far has been directed mainly toward the problem of divisions. Embedded in his argument is the view that these divisions stem ultimately from a defective understanding of God's guidance. Now, and for most of the remainder of the letter, he addresses other specific problems that have the same root cause. At each point he demonstrates that discernment, decision-making, and action in the Christian community requires a synergy that brings together the divine, apostolic, communal, and personal.

II.1 Public Immorality in the Church Community, 5:1–13

⁹I wrote to you in my letter not to associate with sexually immoral persons [*pornois*]— ¹⁰not at all meaning the immoral [*pornois*] of this world, or the greedy and robbers, or idolaters, since you would then need to go out of the world. ¹¹But now I am writing to you not to associate with anyone who bears the name of brother or sister

who is sexually immoral [*pornos*] or greedy, or is an idolater, reviler, drunkard, or robber. Do not even eat with such a one. [12]For what have I to do with judging those outside? Is it not those who are inside that you are to judge? [13]God will judge those outside. "Drive out the wicked person from among you." (1 Cor 5:9–13)

Paul has heard about a situation of public immorality being tolerated within the Corinthian church: a man cohabiting with his stepmother. Like the divisions he heard about through Chloe's people, Paul does not rely here on divine revelations but on having his ear close to the ground. The Corinthians had not told him about this in their letter. But through personal contacts Paul kept himself informed about the real situation hidden behind the Corinthian façade.

Perhaps they thought nothing was wrong and that their tolerance was testimony to their broad-minded freedom in the Spirit (5:1). But Paul insists that both this *porneia* (sexual immorality) and its toleration must be firmly and publicly renounced as incompatible even with conventional Gentile standards of morality, let alone the ethical norms of Scripture (e.g., Lev 18:8, 20:11).[42] Here, in line with Jewish thought, Paul rejects an individualistic approach to guidance. While individuals would of course vary in their devotion and level of spiritual attainment, the community's spiritual health depended on maintaining the maximal standard of life in Christ. They were free to welcome anyone who couldn't reach this high standard (at least not yet), but they were not free to lower the standard itself. And so, while the community had to be a welcoming place of mercy, forgiveness, and spiritual healing for all, it could not tolerate the open undermining of life in Christ. So it would have to be *intolerant* of those who would publicly flout the most basic standards of moral purity—as they were then understood, even by the Gentile public at large.

This was a continuing issue for the Corinthians, one that Paul had addressed before and was now clarifying once again. The lists of forbidden behaviors are not original with Paul but compare to similar lists in circulation among Stoics and also Jews, who saw these as a handy summary of the Bible's ethical teaching (1 Cor 5:9–11, 6:9–10; see also Rom 1:28–31; 2 Cor 12:20ff.; Gal 5:19; Col 3:5; Eph 5:3–5).[43] That Paul views community responsibility for its ethical purity as the biblical norm is underlined when he ends this section by quoting the refrain from Deuteronomy to "drive out the wicked person from among you" (1 Cor 5:13; see, for example, Deut 17:7, 19:19, 22:21, 24:7). While Paul rereads scriptural stories, history, and liturgical commandments as allegories and metaphors—for example, he interprets the Passover lamb as Christ (5:7)—he takes literally the commandments about moral behavior, including sexual purity. These were not to be ignored, made optional, individualized, or spiritualized, as the Corinthians were doing.

Paul's main concern is not to maintain conventional morality but to refocus the community's gaze on the Kingdom of God (1 Cor 4:20, 6:9–10, 15:50). Behavior of the kind they are tolerating is a rejection of the divine guidance of scripture; it is also a rejection of the new life they received at baptism. They risk exclusion from the kingdom of heaven (6:10–11).[44]

Paul does not see their immorality in individualistic terms, as if its effects could be isolated to those directly involved. They are all connected and affect each other, for "a little leaven leavens the whole lump" (5:6). So tolerance in this instance, far from being a virtue, can be like gangrene that spreads from limb to limb in the Body of Christ. Worse, the Corinthians were tolerant to the point of arrogance, insisting on everyone's freedom to act as they wish (5:2, 6:12, 10:23).

Paul insists that they get involved in guiding their community's spiritual health. He refuses to do this alone since God will hold the *community* responsible for how it orders its life. As in the Deuteronomy texts, everyone has to share in this unpleasant task. Leadership of the community, while hierarchal, is not authoritarian. It requires the assent and participation of the whole body. This means that members of the church cannot avoid getting involved in the messy details, and this case of public immorality was a prime example.

But purging and purifying the community is not Paul's sole interest here. He also hopes to save the man in question, and believes that in his case only "the destruction of his flesh will avail to the salvation of his spirit on the day of the Lord" (5:5). Most ancient commentators interpret this as excommunication and exclusion from the community.[45] For example, Tertullian (160–220): "His meaning was, that that Spirit which is accounted to exist in the church must be presented 'saved,' that is, untainted by the contagion of impurities in the day of the Lord, by the ejection of the incestuous fornicator" (*On Modesty* 13).[46] Theodore of Mopsuestia (c. 350–428) elaborates further on the nature of this excommunication and handing over to Satan: "This is not to be taken literally. What Paul means is that the person concerned should be put out of the church and forced to live in the world, which is ruled by Satan. That way he will learn to fear God and escape the greater punishment that is to come."[47] Satan's role here has been debated, but it is sometimes linked to Job and the permission God gives Satan to afflict him. Severian of Gabala (c. 380–425?) comments, "When Paul says that this man must be delivered to Satan, he does not mean that he should be handed over to the power of the evil one. Rather, all evils of this life, for example, diseases, sorrows, sufferings, and other circumstances, were attributed to Satan, and it is in that sense that Paul uses the term here. What he means is that this man should be exposed to the hardships of life."[48] Paul is fully assured of his own authority to make such a judgment and issue directives. He is also certain that his own spirit will be invisibly present in their midst—along with the power of the Lord Jesus—as they carry out his instructions. Nor does he have any hesitancy: the case is clear, the threat real, his judgment certain. Such is the authority of apostolic guidance on questions of morality (5:3–5). Likewise, he reminds them of his earlier instruction, emphasizing yet again that he expects them to hear and heed his guidance to them (5:9–13).

The process described here is a model of synergy between the apostolic and communal, the divine and human. Together they are to take responsibility for delivering the man to Satan. Thus even Satan is part of a process that accomplishes God's purposes, preserves the community's health, *and* saves the man's soul (see also 2 Cor 12:2; 1 Tim 1:20). But Paul limits this process to judgments within the church: judgment of those outside belongs to God alone (5:13).

Paul's Jewish formation leads him to think naturally in terms of divine guidance from liturgical experience, on this occasion the celebration of Passover. Here he reinterprets Passover through Christ, "our Paschal lamb" (1 Cor 5:7): "Do you not know that a little yeast leavens the whole batch of dough? Clean out the old yeast so that you may be a new batch, as you really are unleavened. For our paschal lamb, Christ, has been sacrificed. Therefore, let us celebrate the festival, not with the old yeast, the yeast of malice and evil, but with the unleavened bread of sincerity and truth" (5:7–8). This reference almost certainly points to the new Christian Passover celebration among the Corinthians. As with baptism, Paul wants to ensure that their thought and behavior conform to their liturgical celebration. Theology, liturgy, and ethics are intertwined.

II.2 Litigation among Church Members, 6:1–20

The Corinthians have invited the legal system to intervene in what should have been an internal family squabble. As in the previous case, Paul is concerned here about the church's abdication of responsibility for guiding its own life. Sadly, they have not grasped the fact that they are a community in Christ, a family of brothers and sisters, with the bonds and obligations implied by the notion of family in the Jewish and Greco-Roman world.[49] Once again they have allowed individualism, personal passions, and private self-interest to be tolerated under the banner of spiritual freedom. Their letter to him proclaims, "All things are lawful to me" (6:12). But they are deceived (6:9).

Paul insists once more that they get involved in the potentially messy business of personal relations within the church. In line with the Jewish view that "the law is not in heaven" he is urging them to get their hands dirty with the communal and practical "matters pertaining to this life" (*ta biōtika*, 6:3) and not to stand aloof.

Significantly, Paul does not insist they refer all cases to *him*. By stressing their dignity he reassures the Corinthians of their competence to make difficult decisions. They are the saints who will be judging cosmic events (6:2–3). How much more, then, should they be able to evaluate the relative trivialities of day-to-day life. In a slap at their pride, he wonders if it is possible they have none among them wise enough to make such judgments (6:5). They didn't need to find outside judges, and it is a shame to have done so (6:5). It would have been preferable to swallow the injustice rather than go to a civil court (6:7).

Behind these cases Paul sees a slew of fleshly passions they should have left behind when they were washed in baptism (6:11). He thus points again to the beginning of their life in the church as the touchstone for guidance in decision-making. Baptism has joined the believers to the Lord and made them "one spirit" with Him (6:17). Their own bodies are now inhabited by the Holy Spirit in a union made possible by the Lord's death on the Cross (6:15, 20; 3:16; 2 Cor 6:16). By their own free decision they no longer belong to themselves; they belong to Christ. So they should not act as if they were still independent free agents (6:19). They are not complete in themselves, since they are but single members of the whole Body of Christ. They need the rest of the Body in order to be whole as individuals. Throughout we see Paul using these very physical images to keep pulling the Corinthians back to earthly realities of passions, of suffering, of relationships—in contrast to their besetting temptation to spiritual escapism.

In considering this section of the letter, it is impossible to avoid the single most divisive issue among Christians today: how to understand Paul's statements on homosexual practice, which is mentioned here in the catalogue of behaviors that should have been left behind after baptism: "[9]Do you not know that wrongdoers will not inherit the kingdom of God? Do not be deceived! Fornicators, idolaters, adulterers, male prostitutes, sodomites, [10]thieves, the greedy, drunkards, revilers, robbers—none of these will inherit the kingdom of God. [11]And this is what some of you used to be. But you were washed, you were sanctified, you were justified in the name of the Lord Jesus Christ and in the Spirit of our God" (1 Cor 6:9–11).

Without going into the vast literature on this controversial subject, two points in relation to divine guidance need to be affirmed. First, Paul, in common with the Judaism of his day, was implacably opposed to homosexual practice, along with any other sexual immorality that might have been tolerated among Gentiles. This, together with opposition to pagan religion, was a key distinguishing feature that divided Jew and Gentile. But having said this, it must also be underlined that one of the main themes in this study is the persistence of changing interpretation within the Jewish tradition. Time and again perceptions of God's guidance under new circumstances altered the way Jews understood the commandments and what was required of them to be faithful to the Lord in their time and place.

As E. P. Sanders has shown in his magisterial *Paul: The Apostle's Life, Letters and Thought*, there is no contesting the fact that Paul unambiguously condemned homosexual behavior: "[He] was a first-century Jew, and on ethical questions he ordinarily followed Jewish views precisely; more particularly, he was a Diaspora Jew, and therefore likely to be even more rigid on sexual ethics than were his contemporaries in Jewish Palestine."[50] Paul was a man of his time, but as such his views—like those of the rest of the Bible—are subject to reevaluation in light of later experience and knowledge. Sanders points to polygamy and the levirate (a male relative inseminating a widow so she can bear children for her departed husband) as two prime examples, among others, of parts of the Bible that had fallen into disuse in the first century.

Biblicists, who hold "the view that modern Christians should believe and do precisely what the biblical authors believed and did," ignore this record of reinterpretation. They also are highly selective in how they apply biblical teaching: "Perhaps most to the point, Paul's vice lists are generally ignored in church polity and administration. Christian churches contain people who drink too much, who are greedy, who are deceitful, who quarrel, who gossip, who boast, who once rebelled against their parents, and who are foolish. Yet Paul's vice list condemns them *all*, just as much as they condemn people who engage in homosexual acts."[51]

But while Sanders combats biblicist exclusion of homosexuals, he also warns against a "liberal" biblicism that is equally selective in its revision and quoting of the Bible. Christians, he says, need to be faithful to what Paul actually says, while also taking into consideration contemporary knowledge about sexual identity that Paul and the ancient world simply did not know: "We should let Paul say what he said, and then make the decisions we should make, which should take into account the modern world, rather than the ancient world."[52] I agree with him.

II.3 Social Status, 7:1–39

In this section Paul goes on to answer questions about various social conditions the Corinthians have asked in their letter to him (7:1). In his wide-ranging response he deals with being married or unmarried, slave or free, Jewish or Gentile. While he wants them to take responsibility for their communal life, it is also significant that he never doubts his own authority to give them guidance when necessary. He does not simply throw the questions back to them to decide. Nor does he say "Just read the scriptures" or "Just pray about it" or "Just put your heads together and vote on it" or indeed "Just ask God for guidance."

Paul recognizes his own God-given ministry of leadership and counsel. But he is no autocrat issuing edicts or refusing to be questioned: the tone of his response is one of willing, thoughtful, respectful engagement with the questions put to him. Still, he doesn't agree to make all their decisions or to put himself in the position of all-knowing spiritual guide. Thus he carefully distinguishes between (1) directions from the Lord, (2) his own considered opinion, and (3) questions he leaves to the Spirit-illumined conscience of community and individual (see also Phil 3:15).

Paul's instructions to married couples make clear that *mutual* submission and common agreement are the basis of Christian marital life, including sexuality and spirituality. As David Bentley Hart observes, this "almost unprecedented egalitarianism with regard to the sexes . . . was extraordinary for its time."[53] For Paul, mutual submission is the basis of *all* communal life in Christ and reshapes views on social status, whether one is married, unmarried, Jewish ("circumcised"), Gentile ("uncircumcised"), slave, or free. But Paul does not give detailed rulings for every contingency.

His approach has a number of implications for how the Corinthians are to make decisions:

1. Decision-making about marriage and social status is to be guided not by the norms of Jewish or Greco-Roman society but by the new social patterns shaped by baptism, incorporation into Christ, and preparation for Christ's imminent return (see also 1 Cor 12:13; Gal 3:28; Rom 10:12; Col 3:11). *Everything* is now temporary, "For the present form of this world is passing away" (7:31). This determines the decisions Paul makes on whatever tasks remain in this earthly life. Every social distinction is now to be viewed through the lens of life in Christ, as Paul looks to the far horizon of the Kingdom of God. However, in the present, life in Christ does not obliterate sexual distinctions nor exclude order and hierarchy in regard to either marriage or church life. The new social order brought about by baptism is not the end of hierarchy. But its exercise is no longer in the oppressive or servile terms familiar to the Greco-Roman world of masters and slaves or patrons and clients, but in a Christian spirit of respect, service, collaboration, and mutual submission.

2. Paul gives the Corinthians general norms for marriage and communal life so that they might make later decisions on their own. He isn't interested in keeping them in perpetual childish dependence for every decision they face; instead he promotes a mature relationship between himself and the Corinthians as his grown, adult children in the Lord. His encouragement of independence and freedom is all the more significant given his awareness of their brewing rebellion against his authority.

3. Paul recognizes the "antiguidance" of spiritual forces (Satan) actively working against those who are attempting to lead a more intense spiritual life of prayer and fasting, including fasting from sexual relations. He advises married couples to keep those fasting periods short and by mutual

agreement, "so that Satan may not tempt you because of your lack of self-control" (7:5). His own preference is that all would be single and celibate, but he admits that this isn't for everyone. It's a particular gift from God, and each has his or her own calling (7:6). On the other hand, if they are still unmarried and in the decision-making stage, then if they can live without sexual relations, so much the better. They will be less anxious, less tied to worldly concerns, more focused on Christ. But again, in this highly personal realm Paul is simply advising. He has no wish "to put any restraint" on their decision (7:35); they are free to decide, guided by their own knowledge of themselves, their gifts, and their proclivities (7:6–9, 28, 36, 39). He does not hide his own informed preference "as one who by the Lord's mercy is trustworthy" (7:25), but his emphasis remains on freedom, as each must decide this "in his own heart" (7:37).

4. Paul is careful to distinguish between the Lord's commandment on divorce and remarriage from his own advice on questions about mixed marriages of believers and unbelievers, the unmarried, and widows, for which the Lord had provided no ready answer (7:10–16, 7:25–40). Where the Lord's answer is not obvious he gives his own considered opinions, noting with just a touch of irony, "I too have the Spirit of God" (7:40). However, on the question of divorce between believers, he is following neither his own opinion nor Jewish Law—which permitted divorce—but the command of "the Lord" (7:10), which forbids divorce, as in Mark 10:9 (KJV): "What therefore God hath joined together, let not man put asunder."

(Over the centuries churches have taken a wide range of approaches to divorce, and many found ways to preserve the teaching of Christ while finding forms of pastoral work-around—like annulment in the Roman Catholic tradition—to give a second or third chance where possible, with the understanding that simply coming to the church for a marriage ceremony is not in itself evidence that God has joined the couple together.)

5. Throughout his advice on mixed marriages between believers and unbelievers, and how to decide whether to remain married, Paul says the guiding factor for the believer is the *unbelieving* partner. The believing partner is to live with the decision the other makes. The believer is to approach this decision by giving first consideration to what is best for the *other's* sanctification and salvation (7:14, 7:16). This reinforces Paul's view that the needs and freedom of the other are the general principles guiding decisions in marriage. Christians are coworkers with God not only in the process of their own salvation but in the sacrificial self-emptying that brings salvation to others (see Phil 2:12; Col 1:24).

6. While it is possible to make a decision to change marital status, for other social conditions Paul advises the Corinthians to remain as they are, whether
Jewish or Gentile, slave or free. "[Let] each of you lead the life that the Lord
has assigned, to which God called you. This is my rule in all the churches"
(7:17). The one exception is if a slave has the opportunity to win his or her
freedom. But under no circumstances should a free person willingly enslave
themselves to someone else (7:23). Paul's order may reflect the historical
situation in which self-enslavement was indeed possible,[54] but he was also
metaphorically rebuking the tendency of some in Corinth to allow human
guides to strip them of their freedom. His main concern is the Corinthians'
spiritual stability. They are to focus on serving the Lord, seeking to please
Him and keep His commandments (7:32) regardless of their status as married or unmarried, slave or free, Jew or Gentile (7:19).

II.4 Liturgy and Guidance: Right Living, 8:1–11:1

The Corinthians had a number of questions about food and pagan temples: Was
it permissible to go to social occasions in pagan temples? What about buying
meat in the marketplace, since much that was on sale had first been offered in
a pagan temple? In his extended response Paul puts his answer in the broad
context of baptism and the Lord's Supper, again linking guidance on practical
questions to liturgical experience. For Jews this would have been natural, judging
simply from the sheer amount of space the Torah devotes to liturgical matters
(most of Exodus, Leviticus, Numbers, and Deuteronomy). But for Gentiles, especially those influenced by Roman attitudes (Cicero, for example), the meaning
of liturgical practice could be utterly irrelevant to personal belief and behavior.
The Corinthian Christians had plenty of liturgical life and prided themselves on
a charismatic experience of worship, but they did not think in terms of liturgical
theology, in which faith, theology, liturgy, mission, and behavior were intimately
intertwined. Instead they saw the issue here in terms of their right to personal
spiritual freedom. For Paul the question about food offered to idols opens up
a much broader set of issues and cannot be answered without reference to the
relationships that have been created by God in Christ through baptism and the
Lord's Supper.

The argument of the "strong" Corinthians was that since there is only one true
God, and since idols don't really exist (Paul agrees; 8:4–6), then what is the harm
of participating in meals held in pagan temples (8:10) or eating meat sold in the
marketplace that might have been sacrificed in a pagan temple (10:25)? After
all, these were utterly common social practices with little real belief attached to
them. Paul addresses this objection and reminds them that, at least on this issue,

preserving the bond of relationship within the community is more important than who is right. Christians of weaker, more sensitive conscience will be scandalized at this behavior. He knows that the "weak" are wrong in their thinking (and he will address this later), but their feelings still need to be taken into account by the "strong." Being weaker, their consciences will waver on this matter, especially if those who are reputed to have superior knowledge are giving them a troubling example (8:7). Here, despite his communitarian values, we see the importance Paul also attributes to individual conscience in making decisions. Indeed to go against conscience is to perish (8:11).

The "strong" are correct that idols are meaningless, says Paul. But in this case being right is not enough, and bare truth divorced from love may be the cause of another's spiritual death. He reminds them that while the truth of the "strong" is abstract, the one whose spiritual death they cause is their flesh-and-blood brother or sister for whom Christ died (8:11). Weak and strong have become family through baptism, joined through Christ to each other as members of His Body. Each member no longer has his or her own life entirely apart from Christ and His Body. To wound the other's conscience is therefore to sin against Christ. This implies a genuine interest in knowing and caring what community members think and feel. For Paul there is no spirituality that allows a Christian to live independently of others in the Church. Like it or not, all have been joined to each other in baptism, through which they have all accepted the death of the Lord on their behalf.

This incident again points to Paul's emphasis on the power of human example as guide to either the salvation or the destruction of the other. Paul develops this point in chapter 9 by turning the tables and casting the "strong" Corinthians as in fact the "weak" who are still underdeveloped in their knowledge of rights and responsibilities. For all their boasting of knowledge, they are ignorant of *Paul's* rights as an apostle and their material responsibilities toward him. But he willingly set aside his freedom and rights (9:1–12) to financially support himself (and others) in order to carry out the divinely appointed "necessity" of preaching the gospel (9:12–23). Paul is reticent to speak this way about his own needs, but the Corinthians should have taken an interest in his basic welfare if they wanted to pass the test of spiritual strength.

All Paul's decisions are made in reference to his vocation. This becomes his primary criterion of guidance: "I do it all for the sake of the gospel, that I may share [*synkoinōnos*, 'be a communicant'] in its blessings" (9:23). He is not passive. On the contrary, he is constantly on the lookout for opportunities to actively carry out his mission. We have here the picture of a man with a tremendous sense of direction working toward the goal Christ has given him, racing toward a finish line, not aimlessly running about or boxing the air (9:24–25). At the same time, he realizes that God's guidance to him as an apostle is no substitute for his own ascetic effort in coworking for his salvation: "lest after preaching to others I myself should be disqualified" (9:27).

Paul now returns to the question of rights and responsibilities within the Christian community, and how they ought to relate to the surrounding Greco-Roman culture, where eating in temples was a normal social event (much like renting out a church hall today) and where much of the meat sold in the marketplace routinely came from offerings in local temples. He asks the Corinthians to reshape how they go about thinking and making decisions on practical questions. He wants them to view everything in terms of their participation in the Lord's Supper. Liturgy is to be the theological framework for how they work out their responses to such questions.

Paul knows that the Corinthians have taken to relying on their liturgical celebrations as their guarantee of salvation, but they have disconnected this rite from faith and behavior. So he uses Israel's similar temptation in the wilderness to make his argument. In that ancient example the same false sense of security had prevailed, when they mistakenly assumed that their divine chosenness and their liturgical rites absolved them of further responsibility. Not so, says Paul. "God was not pleased with most of them, and they were struck down in the wilderness" (10:5; see Num 14:26–38; Heb 3:17; Jude 5). Spiritual food and drink didn't protect the Israelites, and baptism and eucharist won't protect the Corinthians if their lives don't also conform to their liturgical rites.

Having established that knowledge alone is an insufficient criterion for decision-making, Paul probes further the apparent knowledge of those "strong" Corinthians who think they can participate in meals in pagan temples with impunity. He has already agreed there is no substance to the idols or to the food sacrificed to them: they are nothing (10:19). But he is not prepared to say that participating in pagan sacrifices is a neutral spiritual experience. On the contrary, the sacrifices are offered to spiritual forces opposed to God, the *daimonia* (10:20).

Although Jews emphasized the uniqueness of the one Creator-God, they also, like Gentiles, accepted that the universe was inhabited by other spiritual forces, both good and evil. But Jews were clear: pagan worship was not worship of God; it was worship of evil demons (Deut 32:17; Ps 90:6; Is 13:21, 34:14, 65:3; Bar 4:7, 35; Tobit passim).[55] Therefore to eat sacrifices within a pagan temple—even if this is merely a social convention—is to have communion with demons (10:21).

The criterion for deciding whether or not to participate in such a meal returns to the meaning of the Lord's Supper (10:16–21). Paul asks the question: With whom do you wish to be in communion? With demons or with the Lord? There is no middle way. For Paul, behavior on this issue must conform to the eucharist. They cannot have communion of the Lord's cup and at the same time be communicating with demons in pagan temples (10:21).[56]

The eucharist is not magical, just as baptism is not magical. Neither can be isolated from faith and behavior. For Paul, using Christian knowledge and freedom as a justification for participating in idolatrous communion is to misunderstand the conditional nature of their election, the meaning of communion in Christ, and the destructive power of demonic forces.

Paul incorporates the mainly Gentile Corinthian community into the people of Israel, telling them it was "our fathers" who were baptized into Moses and ate the spiritual food and spiritual drink (10:1–4). While using the Bible as guide, he has boldly reinterpreted events of the Exodus as "types" (10:6, 11). Whether this is original with him or was already part of a received tradition, he demonstrates that the Christian experience, rather than the original historical situation of the biblical texts, is the new context for interpretation. For Paul, to confine the meaning of the text to its historical context would be to misunderstand its purpose in the *divine* plan, since God ultimately intended the text's full meaning to be disclosed only to the present generation: "[They] were written down for our instruction, upon whom the end of the ages has come" (10:11).

That being said, scriptural interpretation was not the main point of debate here. Paul's message is that the divine election, guidance, "baptism," and spiritual food of their Jewish spiritual ancestors in the wilderness did not absolve them from the need to resist sinful desires or protect them from the consequences of their behavior. The liturgy of these ancestors did not prevent some of them from being seduced by idolatry, *porneia*, and temptation (10:10). If the Corinthians thought they were special, Paul quickly disabuses them of their conceit: in the temptations they face they are no different from these "chosen" ancestors. Therefore anyone among them who is overconfident in his standing must "take heed lest he fall" (10:12).

Yet Paul sees both the temptations and the means of withstanding them as aspects of God's guidance (10:13). Once again Paul's manner of giving guidance is closely connected to his respect for the freedom and integrity of the individual. He wants the Corinthians to willingly accept his argument, not just obey blindly. He regards them as "sensible," capable of judging the truth of what he says (10:15). His letter demonstrates this: they had asked him a question about food offered to idols (8:1), but it is only many pages later, after his full argument has been set out, that he gives them a specific answer.

Paul summarizes everything he has said thus far about the two general criteria for making decisions. They must submit their freedom and knowledge to the double test of building up their relationship (1) with God ("Do all to the glory of God"; 10:31) and (2) with the other ("Let no one seek his own good, but the good of his neighbor"; 10:24). The aim of their decisions must ultimately be the salvation of the other (10:33). But this doesn't mean that they need to engage in debilitating debates. No doubt Paul had this dispute in mind when he later wrote to Rome from Corinth (sometime between 54 and 58):

> Welcome those who are weak in faith, but not for the purpose of quarreling over opinions. ²Some believe in eating anything, while the weak eat only vegetables. ³Those who eat must not despise those who abstain, and those who abstain must not pass judgment on those who eat; for God has welcomed them. ⁴Who are you to pass judgment on servants of another? It is before their own lord that they stand or fall. And they will be upheld, for the Lord is able to make them stand. (Rom 14:1–4)

Accommodating the objections of the "weak" doesn't mean that they should hold everyone else in thrall (1 Cor 10:25–27). Yes, they have tender consciences, but they need to be liberated from their pious fears. While in practice Paul is willing to adapt his behavior to the consciences of the weak for a time (10:28–29), he rebukes them for not accepting their true power and freedom in Christ (10:29–30; 2 Cor 3:17; Gal 5:1–14). This is the example Paul follows in imitation of Christ, and he urges them to do the same (1 Cor 11:1).

II.5 Liturgy and Guidance: Right Worship, 11:2–14:40

We continue to see the centrality Paul gives to worship in the questions the Corinthians raise and the reports he has received about their liturgical order (and disorder). He spends a lot of ink on these liturgical issues: head coverings, abuses at the Lord's Supper, and the exercise of spiritual gifts in the assembly (especially speaking in tongues and prophecy). All this leads to the exhortation that all things be done "decently and in good order" (14:40).

If Paul's concern thus far has been that Corinthians' behavior outside liturgy would reflect their life in the liturgy, now he wants to be sure that their liturgical life itself is *right* worship. By this he means that even an unbeliever might enter the assembly and "declare that God is really among you" (14:25). Liturgy must be a seamless garment, woven together from their faith, their theology, their relations with each other, and their manner of living. Only then can liturgy be the guide for Christian thought and living it is meant to be. Liturgy must reflect their life in Christ, and their life in Christ must reflect their liturgy.

To be such a formational guide, their liturgy must first conform to the tradition Paul received and passed on to them. Paul began his mission by delivering the gospel and liturgical traditions linked with Christ himself (1 Cor 11:2, 11:23, 15:3; see also 2 Thess 2:15, 3:6). It must be emphasized again that he explicitly says he *received* this tradition. Christ revealed Himself to Paul, but He then pointed Paul to the church, and it was in the church that Paul received baptism and the eucharist. Paul's personal revelation was thus incomplete without his life in the community that already had a tradition of faith and worship.

Keeping closely to the traditional form Paul handed on to them might have been the natural conservative inclination of Roman-influenced Corinthians, and Paul praises them for doing exactly as he has taught them liturgically: "I commend you because you remember me in everything and maintain the traditions just as I handed them on to you" (11:2). However, as we have seen, Romans were inclined to take old forms and invest them with new meaning, or no meaning at all. The rite might be kept impeccably but have no practical implications for faith and living. In contrast, Paul's aim is that Christian faith and behavior correspond exactly with the liturgical tradition they have received. Liturgy, faith, and behavior must be a single whole.

Paul's intent is not to maintain tradition as such, but only such practices as were consonant with Christ. Elsewhere he is highly critical when the traditions and teachings of men (Col. 2:8, 22) and the traditions of the fathers (Gal 1:14) obscure Christ and the gospel. His deference to the guidance that comes through the church and its tradition should not be taken to mean that he views every custom or every act and decision by the church's leadership—even the apostles—as coequal to God's. He could be a fierce opponent of such "tradition." Nowhere is this more vividly demonstrated than in Paul's public dispute with Peter over keeping Jewish laws. This is recorded permanently in Galatians for future generations to reflect upon (Gal 2:11–14). But what *is* tradition? And who decides what is inspired tradition, pious custom, or "the traditions of men"? And is there room for new questions (or new answers to old questions)? For new traditions, new interpretations, and change? These are some of the issues around guidance and tradition that emerge in the next section of Paul's letter, 1 Cor 11–14.

II.5.1 Head Coverings, Hairstyles 11:2–16

There is still scholarly debate over the meaning of head coverings in this passage, and no conclusion yet seems possible since the background remains unclear.[57] Nevertheless a few points can be made that relate to divine guidance:

1. A particular liturgical practice or mode of hairstyle was being followed in Corinth—whether this was about head coverings or hairstyles is unresolved. Whatever is happening with the hair, Paul views it as undermining the God-created distinction between male and female. This could have been some social norm to which the Corinthians were accustomed, but they may also have felt justified in blurring liturgical distinctions between male and female. After all, Paul himself accepted and encouraged the equal

status of men and women before God, and he allowed women to prophesy and pray in the assembly with men (11:5). Paul also rejects the traditional Jewish interpretation of Gen 2 that justified the inferiority of woman as created after man (1 Cor 11:8–12).[58] For Paul, both sexes are entirely interdependent (11:11–12). He may well have told the Corinthians the same thing he told the Galatians: "There is no longer Jew or Greek, there is no longer slave or free, there is no longer male and female; for all of you are one in Christ Jesus" (Gal 3:28). As Ben Witherington suggests, "It is possible and likely . . . that some in Corinth thought that through knowledge or other spiritual gifts and experiences they transcended distinctions of gender in Christian worship."[59]

2. However, for all of Paul's support for the equality of men and women before God in Christ, and for all his support of women in ministry, he still wants to affirm (1) the distinction between the sexes and (2) hierarchical order.[60] His rationale for women's head coverings and how this relates to creation, authority, men, and the angels is convoluted. But we need to keep remembering that while some in first-century Corinth might have viewed Paul's inclusion and encouragement of women as shockingly progressive, the fact remains that he was not a social revolutionary on this subject. He was sensitive to the Christian assembly's honor and shame in the wider Corinthian community. As such he was mostly comfortable with the accepted norms, roles, and hierarchy of men and women. This raises the question once again of distinguishing between timeless tradition and socially and historically conditioned tradition.

3. We see Paul willing to engage the Corinthians in conversation and not simply issuing edicts. This is his normal pastoral response. He uses a variety of arguments to convince the Corinthians that their practice is wrong theologically because it is at variance with what it means to be truly human. But their practice is also out of step with the other churches. Thus universal church practice, having a common mind, and preserving relationships among the churches is again seen to be a pattern to guide the behavior of local communities. Theology and liturgy should reflect each other, such that either could be a trustworthy guide to Christian behavior (or in a later formulation, "Lex orandi, lex credendi," The rule of prayer is the rule of faith). Paul's method implies that if theological argument is unconvincing or remains contentious, then universal church liturgical practice is an equally dependable guide. But in giving an answer he does not avoid the hard work of first engaging the Corinthians. He doesn't jump too quickly to the universal practice argument (11:16). This shows remarkable restraint and respect toward the community he founded and toward the individuals whose faith he continues to guide as their father in the Lord.

II.5.2 Social Distinctions at the Lord's Supper, 11:17–34

Paul insists that the Corinthians may not tamper with the sexual distinctions of God's created order. (Here again, however, as with the question of sexual identity, 21st-century knowledge of gender formation raises questions Paul could not have begun to imagine.) But he takes the opposite stand in regard to man-made *socioeconomic* distinctions. He has heard disturbing reports that social and economic class divisions brought in from outside have been deforming their church life (11:21–22), bringing the patronage system of Corinthian society into their liturgical assemblies (11:18).[61] Such values should have no place in guiding the Christian community.

Paul also refuses to be guided by superficial liturgical appearances. The Corinthians may call what they do when they gather "the Lord's Supper," but their individualistic, elitist, and greedy behavior robs their gatherings of that name (11:20). The Lord will indeed be present, says Paul, regardless of their behavior, but the liturgy will be to their condemnation if they do not discern "the body" in both the bread and in the community (11:29; 11:31). It is precisely because the Lord is truly present that Paul takes their behavior at the eucharist so seriously. The Lord's Supper is not simply ritual or religious symbolism; a genuine encounter takes place, whether they accept that or not. What is offered to them through the bread and wine has an effect, with consequences for body and soul because *it is* the Lord's body and blood. This is why so many of them have become weak or sick and some have died (11:30). As Paul warned them earlier, this is what happened to the Israelites with their spiritual food and drink in the desert: "With most of them God was not pleased; for they were overthrown in the wilderness" (10:13). The Corinthians' participation in the eucharist implies their willingness to proclaim the voluntary, self-sacrificial death of the Lord on behalf of all, and to behave in a way that conforms to this. By sharing in the eucharist, they have signaled their willingness to be "in Christ" and to live sacrificially for others. This is exactly the same rationale he used when answering the question about food offered to idols. To treat the scruples of the other with complete disregard is to destroy "the brother for whom Christ died" (8:11) and therefore "to sin against Christ" (8:12).

For Paul, to be baptized is to die to individualism, to accept a new life in Christ no longer on one's own but in His Body. Participation in the Lord's Supper is the continuing manifestation of this. Conversely, to reintroduce individualism is to "not discern the body" (11:29):

> [27]Whoever, therefore, eats the bread or drinks the cup of the Lord in an unworthy manner will be answerable for the body and blood of the Lord. [28]Examine yourselves, and only then eat of the bread and drink of the cup. [29]For all who eat and drink without discerning the body, eat and drink judgment against themselves.

³⁰For this reason many of you are weak and ill, and some have died. ³¹But if we judged ourselves, we would not be judged. (1 Cor 11:27–31)

Although "body" (*sōma*) here also refers to the bread received as Christ's Body (11:24), Paul's purpose is to emphasize the mystical nature not of the bread and wine but of the *community*. The Corinthians were eager to recognize the spiritual power of the bread and wine, but they did not yet connect this with their behavior toward each other. Paul's aim is to correct this imbalance. He shows them that the eucharist is to be the guide to their behavior as a community. Indeed the behavior to which the term "judgment" refers is selfish individualism (11:29, 11:34). The Corinthians should not make the Lord's Supper the occasion for merely satisfying their private spiritual needs. To behave in this way and to shame others is to despise the church (11:22). Paul wants them to be more conscious of the church as a body, as a community in Christ. This makes it very different from a pagan temple. Thus they should wait for each other and celebrate the Lord's Supper together (11:33).

For Paul the main criteria for guiding behavior in the Christian community are Christ and the other person. Or rather, Christ *in* the other person. But Paul is not unrealistic; he understands that members of the Christian community lead lives that differ socially and economically. How and with whom they live and eat in their homes vary greatly from one family to the next. In Corinth we are already far away from the first idyllic Jerusalem community of Acts, when "all who believed were together and had all things in common" (Acts 2:44). But at least their celebration of the Lord's Supper must continue to reflect the new order Christ initiated. Corinthian liturgical life must therefore expel the world's social and economic prejudices and preoccupations.[62]

This disruptive incident about the Lord's Supper and who eats with whom demonstrates that even divisions can be a source of guidance, since they allow "those who are genuine among you to be recognized" (11:19). The eruption of "factions" (*aireseis*, "heresies"; 11:19) indicates that some are faithfully resisting those who are causing division. Peace alone is thus no sure guide to the church's spiritual health, since a community may be harmoniously united around goals and values antithetical to Christ.[63]

Three other observations are worth pointing out:

1. "I received from the Lord what I also delivered to you" (11:23) should not be understood as a form of direct divine revelation to Paul individually. As discussed earlier, it is a reference to the transmission of the tradition about the Lord's Supper in the early church, possibly from the Antiochene liturgy.[64] It implies that Paul viewed this tradition, preserved and passed on by the church even at this very early stage, as divine guidance directly from the Lord.

2. Paul's instructions give an essential place to individual conscience and self-knowledge: "Examine yourselves, and only then eat of the bread and drink of the cup. . . . For if we judged ourselves, we would not be judged" (11:28, 31). In other words, the more honest we are now with ourselves, the less surprised we will be when God judges our hearts at the end.

3. Evidently there were additional minor issues, probably also concerning their liturgical assemblies, but Paul says he will arrange these later when he comes (11:34). This points again to his authority to do so, although he prefers to consult with them in person.

II.5.3 Spiritual Gifts, 12:1–31

Paul's concern about the Corinthian view of the Lord's Supper is closely connected to guidance since the underlying question is this: On what basis are they to make decisions? So when he turns to spiritual gifts in chapters 12–14, his first comment harks back to how they had been guided in the past, *before* they became followers of Christ: "You know that, when you were gentiles, in whatever way you were led, you were being guided away to voiceless idols" (1 Cor 12:2, in Hart, *The New Testament*). As pointed out earlier, the church members were mostly Gentiles, and these former devotees of Greco-Roman religion perhaps now assumed that all spiritual experiences and the emotions that went with them were to be equated with the Holy Spirit. Paul agrees that they may have been moved in some fashion during pagan worship, but this was a delusion. Regardless of the numinous quality they attached to their experience, whatever they felt, they were misguided in trusting their emotions to be a sure test of divine truth.

Scholars still debate the uncertain background to chapter 12, especially "speaking in tongues."[65] What *is* clear is that Paul is trying to insert a new criterion for enabling the Corinthians to evaluate their spiritual experiences. Their new life in the church is not about generic spirituality or spiritual emotions but about Christ. *He* is the key to evaluating the authenticity of spiritual experience, and therefore any experience or person that leads them to curse Christ (or use His name as a curse?) cannot be from the Holy Spirit.[66] Conversely, *without* the Holy Spirit no one can recognize Jesus as Lord (*kyrios*, 12:3). This is the point Paul will elaborate throughout these two chapters: true spiritual experience within the church reflects the intimate connection between the Holy Spirit, Christ, and His Body. But this doesn't mean a narrowing down of spiritual life to the ecclesiastical. On the contrary, as Paul says so expansively in Philippians, being in Christ opens a much bigger world of "whatever is true, whatever is honorable, whatever is just, whatever is pure, whatever is pleasing, whatever is commendable" (Phil 4:8).[67]

Paul's subject in chapter 12 is stated in the first verse: "concerning the *pneumatikōn.*" This is most often thought to refer to spiritual gifts, *ta pneumatika*, as a synonym of *charismata*. But it is equally possible to interpret this as referring to spiritual persons (*oi pneumatikoi*), since Paul refers to the gifts almost exclusively in connection with the persons to whom they are given (12:4–11).[68] His closing arguments in 14:37—"If any one thinks he is a prophet or a spiritual person" (*pneumatikos*)—reinforce the view that he is primarily addressing questions about spiritual persons.[69]

How the Corinthians have been evaluating the relative worth of various spiritual gifts, people, and callings was a major factor in spawning the community's factions and disturbances, and Paul's aim here is to help guide the Corinthians toward healthier discernment. He has also been concerned from the start that the majority is too easily being led astray by excessive dependence on others—including Paul himself. They still have only a poor grasp of the calling and gifts each of them has received from God for the building up of the church. By again insisting on their divine guidance through the variety of spiritual gifts, Paul is trying to alleviate the problem caused by unhealthy dependence upon those who might prey on them through human wisdom, articulate speech, or apparent spirituality.[70]

Paul's argument in chapter 12 makes the following points in relation to guidance:

1. *Each* person is given the manifestation of the Spirit (12:7). As in the early part of the epistle Paul returns to stressing that God is in direct, unmediated relationship with every person in the church, giving a particular gift to each—without exception—for the common good, and in great variety (of which the lists here and in Rom 12 are but examples). The one Lord is active (*energei*) in all as He desires (12:6, 11).

2. The Spirit's gifts serve a single purpose: "the common good" (12:7). One of Paul's favorite words is *oikodomēn* (build up), which he uses in various forms to emphasize this purpose (8:1, 10:23). In chapter 14 he uses it eight times in close succession (14:3, 4, 5, 12, 17, 26). It should be noted that the dominant context here is the church community. The gifts are for "the building up of the church," since the members of the household of faith are to be the special object of Christian service (14:12; see also Gal 6:10). But Paul's outlook on doing good to others is not limited to the church, as he already told the Corinthians (10:31–11:1).[71]

3. No one can claim to have *the* spiritual gift. The variety and distribution of gifts among all the members of the church are designed by God to require them to come together in the exercise of those gifts. Only this communal approach will enable the Body of Christ to act to its full potential.

This applies both to individuals within the community and to relations between communities. This was one of the issues in Corinth, where at least some considered that they and their community were spiritually mature enough that they were beyond needing others. From the start Paul makes it clear to the Corinthians that there are *other* communities of saints calling upon the name of the Lord (1:2, cf. 14:36). In his communal emphasis, Paul may well have been influenced by contemporary Jewish thought, since, as noted earlier, it was widely believed that the Holy Spirit now rested on the Jewish community as a whole rather than on individual prophets.

4. By unpacking at length his understanding of the church as a body Paul makes it clear that relationships between persons are his primary concern, not abstract questions about the relative merit of various gifts. Competition and jealousy over charismatic gifts have become an issue in Corinth only because personal relations have broken down. If this has affected the majority it is only because they have lost a sense of their own direct calling in the Spirit. They have been ignorant regarding spiritual gifts and spiritual persons because they have not recognized their own gifts or not valued them or not exercised them (12:1). As a result they have been unable to carry out their responsibility within the body and have become easy prey for spiritual abusers. By connecting spiritual gifts with being profitable to others, Paul means to avoid the trap that has already led some to be puffed up and others to be servile (8:1).

5. The Corinthians are to be guided not by the social norms and distinctions to which they are accustomed but by the new pattern of relationships that spring from baptism and eucharist: "For by one Spirit we were all baptized into one body—Jews or Greeks, slaves or free—and all were made to drink of one Spirit" (12:13). Again we see Paul turning to the Corinthians' liturgical experience as the blueprint for their behavior. There is no self-sufficiency in the Body, for even the head cannot live apart from His Body (see Col 1:18; Eph 5:23). If there is any distinction of honor to be made among the Corinthians, then God's pattern displayed in the arrangement of the human body is the model. This, Paul says, is the reverse of the world's standard, since God gives greater honor to the weaker members (12:24; see also 1:26–28). There is to be no schism in the body, but the members are to care for each other (12:25). When parts of the body fight each other, that is the very definition of disease.

6. God has gone to the trouble of arranging church life in such a way that it would not depend exclusively on either His direct guidance or on outstanding individuals alone, but requires the collaboration of all the members of the body (12:27). God's guidance to the church has thus been

designed with a strong human and communal component through which the Spirit of God acts.

7. God guides the church through the gifts He distributes to the church as a whole, but there is a hierarchy among the gifts for the good ordering of the community's life. Paul views his ministry as an apostle as just one of the gifts of service in the church, but his outlook on apostolic authority, as already noted, is hardly democratic—though neither is it authoritarian. Thus apostles, prophets, and teachers are set apart from the rest of the vocations (12:27). This is significant and in keeping with Paul's view of his own authority as an apostle.[72] His enumeration gives clear priority to the teaching ministry within the church, since the first three—apostles, prophets, and teachers—are all closely associated with educating the hearts and minds of the faithful. There is a hierarchy in the functional value of gifts for the church's welfare. In this sense some gifts are more valuable, so that Paul can say, "Earnestly desire the higher gifts" (12:31; see also 14:1–25, 14:39). But lest the Corinthian competitive spirit send them running after gifts that their own criteria have decided are "the higher gifts"—namely wisdom, knowledge, ecstatic experiences, revelations, and speaking in tongues—Paul gives them another standard by which to judge the gifts. Rather than stamp out their competitive inclination, in the next section of his letter he redirects them to a new scale of values that will enable them to decide for themselves who is a genuine *pneumatikos*.

II.5.4 Divine Guidance and Love, 13:1–13

If I speak in the tongues of mortals and of angels, but do not have love, I am a noisy gong or a clanging cymbal. [2]And if I have prophetic powers, and understand all mysteries and all knowledge, and if I have all faith, so as to remove mountains, but do not have love, I am nothing. [3]If I give away all my possessions, and if I hand over my body so that I may boast [be burned],[73] but do not have love, I gain nothing.[4]Love is patient; love is kind; love is not envious or boastful or arrogant [5]or rude. It does not insist on its own way; it is not irritable or resentful; [6]it does not rejoice in wrongdoing, but rejoices in the truth. [7]It bears all things, believes all things, hopes all things, endures all things. [8]Love never ends. But as for prophecies, they will come to an end; as for tongues, they will cease; as for knowledge, it will come to an end. [9]For we know only in part, and we prophesy only in part; [10]but when the complete comes, the partial will come to an end. [11]When I was a child, I spoke like a child, I thought like a child, I reasoned like a child; when I became an adult, I put an end to childish ways. ¹²For now we see in a mirror, dimly, but then we will see face to face. Now I know only in part; then I will know fully, even as I have been fully known. ¹³And now faith, hope, and love abide, these three; and the greatest of these is love. (1 Cor 13:1–13)

For Paul the way of love makes relative all divine guidance and all the Spirit's gifts. The gifts he lists as examples in 13:1–3—ecstatic speech, prophecy, knowledge, miracle-working faith, even heroic charity and martyrdom—are without exception of temporary value in comparison to love. God's gift of prophecy—which he says later they should especially pursue (14:1, 14:39)—will also come to an end and be shown to be partial, childish, immature, and imperfect in the light of Christ's appearing at the last day (13:8–10). Paul sees all spiritual gifts in that bright eschatological light from the end of time, when the face-to-face vision of God will replace the dimly lit forms of divine guidance available until then (13:11–12).

If the gifts are imperfect and merely serve temporary purposes, what *does* endure eternally is the faith, hope, and love that inspire the use of one's gifts for the benefit of others (13:13). Thus, in Paul's eyes, how a person cooperates with the gift of God is of incomparably greater value than the gift itself. He therefore urges the Corinthians to make love their aim (14:1; see also 1 Tim 1:5). Although he says, "Earnestly desire the higher gifts" (12:31), he hopes they now understand that these gifts are not ends in themselves. The best gifts profit others by comforting, encouraging, consoling, and building them up (14:3). Paul encourages competitive spirituality but directs the Corinthians to a new idea of the finish line: "Since you are eager for manifestations of the Spirit, strive to excel in building up the church" (14:12).

It is remarkable how often Paul speaks about love, and not just in this well-known passage. John the Evangelist is known as the "Apostle of Love" and uses the word "love" 72 times in his gospel and epistles. But Paul uses the word 103 times, if all the writings attributed him are included (if not, then 62 times). In 1 Corinthians alone, besides chapter 13, he speaks of love in seven other passages:

- "What no eye has seen, nor ear heard, nor the human heart conceived, what God has prepared for those who love him"—these things God has revealed to us through the Spirit (1 Cor 2:9–10).
- "Am I to come to you with a stick, or with love in a spirit of gentleness?" (1 Cor 4:21).
- "Knowledge puffs up, but love builds up" (1 Cor 8:1).
- "[Anyone] who loves God is known by him" (1 Cor 8:3).
- "Let all that you do be done in love" (1 Cor 16:14).

- "Let anyone be accursed who has no love for the Lord" (1 Cor 16:22).
- "My love be with all of you in Christ Jesus" (1 Cor 16:24).

Whatever experience or thoughts Paul had of love in his previous life, everything changed after his encounter with the risen Christ. That unexpected and unmediated personal experience of Christ's love, he claimed, utterly transformed him and shaped the rest of his life, teaching, and ministry (1 Cor 2:2; Gal 1:11-24, 2:20; see also Acts 9, 22, 26).

For Paul, love is no abstract virtue: it takes the very precise shape of Christ on the Cross. It is this crucified, merciful love of Jesus Christ that became the personal foundation for Paul's convictions and way of life. "I am the least of the apostles, unfit to be called an apostle," he says, "because I persecuted the church of God; but by the grace of God I am what I am" (1 Cor 15: 9-10). Paul is ever conscious of this grace, for "it is by God's mercy that we are engaged in this ministry" (2 Cor 4:1). The old Paul the persecutor died, and the new Paul has no other life but the Crucified Christ (1 Cor 2:2). As he told the Galatians, "I have been crucified with Christ and I no longer live, but Christ lives in me. The life I now live in the body, I live by faith in the Son of God, who loved me and gave himself for me" (Gal 2:20-21; see also Col 3:3).

The Corinthian church community was consumed with looking for signs of their special knowledge, insight, and divine power. Paul takes advantage of this to point them to the "more excellent way," imitating the pattern of Christ's self-emptying love (see also Phil 2:5-11).[74] Such humble love for the weakest—not theological bickering, not desire for spiritual signs and wonders—is what will bring God's blessing and at the same time attract unbelievers.

II.5.5 Divine Guidance and the Rational Mind, 14:1-40

By putting God's gifts in the context of their communal purpose, Paul brings a corrective balance to the individualism of Corinthian spirituality. But he still has a battle on another front. If some gave excessive weight to wisdom and rhetoric, others had taken the opposite view and used spirituality as a way to circumvent rational thought entirely. Hence the special value they placed on speaking in tongues. Paul now introduces another counterbalance to assist in discernment: employing the rational mind together with the Spirit, using both faculties to work in tandem (14:15-20).

Paul is entirely unsatisfied with a spirituality that bypasses rational thought. Even the most charismatic liturgical gathering *requires* the mind's engagement so that those present may give their "amen" to the prayers and may be built up through instruction (14:16-19). For Paul this is essential because the liturgical assembly includes unbelievers and uninstructed novices (*idiōtai*, 1 Cor 14:16, 23, 24). Their minds and hearts might be touched by rational words spoken powerfully under the guidance of the Holy Spirit, but not at all by the incomprehensible spiritual experiences of others, such as speaking in tongues (*glossolalia*). If unbelievers or newcomers walk away or remain ignorant of Christian faith, then Paul lays the blame on the church, at least in part. If what the unbeliever hears in the assembly is gibberish, then he or she may rightly be excused for interpreting Christian liturgy as raving madness (14:22–23).

Paul puts prophecy at the top of his list of "the higher gifts," but instead of narrowing this gift to a select few, he opens it to everyone and emphatically desires that *all* would prophesy (14:24: he uses the word "all" three times in the one verse). This is parallel to Moses's response, who had a similar wish when Joshua reported that Eldad and Medad were guilty of unsanctioned prophesying: "And Joshua the son of Nun, the minister of Moses, one of his chosen men, said, 'My lord Moses, forbid them.' But Moses said to him, 'Are you jealous for my sake? Would that all the Lord's people were prophets, that the Lord would put his spirit upon them!'" (Num 11:28–29). In Paul's view, prophecy is not merely one among the spiritual gifts but colors all the other gifts and is accessible to all. Any other gift of the Spirit may be used prophetically to instruct and build up others in the liturgical assembly. This becomes clear in Paul's picture of liturgical life, where each brings some gift for the benefit of all (14:26–33).

Paul makes no fine distinctions between the divine guidance that comes through revelation, knowledge, or prophecy. C. K. Barrett argues that "all these activities . . . shaded into one another too finely for rigid distinctions."[75] But while there is no precise differentiation, they are all inspired utterances or actions that are clearly intelligible.[76] Paul's view of prophecy is thus in line with first-century Jewish thought, where scriptural instruction and prophecy were closely linked (14:31). As with all the gifts, these too work together within the church to promote interdependence and bonding within the Body of Christ. Thus while some speak, others are needed to interpret and discern so that everything may be done in peace and good order (14:29, 32, 33, 40).

Paul is careful to distinguish his view of prophecy from the popular view of pagan prophecy as "madness" (*mania*): "If, therefore, the whole church assembles and all speak in tongues, and outsiders or unbelievers enter, will they not say that you are mad [*mainesthe*]?" (14:23). "Prophet" (*prophētēs*) and its cognates was a word shared by Jews and Gentiles, but Paul never connects prophecy with any other Greek words associated with the *mania* of pagan divination.[77] Far from madness, prophetic words in Paul's definition are rational but divinely inspired words that produce in listeners—whether they welcome it or not—the immediate conviction that God is present. When prophetic words are welcomed they touch the heart and mind and bring people to desire a changed life (14:24–25). Or, in Hans Conzelmann's phrase, prophecy is inspired speech that works the "unmasking of man."[78]

Throughout 1 Cor 12–14 Paul has underlined that each person has divine gifts to bring to the church. All are interdependent in the Body of Christ and thus are jointly responsible for using their gifts peacefully for the benefit of all. In Paul's experience, both rational and mystical are inspired by the same Spirit and must have a home in the church. Thus he ends his teaching on spiritual gifts with encouragement toward balance: "So, my friends, be eager to prophesy, and do not forbid speaking in tongues; but all things should be done decently and in order"(14:39–40).

II.5.6 Divine Guidance and Women in the Assembly, 14:34–35

> As in all the churches of the saints, [34]women should be silent in the churches. For they are not permitted to speak, but should be subordinate, as the law also says. [35]If there is anything they desire to know, let them ask their husbands at home. For it is shameful for a woman to speak in church. (1 Cor 14:34–35, NRSV)

> Wives must not disrupt worship, talking when they should be listening, asking questions that could more appropriately be asked of their husbands at home. God's Book of the law guides our manners and customs here. Wives have no license to use the time of worship for unwarranted speaking. (1 Cor 14:34–35, Eugene Peterson, *The Message*)

> [[34]Let the women in the assemblies be silent, for it is not entrusted to them to speak; rather let them be subordinate, as the Law also says. [35]But, if they want to learn anything, let them inquire of their own husbands at home, for it is an unseemly thing for a woman to speak in an assembly.] (1 Cor 14:34–35, David Bentley Hart, *The New Testament: A Translation*)

The final topic to address in this section on divine guidance and liturgical questions is the role of women in the liturgical assembly. The verses just quoted are controversial. Some scholars and translators, like Eugene Peterson, argue that the context is not about women in general but about disruptive relationships between husbands and wives spilling into the church assembly. (The same Greek word, *gynaika*, is used for both "woman" and "wife," just as *andros* is both "man" and "husband.") But many leading commentators, like David Bentley Hart, have argued persuasively that these two verses were added later by someone else and are not part of Paul's original letter. (Hart's translation brackets these two verses, "as they clearly constitute an interpolation that breaks the flow of the text, and that seems to be written in a voice unlike Paul's, and that contradicts other passages in Paul.")[79] These verses do in fact contradict the internal evidence from the rest of 1 Corinthians, which assumes that women are prophesying, praying, and sharing their spiritual gifts in the assembly (see 1 Cor 11:5, 13, 14:23–24, 26).[80] Added to this is the confusing textual history of 1 Cor 14:34–35, with its varying placement in the manuscript tradition, which further undermines the likelihood of Paul's authorship.

That said, the sentiments expressed in 14:34–35 are clearly in harmony with 1 Timothy 2:11–15: "Let a woman learn in silence with all submissiveness. I permit no woman to teach or to have authority over men; she is to keep silent. For Adam was formed first, then Eve; and Adam was not deceived, but the woman was deceived and became a transgressor. Yet woman will be saved through bearing children, if she continues in faith and love and holiness, with modesty." Once again, however, most scholars discount 1–2 Timothy and Titus (the Pastoral Epistles) as not written by Paul himself. They came from Paul's circle of disciples and may express recollections of his words, but on the whole they reflect a later and less egalitarian phase of the church's development. So I agree with interpreters who believe 1 Cor 14:34–35 was added by later editors to make 1 Corinthians conform to later practice.[81] If this is true, then there is no basis in Paul's own thought for claiming that women do not receive gifts from God that might include praying, speaking, teaching in church, even asking questions, or that they should be forbidden the use of those gifts in church.

Still, even if verses 14:34–35 are not Paul's, this does not eliminate the questions raised by their inclusion in the canon of scripture and the support this view finds elsewhere in the New Testament and in later church tradition. To Paul's understanding of tradition and its place in divine guidance we now return.

II.6 Divine Guidance through Tradition, 15:1–11

Now I would remind you, brothers and sisters, of the good news that I proclaimed to you, which you in turn received, in which also you stand, [2]through which also you are being saved, if you hold firmly to the message that I proclaimed to you—unless you have come to believe in vain. [3]For I handed on to you as of first importance what I in turn had received: that Christ died for our sins in accordance with the scriptures, [4]and that he was buried, and that he was raised on the third day in accordance with the scriptures, [5]and that he appeared to Cephas, then to the twelve. [6]Then he appeared to more than five hundred brothers and sisters at one time, most of whom are still alive, though some have died [fallen asleep]. [7]Then he appeared to James, then to all the apostles. [8]Last of all, as to one untimely born, he appeared also to me. [9]For I am the least of the apostles, unfit to be called an apostle, because I persecuted the church of God. [10]But by the grace of God I am what I am, and his grace toward me has not been in vain. On the contrary, I worked harder than any of them—though it was not I, but the grace of God that is with me. [11]Whether then it was I or they, so we proclaim and so you have come to believe. (1 Cor 15:1–11)

As in the previous section, on liturgical practices, Paul comes back to the nascent Christian tradition, which in turn is rooted in the scriptural tradition of Israel and the direct testimony of living human beings, Paul included, who witnessed the risen Christ. The Corinthians didn't have this direct historical experience themselves, but they trusted, believed, had faith in the apostolic witness. Or at least they had enough trust in the apostolic witness to test for themselves the life in Christ. This was not just about faith; it was about trusting and then imitating the example to personally verify the claims of faith. They were willing to be guided by the claims of others, at first, but then had to confirm for themselves the truth of those claims.

We see here a repeated pattern of receiving and handing on, which is the literal meaning of the Greek *paradosis*, "tradition." In 11:2 Paul explained why he was praising the Corinthians: "Because you remember me in everything and maintain the traditions [*paradoseis*] just as I handed them on to you [*paredōka*]." There he was speaking about liturgical tradition, while here he is talking about the tradition of the gospel, the *evangelion* (15:1). But both these traditions, it should be remembered, were *new* in the eyes of first-century Jews and Gentiles. As a well-trained rabbinic scholar Paul understood the value of ancient tradition, but he also knew that he had experienced in Christ a new dimension of God that overturned his certainties. This is what transformed him from persecutor to apostle.

Excursus on Tradition: Jaroslav Pelikan and Elaine Pagels

As noted throughout this chapter, Paul was simultaneously both a challenger and an upholder of tradition. His intent was not to maintain received tradition as such—that was impossible given his new experience of Jesus Christ—but to pass on an emerging tradition now shaped by the new life in Christ inspired by the Holy Spirit.[82]

The later church, in the face of constant threats to its integrity, sought to defend the apostolic tradition it had received, nurtured, and further developed. This is the main point of Jaroslav Pelikan's monumental study of the Christian creeds, *Credo*.[83] He is positive about this development in Christian history, but is also critical of its potential for ugliness when theological enemies are identified and repelled.

Elaine Pagels, on the other hand, a persistent critic of Christian tradition, is not unsympathetic to some of the features that make tradition attractive in a fragmented, rootless society searching for transcendence, authenticity, warmth, and community. This comes out especially in her 2004 book, *Beyond Belief: The Secret Gospel of Thomas*.[84] Her earlier book, *The Gnostic Gospels* (1979), claimed that the Gnostics were legitimate early interpreters of Jesus who were unfairly suppressed by traditionalists. While this conclusion was controversial, both books raise a number of important questions about tradition and heresy, all of which come down to the question of discernment, which is precisely the faculty Paul was seeking to teach the Corinthians.

As Pelikan points out, the downside of protecting tradition is the demonizing of dissenters. Thus as Christian history unfolded, the laws governing dissent, schismatics, heretics, and followers of other religions became increasingly restrictive, first within the church and then in collaboration with the state under Emperor Constantine (272–337) and his successors. Gradually it became illegal not only to go against the Creed but to go beyond it. By the time of Theodosius the Great (347–395), diversity itself was proof of error, and the Theodosian Code used language that precluded the very idea of any diversity of confessions. This outlook, says Pelikan, found its way into every Christian creed and confession of East and West. Quoting Alfred North Whitehead, he says, "Where there is a creed, there is a heretic round the corner or in his grave."[85] In this sense, instead of being formulas of concord, creeds often became "formulas of discord."[86]

The framework that emerged to protect Christianity's integrity through canon, creed, and hierarchy focused on maintaining a supposedly unchanging Tradition with a capital "T." In this worldview the very words "innovation," "new," and "change" became expletives. Nevertheless both Pagels and Pelikan, from two very different points of view, remark that there was still surprising room for creativity, which Pagels calls disguised innovation.[87] It was innovation by stealth, as succeeding generations of teachers and ecumenical councils kept repeating the mantra of tradition while at the same time actually introducing striking changes. Pelikan cites as examples the First Ecumenical Council at Nicea (325), with its introduction of the nonscriptural term *homoousios* (one in essence) to describe the union of the Father and the Son. The Third Ecumenical Council at Ephesus (431) endorsed the new term *Theotokos* to describe the role of Mary, "the God bearer."[88] My favorite example is the Quinisext Council, also known as "In Trullo" (692), which banned what had heretofore been a perfectly acceptable symbolic depiction of Christ as the victorious Lamb. To combat growing pressure from iconoclasm, with its excessive preference for the symbolic and metaphorical, the Council decided that new emphasis was needed on the historical and incarnational. Icons of Jesus Christ as God incarnate in history were therefore to be promoted. But the *traditional* symbolic image of the Lamb would cause confusion and had to go.[89]

Each time such an innovation was introduced, past texts were reread to find the inspired "new" doctrine or practice in the ancient tradition, thus showing unbroken continuity. This, of course, was the basic hermeneutical method in the New Testament's use of the Old Testament. It was also fundamental to rabbinic interpretation because it allowed the biblical text to remain sacredly unchanging while introducing new interpretations adapted to new contexts (the Messianic rereading of prophecy being the prime example).

It has been said that the church changed in order to remain the same.[90] It was this ability to adapt to new situations and challenges that often resulted in schism with the most conservative groups, who were gradually left behind. This was the case of those who opposed the new Trinitarian formulation or who objected to calling Mary *Theotokos*. But it was also true of the Novationists (third century) and Donatists (fourth to sixth century), who broke communion with the rest of the church not on theological grounds but for being too lax toward sinners. These rigorists resisted the tide of compassion that swept through the wider church as it sought to deal with the thousands of Christians who had compromised or lapsed during times of persecution. The discipline of the church, says Pelikan, was obliged to deal with violations of unity and love as well as with violations of faith and doctrine. Sadly, in their rigidity the traditionalists found themselves on the wrong side of both history and the church's Tradition.

II.7 Divine Guidance through the Resurrection, 15:12–58

For Paul, faith in Christ is pointless without the resurrection of Christ. This was central to his proclamation of the gospel. But some in Corinth were denying belief in resurrection of the dead (15:12), probably as part of a general tendency to downplay the physical, bodily, and material in favor of the spiritual, incorporeal, and immaterial. They might have accepted Christ's own resurrection and appearances, but why this meant *everyone* would be physically resurrected was unclear to them. And for Gentiles, resurrection was an odd idea. (It was a familiar though disputed belief among Jews, with Sadducees denying resurrection: Matt 22:23; Mark 12:18; Luke 20:27; see also Dan 12:1; 2 Macc 7:14, 12:43; 2 Esdras 2:23.) Some sort of life for the soul after death they could understand, even the transmigration of souls (*metempsychosis*), as taught by Plato and Pythagoras. This was commonly accepted in the Greco-Roman world, but not bodily resurrection.

Corinthians' assumptions about the body—and specifically their hesitancy about resurrection of the body—had important consequences for their attitudes toward bodily action, sacrifice, service, sexuality, and ascetic practice. Paul wants their thinking and behavior to be grounded in and guided by the resurrection. So he underlines the bodily reality of the death, burial, and resurrection of Christ as verified by human witnesses and received by the Corinthians through the preaching of the apostles. Jesus Christ truly died, was buried, was raised, and was seen by witnesses (15:1–11).

Christ's bodily resurrection implies that the body is central to the spirituality of the Christian. Paul stresses this by his repeated use of *sōma* and related words: 9 times just in chapter 15 and 35 times in 1 Corinthians, which is almost three times more often than he uses the word in Romans (13 times), the letter where it is cited next most often. For Paul, denial of the body is a sign that these Corinthians are advocating a form of spirituality that cuts itself off from the realities of life and death. Denial of the body also empties of significance the present efforts and suffering of believers (15:30–34). Just as the "strong" Corinthians argued that the nonexistence of pagan "gods" justified eating in temples, so—if the body is of no eternal significance—they could also justify doing what they liked with it (15:32). Likewise, such a view of the body could allow them to dismiss the real physical and material needs of others, since what really matters is only the spiritual. But if the Lord's Body is risen, then not only are the dead raised, but the body is of permanent and divine value. And no bodily labor or suffering or ascetic effort "in the Lord" is thus in vain. Paul can even state in Colossians, "I am now rejoicing in my sufferings for your sake, and in my flesh *I am completing what is lacking in Christ's afflictions* for the sake of his body, that is, the church" (Col 1:24, my emphasis). Such is the redemptive and eternal value Paul attributes to the body.

Paul uses "labor" (*kopos*) to highlight the physical, strenuous, bodily dimension of apostolic work (15:58).[91] His argument about the resurrection of the body is directly related to his concern about what is guiding Corinthian decision-making on a host of daily work-life issues. While insisting on the permanent value of labor for the Lord, he is also certain that such work is accomplished successfully only with God's grace and guidance. Paul is able to state unequivocally that in comparison with the rest of the apostles he "worked harder than any of them," but he remains conscious that his calling is an undeserved gift from God, whose overwhelming grace working in him and with him makes his labor possible: "It was not I, but the grace of God which is with me" (15:10). Paul can no longer attribute to himself the slightest credit for who he is and what he has done, with the single exception of his sins: "For I am the least of the apostles, unfit to be called an apostle, because I persecuted the church of God" (15:9). Without offering us any further details, he makes it clear that he depends on God's grace at all times. In all his varied movements, decisions, arguments, reasoning, writing, labors, and suffering he is continually aware of God's presence, even if he doesn't always have a direct word of assured guidance.

However, on this occasion Paul does say that his insight into the resurrection did come through the mystery of direct divine guidance:[92]

> [51]Listen, I will tell you a mystery! We will not all [fall asleep], but we will all be changed, [52]in a moment, in the twinkling of an eye, at the last trumpet. For the trumpet will sound, and the dead will be raised imperishable, and we will be changed. [53]For this perishable body must put on imperishability, and this mortal body must put on immortality. [54]When this perishable body puts on imperishability, and this mortal body puts on immortality, then the saying that is written will be fulfilled:
>
> "Death has been swallowed up in victory."
> [55]"Where, O death, is your victory?
> Where, O death, is your sting?"
> [56]The sting of death is sin, and the power of sin is the law. [57]But thanks be to God, who gives us the victory through our Lord Jesus Christ.
>
> [58]Therefore, my beloved, be steadfast, immovable, always excelling in the work of the Lord, because you know that in the Lord your labor is not in vain. (1 Cor 15:51–58)

Paul links this new revelation with past prophecies in Isaiah and Hosea: "Then shall come to pass the saying that is written: 'Death is swallowed up in victory'" (Isa 25:8). As is his pattern, Paul's citation of scripture is adapted to his purposes. Here he combines an idiosyncratic text of Isaiah 25:8 with Hosea 13:14, but modifies the latter. Thus "O Death, where is your sentence [LXX, or "your plagues," Heb.]?" is transformed into "O Death, where is your *victory*."[93] Inserting a single changed word into the text may seem like a minor point, and as we have seen, such interpretive freedom was common in Judaism. But it is one more piece of evidence that while Paul abhors the thought of "misrepresenting God" (15:15), his sense of divine guidance frees him from slavery to the letter of the law and the text.

II.8 Divine Guidance through the Needs of Others, 16:1–4

Having ended his defense of bodily resurrection and bodily spirituality with the exhortation to abound in the work of the Lord (15:58), Paul now offers the

Corinthians a practical opportunity to apply this message by putting in front of them the plight of the Jerusalem poor.[94] They had obviously heard of this before since Paul immediately jumps into the administrative details of the collection. They had already agreed to send relief (see 2 Cor 9:1–2); Paul is merely setting up the procedure that will enable them to make good. They apparently needed a push, perhaps because the Corinthian Christians were more at home in spirituality than in the mundane demands of helping people in distress. They are dragging their feet and need clear instructions on how and when to collect. The process Paul follows is instructive for understanding his approach to guidance and decision-making in practice:

1. He issues an order, the same order he gave to churches in Galatia, about the mechanics of making a collection for the saints in Jerusalem, showing the Corinthians that there is good precedent. By the time he wrote 2 Corinthians they still hadn't delivered, so Paul once again points to another community—the poverty-stricken Macedonians—who despite their meager resources in comparison to the Corinthians, "overflowed in a wealth of liberality" (2 Cor 8:2). They gave "beyond their means, of their own free will, begging us earnestly for the favor of taking part in the relief of the saints" (2 Cor 8:3–4). He thus guides them with the example of others through some healthy competition and modest shame.

2. Each of them, not merely the wealthy, is to set aside *something*. But what they give is to be their own decision, based on how they have prospered (16:2). In a society accustomed to wealthy patrons footing the bill, this may have been regarded as novel, but Paul consistently seeks to spread to everyone both the responsibility for the church's welfare and the spiritual satisfaction of generous giving.[95]

3. Paul links the collection with the liturgical week, telling them to set something aside "on the first day of every week" (*kata mian sabbatou*), i.e., on Sunday. Although nothing is said here about the collection being taken at the liturgical assembly, this is a reasonable assumption given that Paul did not want to make the collection when he arrived (16:2). This is more than just a practical way to collect money; it underlines the connection Paul has repeatedly emphasized between their liturgical celebration of the Lord's Supper and how they relate to each other in the Body of Christ.

4. The collection is to be made before he arrives. Three reasons may stand behind this. First, it could spare them the embarrassment of making a small collection when he arrived. Second, it could be Paul's way of keeping his preaching separate from financial appeals (see 1 Cor 9:15; 1 Thess 2:5–9). Third, by making the collection over a period of weeks the

Corinthians could get practice in making social action a regular part of their communal life.

5. *They* are to choose who will go to Jerusalem with their gift, although Paul will also send a letter of commendation (16:4). This keeps the transaction honest, maintains Paul's authority, and reinforces their responsibility—and credit—for the collection.

6. Paul is still unsure whether or not he will go to Jerusalem. The various English translations for the Greek *ean de axion* are all variations on "if it is advisable," "if it is meet," "if it is fitting, "if it is suitable." But John Chrysostom understands this more concretely: he says that the decision hinges on whether the donation is worthy (*axios*), in other words, if it's big enough. If the collection is good, then Paul will accompany the delegation from Corinth to Jerusalem. Again Paul seems to be taking gentle advantage of their competitive pride.

7. The Corinthians finally make a sizable collection, but only after much further stalling and more cajoling from Paul, who tells them he was on the cusp of serious shame, having boasted to others about their big intentions (2 Cor 9:1–15). In the end they came through with a decent gift, so he postpones his visit to Rome. Writing from Corinth he tells the Roman community that he can't visit them right away, as originally planned, explaining, "I am going to Jerusalem with aid for the saints": "For Macedo'nia and Acha'ia have been pleased to make some contribution for the poor among the saints at Jerusalem; they were pleased to do it, and indeed they are in debt to them, for if the Gentiles have come to share in their spiritual blessings, they ought also to be of service to them in material blessings" (Rom 15:25–28).

II.9 Uncertain Guidance, 16:5–12

Paul's travel plans give us a window into his decision-making when conditions are uncertain:

1. Paul was based at Ephesus in Asia Minor while he was writing to the Corinthians. Ephesus was almost directly across the Aegean Sea from Corinth, about a week away if traveling briskly by sea. The land route north from Ephesus, through Macedonia and south to Athens and then Corinth, would take much longer (it was about 1,400 kilometers), but Paul planned to makes short stops at the Macedonian congregations and then stay on in Corinth for a substantial visit, perhaps even through the winter, rather than rushing through a brief stop now. His guiding motivation is to spend an

extended period of time with the Corinthians. He has a plan, but it remains conditional on the Lord's permission (16:7).

2. His intention is to remain in Ephesus through the spring. He is motivated by awareness that (1) a large door for effective work has been opened to him and that (2) there are many "adversaries" (16:2). What is notable here is that while Paul views the positive response to his preaching and teaching as God's guidance to pursue his mission (2 Cor 2:12; Col 4:3), he does not view opposition as a sign to redirect or abandon his work. This is a key point that is repeated throughout his writing. Far from basing his mission on signs of prosperity, he has founded his ministry on what many would have viewed as the most inauspicious signs of opposition from Jews and Gentiles, from church members, from the Roman state, and from his own fears and anxieties:

> [24]Five times I have received at the hands of the Jews the forty lashes less one. [25]Three times I have been beaten with rods; once I was stoned. Three times I have been shipwrecked; a night and a day I have been adrift at sea; [26]on frequent journeys, in danger from rivers, danger from robbers, danger from my own people, danger from Gentiles, danger in the city, danger in the wilderness, danger at sea, danger from false brethren; [27]in toil and hardship, through many a sleepless night, in hunger and thirst, often without food, in cold and exposure. [28]And, apart from other things, there is the daily pressure upon me of my anxiety for all the churches. [29]Who is weak, and I am not weak? Who is made to fall, and I am not indignant? (2 Cor 11:24–29; see also 1 Cor 4:9–13; Acts 18:9–11)

This identification with the weak conforms to Paul's driving motivation to shape his life around "Christ and him crucified" (1 Cor 2:2). Far from being dissuaded or discouraged by weakness and opposition or thinking that God must be against him, Paul most often takes adversity as the paradoxical sign that he is on the path of grace and divine power. Indeed it was his experience of weakness—more than divine revelations—that strengthened his identity with the Crucified Christ. He famously learned this when he was asking God to remove his persistent "thorn in the flesh":

> [8]Three times I besought the Lord about this, that it should leave me; [9]but he said to me, "My grace is sufficient for you, for my power is made perfect in weakness." I will all the more gladly boast of my weaknesses, that the power of Christ may rest upon me. [10]For the sake of Christ, then, I am content with weaknesses, insults, hardships, persecutions, and calamities; for when I am weak, then I am strong. (2 Cor 12:8–10)

3. This paradoxical approach to weakness turns upside down the popular divine guidance calculations of the ancient world, both Jewish and Gentile. Bad things happen to bad people; good things happen to good people; and if something bad happens to someone who *appears* to be good, then there must be some hidden, secret sin lurking in his or her life. Job's friends took this view of his suffering, and Proverbs 12:21 puts this view succinctly: "No harm happens to the righteous, but the wicked are filled with trouble."

The reactions of the Maltese to Paul after the wreck of the ship carrying him and other prisoners is typical of this outlook (Acts 28):

> [3]Paul had gathered a bundle of sticks and put them on the fire, when a viper came out because of the heat and fastened on his hand. [4]When the natives saw the creature hanging from his hand, they said to one another, "No doubt this man is a murderer. Though he has escaped from the sea, justice has not allowed him to live." [5]He, however, shook off the creature into the fire and suffered no harm. [6]They waited, expecting him to swell up or suddenly fall down dead; but when they had waited a long time and saw no misfortune come to him, they changed their minds and said that he was a god. (Acts 28:3–6)

For the Maltese, only a god could thwart the otherwise inexorable justice of the universe.

4. Paul deflects attention away from himself in order to magnify the ministry of his younger protégé Timothy. This demonstrates that Paul is not interested in becoming the sole repository of divine grace for the Corinthians. He is on the lookout for God's hand at work in the ministries of others. Likewise he refuses to accept the adversarial relationship the Corinthians have set up between himself and Apollos, although he is keenly aware of the trouble Apollos's presence has caused through no fault of his own. Instead he reminds them that he and Apollos are brothers and very much on speaking terms (16:12). Far from preventing Apollos from returning to Corinth, Paul encourages him to go, leaving the final decision entirely up to him.

This freedom to decide is a point John Chrysostom develops in connection with Titus's decision to visit Corinth (2 Cor 8:16–17). The decision-making process is one of synergy between God and Titus. God puts concern for the Corinthians in Titus's heart, but it is Titus's own decision to act on that concern and go to Corinth: "Observe how [Paul] also represents [Titus] as fulfilling his own part, and needing no prompting from others. And having mentioned the grace of God, he does not leave the whole to be

God's; again, that by this also he may win them unto greater love, having said that he was stirred up from himself also" (John Chrysostom *Homilies on 1 Corinthians*, 18.1).

5. Paul regards his process of decision-making on travel plans at the end of 1 Corinthians important enough to address again at the start of 2 Corinthians, by which time it has become apparent to everyone that his initial plans had changed:

> [16]I wanted to visit you on my way to Macedo'nia, and to come back to you from Macedo'nia and have you send me on my way to Judea. [17]Was I vacillating when I wanted to do this? Do I make my plans like a worldly man, ready to say Yes and No at once? [18]As surely as God is faithful, our word to you has not been Yes and No. . . . [23]But I call God to witness against me—it was to spare you that I refrained from coming to Corinth. [24]Not that we lord it over your faith; we work with you for your joy, for you stand firm in your faith. (2 Cor 1:12–24)

Paul is at pains to convince the Corinthians he is not being two-faced. He simply wanted to spare them what might have been an awkward and painful encounter. Such was his anxiety that he even abandoned the promising mission he says God opened to him in Troas. Instead he goes to Macedonia to meet Titus in order to hear the latest news from Corinth (2 Cor 2:12–13). This little incident is illuminating because it demonstrates once again Paul's conviction that all forms of divine guidance are secondary to restoring the bonds of love between people and communities. Even God's clear guidance, which led him to the Troas mission, is less important than repairing, preserving, and building his relationship with the Corinthians (see also 1 Cor 16:14; 2 Cor 5:14ff.).

II.10   Final Instructions and Greetings, 16:13–24

[13]Keep alert, stand firm in [the] faith, be courageous, be strong. [14]Let all that you do be done in love. [15]Now, brothers and sisters, you know that members of the household of Stephanas were the first converts in Achaia, and they have devoted themselves to the service of the saints; [16]I urge you to put yourselves at the service of such people, and of everyone who works and toils with them. [17]I rejoice at the coming of Stephanas and Fortunatus and Achaicus, because they have made up for your absence; [18]for they refreshed my spirit as well as yours. So give recognition to such persons.

[19]The churches of Asia send greetings. Aquila and Prisca, together with the church in their house, greet you warmly in the Lord. [20]All the brothers and sisters send greetings. Greet one another with a holy kiss. [21]I, Paul, write this greeting with my own hand. [22]Let anyone be accursed who has no love for the Lord. Our Lord, come [*Marana tha*]! [23]The grace of the Lord Jesus be with you. [24]My love be with all of you in Christ Jesus. (1 Cor 16:13–24)

These simple final instructions and greetings act as a summary of much that Paul has been telling the Corinthians about divine guidance:

1. He reminds them that they all need to take responsibility for their lives in Christ and for the health of the church. He uses a string of strong active verbs antithetical to the passive spirituality to which they had fallen prey: "Be watchful, stand firm in the faith, be courageous, be strong" (*Grēgoreite, stēkete en tē pistei andrizesthe, krataiousthe*; 16:13; see Figure 13.2).[96]

2. Love is to be the controlling guide to their decisions: "Let all that you do be done in love" (16:14). By this point in the letter the Corinthians should understand that Paul's image of love is very specific: Christ on the Cross.

3. They are responsible for discerning who are the ones among them capable of leadership in the community, the genuinely spiritual persons (*pneumatikoi*) to whose voices and examples they should give heed. He gives them Stephanas's household as a model because (1) they are longtime converts, (2) "they have devoted themselves to the service of the saints" (16:15), and (3) they have remained in generous fellowship with everyone, including Paul. With this example—and others, like Fortunatus and Achaicus—Paul now leaves the Corinthians to decide for themselves who else are the servant-leaders to whom they should submit (16:16, 18). Thus, for Paul, hierarchical, communal, and personal are woven together as the people follow leaders they choose on the basis of their public record of life and service in the church.

4. The greetings from the church in Asia, from Aquila, Prisca, the church in their house, and all the brethren are more than conventional for Paul (16:19). These personal bonds underline the point he has been making throughout the letter: the church is the Body of Christ. In Christ the church is a network of new family relationships, not merely a common faith, doctrine, liturgy, or spirituality. And certainly not a racial, ethnic, tribal, socioeconomic, or political enclave. The Corinthians are not their own; they "have been bought with a price" (1 Cor 6:20). But neither are

Fig. 13.2. Gate of Selwyn College, Cambridge. (Wikimedia Commons).

they *on* their own; they belong to a communion of local churches, with whose members they have all become brothers and sisters through baptism (16:19–20).

5. Paul underscores this personal dimension by telling them, "Greet one another with a holy kiss" (16:20; see also Rom 16:16; 2 Cor 13:12; 1 Thess 5:26). This would have had special poignancy in light of the divisions he has addressed as their main problem. Some scholars see here the origins of the "kiss of peace" at the eucharist, although as a liturgical act this can be dated with certainty only from the second century (Justin Martyr, *Second Apology* 165).[97] At this early stage of liturgical development the "holy kiss" was probably not a liturgical rite, and this makes it even more significant as a sign of genuine personal communion within the church. On the other hand, if it was a liturgical gesture, then Paul's insistence on a *holy* kiss would be entirely in keeping with his view that liturgy and behavior must conform to each other.

6. In his own hand Paul adds the final greeting: "If any one has no love for the Lord, let him be accursed [*anathema*]" (16:22). This curse would have come as a shock if the Corinthians had been lulled into thinking that Paul's view of love was all too soft, or if they were tempted to interpret love in any way other than as Christ on the Cross. *Anathema* was not a vague imprecation but a technical term used in the Septuagint to translate the Hebrew *herem*, the holy ban used in the Torah for sacred destruction at the command of God. In Paul's day it meant banishment from the community. Nor was this mere hyperbole: exclusion was precisely what Paul had prescribed to be carried out by the assembly in 1 Cor 5:1–5 (see Gal 1:8, 9; Ezra 10:8). Thus Paul puts love and *anathema* together in one sentence, without any hint of apology (16:22). It might be temporary exclusion (as in that earlier case), but it was a form of tough love he was not hesitant to apply if necessary as a last resort to both protect the community and correct the individual. For Paul, love for the Lord is what ultimately must guide decision-making in the church, but this love is a double-edged sword that paradoxically both separates and unites.[98]

7. "Our Lord, come!" (*Marana tha*, Aramaic; 16:22): Paul sees everything in light of the eschaton, the Lord's return at the last day. For now, that eternal Kingdom is known only "through a glass, darkly" (13:12). In the light of that never-ending day *all* guidance in this age is partial and imperfect and leads to decisions no less partial and imperfect, the inadequacies of which will be corrected at the coming of the Lord, for "when the perfect comes the imperfect will pass away" (13:10). In the meantime Paul desires that the Corinthians would have the grace of the Lord Jesus with them in everything, as they look forward to His return (16:23).

8. "My love be with you all in Christ Jesus. Amen" (16:24). Paul's final words bring the Corinthians back from the eschaton to Paul's own earnest love for them in the present. His example, more than anything he said or wrote, revealed to them the true meaning of divine guidance in this life.

Summary: Decisions and Divine Guidance in 1 Corinthians

This survey of 1 Corinthians has shown that questions about divine guidance are explicitly and implicitly woven throughout the varied topics Paul addresses. While he is firmly rooted in the Jewish tradition, he charts a new and distinctive approach to divine guidance based not on the Torah but on direction by the Spirit revealed to all who put their faith in the Crucified Christ and seek to follow His example in their life. 1 Corinthians is an extended attempt to rebuild the confidence of the majority in the personal and communal direction of Christ through the Spirit, to awaken their sense of responsibility for the community's life, and to wean them from excessive dependence on human guides.

The Spirit's presence and direction are basic to Paul's view of Christian life. But decision-making for Paul (as in Judaism) involves much more than individual and immediate divine guidance. He firmly upholds the role of rational thought in making decisions. Likewise he understands that the Spirit's direction can be experienced in a variety of ways, and especially in the community: through Scripture, preaching, service, apostolic and hierarchical order, teachers, and liturgical life. These communal modes of divine guidance balance the potential deceptions of individual claims. Yet neither his own apostolic authority nor these communal checks and balances are ever allowed to eclipse the mystery of God's direct and unpredictable guidance in the new age of the Spirit.

For Paul access to the Spirit comes through following Christ Crucified. All other divine guidance is secondary to being a disciple of the Crucified Christ. As he said in 1 Cor 2:2, "I decided to know nothing among you except Christ, and him crucified." The link between Christ's Cross and the Spirit cannot be overemphasized when looking at Paul's view of divine guidance in the context of Jewish and Greco-Roman thought. The Cross was a "stumbling block" to the Jews and utter foolishness to the Gentiles (1 Cor 1:23). The preaching of the Cross turned upside down conventional Jewish and Gentile notions of divine guidance, since Paul was proclaiming that the worst possible sign—horrific and shameful death by crucifixion—was the very sign God had chosen to overturn the world's expectations and bring victory over sin and death. Through the Cross of Christ and all it represents the point of greatest weakness is revealed as the channel of God's most profound guidance and grace.

The joining of the Cross and the Spirit has implications at every level for Paul's understanding of divine guidance. Above all, it means that he does not view adversity and suffering as signs that his course of action is wrong or that God is displeased. On the contrary, to share in the suffering of Christ is Paul's glory, just as the Crucified Christ is "the King of Glory," as inscribed on Byzantine icons of Christ on the Cross. The Cross and the Spirit bound together in Paul reveal what Alexander Schmemann called the "bright sadness" of the Christian way.[99] For Paul, the Cross of Christ is God's most profound guidance, paradoxically transforming weakness, adversity, and death into strength, joy, and unending life.

PART IV
REPRISE: DIVINE GUIDANCE IN THE FIRST AND 21ST CENTURIES

14

Divine Guidance

Continuing the Conversation into the 21st Century

I recently came across an account of a Roman Catholic man, the son of an ex-priest and an ex-nun, trying to decide whether he should pursue a vocation as a monk. After years of questioning and exploration he finally came to the point of visiting a monastery to immerse himself in the monastic life for several months. At the end of that time he still wasn't sure, and as he sat alone in the chapel competing thoughts came crowding in.

> Dear God, I prayed, couldn't you for once make something simple?
> "Please," I said.
> For a moment there was only silence, but then I heard a voice above me, an
>   answer to all my prayers. The biblical cliché for such pronouncements
>   is that it comes in the kind of "still, small voice" heard by the prophet
>   Elijah. This one rang out like an Irish whisper.
> "You don't belong here," it said.
> Just a simple, obvious statement, but I felt a flood of relief wash over me.
> No, I thought, I don't.[1]

This positive contemporary experience of divine guidance stands in stark contrast with another story I heard recently, on *The Moth Radio Hour*, this one from a preacher's daughter, now an adult, who recounts being terrified of God as a child:

> I am the third daughter of a violent, fundamentalist, Presbyterian preacher.
>   And I'm telling you this because I want you to understand that growing
>   up I knew that God is love.
> *But,* if you cross him, he will burn you with fire, send you to hell and you
>   will burn forever.
> *But,* he does other things before that, like give you terrible diseases. One is
>   leprosy. Sunday school literature was full of pictures of lepers.

One day, she stole a couple of pennies from the children's "Leper Pig," the piggy-bank collection for leprosy relief, and with a friend secretly went to a penny-candy store. When conscience later smote her, she was fearful of

Divine Guidance. John A. Jillions, Oxford University Press (2020). © Oxford University Press.
DOI: 10.1093/oso/9780190055738.001.0001

the retribution God would exact. Surely she would be struck with leprosy, her skin would turn white, she would lose her fingers, her toes, her nose, and "maybe [her] whole face." When she discovered some white spots on her skin she knew she had the terrible disease. "I was terrified. I couldn't sleep. I couldn't pay attention in school. All I could think about was my leprosy." But she had also learned a test in Sunday school: "If you stick a pin in it and it doesn't hurt, you know you have leprosy." In fear and trembling she shut herself up in the bathroom, locked the door, took a pin and prepared for the worst.

> I sat down on the floor to do the dreaded test. I couldn't breathe. I held the pin over the spot. And then I prayed, "God, dear God, please, please let it hurt. I'll never steal from Pete the Leper Pig again. Please let it hurt."
> Ow. It *hurt*.
> God is *love*.[2]

Such 21st-century interpretations of good and bad divine guidance would be familiar to first-century people. Each of the cultures described in this study—Greek, Roman, Jewish, Christian—produced thinkers who wrestled with divine guidance within their own contexts.

Corinth has given us a varied set of pathways into Paul's first-century world. It should be clear by now that many forms of perceived divine guidance were at play in the Roman Empire, of which Corinth was a prime expression, where Greco-Roman religion and philosophy mixed with Judaism and Paul's early Christianity. Healing temples and synagogues, various forms of public worship and household shrines, astrology, oracles, dreams, sacred scriptures, and literary texts (including Homer and Virgil), professional rhetoricians, revered teachers and rabbis—these all had a role in popular approaches to divine guidance among people who rubbed shoulders in the marketplace and streets of ancient Corinth. Perhaps they also patronized Paul's tent-making business, heard him speak in the synagogue, or looked in on the new worshipping community he was planting next door in the house of Titius Justus (Acts 18:7).

In this final chapter I recap the findings of this study and then conclude by briefly considering the experience of divine guidance in the 21st century. First-century religious practices, while of interest to some, are much less germane to the 21st century than the attitudes expressed by the array of ancient writers, historians, philosophers, and poets who reflected on those practices. Their views are attractive because they engage perennial philosophical and spiritual questions still being raised in our own time.

Greco-Roman Views

For a minority of critics, such as Lucretius, the abuses of popular religion were enough to abandon religion entirely. Instead of practicing religion, with its foolishness and fears, human beings should peacefully develop their sense of wonder at the universe and dedicate themselves to simple virtue:

> Poor humanity, to saddle the gods with such responsibilities and throw in a vindictive temper! What griefs they hatched then for themselves, what festering sores for us, what tears for our posterity! This is not piety, this oft-repeated show of bowing a veiled head before a graven image; this bustling to every altar; this kow-towing and prostration on the ground with palms outspread before the shrines of the gods; this deluging of altars with the blood of beasts; this heaping of vow upon vow. True piety lies rather in the power to contemplate the universe with a quiet mind. (*The Nature of the Universe* 5.1190ff.)

Diogenes, on the other hand, was more forgiving of popular divine guidance. It couldn't do much harm, as long as people didn't put much store by it. But they should be taught first to do the more difficult inner work of learning to know oneself and to trust their intelligence: "If you are possessed of intelligence, you will know of yourself what you ought to do and how to go about it. . . . Aim first to know thyself; afterwards, having found wisdom, you will then, if it be your pleasure, consult the oracle. For I am persuaded that you will have no need of consulting oracles if you have intelligence" (Dio Chrysostom, *Servants* 10:28).

Cicero took a similar view but made a much clearer distinction between practice and belief. He advocated active involvement in religious life as a pillar of cultural tradition and out of respect "for the opinion of the masses" but felt no qualms about believing none of it. Tradition is good, he says in effect, but let's not pretend that the ancients were right about everything, including their superstitious views on divine guidance. But rejecting belief in popular religion doesn't mean Cicero rejects belief in a divine force: "The celestial order and the beauty of the universe compel me to confess that there is some excellent and eternal Being who deserves the respect and homage of men" (*Div.* 2.71.148).

Seneca goes further. He thinks it is disingenuous to cherish the god of the philosophers while still maintaining false religious practices, even for reasons of state and pandering to the masses. He argues instead for a Stoic philosophical commitment to the divine, but without all the trappings of popular religion:

> [Let] us forbid lamps to be lighted on the Sabbath, since the gods do not need light, neither do men take pleasure in soot. Let us forbid men from offering

morning salutation and to throng the doors of temples; mortal ambitions are attracted at such ceremonies, but God is worshipped by those who truly know him. Let us forbid bringing towels and flesh-scrapers to Jupiter, and proffering mirrors to Juno; for god seeks no servants. Of course not; he himself does service to mankind, everywhere and to all he is at hand to help. (*Epistles* 95:47)

Seneca believes in an ultimately kind Fate whose ways—for now—are unknown and simply require peaceful acceptance of whatever happens, in imitation of the impassible, imperturbable peace that governs "the great creator and ruler of the universe":

What then is the part of a good man? To offer himself to Fate. It is a great consolation that it is together with the universe that we are swept along; whatever it is that has been ordained us so to live, so to die, by the same necessity it binds also the gods. One unchangeable course bears along the affairs of men and gods alike. Although the great creator and ruler of the universe himself wrote the decrees of Fate, yet he follows them. He obeys forever, he decreed but once. (*De prov* 5:8)

For God also, the all-embracing world and the ruler of the universe, reaches forth into outward things, yet, withdrawing from all sides returns unto himself. And our mind should do the same; when, having followed the senses that serve it, it has through them reached to things without, let it be master both of them and of itself. In this way will be born an energy that is united, a power that is at harmony with itself, and that dependable reason which is not divided against itself, nor uncertain either in its opinions, or its perceptions, or its convictions; and this reason, when it has regulated itself, and established harmony between all its parts, and, so to speak, is in tune, has attained the highest good. (*De vita beata* 8.6)

The ideal path is thus the harmony of inward and outward being. In Seneca's outlook there is no need for special divine guidance, since accepting with equanimity the good, bad, or indifferent is the way to inner peace.

Plutarch is unsatisfied with this kind of bloodless philosophical religion. Unique among the Greco-Roman writers surveyed here, he sought to balance rejection of the bad religion of superstition with heartfelt embracing of mystical communion with the divine. He is most disturbed by the fears that undergird so much popular religion. This instinctive sense of dread among those who serve the gods with such devotion reveals a hidden hatred:

They assume that the gods are rash, faithless, fickle, vengeful, cruel, and easily offended; and as a result, the superstitious man is bound to hate and fear the gods. Why not, since he thinks that the worst of his ills are due to them, and will be due to them in the future? As he hates and fears the gods, he is an enemy to them. And yet, though he dreads them, he worships them and sacrifices to them and besieges their shrines. (*On Superstition* 170E)

The atheist thinks there are no gods; the superstitious man wishes there were none, but believes in them against his will, for he is afraid not to believe. . . . The superstitious man by preference would be an atheist, but is too weak to hold the opinion about the gods that he wishes to hold. (*On Superstition* 170F)

Given the excesses, fears, and ignorance found in popular religion, Plutarch has no trouble understanding why thoughtful people would rather be atheists. Indeed the gods themselves might prefer to have their existence denied than to be so maligned:

Why for my part, I should prefer that men should say about me that I have never been born at all, and there is no Plutarch, rather than that they should say "Plutarch is an inconstant fickle person, quick-tempered, vindictive over little accidents, pained at trifles. If you invite him to dinner and leave him out or if you haven't the time and don't go to call on him, or fail to speak to him when you see him, he will set his teeth into your body and bite it through, or he will get hold of your little child and beat him to death, or he will turn the beast that he owns into your crops and spoil your harvest." (*On Superstition* 170A)

If superstition is worse than atheism, for Plutarch it is still deeply sad when all sense of God's presence has been lost. It is "a great misfortune for the soul . . . for it is as if the soul had suffered the extinction of the brightest and most dominant of its many eyes, the conception of God" (*On Superstition* 167B). Rejecting the extremes of credulity and atheism Plutarch pursues a middle way that brings rational and mystical together.

Jewish Views

Jewish approaches to divine guidance display some variety, but nothing like the polarities seen among Gentiles in the Greco-Roman world. They were fundamentally united around devotion to the written and oral Torah, and this, according to Josephus, was one of the great strengths of Judaism:

Among us alone will be heard no contradictory statements about God, such as are common among other nations, not only on the lips of ordinary individuals under the impulse of some passing mood, but even boldly proclaimed by philosophers; some putting forward crushing arguments against the very existence of God, others depriving him of his providential care for mankind. Among us alone will be seen no difference in the conduct of our lives. With us all act alike, all profess the same doctrine about God, one which is in harmony with our Law and affirms that all things are under his eye. Even our womenfolk and dependants would tell you that piety must be the motive of all our occupations in life. (*Against Apion* 2.179–181)

The community's written and oral law worked together. Through the centuries oral law interpreted the written law and showed Jews how to understand and carry out God's commandments in their own time and place. Over time, this constant rereading, reinterpretation, and reapplication resulted in a body of communal tradition that itself became a form of divine guidance.

But this view did not exclude immediate divine guidance—through angels, a "heavenly voice," dreams, prophetic words—as we see in the Hebrew Bible, intertestamental writing, Philo, Josephus, and early rabbinic thought. King Solomon, for example, known for his rational wisdom, was equally at home in the world of mystical inspiration. His famous prayer at the start of his reign, asking God to give him "an understanding mind" (or a "hearing heart," in the Septuagint Greek), takes place "in a dream by night," when God says, "Ask what I shall give you" (1 Kings 3:5):

[7]"And now, O Lord my God, you have made your servant king in place of my father David, although I am only a little child; I do not know how to go out or come in. [8]And your servant is in the midst of the people whom you have chosen, a great people, so numerous they cannot be numbered or counted. [9]Give your servant therefore an understanding mind to govern your people, able to discern between good and evil; for who can govern this your great people?" [10]It pleased the Lord that Solomon had asked this. [11]God said to him, "Because you have asked this, and have not asked for yourself long life or riches, or for the life of your enemies, but have asked for yourself understanding to discern what is right, [12]I now do according to your word. Indeed I give you a wise and discerning mind; no one like you has been before you and no one like you shall arise after you. [13]I give you also what you have not asked, both riches and honor all your life; no other king shall compare with you. [14]If you will walk in my ways, keeping my statutes and my commandments, as your father David walked, then I will lengthen your life." [15]Then Solomon awoke; it had been a dream. (1 Kings 3:7–15)

The story of Solomon was written down sometime in the sixth century BCE during the Babylonian Exile of the Jews. Five hundred years later, early in the first century CE, the sophisticated, philosophically trained Philo also accepts that

God can directly illumine the soul—even when it is weak or lazy—to discern what is right, especially when reading the scriptures: "[Even] if we do close the eye of our soul and either will not take the trouble or have not the power to regain our sight, do thou thyself, O Sacred Guide, be our prompter and preside over our steps and never tire of anointing our eyes, until conducting us to the hidden light of hallowed words thou display to us the fast-locked loveliness invisible to the uninitiate" (*On Dreams*, 1.165).

Not unlike Paul a few decades later, Philo insists that having such a sense of weakness is the *prerequisite* for perceiving God's presence and direction, as a counterweight to human pride: "For so long as mind and sense-perception imagine that they get a firm grasp . . . the divine word is far away. But when each of them acknowledges its weakness, and going through a kind of setting passes out of sight, right reason is forward to meet and greet at once the practicing soul, whose willing champion he is when it despairs of itself and waits for him who invisibly comes from without to its succour" (*On Dreams* 1.118).

Yet dreams, the "heavenly voice," and mystical experiences played a relatively minor role in rabbinic thought. Preoccupation with heavenly voices was a distraction. Indeed it became a pillar of community decision-making that divine guidance was no substitute for rational human debate, "for the law is not in heaven." As Isaiah had written, the clearest path to divine guidance is to follow the commandments, to do no harm, and to open one's eyes to the real needs of others. *Then* God will "guide you continually and satisfy your soul" (Isa 58:11).

It must also be noted that while Jewish thought was biting in its criticism of pagan religion (in terms similar to those of Greek and Roman critics), it was equally critical of deformed religious life *within* Judaism. Isaiah famously begins his prophecy by denouncing Israel's religious practices, made corrupt by their violence, injustice, and mistreatment of the oppressed, the orphan, and the widow:

> [14]Your new moons and your appointed festivals
>   my soul hates;
> they have become a burden to me,
>   I am weary of bearing them. . . .
> [16]Wash yourselves; make yourselves clean;
>   remove the evil of your doings
>   from before my eyes;
> cease to do evil,
> [17]learn to do good;
> seek justice,
>   rescue the oppressed,
> defend the orphan,
>   plead for the widow. (Isa 1:14, 16–17; see also Ezek 34; Amos 5:21–27)

Perhaps the best summary of the multifaceted Jewish approach to divine guidance is found in the story of Susanna, who refuses the lecherous advances of two respected Jewish sages (Daniel 13 Septuagint). She is saved from their false accusations and execution only when the prophet Daniel, prompted by divine inspiration, suddenly intervenes. The moral of the story is that the divinely ordained institutions of law are not meant to permanently silence the God of Israel.

From a human perspective this unexpected, untamed, undomesticated, unfinished character of the God of the Bible is also unsettling. But that is precisely the experience of God that the Bible seeks to convey and preserve. This is the key conclusion of Walter Brueggemann's monumental *Theology of the Old Testament*: "Israel's knowledge of God is endlessly elusive, under challenge, and in dispute. Israel thereby refuses the kind of certitude that either historical positivism or theological positivism can give."[3]

Paul's Christian View

Paul's Christian community in Corinth was drawn from both the Greco-Roman and Jewish worlds, and where he finds most common ground with them is in their shared critique of pagan divination and religion. He tells his mainly Gentile flock of converts that they were led astray by their past pagan practices, regardless of whatever spiritual feelings they may have experienced (1 Cor 12:2). However, Paul reserves his sharpest criticism for his own Christian coreligionists. In none of his letters—and especially in 1 Corinthians—does he cover up or minimize the failures of the early Christian communities. Equally significant, these very churches preserved, displayed, and circulated his written critiques for all future generations to see. Such is the value that Paul and the early church placed on honesty, self-examination, confession, and humility.

In the same spirit of openness, Paul does not hide or justify his own deeply flawed past as a persecutor or his current weaknesses and struggles. This kind of open self-criticism is characteristic of the entire Judeo-Christian tradition of the Bible, which is as much a record of the failings of patriarchs, princes, prophets, and apostles as it is of God's guidance.

Paul's approach to divine guidance shares many elements with Jewish tradition, but his single-minded devotion to "Jesus Christ and him crucified" (1 Cor 2:2) brings about a sharp divergence. For Paul, Christ initiates the age of the Messiah and thus opens access to the outpouring of the Holy Spirit. The Holy Spirit's guidance comes in response to being a disciple of the Crucified Christ. All other divine guidance is secondary. This link between Christ's Cross and the Spirit cannot be overemphasized when looking at Paul's understanding of divine guidance in the context of Jewish and Greco-Roman thought.

The survey of 1 Corinthians in the previous chapter showed that questions about divine guidance are explicitly and implicitly woven throughout Paul's many topics. The Spirit's presence and direction are basic to his view of decision-making in Christian life, but this means more than God speaking directly to individuals. Paul upholds the role of rational thought, scripture, preaching, service, apostolic and hierarchical order, church tradition, teachers, and liturgical life. These modes of thinking, communal mentoring, and discernment preserve the value of initiative and action while acting as guardrails to protect the community from deception and spiritual abuse. Yet neither Paul's own apostolic authority nor these communal checks and balances are allowed to eclipse the mystery of God's direct and unpredictable guidance to individuals and communities in the new age of the Spirit.

Conclusions

Before moving on to consider divine guidance in the present, let me summarize this study's conclusions about the past.

First, divine guidance was a major topic of reflection, writing, and debate in the Greco-Roman and Jewish worlds that shaped St. Paul's Corinth.

Second, while Gentiles displayed a wide range of attitudes toward divine guidance, Jews were much more closely united. Divine guidance for them was centered on devotion to the Torah as interpreted within the community of faith. For Jews and for Paul, the communal context of divine guidance is an important distinguishing feature vis-à-vis the Greco-Roman world. But even here the distinctions are not absolute: official policy in Augustan Rome clearly regarded the civic and communal role of divine guidance as paramount.

Third, for Paul divine guidance was central in his approach to decision-making and links all the topics he addresses in 1 Corinthians. His Christian view of divine guidance is firmly rooted in the Jewish experience of revelation, prayer, scripture, study, hierarchy, community, and liturgy, but all seen through a new filter: faith in the crucified and risen Christ who opens the new age of the Spirit.

Fourth, the Cross for Paul stands as a paradoxical and contradictory sign of divine guidance through weakness, humility, and self-emptying (*kenosis*) and most sets apart his Christian view from the Greco-Roman and Jewish worlds.

Fifth, there was a remarkable degree of common ground in the "community of discourse" that shaped first-century Corinth. Most people would have shared the assumption that divine guidance in one form or another was a normal feature of human life and decision-making. There was also a shared critique of popular views of divine guidance that crossed the divides of Gentile, Jew, and Christian.

Sixth, this common ground should not be exaggerated: Gentile, Jewish, and Pauline approaches to divine guidance could also appear so alien to each other as to lead to mutual condemnation, persecution, and martyrdom.

Seventh, all the writers surveyed, whatever their attitudes, reveal a culture that reflected deeply upon the realities, ambiguities, and snares posed by divine guidance in decision-making. The first-century world asked questions about the existence and character of God or the gods; the possibility of divine guidance and how to distinguish it from delusion; factors impeding awareness of spiritual forces both good and evil; how to refine one's faculties of spiritual perception; how reason, initiative, rational decision-making, and action combine with a sense of divine presence and direction; the role played by mentoring and community life. This widespread preoccupation with such questions is especially striking in light of the contemporary Western world where rational and mystical are rarely permitted to share the same space.

Religious Experience and Divine Guidance in the 21st Century

It should be obvious to anyone who is even superficially aware of spiritual currents around the world today that the first-century questions about religious experience—despite the vast historical and cultural gulf that separates us from that time—still resonate in the 21st century. So what can we say about divine guidance today?

To begin to frame an answer, consider a pivotal experience in the life of an American icon, the Rev. Dr. Martin Luther King Jr. On Friday night, January 27, 1956, King was in Montgomery, Alabama, during the tense early weeks of the bus boycott. He was 27 years old and had been pastor of the Dexter Avenue Baptist Church less than two years, but already he was feeling the weight of pastoral leadership, injustice, oppression, and threats of violence even as he was determined to lead a nonviolent protest. He got home very late at night after a long, demoralizing, and tiring day. The family was asleep. Then a phone call came and a threatening voice said, "Leave Montgomery immediately if you have no wish to die." In *Stride toward Freedom,* King describes what happened next:

> I was ready to give up. With my cup of coffee sitting untouched before me,
> I tried to think of a way to move out of the picture without appearing a coward.
> In this state of exhaustion, when my courage had all but gone, I decided to take

my problem to God. With my head in my hands, I bowed over the kitchen table and prayed aloud.

The words I spoke to God that midnight are still vivid in my memory. "I am here taking a stand for what I believe is right. But now I am afraid. The people are looking to me for leadership, and if I stand before them without strength and courage, they too will falter. I am at the end of my powers. I have nothing left. I've come to the point where I can't face it alone."

At that moment, I experienced the presence of the Divine as I had never experienced God before. It seemed as though I could hear the quiet assurance of an inner voice saying: "Stand up for justice, stand up for truth; and God will be at your side forever." Almost at once my fears began to go. My uncertainty disappeared. I was ready to face anything.[4]

Martin Luther King's experience takes us from the first century to the present.

Some will dismiss divine guidance and its attendant questions as the moldy leftovers of a backward, superstitious, and dangerous set of religious views that have no place in forming a flourishing humanity today. And of course it is possible to point to stories almost anywhere in the world where religious credulity is exploited and manipulated, and how it inspires the most heinous acts of violence.

We are most familiar with the big headlines of dramatic religion-inspired bombings. But there are scores of disturbing examples at the local level around the world. A news story from tribal Nigeria, for example, reported on families of sex-trafficking victims who are too fearful of native witch doctors to report the crimes. They are terrified of voodoo threats that "their relatives will die if they go to the police or fail to pay off their debt." To combat this widespread fear the traditional ruler of the kingdom of Benin, Oba Ewuare II, proclaimed a curse on these shamans and anyone caught aiding and abetting the traffickers. According to Nigerian antitrafficking officials, this is a bold weapon, "because the Edo people's belief system is strongly rooted in traditional worship."[5]

Religious or superstitious anxieties still have a place in the outlook of people in many parts of the world. A 2006 study of 13–15-year-old girls in Wales, for example, found a significant proportion—especially among the unchurched—who believed in the afterlife, supernatural forces, good luck, and ways to protect against bad luck and harm from supernatural forces. Among non-churchgoers, 20% believed that fortune-tellers can tell the future and 36% believed in their horoscope.[6] Anecdotally, a man in Canada told me that as a university student he went out one Saturday night with friends, and after a few beers they stopped "for fun" to see a fortune-teller. "Years later," he said, "in church on the day of my wedding, as I was walking up the aisle I was still thinking about that fortune-teller, because she had predicted that I would never get married."

But religious unbelief is also sharply on the way up. In the USA, according to the 2015 Pew Religious Landscape Study, the growth of the "nones" is especially dramatic among the younger generations. More than a third of all millennials (born 1981–1996) now consider themselves atheist, agnostic, or "religiously unaffiliated."[7] This phenomenon has been paralleled by a spate of books in recent years debunking religion in general and Christianity in particular (see works by Richard Dawkins, Christopher Hitchens, Daniel Dennett, and Sam Harris, for example).

Although the scientific community is well represented in the "nones" category, many scientists find it possible to combine rational thought, religious faith, and spiritual experience. This is the focus, for example, of the John Templeton Foundation, which seeks to promote intellectual humility and cross-pollination in the various realms of thought, both scientific and religious/spiritual. They are interested in "big questions" that require collaboration, such as "Is there a divine reality, and how is it related to the cosmos? Do we have free will? Are minds wholly material? What are the virtues and how do we acquire them?"[8]

Perhaps the most trenchant rebuttal to the new atheists has come from the learned and acid pen of David Bentley Hart in *Atheist Delusions: The Christian Revolution and Its Fashionable Enemies*. But Hart shares some of their critique of religion and Christianity, much as Plutarch sympathized with detractors of superstition in the first century:

> To be honest, my affection for institutional Christianity as a whole is rarely more than tepid; and there are numerous forms of Christian belief and practice for which I would be hard pressed to muster a kind word from the depths of my heart, and the rejection of which by the atheist or skeptic strikes me as perfectly laudable. . . .
>
> I can honestly say that there are many forms of atheism that I find more admirable than many forms of Christianity or of religion in general. But atheism that consists entirely in vacuous arguments afloat on oceans of historical ignorance, made turbulent by storms of strident self-righteousness, is as contemptible as any other form of dreary fundamentalism.[9]

Surprisingly, the growing swath of doubters doesn't mean that they have all given up on spiritual life or even churchgoing. The Pew findings on attendance at religious services show 28% of the unaffiliated ("nones") attend at least once or twice a month or a few times a year (and 4% go weekly); 20% of the "nones" pray at least daily, and 38% pray monthly or weekly.[10] These are the "spiritual but not religious" who are spiritually thirsty but can't seem to find a water fountain in the religions they have encountered. Even Sam Harris, the most vehement of the modern despisers, has discovered a path for atheists to a meditative spirituality in his *Waking Up: A Guide to Spirituality without Religion*. This is touching a chord, which by his own admission is causing alarm to some of his fellow nonreligionists:

> For many years, I have been a vocal critic of religion, and I won't ride the same hobbyhorse here. I hope that I have been sufficiently energetic on this front that even my most skeptical readers will trust that my bullshit detector remains well calibrated as we advance over this new terrain. Perhaps the following assurance can suffice for the moment: Nothing in this book needs to be accepted on faith. Although my focus is on human subjectivity—I am, after all, talking about the nature of experience itself—all my assertions can be tested in the laboratory of your own life. In fact, my goal is to do just that.[11]

Yet testing and verifying "in the laboratory of your own life" is not a new invention; it is historically at the heart of virtually every enduring path of spiritual life, including Christianity.[12] And despite the apparent growth of the "nones," the fact remains that there are few experiences more common across cultures around the world than spiritual intuition and practice. There is an undeniable hunger for a personal connection with the divine, however this might be understood. Indeed among psychiatrists, psychologists, social workers, and counselors it is now routine to take into consideration a person's spiritual dimension.[13]

Religion and its institutions, intricacies, and politics are of only minor interest in comparison to this thirst for a deeper spiritual life. Paradoxically it is religious leaders who often miss this. This was precisely Evelyn Underhill's critique of church life in 1930, when she wrote to the archbishop of Canterbury, Cosmo Lang. If clergy aren't nurturing awareness of spiritual life, then they and their churches risk becoming irrelevant. She thought that the church was distracted by too many secondary tasks and was thus failing miserably at its primary mission, the nurturing of "theocentric souls." Underhill believed that if the church were to consciously refocus on communion with God, it might find a lot more devotion among people at the grassroots. As she told the archbishop, "*God* is the interesting thing about religion."[14]

Testing Divine Guidance Today

As a counterpoint to what might be called the mystically challenged academic environment described in the introduction, in which scholars and even religious leaders have discomfort entering sympathetically into a world where divine guidance is possible, I would like to suggest that the views of two Eastern

Orthodox scholars may open a door to a new perspective on religious experience and discernment.

In the early 1970s Kallistos Ware (b. 1934) and Lev Gillet (1893–1980) gave separate lengthy interviews to researchers as part of a decades-long study conducted by the Alister Hardy Religious Experience Research Centre, then based in Oxford and now at the University of Wales.[15] As noted in the introduction, the Centre continues to do research and publishing in the field of religious experience and has collected over 6,000 accounts from people who had a spiritual or religious experience that was significant in shaping their lives. At the time, both Ware and Gillet were Orthodox priests living in England. (Ware was the Spalding Lecturer of Eastern Orthodox Studies at the University of Oxford for 35 years, ordained a bishop in 1982, and is now Metropolitan Kallistos of Diokleia. Lev Gillet was a well-known writer on the spiritual life, often writing under the name "A Monk of the Eastern Church.") Both insisted on the reality of personal encounters with God, but also the need to carefully test such experiences and assess whether they are indeed encounters with God.

Lev Gillet

In his interview Gillet said he often experienced divine guidance through the inward hearing of silent words: "Many times in my life when I have asked for guidance, asking for an answer in concrete terms, this has been given to me, in words: words innerly spoken, without a sound, but in a way which left me in no doubt about the superhuman origin of those answers. I have some criteria which allowed me to discriminate such words from other words, purely human words."[16] He lists four criteria for discerning whether such experiences are in fact "divine" guidance.

First, it must be repeated.

Second, it must be spoken "in the style of God": "God speaks always in very short sentences, very short. He does not generally go further than five or six words. They are spoken in a way for which I can only find one adjective: FINAL. He doesn't leave the door open to any argument, contestation or question. I think these are the two characteristics: great brevity and the absoluteness of it."[17]

Gillet expands on this, saying that there are other experiences that can be described as "infiltration by God," illustrated by the conversation that the risen Jesus has with two disciples on the road to Emmaus (Luke 24:13–35). "He follows them, listens to them, and hears them, and enters into their talk. This is not the way of speaking with authority, but the method of infiltration. He can enter us as ink can penetrate blotting paper."[18]

The third way test to the experience is to ask others: "Ask four or five people who understand your problem to pray for a solution and to ask for guidance, and see whether the answers are convergent."

The fourth and "most definitive" criterion for evaluating the experience is to pay attention to the feelings and actions that the experience produces: "Does this guidance create in you sorrow, bitterness, hatred? Or does it create in you joy and love for God and other people? Judge the tree according to its fruit."[19]

Kallistos Ware

Interviewed independently, Ware's responses are similar to Gillet's, which might be expected from two respondents deeply immersed in the same religious tradition. He is intrigued by research on religious experience and sees it as having the potential to show that "man can experience and know things in ways not normally allowed for . . . ways of understanding apart from those based on sense-perception and the reasoning of the conscious mind."[20] Within the framework of institutional religion, he says, *personal experience* (his emphasis) is essential. Even in strictly human terms this is fundamental to becoming a person. "You become a real person by having contact with others, by living in them and for them, by your sharing in their experience and by their sharing in yours. . . . [There] can be no genuine knowledge of other people without love for them."[21] But like Gillet, he sees the need for "outside standards by which you are going to interpret the experiences."[22] He is likewise wary of all descriptions of experience: "Any statement in human language about God or religious experience is inevitably inadequate; not necessarily untrue, but inadequate."[23]

Ware is especially interested in experiences that "express some feeling that our encounter with this reality is not just an experience of impersonal power but is in some sense a personal meeting similar to that which human beings have with each other."[24] If someone claims to have had a religious experience, then to test whether this was genuinely personal, the criterion he applies is this: Does this religious experience "manifest in some way an awareness that this greater reality—around them and in them—in some sense loves them, and that they are called to love in return?"[25] And then he would want to know what difference the experience made to the person's life: "Did it make a decisive difference to the quality of their life? . . . Is it an experience such that they never forget it, and they feel that the experience has altered the whole direction of their life and has given them a new way of looking at the world?"[26]

Ware acknowledges that church tradition is cautious about extraordinary religious experiences and psychic phenomena, and considers that they can fall into three categories: evil, neutral, or from God. "The experiences originating from the devil are to be at once repelled; those from God are to be accepted; those that are neutral are to be ignored."[27] There are a number of tests to distinguish between these three sources of religious experience. The first test is to simply take no notice and to continue praying; if the experiences go away, then they are not important. "Two other tests can also be applied. The first is external: What effect do these experiences have on your daily life? Do they make you a better person in your dealings with other people? If they do not, then this would be an indication that there is something wrong in these experiences. Here we have the old test of 'by their fruits you will know them.' " He adds that we might indeed have a true religious experience, "but we for our part proved false to it" and thus did not bring forth fruit.[28]

> The third test is interior:
> [If] a thing is from God, it is absolutely convincing; it leaves no element of doubt in your mind that this is God, that now I am face to face with the true reality in the universe and beyond the universe. If there is doubt in your mind, then you should ignore the experience. If you can ignore it and forget about it, this again is generally an indication that it is not from God. When a true experience from God comes, it will have such power in it that it cannot be ignored. The basic inward criterion is summed up in the Greek term *plērophoria*, meaning assurance, an overwhelming conviction.[29]

Ware then adds a fourth test for discernment: seeking out a spiritually experienced person to assist in evaluating one's experience. With this help, learning how to discern in this way is a basic aspect of the spiritual life and is gradually developed over time. "[If] someone is sincerely pursuing the spiritual way, then gradually—through prayer, study, fasting, obedience and active service to others—he will develop a spiritual 'taste' which directly and intuitively enables him to distinguish the genuine or divine from the counterfeit or demonic, just as our natural taste enables us immediately to distinguish wholesome food from food that has gone mouldy."[30]

Ware's description of acquiring a spiritual sense of taste is comparable to Gillet's "grammar of God." One learns how to listen and recognize the voice of God when He speaks. Nevertheless even with these criteria of discernment and with an experienced spiritual guide, "the dangers of delusion remain very great," and therefore extraordinary experiences ought to be treated with great caution. But just as Gillet spoke also of God's gradual "infiltration" rather than dramatic experiences, so Ware also recognizes that "there must be many people who consider that they have religious experience in a wider sense, as something which extends through their whole life, though they could not point to any extraordinary experience for which they could send you a description."[31]

While speaking cautiously about spiritual experiences, Ware is still persuaded that direct personal experience of God is essential to a spiritual life:

[We] ought to impress on people that Christianity is not just a question of ritual, moral rules and abstract adherence to verbal doctrinal formulations; each is called to relive the Tradition in his own personal experience. We should tell people that remarkable experiences do happen, and that, while they may be a delusion from the devil, they may be a gift from God. We should however, always be seeking not God's gifts, but God Himself. The experiences are important, not in isolation, but because they may point beyond themselves to Him. . . .

There is an ever-present danger of reducing religion to a philosophical theory or moral code; whereas the primary purpose of the Church on earth is to bring people, through prayer, to a direct apprehension of the living God. Of course such apprehension should then transform our personal relations to others and inspire us to serve them in a new way. But if in our religious teaching we speak only of service to others, divorced from the direct apprehension of God through prayer, then we reduce the Church to a kind of social welfare organization.[32]

* * *

Why doesn't everyone have this experience of divine guidance? Or why doesn't the experience stay with them? These are questions posed by Alexander Schmemann, another leading Eastern Orthodox thinker of the 20th century:

I see that everything in the world speaks of God, reveals God, radiates with his presence: the darkness of night, as much as the sunlight of morning; suffering and sorrow, as much as happiness and joy. And if so many people do not see this, then it is because I—and believers like me—am too weak a witness of faith; it is because from earliest childhood we surround the person with triviality and lies; we encourage him not to search and not to thirst for the depths, but to desire instead a petty and illusory success; it is because we rivet his attention to things that are vain and futile. And therefore his mysterious inner faculty of light and love is suffocated and the world is filled with the clinging darkness of unbelief, skepticism and their offspring: self-conceit, hatred and malice.[33]

And yet, despite all of these stumbling blocks, despite the failings of people of faith and their institutions, despite everything that conspires to suffocate their "mysterious inner faculty of light and love," many still find themselves with a wistful longing for God that won't go away.

In first-century Corinth, Paul expected that such people would be found on the margins of church life: curious, looking in, testing the waters. The same is surely true in the 21st century. Whatever it is that mysteriously stirs these thoughts and feelings in a person's soul, it was Paul's hope that the church community would be ready to welcome them, for their own encounter with the living God.

Notes

Introduction

1. Margalit, "Israel's Jewish-Terrorist Problem."
2. Beech, "The Face"; Di Pane and Enos, "Festering."
3. Henderson, "10 Worst Examples."
4. Stern, *Terror*, 12. Stern goes on to note: "Faith must also have played a role, then, when he drove to Kansas City with plastic explosives and a. 22 pistol to shoot some 'queers and niggers,' bomb a pornographic bookstore, and blow up a church frequented by homosexuals" (12).

   For two additional superb studies of religious violence, see Armstrong, *Fields of Blood*; Sacks, *Not in God's Name*.
5. Cited in Lampe, *Cambridge History*, 146.
6. Pew Research Center, "Age Gap in Religion,"
7. "A Nation." See also Robinson, "Lobbying."
8. Sherwood, "Attendance." Compare attendance at football matches: Statista, "Number of Football Attendances."
9. Luhrmann, *Persuasions*, 339.
10. Paul's views on divine guidance have been given only limited attention among scholars. Markus Bockmuehl's important study, *Revelation and Mystery in Ancient Judaism and Pauline Christianity*, considers the issue tangentially under what he calls "occasional revelation." Under this heading he includes prophetic and other manifestations of the Spirit in the course of congregational worship (1 Cor. 12:7–11, 14:6, 26, 30), heavenly visions (2 Cor 12:1–4), conviction of sin (1 Cor 14:24) or of improper disposition of life (Phil 3:15), concrete instruction (Gal 2:2), and prompting of prayer (Rom 8:15f., 26f.; Gal 4:6). He says that "this type of divine disclosure was certainly important and recurrent in the experience of Paul and his churches" (144). He also notes the frequency of such phenomena in Acts (13:2, 16:6–10, 18:9–11, 22:17–21, 23:11, 27:23ff). All of this is particularly significant "against a background of Jewish and Old Testament eschatology and how the presence or absence of the Spirit, Shekinah was perceived in Judaism" (144). While he agrees that "in the message and apostolic ministry of the gospel the present dimension of revelation remains essential for Paul," he devotes only four paragraphs to this subject and does not regard it as "foundational" for Paul's understanding of revelation: "The significance of contemporary revelations in the larger pattern of God's saving design is in the final analysis theologically secondary and transient" (144). For more on occasional revelation he refers readers to other studies of New Testament prophecy (145): Aune, *Prophecy*; Hill, *New Testament Prophecy*; Grudem, *The Gift of Prophecy in 1 Corinthians* (1982),

revised as *The Gift of Prophecy in the New Testament and Today* (1988); Müller, *Prophetie und Predigt* (1975). However, these studies are primarily concerned with public prophecy. This is an important aspect of divine guidance, but the focus here will be on God's perceived guidance for individual as well as communal decision-making in concrete circumstances.

11. Other writers not included here also similarly reflect this era. The Neopythagorean philosopher Apollonius of Tyana (c. 15–c. 100) is associated with personal holiness, healing, and the understanding that all true philosophy comes as divine revelation. The Stoic philosopher Musonius Rufus (25–95) and his most famous student, Epictetus (55–135), influenced Emperor Marcus Aurelius (161–180), who believed that following one's inner "daimon" (genius) was the key to a philosophical life (see *Meditations* 2:17).

12. Cross-reference will also be made to Paul's other epistles. Following the most conservative view for purposes of this study, I take as authentic the seven epistles most widely accepted by scholars as written by Paul: Romans, 1–2 Corinthians, Galatians, Philippians, 1 Thessalonians, and Philemon. However, I would also regard Ephesians, Colossians, and 2 Thessalonians as genuine. The Pastoral epistles (1–2 Timothy, Titus), while authentic reflections of much of Paul's thought, closely connected to him, and based on direct communication with him, come from a slightly later period of church life. Hebrews is anonymous, never claims to be Pauline, and its authorship was debated even in the early church.

13. See the website of the Alister Hardy Religious Experience Research Centre.

14. Dunn, "In Quest," 103–104.

15. See, for example, Brown, "Our New Approach."

16. Kesich, *The Gospel Image*, 115.

17. Kraftchick, "An Asymptotic Response," 133. Frances Young makes the same point in reference to patristic studies: "Underlying modern discussions is the suspicion that God-talk is somehow all a misleading hoax, that in the absence of empirical tests theology can have no claim to be a formal discipline of enquiry into reality; whereas in the ancient world the issue was how to talk about a being defined as inexpressible" ("The God," 45).

18. Bockmuehl was a professor of theology and ethics at Regent College in Vancouver, Canada, until his death in 1989. His interest in divine guidance and "listening to God" was inspired in part by Frank Buchman (1878–1961) and the Oxford Group (Moral Re-Armament). In his introduction he cites Buchman: "Divine guidance must become the normal experience.... Definite, accurate, adequate information can come from the mind of God to the minds of men. This is normal prayer" (Buchman, *Remaking*, 43 quoted in Bockmuehl, *Listening*, 8).

19. Markus Bockmuehl, Klaus Bockmuehl's son, is an internationally known biblical scholar. He taught for many years at the University of Cambridge, where I had the opportunity in the 1990s to speak with him about his father's work. He is currently the Dean Ireland's Professor of the Exegesis of Holy Scripture at the University of Oxford.

20. Klaus Bockmuehl does not, however, take into account the Pentecostal and Charismatic movements, which had a deep impact on Protestant and Roman

Catholic spirituality in the second half of the 20th century. This has led to a much more positive attitude toward direct divine guidance.

21. Bruce Waltke (b. 1930), an Evangelical biblical scholar and colleague of Klaus Bockmuehl at Regent College, developed this point in *Finding the Will of God*. Waltke is critical of Evangelical biblical scholarship (and he includes himself here) that too often has avoided speaking about the Holy Spirit's illumination in biblical understanding (182). He cites John Calvin: "The Holy Spirit enlightens us to make us capable of understanding what would otherwise be incomprehensible" (181). But Waltke is also leery of too much emphasis on personal divine guidance.

22. Bockmuehl, *Listening*, 125.

23. Bockmuehl, *Listening*, 126, citing Luther's *Against the Heavenly Prophets* (1524/25).

24. Bockmuehl, *Listening*, 132.

25. Bockmuehl, *Listening*, 127.

26. In *Revelation and Mystery* Bockmuehl cites *Institutes of the Christian Religion* of 1539 (*Institutio*, I, 9 and III, 3, 14); *Treatises against the Anabaptists and against the Libertines* (1545); *Letter to Edward Seymour, Duke of Somerset and Lord Protector* (1548).

27. Bockmuehl, *Listening*, 129.

28. Bockmuehl, *Listening*, 130.

29. Bockmuehl, *Listening*, 132.

30. Bockmuehl, *Listening*, 133.

31. Quoted in Bockmuehl, *Revelation and Mystery*, 134. It is worth remembering that Calvin's Geneva was later home to Voltaire.

32. Bockmuehl, *Listening*, 137.

33. Bultmann, "New Testament," 5, quoted in Lane, *Unseen World*, ix.

34. Pelikan, *The Emergence*, 99.

35. Pelikan, *The Emergence*, 99.

36. Pelikan, *The Emergence*, 105–106.

37. Pelikan, *The Emergence*, 107.

38. See Meyendorff, *St Gregory Palamas*.

Chapter 1

1. For the dating of Paul's visit, see Murphy-O'Connor, *St. Paul's Corinth*, 129–152.

2. MacMullen and Lane, *Paganism and Christianity*, viii.

3. MacMullen and Lane, *Paganism and Christianity*, xii.

4. Kent, *The Inscriptions*.

5. Witherington, *Conflict and Community*, 48; Osler, "Use, Misuse."

6. Lane, "Corinth," 94.

7. In Murphy-O'Connor, *St. Paul's Corinth*, 45–46.

8. For discussions of the refounding of Corinth, see Murphy-O'Connor, *St. Paul's Corinth*, 66–67; Wiseman, "Corinth and Rome," 497; Engels, *Roman Corinth*, 16–19; Alcock, *Graecia Capta*, 168–170; Witherington, *Conflict and Community*, 6.

9. Alcock, *Graecia Capta*, 168.

10. Zanker, *The Power*, 330.

11. Crinagoras, *Greek Anthology, Volume III: Book 9,* IX:284.

12. Alcock, *Graecia Capta*, fig. 5, 23.

13. Engels, *Roman Corinth*, 69.

14. Walbank, "The Nature," 221; see also Romano, "Post 146 B.C.," 9–30.

15. Williams, "The Refounding," 26, in Macready and Thompson.

16. Engels, *Roman Corinth*, 71.

17. Alcock, *Graecia Capta*, 168.

18. Murphy-O'Connor, "The Corinth," 152, supported by Engels, *Roman Corinth*, 99.

19. Zanker, *The Power*, 195–197.

20. C. K. Williams, "The Refounding of Corinth," 157, in Alcock, *Graecia Capta*, 169.

21. Witherington, *Conflict and Community*, 18.

22. Engels, *Roman Corinth*, 72. On the evolution of the imperial cult, see Agourides, *Istoria*, 52–56, 225–235.

23. Engels, *Roman Corinth*, 34.

24. In Witherington, *Conflict and Community*, 11.

25. Walbank, "Pausanias, Octavia," 29n, 372.

26. Spawforth, "Corinth, Argos," 211. For more on Greek and Roman attitudes toward each other, see Petrochilos, *Roman Attitudes*.

27. Alcock, *Graecia Capta*, 217.

28. Wiseman, "Corinth and Rome," 541.

29. Williams, "The Refounding," 31, in Macready and Thompson.

30. Williams, "The Refounding," 32, in Macready and Thompson.

31. Engels, *Roman Corinth*, 69.

32. Engels, *Roman Corinth*, 71.

33. In Wiseman, "Corinth and Rome," 508.

34. Dodds, *The Greeks*.

35. Fox, *Pagans and Christians*, 201.

36. Fox, *Pagans and Christians*, 202.

37. Williams, "The Refounding," 35.

38. Syme, *The Roman Revolution*; see also Zanker, *The Power*; Ogilvie, *The Romans*.

39. Zanker, *The Power*, 57.

40. Ogilvie, *The Romans*, 59, 124.

41. Ogilvie, *The Romans*, 101.

42. Ogilvie, *The Romans*, 10.

43. Zanker, *The Power*, 64, 2–3, 4.

44. For more on the moral evaluation of art in ancient Greece and Rome, see Zanker, *The Power*, 245–252.

45. Zanker, *The Power*, 92.

46. *Res Gestae* 34 in Velleius Paterculus, *Compendium*.

47. Zanker, *The Power*, 156.

48. J. R. Lanci, "Roman Eschatology in First-Century Corinth," unpublished paper, Society of Biblical Literature, 1992, quoted in Witherington, *Conflict and Community*, 297.
49. Witherington, *Conflict and Community*, 295.
50. W. Dittenberger, *Orientis graeci inscriptiones selectae* (Hildesheim: Olms, 1960), II, no. 458, lines 40–42, in Witherington, *Conflict and Community*, 296.
51. MacMullen, *Roman Empire* (1981), 13.
52. Ernst Lornemann, *Neu Dokumente zum lakonischen Kaiserkult* (Breslau: M. and H. Marcus, 1929), 7–10, in MacMullen and Lane, *Paganism and Christianity*, 74–76.
53. Zanker, *The Power*, 35–36. The star leading the Magi to the newborn Son of God and King of the Jews in Bethlehem is an obvious parallel (Matt 2:2).
54. In Zanker, *The Power*, 47–48.
55. Zanker, *The Power*, 96.
56. Zanker, *The Power*, 98.
57. Zanker, *The Power*, 307–308.
58. Zanker, *The Power*, 332; see also 297ff.
59. Zanker, *The Power*, 232.
60. Papahatzis, *Ancient Corinth*, 95.
61. See Winter, *Seek the Welfare*.
62. See Gill, "Erastus the Aedile."
63. MacMullen and Lane, *Paganism and Christianity*, 34. For further examples, see 34–36.
64. In Engels, *Roman Corinth*, 224n92.
65. Engels, *Roman Corinth*, 224n92.
66. Quoted in Ogilvie, *The Romans*, 8.
67. Engels, *Roman Corinth*, 87.
68. Engels, *Roman Corinth*, 19.

Chapter 2

1. Compare Paul's use of *epitagēn* in 1 Cor 7:25 and 2 Cor 8:8.
2. In MacMullen, *Roman Empire*, 61.
3. *Abaton* is also one of the terms for the sanctuary in a Greek Orthodox Church.
4. Murphy-O'Connor, *St. Paul's Corinth*, 156.
5. Lang, *Cure and Cult*, 14.
6. In Lang, *Cure and Cult*, 15.
7. In Lang, *Cure and Cult*, 20. For other examples, see MacMullen and Lane, *Paganism and Christianity*, 31–33.
8. British Museum GR 1912. 0311.1, Roman first–second century. Similarly a Jewish hospital I once visited in Newark, New Jersey, had a sign near the front door quoting Exodus 15:26: "I the Lord am your healer."
9. Paul Maas, *Epidaurische Hymnen* (Halle: Max Niemeyer, 1933), in MacMullen and Lane, *Paganism and Christianity*, 57.

10. Broneer, "Corinth," 93. The Isthmian games were held in Corinth in the year before and after the Olympic games. They were held in honor of Poseidon/Neptune and took place at his temple on the Isthmus of Corinth.

11. See Wiseman, "Corinth and Rome," 540–541.

12. See Edwards, "Tyche at Corinth."

13. Edwards, "Tyche at Corinth," 532n16.

14. Edwards, "Tyche at Corinth," 533.

15. Edwards, "Tyche at Corinth," 532.

16. Edwards, "Tyche at Corinth," 533.

17. Edwards, "Tyche at Corinth," 541.

18. Edwards, "Tyche at Corinth," 542.

19. British Museum GR 1995.12–15.1, second century CE, Cyprus.

20. Ogilvie, *The Romans*, 47.

21. In an intriguing Corinthian connection here, Pliny views the fact that the Corinth canal was started by several emperors but not completed by any of them—all died shamefully, he says—as proving that the attempt was an "act of sacrilege" (*Natural History*, 4.4.9).

22. Fowler, *Roman Ideas*, 65.

23. Williams, "The Refounding," 31, cites this as evidence that "some Greek cult ritual, although known to the Romans, was not reinstated by the Roman colonists, even though the cult or cult monuments were reestablished."

24. In Murphy-O'Connor, "The Corinth," 152.

25. Aphrodite and the other gods had various surnames corresponding to aspects of her character. Pausanias has this to say about Melainis in his *Description of Greece* 8.6.5: "Near the well is a hall of Dionysos and a sanctuary of Aphrodite Melainis. The surname of the goddess is simply due to the fact that men do not, as beasts do, have sexual intercourse always by day, but in most cases by night."

26. Spitzer, "Roman Relief Bowls," 186–187.

27. Parke and Wormell, *The Delphic Oracle*, vol. 2, no. 7, 199, 398, 547.

28. Parke and Wormell, *The Delphic Oracle*, vol. 1, 262.

29. In Forbes, *Prophecy*, 300.

30. Parke and Wormell, *The Delphic Oracle*, vol. 1, 262.

31. Levin, "The Old Greek Oracles," 1605.

32. In Murphy-O'Connor, *St. Paul's Corinth*, 141. The addressee was not recovered in the inscription, and the Greek text is discussed in an appendix, 173–176.

33. Murphy-O'Connor, *St. Paul's Corinth*, 149.

34. Levin, "The Old Greek Oracles," 1604.

35. Murphy-O'Connor, *St. Paul's Corinth*, 145.

36. Levin, "The Old Greek Oracles," 1614. This conclusion is strongly supported by Forbes: "What we have seen of oracular practice, both at Delphi and Didyma, suggests a calm and aristocratic concern for detail rather than intense emotional involvement" (*Prophecy*, 282).

37. Kent, *The Inscriptions*, nos. 66 and 67, date uncertain.

38. Paige, "Spirit," 264ff., 288 ff.

39. Paige, "Spirit," 264.
40. In Rice and Stambaugh, *Sources*, 143.
41. Rice and Stambaugh, *Sources*, 143.
42. In Rice and Stambaugh, *Sources*, 139.
43. Fowler, *Roman Ideas*, 159.
44. Fowler, *Roman Ideas*, 160.
45. Petit, *Pax Romana*, 118.
46. Murphy-O'Connor, "The Corinth," 41.

Chapter 3

1. Agourides, *Istoria*, 31.
2. See, for example, Sampley and Lampe, *Paul and Rhetoric*.
3. Mortley, "The Past," 195. He has an insightful discussion of Clement's comparison of Greek *manteia* and Jewish prophecy (*Stromateis* I.21.134.1ff.). Mortley points out that the sense of connection between cultures was part of a common worldview that existed long before Clement: "Truth was universal, and was therefore to be found everywhere" (200).
4. In Winter, *Philo and Paul*, 78n66.
5. Winter, *Philo and Paul*, 79n70.
6. For more evidence of Plutarch's feelings toward the Roman subjugation of Greece, see *Praecepta gerendae rei publicae* 813 D–F, 824 E–F, in Alcock, *Graecia Capta*, 150.
7. See Xenophon, *Symposium*, 3.5; Dio Chrysostom, *Borysthenic Discourse* (Oration 36).9; both noted in van der Valk, "The Homeric Quotations," 285, and Householder, *Literary Quotations*, 57. See also Ibrahim, "The Study."
8. In Winter, *Philo and Paul*, 78.
9. Coxon, "Xenophanes," 1141.
10. See also *Isis and Osiris* 367, 373: "Hermes . . . that is to say Reason."
11. Levinskaya cites Roberts, "Reliefs," 112–122, in *The Book of Acts*, 93n66.
12. Fowler, *Roman Ideas*, 161. See also Agourides, *Istoria*, 44–56.
13. For more on Greek "disbelief" in Homer, see Caragounis, "Greek Culture."
14. Kristof, "Cardinal Tobin."
15. Rice and Stambaugh, *Sources*, 147.
16. British Museum, P. Hawara 24.
17. MacMullen and Lane, *Paganism and Christianity*, viii.
18. Griffin, introduction, xviii.
19. Griffin, introduction, xviii.
20. Griffin, introduction, xviii.
21. Griffin, introduction, xix.
22. Griffin, introduction, xxi.
23. Horace *Epistles,* in Horace, *Odes,* introduction by B. Radice, 29.
24. Similarly, *Odes* 2.11.11–12: "Why tire your mortal mind with counsels of eternity? Better to drink while we may."

Chapter 4

1. The translation of Propertius by H. E. Butler is slightly altered here to eliminate archaisms.
2. A. L. Wheeler in Ovid, *Tristia*, xxi.
3. The legend arose that these birds built their nests on the sea, bringing two weeks of calm in early winter, known as "halcyon days," in order to lay their eggs.
4. In Fowler, *Roman Ideas*, 157.
5. Foster, in Livy, *History*, xxi.
6. Foster, in Livy, *History*, xxi.
7. J. D. Duff in Lucan, *The Civil War*, xiv.
8. Anderson, "Lucan," 620.
9. See Sullivan, *The Satyricon*, 27ff., for discussion of Petronius's identity. For the minority view that he was primarily a moral philosopher, see 106ff.
10. Sullivan's close comparison of passages from Petronius and Seneca shows convincingly that Seneca is often the butt of the satire. The *Satyricon*, he says, is a "a free pastiche of the philosopher" (*The Satyricon*, 198).
11. The translation is Sullivan's. Other passages include 104.3; fragments xxvii, xxx.
12. For example, see Petronius, *Satyricon* 1, 90, 126.
13. Sullivan, *The Satyricon*, 212–213.

Chapter 5

1. Treves, "Posidonius," 868.
2. See the extensive index of ancient sources Kidd adduces in *Posidonius*, vol. 1, 257–264.
3. Kidd, *Posidonius*, I, 257.
4. Kidd, *Posidonius*, II (i), 427.
5. Kidd, *Posidonius*, II (i), 430.
6. See also On Fate 5–7; Div. II.33–35; II.47; I:125, 1:64, I:129–130.
7. Treves, "Posidonius," 868.
8. Posidonius, cited by Galen, *De Hippocratis et Platonis Decretis*, iv.7, in Barrett, *The New Testament Background*, 65.
9. Luck, 230–231.
10. Ogilvie, *The Romans*, 54.
11. Manilius, *Astronomica* 2.65ff., trans. G. P. Goold, LCL, in MacMullen and Lane, *Paganism and Christianity*, 18–19.
12. Kidd, *Posidonius*, II (i) 339.
13. Barrett, *The New Testament Background*, 65.
14. See also *Republic* 364B; *Laws* 772D; *Phaedrus* 244Aff.
15. Ibycus was a Greek lyric poet of the sixth century BCE.
16. In Alexander, "Acts," 59.
17. Note that in the LCL *Moralia* (vol. 7) the title is translated "On the Sign of Socrates."
18. Cited in Alexander, "Acts," 58.

19. Jones, in Strabo, *Geography*, xviii.
20. Dodds, *The Greeks*, 120.
21. In Aristotle, *On the Soul*.
22. Aristotle, "Prophesying by Dreams," in *On the Soul*.
23. Kidd, "Posidonius," 1232.

Chapter 6

1. Latham, introduction, 13.
2. Latham, introduction, 9.
3. "Cicero, of course was extensively read, then and later, by Christians, and has carried his Academicism down the centuries with him." Armstrong, "The Self-Definition," 99.
4. H. Rackam, introduction to Cicero, *On Fate*, 189.
5. *De officiis* 2.6.19, noted by Fowler, *Roman Ideas*, 67.
6. Grant, *Ancient Roman Religion*, 79.
7. Agourides, *Istoria*, 68.
8. James, "The Correspondence," 480–484.
9. Surprisingly, it is precisely some of these pagan practices criticized by Seneca that are found in a rare instance of Christian praise for the pagans, in the *Didascalia Apostolorum* (Syria, mid-third century ce): "The heathen, when they daily rise from their sleep, go in the morning to worship and minister to their idols; and before all their works and undertakings they go first and worship their idols. Neither at their festivals and fairs are they wanting, but are constant in assembling—not only they who are of the district but even those who come from afar; and all likewise assemble and come to the spectacle of their theatre." *Didascalia Apostolorum* 13, in MacMullen and Lane, *Paganism and Christianity*, 84.
10. MacMullen and Lane, *Paganism and Christianity*, 81–82.
11. In 62 ce at the latest, since that is the date of death for Lucilius, to whom the essay is addressed. Seneca, *Moral Essays*, vol. 1, xi.
12. *To Lucilius* 41.5, trans. Robin Campbell, in *Letters from a Stoic* (Harmondsworth, UK: Penguin, 1969), 87, in MacMullen and Lane, *Paganism and Christianity*, 79–80.
13. Pliny, *Natural History* 28.4.228, 28.6.30, trans. W. H. S. Jones, LCL, in MacMullen and Lane, *Paganism and Christianity*, 22–24.

Chapter 7

1. Petit, *Pax Romana*, 117.
2. Bernadotte Perrin, in Plutarch, *Lives* I, xii.
3. D. A. Russell, "Plutarch," OCD, 849.
4. Interestingly, Plutarch contrasts Ajax's actions with the superstitious inaction of Jewish forces in one of the Roman campaigns (the incident is of uncertain date, but possibly refers to the capture of Jerusalem in 63 BCE [Pompey] or 38 BCE [Antony]): "These Jews, because it was the Sabbath day, sat in their places immovable,

while the enemy were planting ladders against the walls and capturing the defenses, and they did not get up, but remained there, fast bound in the toils of superstition as in one great net" (*Superstition* 169C).

5. In *Isis and Osiris* Plutarch notes, "In Crete there was a statue of Zeus having no ears; for it is not fitting for the Ruler and Lord of all to listen to anyone" (381E).

6. In Alcock, *Graecia Capta*, 150.

7. In Rice and Stambaugh, *Sources*, 158.

8. Dodd, *According to the Scriptures*, 12.

9. Brown, *The Body*, 22.

10. Petit, *Pax Romana*, 112.

11. Fox, *Pagans and Christians*, 123.

Chapter 8

1. See also 1 Sam 15:23; 2 Kgs 17:17; 2 Chr 33:6; Isa 2:6; Wis 12:4; Sir 34:5.

2. Stulmacher, "The Significance," 12. See also Oikonomos, "The Significance," which shows the diversity of answers given in church history to questions about the authority of various Old Testament apocryphal writing. See also Pentiuc, *The Old Testament*, especially 132–133.

3. Stern, "Introduction," 1.

4. The technical term *theosebeis* (translated as "worshipper of God" or "God-fearer") refers to sympathetic Gentiles who were attracted to Jewish worship but had not converted. For the debate surrounding its use, see Levinskaya, *The Book of Acts*, chapter 4.

5. The date of the expulsion that forced Aquila and his wife Priscilla to leave Rome and move to Corinth (Acts 18:2) is disputed, most scholars opting for 49.

6. "And they all [*pantes*] seized Sosthenes" (Acts 18:17). Most scholars say the crowd doing the beating was made up of anti-Jewish Gentiles. But I. H. Marshall (*Acts*, 299) suggests that Sosthenes could well have been a Christian sympathizer. This is also the view of John Chrysostom (*Homilies on Acts* 39).

7. The earliest Jewish finds date from the second to fifth centuries CE.

8. See also *Vita Mosis*, II, 27 in Stern, "The Jewish Diaspora," 118. For a summary of what is known of Jewish Corinth in the first century, see Witherington, *Conflict and Community*, 24–28; Murphy-O'Connor, *St. Paul's Corinth*, 77–80. For a thorough evaluation of Jewish inscriptions from Corinth, see Levinskaya, *The Book of Acts*, 162–166.

9. Safrai, "Relations," 184.

10. Stern, "The Jewish Diaspora," 159. Based on evidence from Philo, Murphy-O'Connor says, "Despite the complete silence of all other ancient sources, it would appear that we must conclude that [Corinth and Argos] had particularly large and vital Jewish communities." Otherwise, "we are forced to extrapolate from what is known elsewhere in the Diaspora" (*St. Paul's Corinth*, 78, 79).

11. Applebaum, "The Organization," 464.

12. Applebaum, "The Organization," 492. He notes that the Jewish community attracted the unflattering attention of Cicero, who was defending L. Valerius Flaccus on trial in

Rome in 59 BCE for, among other charges, confiscating gold collected for the Temple at Jerusalem while Flaccus was governor of Asia. Cicero was aware of a large Jewish audience in the court and hence spoke in a low voice for the benefit of the jury alone so his words of contempt for the Jews and their "barbaric superstition" would not provoke a riot (*Pro Flacco* 28:67). See also Feldman, *Jew and Gentile*; Levinskaya, *The Book of Acts*.

13. Applebaum, "The Organization," 492. See also Safrai and Stern, *The Jewish People*, 2:701–727.

14. Suetonius, *Divus Julius* 42.3, in *Lives of the Caesars*; Josephus, *Antiquities* xiv.215, in Stern, "The Jewish Diaspora," 163.

15. *Hullin* 84.5, in Stern, "The Jewish Diaspora," 163.

16. Stern, "The Jewish Diaspora," 163.

17. Stern, "The Jewish Diaspora," 163. He cites Josephus, *Antiquities* xviii,65–84; Tacitus, *Annals II*, 85; Suetonius, *Life of Tiberius* 36.

18. For a summary of the evidence for the expulsion of Jews from Rome in 49, see Witherington, *Conflict and Community*, 29n74. He concludes that the Chrestus in question was probably not Jesus Christ, but a Roman Jew.

19. Safrai and Stern, *The Jewish People*, 2:793. See also Feldman, *Jew and Gentile*; Stern, "The Jewish Diaspora"; Levinskaya, *The Book of Acts*. The historian Simon Schama, in his popular BBC documentary, *The Story of the Jews*, emphasizes that Jewish identity continues to be shaped around the Torah, both written and oral, however that has been interpreted. See also Schama's book by the same title.

20. Neusner, *The Classics*, ix–x, citing *Abot* 1:1.

21. Susan Niditch, in *Oral World and Written Word*, argues that both written and oral Torah existed together from the start.

22. Safrai and Stern, *The Jewish People*, 2:793. Bamberger says that in the first century, literalists like the Sadducees were very much in the minority ("The Torah," xxxi).

23. Safrai, "Relations," 185.

24. Maccoby, *Early Rabbinic Writings*, 28.

25. Maccoby, *Early Rabbinic Writings*, 28.

26. Maccoby, *Early Rabbinic Writings*, 28–29. Jacob Neusner has a similar view of the development of oral and written Torah: see *The Mishnah*, xxxv–xl.

27. Maccoby, *Early Rabbinic Writings*, 4.

28. Maccoby, *Early Rabbinic Writings*, 4.

29. Maccoby, *Early Rabbinic Writings*, 4.

30. The Mishnah was codified in the third century CE. However, there is evidence of written Mishnah material in the Dead Sea Scrolls (first century BCE), indicating some departure at an early date from the requirement that the oral law not be written down.

31. Schreiber, *Jewish Law*, 203.

32. Schreiber, *Jewish Law*, 203. Rabbi Martin S. Cohen gives an intriguing example of how this process might work today. Leviticus 14 specifies that for purification of a leper, sacrificial blood must be daubed on the right thumb, right big toe, and right ear. But what if the leper is missing any one of these? The Mishnah discusses the accommodations that could be made in the case of an earless man, a *metzora* ("one

being diseased"; *Tractate Negaim* 14:9). Rabbi Cohen unpacks this for present-day application and says that the Mishnah is composed as it is in order "to give the formal nod to *halakhic* authority [*halakha* is the Jewish law] to the principle of allegiance to the letter of the law," but also to give support to the voices of compromise so that the law may be "kind and reasonable." To apply this precedent to a contemporary question he asks, "Should gay people who cannot participate in heterosexual marriage, just sit it out and skip the *mitzvah* [commandment] entirely, or should we applaud any effort to find a suitable alternative that embodies the spirit, if not the precise letter, of the law?" (*The Boy*, 97–98).

33. For discussion of worship in this period, see Safrai and Stern, *The Jewish People*, vol. 2, chapters 14–18.

34. See Levine, "The Nature."

35. Safrai and Stern, *The Jewish People*, 2:922.

36. Safrai and Stern, *The Jewish People*, 2:917.

37. Safrai and Stern, *The Jewish People*, 2:918–919. See also Rajak and Noy, "Archisynagogoi."

38. Safrai and Stern, *The Jewish People*, 2:915.

39. Safrai and Stern, *The Jewish People*, 1:432. See also Momigliano, *On Pagans*, 90; Baumgarten, "The Torah"; Levine, "The Nature." For more on the changes between first and second temple periods, see Davies and Finkelstein, *The Cambridge History*, 1.130–161; Grabbe, *Judaism*, 1.119–145.

40. "While Israel dwelt in that land Reuben went and lay with Bilhah his father's concubine; and Israel heard of it."

41. In Bromiley, *International*, 729, citing *Qiddushin* 49a.

42. Safrai and Stern, *The Jewish People*, 2:931.

43. Safrai and Stern, *The Jewish People*, 2:973.

44. Maccoby, *Early Rabbinic Writings*, 15–16.

45. Fishbane, "Inner-Biblical Exegesis," 48.

46. For discussion of Paul's use of LXX and Hebrew texts, see Ellis, *Paul's Use*, 10–20. Ellis counts 51 citations of the LXX (22 at variance with the Hebrew, mostly from Isaiah and Genesis), 4 citations of the Hebrew against LXX, and 38 citations that diverge from both. The reasons for these variations are still a matter of debate.

47. Avi-Yonah, "Archeological Sources," 54.

48. How well Philo knew Hebrew is also under debate. See Instone-Brewer, *Techniques*, 202.

49. Instone-Brewer, *Techniques*, 209–210.

50. The text cited here is that of Charles, *The Apocrypha*.

51. For a summary of the main differences between the LXX and Hebrew texts, see Melvin Peters, ABD V:1093–1104.

52. ABD V:1017. As Fishbane has shown, this approach is found much earlier than Tannaitic times, in the OT itself.

53. For a detailed account see Charlesworth, "Old Testament Apocrypha."

54. Metzger, *An Introduction*, 31. Tobit was also widely referenced by church fathers as a prototype of the Christian who prays, fasts, and does good works in faith and

patience (Polycarp, Hermas, Cyprian, Clement of Alexandria). Cyprian notes Tobit's continual prayer combined with acts of justice (*De dominica oratione* 33), while Clement of Alexandria (*Stromata* I.123) considers Tobias "a symbol of the soul led by its guardian angel" (L. Vanyo, "Tobias," in Ferguson, *Encyclopedia*).

55. NJBC 38:29. Possible dates range from fifth century BCE to first century CE.
56. "Judith," in *OAB Apocrypha*, 76.
57. Metzger, *An Introduction*, 52–53.
58. Like Tobit and Judith, the story of Susanna was popular in early Christianity, when it was depicted in catacombs and cited by a number of prominent writers (Irenaeus, Origen, Tertullian, Athanasius, Cyril of Jerusalem, and Gregory Nazianzus). See Pamela Bright, "Susanna," in Ferguson, *Encyclopedia*, 1097.

Chapter 9

1. Neusner and Green, *Dictionary*, 2.481. For the debate over Philo's significance, see ABD V:341.
2. On the centrality of Philo's Jewish identity, see Runia, *Philo*, 540.
3. Winter, *Philo and Paul*, 111, citing numerous references in Philo.
4. Runia, *Philo*, 536.
5. Winter, *Philo and Paul*, 241–242. For further comparison of the exegetical techniques of Philo and Paul, see Wan, "Charismatic Exegesis."
6. In this particular passage the question was this: Why in Exodus 7:15 does Moses refer to the Nile as having "lips" (*cheilos*) but does not apply this term to other sacred rivers? Philo's answer: human lives, not river currents are the concern here. "For the lives of the good and the bad are shown, one in deeds, the other in words, and words belong to the tongue, mouth and *lips*" (*Dreams* 2.302; the rest of the text is missing).
7. Instone-Brewer, 426.
8. Stern, "The Greek and Latin," 19. He cites as examples Philo's *On the Embassy to Gaius* 3 and *Against Flaccus* 102, 170.
9. Runia, *Philo*, 541. Runia cites the Talmud tractate Megillah 9a.
10. Colson and Whittaker note that *ypechei* (prompter), "which is frequently used by Philo, seems to carry with it the thought of a voice heard inwardly and not audible in the ordinary sense" (in *On Dreams*, 601).
11. See Sandmel, *Philo*, 87–89.

Chapter 10

1. Elsewhere Josephus defends attention to dreams in the face of Greek ridicule (*Against Apion* 1.205–212). But he then rejects an Egyptian claim to a divine appearance in a dream, saying, "He invents his own story" (*Against Apion* 1.295, 298).
2. Urbach, *The Sages*, 593.

3. Feldman, "Josephus," ABD III:985–986. For extensive discussion of how Josephus approaches the Hebrew Scriptures, see Feldman, *Josephus's Interpretation*; Klawans, *Josephus*.

4. Feldman, "Josephus," ABD III:985–986.

5. Feldman, "Josephus," ABD III:985–986.

6. See also Flusser, *Judaism*, 224.

7. Josephus connects Essene belief in fate with the ability of some of their prophets to foretell the future: "There are some among them who profess to foretell the future, being versed from their early years in the holy books, various forms of purification and apothegms of the prophets; and seldom, if ever, do they err in their predictions" (*Jewish War* 2.8.12).

8. Urbach, *The Sages*, 284–285.

9. Neusner and Green, "Philo," in *Dictionary*, 481.

10. Feldman, "Josephus," ABD, III:993.

11. However, Feldman views Josephus as much more representative of mainstream Judaism than Philo (ABD, III:993).

Chapter 11

1. Dead Sea Scrolls texts are taken from Martinez, *The Dead Sea Scrolls*. See also Vermes, *The Complete*. For an introduction to the Scrolls and their discovery, see Vermes, *The Story*. For access to digital views and extensive information, see the Leon Levy Dead Sea Scrolls Digital Library, operated under the Israel Antiquities Authority, https://www.deadseascrolls.org.il/?locale=en_US.

2. Instone-Brewer, *Techniques*, 198.

3. Instone-Brewer, *Techniques*, 197.

4. Englezakis, *New and Old*, 53.

5. It is generally acknowledged that no satisfactory term has been found to describe this literature, since "apocrypha" is understood in widely differing ways, with Roman Catholics and Orthodox including Protestant "apocryphal" books as part of the Old Testament canon. "Pseudepigrapha" is also often misleading. Other proposed terms include "extra-biblical books," "the writings contemporaneous with Jesus," and "intertestamental books." For a review of this material and its dating, see NJBC 67. For a more extensive discussion, see Charlesworth, *The Pseudepigrapha*. For texts and commentary in English, see Charlesworth, *The Old Testament Pseudepigrapha*, vol. 1 and vol. 2. For the latest research, see the *Journal for the Study of the Pseudepigrapha*, https://us.sagepub.com/en-us/nam/journal/journal-study-pseudepigrapha.

6. Metzger, *The Oxford Annotated Apocrypha*, xxii.

7. Charlesworth, *Old Testament Pseudepigrapha*, vol. 1, xxviii.

8. NRSV (Anglicized version) National Council of Churches of Christ USA, 1989/1995.

9. Metzger, *The Oxford Annotated Apocrypha*, 219.

10. Metzger, *The Oxford Annotated Apocrypha*, 500.

11. Charlesworth, *Old Testament Pseudepigrapha*, vol. 1, xxviii.

12. Collins, "The Sibylline Oracles," 322.

13. Collins, "The Sibylline Oracles," 322.

14. JBC 67:35.

15. Compare Paul: "You know that when you were heathen, you were led astray to dumb idols, however you may have been moved" (1 Cor 12:2).

16. Charlesworth, *Old Testament Pseudepigrapha*, vol. 1, xxxi.

Chapter 12

1. See Instone-Brewer, *Techniques* and *Traditions*. See also Maccoby, *Early Rabbinic Writings*.

2. Maccoby, *Early Rabbinic Writings*, 15.

3. Neusner, *Rabbinic Literature*, 169. Similarly, Paul took the view that the human examples of the Hebrew scriptures were written "for our instruction" (Rom 15:4; 1 Cor 10:11).

4. The following section on the Bat Kol draws heavily on rabbinic material found in Montefiore and Loewe, *A Rabbinic Anthology*, and Urbach, *The Sages*. I am grateful to Dr. David Instone-Brewer of Tyndale House in Cambridge for these suggestions and for conversations regarding the Bat Kol.

5. In Montefiore and Loewe, *Rabbinic*, 16, citing *Pesiqta Rabbati* 160a.

6. Montefiore and Loewe, *Rabbinic*, 739; see also Lieberman, *Hellenism*, 194–199; Sperling, "Akkadian Egerru."

7. *b. Sotah* 33a, cited at http://www.come-and-hear.com/sotah/sotah_33.html. The *Shema* was originally just this single verse but was expanded to include liturgically the following verses as well: Deut 6:4–9, 11:13–21; Num 15:37–41.

8. *b. Ta'anit* 25b, in Montefiore and Loewe, *Rabbinic*, 372.

9. In Montefiore and Loewe, *Rabbinic*, 431. Compare Luke 10:25–37, "The Good Samaritan."

10. Urbach, *The Sages*, 579.

11. Lachs, *A Rabbinic Commentary*, 214. The same phenomenon is frequently found in the Christian tradition. Compare the parallel in the *Confessions* of St. Augustine (354–430), whose conversion was prompted by the words he overheard of a child playing in the garden: "Tolle, lege"—Pick it up and read. He understood this to be divine guidance to read the scriptures in front of him, just as Anthony the Great had done (251–356). In both cases their lives changed dramatically in response to following divine guidance. See Augustine, *Confessions* 12.28–29.

12. In Montefiore and Loewe, *Rabbinic*, 692, citing *Pesiqta Rabbati* 152a.

13. In Montefiore and Loewe, *Rabbinic*, 692. Citing tractates Berakhot 4a, 20a and Sanhedrin 94b.

14. Montefiore and Loewe *Rabbinic*, 692, citing Exodus Rabbah, Beshallah, 23, 5; Midrash Psalm 145, I (267b, 1).

15. Schreiber, *Jewish Law*, 212, citing Baba Metzi'a 59b.

16. Schreiber, *Jewish Law*, 212.

17. Maccoby, *Early Rabbinic Writings*, 5.
18. Schreiber, *Jewish Law*, 211–212, citing Levi Yitzhak of Berditchev.
19. Urbach, *The Sages*, 1:118–119, citing Sifra, end of Lev., T. B. Temura 16a, and T. B. Yevamot 102a.
20. Schreiber, *Jewish Law*, 212, citing Sefer Ha'Ikarim, 3.23. He also cites the medieval Jewish philosopher Albo.
21. Schreiber, *Jewish Law*, 214.
22. Schreiber, *Jewish Law*, 214.
23. Schreiber, *Jewish Law*, 214.
24. Maccoby, *Early Rabbinic Writings*, 38.
25. Maccoby, *Early Rabbinic Writings*, 18–19.
26. Urbach, *The Sages*, 1:119.
27. Englezakis, *New and Old*, 45.
28. Urbach, *The Sages*, 1:577.
29. In Urbach, *The Sages*, 1:577, citing *Tosefta Sota* xiii, 3, 318.
30. In Urbach, *The Sages*, 1:578, citing Sukkah 28a; Bava Batra 134a.
31. Urbach, *The Sages*, 1:578.
32. Urbach, *The Sages*, 1:578, citing *b. Bava Batra* 12a.
33. Urbach, *The Sages*, 1:578.
34. Urbach, *The Sages*, 2:949–950n28, citing Tosefta Pesahim i, 27, p. 157 and T. P. Shevi'it ix, 1, p. 38d.
35. Urbach, *The Sages*, 2:950n29, citing *b. Bava Batra* 12b.
36. Englezakis, *New and Old*, 55.
37. Englezakis, *New and Old*, 55.
38. Fishbane, *Biblical Interpretation*. For a summary of his evidence and results, see 525–543.
39. The late W. Gunther Plaut, a prominent Canadian rabbinical scholar and editor of *The Torah: A Modern Commentary*, noted that this freedom of interpretation didn't last into the modern world: "Halakhah ran into serious difficulties only in modern times when the rabbis no longer considered themselves qualified to interpret the law freely" (*The Torah*, 1085).
40. Childs, *Introduction*, 445.
41. See Childs, *Introduction*.
42. Guillaume, *Prophecy and Divination*, 364. While God is "persuadable" in Hebrew thought, he is not "coercible." Guillaume refuses to exaggerate the differences between Hebrew and other forms of prophecy, and prefers to see them all sharing the conviction that divine guidance is a normal feature of human life (see especially 362–367). I am grateful to Dr. David Instone-Brewer for this reference.

Chapter 13

1. Peter Marshall says, "It is difficult for us to grasp how pervasive and influential rhetoric was in Greco-Roman society" (*Enmity*, 383). For a summary on Paul and rhetoric, see Winter, "Rhetoric," 820–822; Witherington, *Conflict and Community*, 39–43.

2. The negative connotation linking guides with blindness is also found in Greco-Roman and Jewish literature of the period (Plutarch, *Chance* 98B; Josephus, *Jewish War* 6.2.6), but this was not its only sense. The term was also associated with guidance from a god or goddess. Pausanias gives an example of this in his description of the temple of Hera at Sikyon, not far from Corinth (*Description of Greece* 2.11.2). Hermes is associated with guidance of the soul at death, and the Corpus Hermeticorum makes reference to the mind (*nous*) as guide of the soul (TDNT 5:97).

3. The two terms are linked in Ps 42:3: "Oh send out thy light and thy truth; let them lead [*odēgeō*] me, let them bring [*agō*] me to thy holy hill and to thy dwelling!" This verse is used as the liturgical entrance hymn (introit) on the feast of Mid-Pentecost in the Orthodox Church, celebrating the midpoint between Easter and Pentecost.

4. Paul also uses the word *agō* in reference to being led astray by idolatry (1 Cor 12:2).

5. Dunn, "Discernment," 91. Dunn acknowledges the roles of authority and past revelation in the process of discernment but admits the elusive quality of divine guidance when he gives special weight to "the dialectic of liberty" through which decisions are based on the criterion of love, "something much more spontaneous than can be tested by simple reference to the rule book and precedent" and "much more in the nature of obedience to an inward compulsion" (91).

6. JBC 47:1. Alternatively, the phrase may have been Paul's creation (Witherington, *Conflict and Community*, 80).

7. JBC 51:9; TDNT 1:112.

8. NJBC, 82: 77; Fee, *The First Epistle*, 32n21. The centrality of baptism in St. Paul's thought and its connection with the reception of the Spirit is well known. See NJBC 82:112–115; Schnackenburg, *Baptism*; Dunn, *Baptism*.

9. JBC 79:138.

10. The most frequent use of the phrase *klētois agiois* is Lev 23, where it occurs seven times in reference to the assembly on the seventh day (Lev 23:3, 7, 8, 24, 27, 35, 36; see also Exod 12:16 and Num 28:25).

11. NJBC 49:12; TDNT 3:804–809.

12. In 1–2 Cor Paul uses *gnosis* (knowledge) and its cognates 19 times, which is more than twice the use in all his other epistles combined (9 times); *sophia* (wisdom) and related words are similarly used much more than in his other writing: in 1 Cor 15 times, elsewhere 12 times. Words related to *pneuma* (spirit) occur 57 times in 1–2 Cor, accounting for more than a third of all the usages (Rom 30 times, Eph 17, Gal 15, the other epistles fewer).

13. TDNT 2:61–62. The word could also be used apart from religious connotations, but in the Septuagint and in Greek literature it is associated with divine revelations.

14. JBC 51:16; Fee, *The First Epistle*, 74; Agourides, *Apostolou Pavlou*, 54–55 (see Matt 11:38–39; Mark 8:11; Luke 11:16; John 6:30). Others suggest "signs" are miracles generally (NJBC 49:22).

15. So also Barrett, *The First Epistle*, 54–55; Conzelmannn, *First Corinthians*, 47.

16. How accurately Paul understood Judaism is still the subject of debate. See Sanders, *Paul and Palestinian Judaism*; Ellis, *Paul's Use*; Davies, *Paul*.

17. The survey here covers 10 epistles, excluding the Pastorals, using the list in UBS-4.

18. While some have argued for possible allusion to 1 Enoch (for example, in Rom 3 and 1 Cor 3), there are no certain references in Paul's writing to *any* texts in the vast body of intertestamental literature. See Herms, " 'Being Saved' "; Linebaugh, "Debating."

19. However, it is also possible that Paul's allusions to deutero-canonical books may have been more extensive than suggested in the UBS-4. Other possible allusions: Ps 31:4, 11 LXX (2 Cor 12:1, 7, 9), Isa 65:11 LXX (1 Cor 10:21), 4 Macc 7:14 (2 Cor 4:2, 8), 4 Macc 7:19 (Mark 12:26; Rom 6:10, 14:8; Gal 2:19), Sir 5:5–6 (Rom 2:4), Sir 7:34 (Rom 12:15), Sir 7:29–31 (1 Tim 5:17), Sir 33:2 (James 1:6; Eph 1:10), Sir 43:26 (Col 1:17), Wis 2:22 (Rom 6:23; Phil 3:14?), Wis 9:15 (2 Cor 5:1, 4), Wis 13:5, 8, and 14:24, 27 (Rom 1:20–29, 9:21–23, 12:12, 20, 15:7), Wis 19:4 (1 Thess 2:16).

20. Hart, *The New Testament,* 376. Hart is commenting on Gal 4:21–31, Paul's allegory of Hagar and Sarah.

21. See Georges Florovsky, "Revelation and Interpretation," in *Bible, Church,* 33–36, on the need to distinguish carefully between the "provisional" and permanent in scripture.

22. Dodd, *According,* especially 126–127.

23. Fee, *The First Epistle,* 114, 110n13; Agourides, *Apostolou Pavlou,* 65.

24. Conzelmann, *First Corinthians,* 57.

25. Barrett, *Corinthians,* 76.

26. Conzelmann, *First Corinthians,* 59.

27. Orr and Walther, *1 Corinthians,* 158.

28. JBC 51:19.

29. Tarazi, *1 Thessalonians,* 142–143. See also Witmer, " 'Taught by God' and 'θεοδιδακτοι' in 1 Thessalonians 4.9."

30. John Chrysostom understands Paul to be including the whole body of Corinthian believers among those who have been "taught by God" (*Homilies on 1 Corinthians,* 36.7–8).

31. NJBC 49:20.

32. Fee, *The First Epistle,* 107–109.

33. Orr and Walther, *1 Corinthians,* 157.

34. Paul warns about deception repeatedly: 1 Cor 6:9, 15:33; Gal 6:7; Eph 4:14; 1 Thess 2:3; 2 Tim 3:13; Titus 3:3.

35. Moffat, *Corinthians,* 46.

36. Conzelmann, *First Corinthians,* 86.

37. Fee, *The First Epistle,* 166.

38. Morna Hooker, "Beyond the Things Which Are Written: An Examination of 1 Cor 4:6," cited in Agourides, *Apostolou Pavlou,* 87–88.

39. Bruce, *1 and 2 Corinthians,* 48; Hays, *First Corinthians,* 69.

40. If the Corinthians were tempted to abandon scripture and commandments, the Galatians had the opposite temptation: *excessive* reliance on written texts and pious traditions. So in writing to the Galatians Paul doesn't emphasize keeping the commandments but rather "faith working through love" (Gal 5:6) and "a new creation" (Gal 6:15). In other words, Paul has two different pastoral aims with these two different communities. In their relationship to "what is written" he needs to tighten the Corinthians but loosen the Galatians.

41. Plutarch, *Fabius Maximus* 5, LSJ, παιδαγωγός (*paidagōgós*). He is still known as "Cunctator," the Procrastinator. But Fabius's patience eventually overcame Hannibal's threat to Rome. Fabius was then more appreciated and was called "the Shield of Rome" (OCD, 427).

42. JBC 51:27 cites Caius (or Gaius, c. 130–180), *Institutes*, 1.63–64, a compendium of Roman law, c. 170. Such unions are treated severely, and any children are regarded as illegitimate.

43. JBC, 79:161.

44. Agourides, *Apostolou Pavlou*, 102.

45. See later on 1 Cor 16:22, "If any one has no love for the Lord, let him be accursed [*anathema*]." See also Jillions, "Love and Curses."

46. In Collins, "The Function," 260.

47. ACCS-NT, VII.*1-2 Corinthians*, 46.

48. ACCS-NT, VII.*1-2 Corinthians*, 46.

49. See Nathan, *The Roman Family*; Osiek and Balch, *Families*; Wright, "Family."

50. Sanders, *Paul: The Apostle*, 373.

51. Sanders, *Paul: The Apostle*, 372.

52. Sanders, *Paul: The Apostle*, 370.

53. Hart, *The New Testament*, 345n.x.

54. See Winter, *Seek the Welfare* for historical background on removing marks of circumcision (147–152); on manumission and self-enslavement (152–159).

55. TDNT, II:1–20. For the connection of daimons with spirits of the dead, see Bolt, "Jesus."

56. This is a much less irenic attitude toward pagans than Luke's portrayal of Paul in conversation with Athenians on the Areopagus (Acts 17). There Paul sees Greek piety—and especially the temple dedicated to the "unknown God" (Acts 17:23)—as a bridge to faith in Christ.

57. See Finney, "Honour"; Witherington, *Conflict and Community*, 231–240; Thompson, "Hairstyles." Murphy-O'Connor, "Sex and Logic," contends that the question here is about hairstyles, not hair coverings. John Chrysostom sees covering as the issue in regard to women, but long hair in regard to men. Both see the fundamental point as preservation of sexual distinction, although Chrysostom also is aware that long hair among men had additional connotations that made it undesirable in Paul's eyes: its association with homosexuality (*Homilies on 1 Corinthians*, 26.6) and pretensions to being a philosopher (*Homilies on 1 Corinthians*, 26.2).

58. NJBC 49:54.

59. Witherington, *Conflict and Community*, 236.

60. See Hopko, "Galatians 3:28."

61. See Witherington, *Conflict and Community*, 241–252.

62. As Hart notes ironically, "[Luke's] description in Acts of the early church's communism of goods in Jerusalem is one that good Christians have striven heroically for the better part of two millennia to pretend not to notice" (*The New Testament*, 569).

63. See later discussion on 1 Cor 16:22; Jillions, "Love and Curses."

64. Witherington, *Conflict and Community*, 250; JBC, 51:71 (NJBC, 49:57). See Luke 22:19–20.

65. Conzelmann, *First Corinthians*, 204; Fee, *The First Epistle*, 575.

66. The Gospels of Luke and Matthew are more charitable on this point and allow that opposing Christ is forgivable. Not so with blaspheming the Holy Spirit: "And everyone who speaks a word against the Son of Man will be forgiven; but whoever blasphemes against the Holy Spirit will not be forgiven" (Luke 12:10; Matt 12:31; compare Mark 3:28–30 and Isaiah 5:20). "The sin against the Holy Spirit" can be interpreted as a perversion of basic human criteria for judging experience, leading to an Orwellian world of Newspeak, where "war is peace, freedom is slavery, ignorance is strength."

67. In Johannine terms, to know Christ as the incarnate Logos is to be able to recognize his presence everywhere. Or, as one of the unwritten sayings of Jesus puts it, "It is I who am the light which is above them all. It is I who am the all. From me did the all come forth, and unto me did the all extend. Split a piece of wood, and I am there. Lift up the stone, and you will find me there" ("The Gospel of Thomas," 77). See also Hart, *The New Testament*, 194–195n.v, 549–551.

68. Bruce, *1 and 2 Corinthians*, 116; Barrett, *The First Epistle*, 278.

69. Hart also takes the view that Paul is primarily speaking about spiritual persons (1 Cor 2:15, 3:1, 14:37; Gal 6:1). He thus translates *pneumatikos* as "Spiritual man" (*The New Testament*, 564). Later Greek Christian tradition and contemporary practice use the term *pneumatikos* to refer to one's confessor and spiritual father, usually meaning a priest or monastic.

70. John Chrysostom also sees the subject here as discernment of false prophets (*Homilies on 1 Corinthians*, 29.5).

71. This is highlighted in Winter, *Seek the Welfare*.

72. NJBC 49:60: "The first three gifts, set off from the others by being numbered and personalized, constitutes the fundamental threefold ministry of the word by which the Church is founded and built up." Gordon Fee sees the ranking in similar terms, as the order in which a community is established: first by apostles, then prophets and teachers, in a process that leads from founding to consolidation of community life (*The First Epistle*, 619).

73. In 13:3 the text is uncertain, although the critical text of the Greek New Testament (UBS-4) on balance opts for *kauchisōmai* (boast) instead of the more frequently attested *kauthēsōmai* (burn). Paul's main point in 13:1–3 is that an underlying motivation of love is what matters most, regardless of whatever actions may be undertaken—even the most heroic This point remains true with either reading.

74. John Chrysostom develops this point: "But even when He was on high upon the cross, He says, Father, forgive them their sin. But the thief who before this reviled Him, He translated into very paradise; and made the persecutor Paul, an Apostle" (*Homilies on 1 Corinthians*, 32:14).

75. Barrett, *The First Epistle*, 317, in Fee, *The First Epistle*, 663.

76. Fee, *The First Epistle*, 662–663.

77. For example, *mantis* (diviner), *chrēsmologos* (soothsayer), *mainomai* (to be mad), *enthousiasmos* (frenzy, inspiration). TDNT VI:851.

78. Conzelmann, *First Corinthians*, 243. John Chrysostom too says that the rational element in Pauline prophecy is what most distinguished it from pagan oracles. The oracles lose their natural reason and act under compulsion as slaves, not understanding what they say, while the Pauline prophet remains sober, free, and aware of what he is saying. Paul's prophet is "not bound by necessity but honored with a privilege, for God chooses prophets not by compulsion, but by advising, exhorting, warning, not darkening their mind; for to cause destruction and madness and great darkness is the proper work of a demon; but it is God's work to illuminate and with consideration to teach things needful" (*Homilies on 1 Corinthians*, 29.2).

79. Hart, *The New Testament*, 345n.x.

80. However, recent scholarship on the Greco-Roman and Jewish contexts may show that these apparently contradictory points of view could be compatible. See Baum, "Paul's Conflicting Statements."

81. Hart, *The New Testament*, 345n.x; Fee, *The First Epistle*, 609–705; NJBC 49:64; Conzelmann, *First Corinthians*, 246, Agourides, *Apostolou Pavlou*, 246–247. Barrett favors this conclusion but is not certain (*The First Epistle*, 333). Hart says, "[The] whole tenor of Paul's genuine writings is one of almost unprecedented egalitarianism with regard to the sexes (Galatians 3:28 being perhaps the most famous instance, but [1 Corinthians] 7:4 above being no less extraordinary for its time)" (*The New Testament*, 345n.x). Orr and Walther take the view that the passage concerns not women generally but the particular situation in Corinth, where disruptive public disputes of wives with their husbands during worship was creating chaos (*1 Corinthians*, 312–313). This is an attractive solution but makes complete sense only if Paul, without telling us, has not included wives among the women or the "all" of 11:5, 13, 14:23–24, 26.

82. This section is adapted from Jillions, "The Language of Enemies," 324–330.

83. See also Pelikan and Hotchkiss, *Creeds*.

84. Elaine Pagels's most recent book, *Why Religion: A Personal Story* (2018), builds on her tragic personal losses and the persistent questions about the continuing attraction of religious faith.

85. Pelikan, *Credo*, 187.

86. Pelikan, *Credo*, 187.

87. Pagels, *Beyond Belief*, 183; see also Pelikan, *Credo*, 18, 19, 189.

88. Pelikan, *Credo*, 330ff., 18, 346ff.

89. In Trullo, canon 82.

90. Attributed to Alexander Schmemann.

91. See TDNT III, 827–830. The article notes that the use of *kopian* in connection with Christian ministry declined in the second century: "With increased esteem for the officers of the church it was perhaps felt that *kopian*, with its sense of manual work, was not wholly fitting" (830).

92. In commenting on "Lo! I tell you a mystery" (15:51), John Chrysostom understands that Paul is introducing "something awful and ineffable and which all know not" (*Homilies on 1 Corinthians*, 42.3). Fee in *The First Epistle* likewise sees this as a special revelation that reflects Paul's role as a prophet (12:8, 13:2).

93. Witherington, *Conflict and Community*, 310; NJBC 49:75.
94. Petros Vassiliadis emphasizes that the collection was an appropriate follow-up to their questions about liturgy: "In fact, [the collection] was identified with a 'true and spiritual liturgy' " ("Equality and Justice," 56).
95. Witherington, *Conflict and Community*, 315.
96. *Stēkete en tē pistē, andrizesthai* (Stand firm in the faith, be courageous): these words in Greek are emblazoned over the great wooden gate at the entrance to Selwyn College in the University of Cambridge. I used to see them almost every day bicycling past on my way to Tyndale House Library, where I was doing the research for this study.
97. JBC 49:79.
98. See Jillions, "Love and Curses."
99. Schmemann, *Great Lent*, 33–36.

Chapter 14

1. Manseau, *Vows*, 296–297.
2. Schaffer, "Pete."
3. Brueggemann, *Theology*, 725. This "wild" character of the biblical God is the theme as well of Paul Tarazi's *The Rise of Scripture*.
4. King, *Stride*, 124–125.
5. Nwaubani, "A Voodoo Curse."
6. Francis, Robbins, and Williams, "Believing."
7. Pew Research Center, *America's Changing*.
8. See John Templeton Foundation, "Science."
9. Hart, *Atheist Delusions*, x, 4.
10. Pew Research Center, "Attendance at Religious Services," *America's Changing Religious Landscape*, May 12, 2015, https://www.pewforum.org/religious-landscape-study/attendance-at-religious-services/; Pew Research Center, "Frequency of Prayer," *America's Changing Religious Landscape*, May 12, 2015, https://www.pewforum.org/religious-landscape-study/frequency-of-prayer/.
11. Harris, *Waking Up*, 7.
12. See, for example, John 4, where Samaritans are willing to give an initial hearing to Jesus based on what one of their fellow citizens told them about her experience. But having listened to Jesus for themselves, they come to their own conclusion based on their own personal experience.
13. See, for example, Mabry, *Spiritual Guidance*. I have a chapter in this book, "Spiritual Guidance in Eastern Orthodox Christianity," 247–261.
14. Underhill, "A Letter."
15. See the Centre's website: http://www.uwtsd.ac.uk/library/alister-hardy-religious-experience-research-centre/.
16. Robinson, *This Time-Bound Ladder*, 33.
17. Robinson, *This Time-Bound Ladder*, 46.
18. Robinson, *This Time-Bound Ladder*, 46.

19. Robinson, *This Time-Bound Ladder*, 45.

20. Robinson, *This Time-Bound Ladder*, 107.

21. Robinson, *This Time-Bound Ladder*, 115.

22. Robinson, *This Time-Bound Ladder*, 107.

23. Robinson, *This Time-Bound Ladder*, 110.

24. Robinson, *This Time-Bound Ladder*, 110–111.

25. Robinson, *This Time-Bound Ladder*, 111.

26. Robinson, *This Time-Bound Ladder*, 114.

27. Robinson, *This Time-Bound Ladder*, 116.

28. Robinson, *This Time-Bound Ladder*, 120.

29. Robinson, *This Time-Bound Ladder*, 116–117.

30. Robinson, *This Time-Bound Ladder*, 117.

31. Robinson, *This Time-Bound Ladder*, 119.

32. Robinson, *This Time-Bound Ladder*, 122, 123.

33. Schmemann, *Celebration*, 30.

Bibliography

Agourides, Savvas. *Apostolou Pavlou Prōtē Pros Korinthious Epistolē*. Thessaloniki: Pournara, 1982.

Agourides, Savvas. *Istoria tōn Chronon tēs Kainēs Diathēkēs*. Thessaloniki: Pournara, 1980.

Aland, Barbara, Kurt Aland, Johannes Karavidopoulos, Carlo Martini, and Bruce Metzger. *The Greek New Testament*, 4th revised edition. Stuttgart: United Bible Societies, 1993.

Alcock, Susan E. *Graecia Capta: The Landscapes of Roman Greece*. Cambridge, UK: Cambridge University Press, 1993.

Alexander, L. C. A. "Acts and Ancient Intellectual Biography." In *The Book of Acts in Its Ancient Literary Setting*, edited by Bruce Winter and Andrew Clarke. Grand Rapids, MI: Eerdmans, 1993.

Alister Hardy Religious Experience Research Centre. Online: http://www.uwtsd.ac.uk/library/alister-hardy-religious-experience-research-centre/.

Anderson, William Blair. "Lucan." In *The Oxford Classical Dictionary*, 2nd edition, edited by N. G. L. Hammond and H. H. Scullard. Oxford: Clarendon Press, 1970.

Antipater of Sidon. In *Greek Anthology, Volume I. Book 1: Christian Epigrams. Book 2: Description of the Statues in the Gymnasium of Zeuxippus. Book 3: Epigrams in the Temple of Apollonis at Cyzicus. Book 4: Prefaces to the Various Anthologies. Book 5: Erotic Epigrams*. Translated by W. R. Paton. Revised by Michael A. Tueller. Loeb Classical Library 67. Cambridge, MA: Harvard University Press, 2014.

Applebaum, S. "The Organization of the Jewish Communities in the Diaspora." In *The Jewish People in the First Century*, Volume 1, edited by S. Safrai and M. Stern. Assen: Brill, 1974.

Aristotle. *On the Soul. Parva Naturalia: On Breath*. Translated by W. S. Hett. Loeb Classical Library 288. Cambridge, MA: Harvard University Press, 1957.

Armstrong, A. Hilary. "The Self-Definition of Christianity in Relation to Later Platonism." In *Jewish and Christian Self-Definition, Volume 1: The Shaping of Christianity in the Second and Third Centuries*, edited by E. P. Sanders et al. London: SCM Press, 1980.

Armstrong, Karen. *Fields of Blood: Religion and the History of Violence*. New York: Anchor, 2015.

Augustine. *Confessions and Enchiridion*. Edited and translated by Albert C. Outler. Philadelphia: Westminster Press, 1955.

Aune, David E. *Prophecy in Early Christianity and the Ancient Mediterranean World*. Grand Rapids, MI: Eerdmans, 1981.

Avi-Yonah, M. "Archeological Sources. " In *The Jewish People in the First Century*, Volume 1, edited by S. Safrai and M. Stern. Assen: Brill, 1974.

Bamberger, Bernard J. "The Torah and the Jewish People." In *The Torah: A Modern Commentary*, edited by Gunther Plaut. New York: Union for Reform Judaism, 1981.

Barrett, C. K. *The First Epistle to the Corinthians*, 2nd revised edition. London: Black, 1992.

Barrett, C. K. *The New Testament Background: Selected Documents*, revised edition. London: SPCK, 1987.

Baum, Armin Daniel. "Paul's Conflicting Statements on Female Public Speaking (1 Cor 11:5) and Silence (1 Cor 14:34–35): A New Suggestion." *Tyndale Bulletin* 65:2 (2014): 247–274.

Baumgarten, A. I. "The Torah as a Public Document in Judaism." *Studies in Religion* 14 (1985): 17–24.

Beech, Hannah. "The Face of Buddhist Terror." *Time*, July 1, 2013. Online: http://content.time.com/time/subscriber/article/0,33009,2146000,00.html.

Bockmuehl, Klaus. *Listening to the God Who Speaks: Reflections on God's Guidance from Scripture and the Lives of God's People.* Colorado Springs, CO: Helmer and Howard, 1990.

Bockmuehl, Markus. *Revelation and Mystery in Ancient Judaism and Pauline Christianity.* Tubingen: Mohr Siebeck, 1990.

Bookidis, Nancy, and R. S. Stroud. *Demeter and Persephone in Ancient Corinth.* Princeton, NJ: American School of Classical Studies at Athens, 1987.

Bolt, Peter. "Jesus, the Daimons and the Dead." In *The Unseen World: Christian Reflections on Angels, Demons, and the Heavenly Realm,* edited by Anthony N. S. Lane. Grand Rapids, MI: Eerdmans, 1996.

Bray, Gerald. *Biblical Interpretation: Past and Present.* Leicester, UK: IVP Academic, 1996.

Breck, John. "Exegesis and Interpretation: Orthodox Reflections on the 'Hermeneutic Problem.'" *SVTQ* 27:2 (1983): 75–92.

Breck, John. "Orthodox Principles of Biblical Interpretation." *SVTQ* 40:1–2 (1996): 77–93.

Breck, John. *The Power of the Word in the Worshipping Church.* Crestwood, NY: St. Vladimir's Seminary Press,1986.

Breck, John. *Scripture in Tradition: The Bible and Its Interpretation in the Orthodox Church.* Crestwood, NY: St. Vladimir's Seminary Press, 2001.

Breck, John. "The Two Hands of God: Christ and the Spirit in Orthodox Theology." *SVTQ* 40:4 (1996): 231–246.

Brenton, L. C. L. (translator). *The Septuagint with Apocrypha.* London: Samuel Bagster and Sons, 1884.

Bromiley, Geoffrey William. *International Standard Bible Encyclopedia,* Volume 4. Grand Rapids, MI: Eerdmans, 1995.

Broneer, Oscar. "Corinth: Center of St. Paul's Missionary Work in Greece." *Biblical Archeologist* 14:4 (1951): 77–96.

Brown, Peter. *The Body and Society: Men, Women and Sexual Renunciation in Early Christianity.* New York: Columbia University Press, 1988.

Brown, Raymond E. "Our New Approach to the Bible." In *New Testament Essays,* edited by Raymond E. Brown and introduced by Ronald D. Witherup. New York: Image Books, 2010.

Brown, Raymond E., Joseph A. Fitzmyer, and Roland E. Murphy, editors. *The Jerome Biblical Commentary.* Englewood Cliffs, NJ: Prentice-Hall, 1968.

Brown, Raymond E., Joseph A. Fitzmyer, and Roland E. Murphy, editors. *The New Jerome Biblical Commentary.* Englewood Cliffs, NJ: Prentice-Hall, 1990.

Bruce, F. F. *1 and 2 Corinthians.* London: Oliphants, 1971.

Brueggemann, Walter. *Theology of the Old Testament: Testimony, Dispute, Advocacy.* Minneapolis, MN: Fortress Press, 1997.

Buchman, Frank N. D. *Remaking the World,* London: Blandford, 1947.

Bultmann, R. "New Testament and Mythology." In *Kerygma and Myth,* Volume 1, 2nd edition, edited by H. W. Bartsch. London: SPCK, 1964.

Caragounis, Chrys C. "Greek Culture and Jewish Piety: The Clash of the Fourth Beast of Daniel 7." *Ephemerides Theologicae Lovanienses* 65 (1989): 280–308.

Charles, R. H. *The Apocrypha and Pseudepigrapha of the Old Testament in English.* Oxford: Clarendon Press, 1913. Online: http://www.ccel.org/c/charles/otpseudepig/aristeas.htm.

Charlesworth, James H. "Old Testament Apocrypha." *ABD* 1.292–294.

Charlesworth, J. H., editor. *The Old Testament Pseudepigrapha, Volume 1: Apocalyptic Literature and Testaments.* New Haven, CT: Yale University Press, 1983.

Charlesworth, J.H., editor. *The Old Testament Pseudepigrapha, Vol. 2: Expansions of the Old Testament and Legends, Wisdom and Philosophical Literature, Prayers, Psalms, and Odes, Fragments of Lost Judeo-Hellenistic works.* New York: Doubleday, 1985.

Charlesworth, J. H. *The Pseudepigrapha and Modern Research with a Supplement.* Ann Arbor, MI: Borchardt Library, La Trobe University, 1991.

Childs, Brevard. *Introduction to the Old Testament as Scripture.* Philadelphia: Fortress Press, 1979.

Cicero. *The Letters to His Brother Quintus.* Translated by W. Glynn Williams. *The Letters to Brutus.* Translated by M. Cary. *Handbook of Electioneering. Letter to Octavian.* Translated by Mary Henderson. Loeb Classical Library 462. Cambridge, MA: Harvard University Press, 1972.

Cicero. *On Duties.* Translated by Walter Miller. Loeb Classical Library 30. Cambridge, MA: Harvard University Press, 1913.

Cicero. *In Catilinam 1-4. Pro Murena. Pro Sulla. Pro Flacco.* Translated by C. Macdonald. Loeb Classical Library 324. Cambridge, MA: Harvard University Press, 1976.

Cicero. *On Old Age. On Friendship. On Divination.* Translated by W. A. Falconer. Loeb Classical Library 154. Cambridge, MA: Harvard University Press, 1923.

Cicero. *On the Nature of the Gods. Academics.* Translated by H. Rackham. Loeb Classical Library 268. Cambridge, MA: Harvard University Press, 1933.

Cicero. *On the Orator: Book 3. On Fate. Stoic Paradoxes. Divisions of Oratory.* Translated by H. Rackham. Loeb Classical Library 349. Cambridge, MA: Harvard University Press, 1942.

Clark, Stephen B. *Unordained Elders and Renewal Communities,* New York: Paulist Press, 1976.

Clarke, M. L. *Higher Education in the Ancient World.* London: Routledge, 1971.

Clement of Alexandria. *Stromateis, Books 1-3.* Translated by John Ferguson. Fathers of the Church Patristic Series 85. Washington, DC: Catholic University of America, 2005.

Cohen, Martin Samuel. *The Boy on the Door on the Ox: An Unusual Spiritual Journey through the Strangest Jewish Texts.* New York: Aviv Press, 2008.

Collins, Adelea Yarbro. "The Function of 'Excommunication' in Paul." *Harvard Theological Review* 73:1–2 (1980): 251–263.

Collins, J. J. "The Sibylline Oracles." In *The Old Testament Pseudepigrapha, Volume 1 Apocalyptic Literature and Testaments,* edited by James H. Charlesworth. New York: Doubleday Anchor, 1983.

Conzelmann, Hans. *First Corinthians: A Commentary on the First Epistle to the Corinthians.* Philadelphia: Fortress Press, 1988.

Coxon, A. H. "Xenophanes." In *The Oxford Classical Dictionary,* 2nd edition, edited by N. G. L. Hammond and H. H. Scullard. Oxford: Clarendon Press, 1970.

Davies, W. D. *Paul and Rabbinic Judaism.* London: SPCK, 1948.

Davies, W. D., and L. Finkelstein, editors. *The Cambridge History of Judaism, Volume 1: Introduction: The Persian Period* (1984); *Volume 2: The Hellenistic Age* (1990). Cambridge, UK: Cambridge University Press.

Di Pane, James, and Olivia Enos. "The Festering Religious Violence That Underpins Modi's India." *Newsweek*, April 1, 2017. Online: http://www.newsweek.com/ festering-religious- violence-underpins-modis-india-583835.

Dio Chrysostom. *Discourses 1–11*. Translated by J. W. Cohoon. Loeb Classical Library 257. Cambridge, MA: Harvard University Press, 1932.

Dio Chrysostom. *Discourses 37-60*. Translated by H. Lamar Crosby. Loeb Classical Library 376. Cambridge, MA: Harvard University Press, 1946.

Dodd, C. H. *According to the Scriptures: The Sub-structure of New Testament Theology.* London: Nisbet, 1952.

Dodds, E. R. *The Greeks and the Irrational.* Berkley: University of California Press, 1971.

Dunn, James D. G. *Baptism in the Holy Spirit.* London: SCM, 1970.

Dunn, James D. G. "Discernment of Spirits—A Neglected Gift." In *Witnesses to the Spirit: Essays on Revelation, Spirit, Redemption,* edited by W. Harrington. Dublin: Irish Bible Association, 1979.

Dunn, James D. G. "In Quest of Paul's Theology: Retrospect and Prospect." In *Pauline Theology,* volume 4, edited by E. E. Johnson and David M. May. Atlanta, GA: Scholar's Press, 1997.

Dunn, James D. G. *The Theology of Paul the Apostle.* Grand Rapids, MI: Eerdmans, 1998.

Edwards, C. M. "Tyche at Corinth." *Hesperia* 59 (1990): 529–542.

Ellis, E. Earl. *Paul's Use of the Old Testament.* Edinburgh: Oliver and Boyd, 1957.

Engels, Donald. *Roman Corinth: An Alternative Model for the Classical City.* Chicago: University of Chicago Press, 1990.

Englezakis, Benedict. *New and Old in God's Revelation: Studies in Relations between Spirit and Tradition in the Bible.* Crestwood, NY: St. Vladimir's Seminary Press, 1982.

Evans, C. A., and W. F. Stinespring, editors. *Early Jewish and Christian Exegesis.* Atlanta, GA: Scholars Press, 1987.

Fee, Gordon. *The First Epistle to the Corinthians.* Grand Rapids, MI: Eerdmans, 1987.

Feldman, Louis H. *Jew and Gentile in the Ancient World: Attitudes and Interactions from Alexander to Justinian.* Princeton, NJ: Princeton University Press, 1993.

Feldman, Louis H. *Josephus's Interpretation of the Bible.* Berkeley: University of California Press, 1998.

Ferguson, Everett, editor. *Encyclopedia of Early Christianity,* 2nd edition. New York: Garland, 1998.

Finney, Mark. "Honour, Head-Coverings and Headship: 1 Corinthians 11:2–16 in Its Social Context." *JSNT* 33:1 (September 2010): 31–58.

Fishbane, Michael. *Biblical Interpretation in Ancient Israel.* Oxford: Oxford University Press, 1985.

Fishbane, Michael. "Inner-Biblical Exegesis." In *Hebrew Bible/Old Testament: The History of Its Interpretation, Volume 1: From the Beginnings to the Middle Ages, Part I: Antiquity,* edited by Magne Saebo. Gottingen: Vandenhoek and Ruprech, 1996.

Florovsky, Georges. *Bible, Church, Tradition: An Eastern Orthodox View.* Belmont, MA: Nordland, 1972.

Flusser, David. *Judaism of the Second Temple Period, Volume 2: Sages and Literature.* Translated by A. Yadin. Grand Rapids, MI: Eerdmans, 2009.

Forbes, Christopher. *Prophecy and Inspired Speech in Early Christianity and Its Hellenistic Environment*. Tubingen: Mohr Siebeck, 1995.

Ford, Mary. "Seeing, but Not Perceiving: Crisis and Context in Biblical Studies." *SVTQ* 35:2–3 (1991): 107–125.

Fowler, W. Ward. *Roman Ideas of Deity in the Last Century before the Christian Era*. London: Macmillan, 1914.

Fox, Robin Lane. *Pagans and Christians*. New York: HarperCollins, 1988.

Francis, Leslie J., Mandy Robbins, and Emyr Williams. "Believing and Implicit Religion beyond the Churches: Religion, Superstition, Luck and Fear among 13–15 Year-Old Girls in Wales." *Implicit Religion* 9:1 (2006): 74–89.

Freedman, D. N., et al., editors. *The Anchor Bible Dictionary,* 6 volumes. New York: Anchor Bible, 1992.

Gadberry, L. M. "Roman Wall-Painting at Corinth: New Evidence from East of the Theater." In *The Corinthia in the Roman Period*, edited by Timothy E. Gregory. Ann Arbor: University of Michigan Press, 1993.

Gaius. *The Institutes of Gaius*. Online: http://thelatinlibrary.com/law/gaius1.html.

Gebhard, E. R. "The Isthmian Games and the Sanctuary of Poseidon in the Early Empire." In *The Corinthia in the Roman Period*, edited by Timothy E. Gregory. Ann Arbor: University of Michigan Press, 1993.

Gill, D. W. J. "Erastus the Aedile." *Tyndale Bulletin* 40 (1989): 293–301.

Gill, D. W. J., and Bruce Winter. "Acts and Roman Religion." In *The Book of Acts in Its Graeco- Roman Setting*, edited by D. W. J. Gill and C. Gempf. Volume 2 *of The Book of Acts in Its First Century Setting,* edited by Bruce W. Winter. Grand Rapids, MI: Paternoster/Eerdmans, 1994.

Gordon, R. "Religion in the Roman Empire: The Civic Compromise and Its Limits." In *Pagan Priests: Religion and Power*, edited by M. Beard and J. North. Ithaca, NY: Cornell University Press, 1990.

"The Gospel of Thomas." In *The Nag Hammadi Library in English*. Revised edition. Translated by Thomas O. Lambdin and edited by James M. Robinson and Richard D. Smith. New York: HarperCollins, 1990.

Grabbe, L. *Judaism from Cyrus to Hadrian*, 2 volumes. Minneapolis, MN: Fortress Press, 1992.

Grant, F. C. *Ancient Roman Religion*. New York: Macmillan, 1957.

Crinagoras. *The Greek Anthology, Volume III: Book 9: The Declamatory Epigrams*. Translated by W. R. Paton. Loeb Classical Library 84. Cambridge, MA: Harvard University Press, 1917.

Griffin, Jasper. Introduction to Virgil, *The Aeneid*. Oxford: Oxford University Press, 1986.

Grudem, Wayne. *The Gift of Prophecy in 1 Corinthians*. Lanham, MD: University Press of America, 1982.

Grudem, Wayne. *The Gift of Prophecy in the New Testament and Today*. Westchester, IL: Crossway Books, 1988.

Guillaume, Alfred. *Prophecy and Divination among the Hebrews and Other Semites*. London: Hodder and Stoughton, 1938.

Hammond, N. G. L., and H. H. Scullard, editors. *The Oxford Classical Dictionary,* second edition. Oxford: Clarendon Press, 1970.

Harris, Sam. *Waking Up: A Guide to Spirituality without Religion*. New York: Simon and Schuster, 2014.

Hart, David Bentley. *Atheist Delusions: The Christian Revolution and Its Fashionable Enemies*. New Haven, CT: Yale University Press, 2009.

Hart, David Bentley. *The New Testament: A Translation*. New Haven, CT: Yale University Press, 2017.

Hayes, J. H. "Provisional Thoughts on Roman Pottery from the Sanctuaries of Isthmia." In *The Corinthia in the Roman Period,* edited by Timothy E. Gregory. Ann Arbor: University of Michigan Press, 1993.

Hays, R. B. *First Corinthians*. Louisville, KY: Interpretation, 1997.

Henderson, Alex. "10 Worst Examples of Christian or Far-Right Terrorism." *Salon,* August 3, 2013. Online: https://www.salon.com/2013/08/03/the_10_worst_examples_of_christian_or_far_right_terrorism_partner/.

Herms, Ronald. "'Being Saved with Honor': A Conceptual link between 1 Corinthians 3 and 1 Enoch 50?" *Journal for the Study of the New Testament* 29:2 (December 2006): 187–210.

Hill, A. E. "The Temple of Asclepius: An Alternative Source for Paul's Body Theology?" *Journal of Biblical Literature* 99 (1980): 437–139.

Hill, David. *New Testament Prophecy*. Atlanta, GA: Knox, 1979.

Homer. *Odyssey, Volume 1: Books 1–12*. Translated by A. T. Murray. Revised by George E. Dimock. Loeb Classical Library 104. Cambridge, MA: Harvard University Press, 1919.

Homer. *Iliad, Volume 1: Books 1–12*. Translated by A. T. Murray. Revised by William F. Wyatt. Loeb Classical Library 170. Cambridge, MA: Harvard University Press, 1924.

Homer. *Odyssey, Volume 2: Books 13–24*. Translated by A. T. Murray. Revised by George E. Dimock. Loeb Classical Library 105. Cambridge, MA: Harvard University Press, 1919.

Homer. *Iliad, Volume 2: Books 13–24*. Translated by A. T. Murray. Revised by William F. Wyatt. Loeb Classical Library 171. Cambridge, MA: Harvard University Press, 1925.

Hooker, Morna. "Beyond the Things Which Are Written: An Examination of 1 Cor 4:6." *New Testament Studies* 10:1 (1963–1964): 127–132.

Hooker, Morna. *Paul: A Short Introduction*. Oxford: Oneworld, 2003.

Hopko, Thomas. "The Bible in the Orthodox Church." *SVTQ* 14:1–2 (1970): 66–99.

Hopko, Thomas. "Galatians 3:28: An Orthodox Interpretation." *SVTQ* 35:2–3 (1991): 169–186.

Horace. *The Complete Odes and Epodes with the Centennial Hymn*. Translated by B. Radice and W.G. Shepherd. Harmondsworth, Middlesex, UK: Penguin, 1983.

Horace. *Satires. Epistles. The Art of Poetry*. Translated by H. Rushton Fairclough. Loeb Classical Library 194. Cambridge, MA: Harvard University Press, 1926.

Horbury, William, W. D. Davies, and John Sturdy, editors. *The Cambridge History of Judaism, Volume 3: The Early Roman Period*. Cambridge, UK: Cambridge University Press, 1999.

Hornblower, S., and A. Spawforth, editors. *The Oxford Classical Dictionary,* 3rd edition. Oxford: Oxford University Press, 1996.

Householder, F. W., Jr. *Literary Quotations and Allusions in Lucian*. New York: King's Crown Press, 1941.

Ibrahim, M. H. "The Study of Homer in Graeco-Roman Education." *Αθήνα* (Athēna) 76 (1976–1977): 187–195.

Instone-Brewer, David. *Techniques and Assumptions in Jewish Exegesis before 70 CE*. Tubingen: Mohr, 1992.

Instone-Brewer, David. *Traditions of the Rabbis from the Era of the New Testament*. Grand Rapids, MI: Eerdmans, 2004.

James, M. R. (trans. and editor). "The Correspondence of Paul and Seneca." In *The Apocryphal New Testament*, corrected edition. Oxford: Oxford University Press, 1953.

Jillions, John A. "Kenotic Ecumenism." In *The Oxford Handbook of Ecumenical Studies*, edited by Geoffrey Wainwright and Paul McPartlan. Oxford: Oxford University Press, 2019. Published online 2017: http://www.oxfordhandbooks.com/view/10.1093/oxfordhb/9780199600847.001.0001/oxfordhb-9780199600847.

Jillions, John A. "The Language of Enemies." *Logos: A Journal of Eastern Christian Studies* 50:3–4 (2009): 271–368.

Jillions, John A. "Love and Curses: Searching St Paul for a Vision of Ecumenism." *Sobornost* 20:1 (1998): 49–63.

Jillions, John A. "An Orthodox Response to N. T. Wright, 'Learning from Paul Together.'" *SVTQ* 62:4 (2018): 333–347.

Jillions, John A. "Spiritual Guidance in the Eastern Orthodox Tradition." In *Spiritual Guidance across Religions: A Sourcebook for Spiritual Directors and Other Professionals Providing Counsel to People of Differing Faith Traditions*, edited by John R. Mabry. Nashville, TN: Skylight Paths, 2014.

John Chrysostom. *Homilies on Acts*. Translated by J. Walker, J. Sheppard, and H. Browne. Revised by George B. Stevens. *Nicene and Post-Nicene Fathers*, First Series, Volume 11, edited by Philip Schaff. Buffalo, NY: Christian Literature, 1889.

John Chrysostom. *Homilies on 1 Corinthians*. Translated by Talbot W. Chambers. *Nicene and Post-Nicene Fathers*, First Series, Volume 12, edited by Philip Schaff. Buffalo, NY: Christian Literature, 1889.

John Chrysostom. *Homilies on 2 Corinthians*. Translated by Talbot W. Chambers. *From Nicene and Post-Nicene Fathers*, First Series, Volume 12, edited by Philip Schaff. Buffalo, NY: Christian Literature, 1889.

Johnson, Luke Timothy. *Scripture and Discernment: Decision-Making in the Church*, revised edition. Nashville, TN: Abingdon, 1996.

John Templeton Foundation. "Science and the Big Questions." Accessed September 20, 2019. Online: https://www.templeton.org/funding-areas/science-big-questions.

Josephus. *Jewish Antiquities, Volume 9: Book 20*. Translated by Louis H. Feldman. Loeb Classical Library 456. Cambridge, MA: Harvard University Press, 1965.

Josephus. *The Jewish War, Volume 1: Books 1–2*. Translated by H. St. J. Thackeray. Loeb Classical Library 203. Cambridge, MA: Harvard University Press, 1927.

Josephus. *The Jewish War, Volume 2: Books 3–4*. Translated by H. St. J. Thackeray. Loeb Classical Library 487. Cambridge, MA: Harvard University Press, 1927.

Josephus. *The Life. Against Apion*. Translated by H. St. J. Thackeray. Loeb Classical Library 186. Cambridge, MA: Harvard University Press, 1926.

Judge, E. A. "Judaism and the Rise of Christianity: A Roman Perspective." *Tyndale Bulletin* 45:2 (1994): 356–359.

Karavidopoulos, I. *Apostolou Pavlou Epistoles Pros Ephesious, Philippēsious, Kolossaeis*. Thessaloniki: Pournara, 1981.

Karavidopoulos, I. *Biblikes Meletes*. Thessaloniki: Pournara, 1995.

Karavidopoulos, I. *Eisagogē stēn Kainē Diathēkē*. Thessaloniki: Pournara, 1993.

Karavidopoulos, I. "The Interpretation of the New Testament in the Orthodox Church." In *Jesus Christus als die Mitte der Schrift: Studien zur Hermeneutik des Evangeliums*, edited by Christof Landmesser et al. Berlin: de Gruyter, 1997.

Kent, J. H., editor. *The Inscriptions: 1926–1950*, Corinth VIII/3. Princeton, NJ: ASCSA, 1966.

Kesich, Veselin. *Formation and Struggles: The Birth of the Church AD 33–200*. Crestwood, NY: St. Vladimir's Seminary Press, 2007.

Kesich, Veselin, *The Gospel Image of Christ: The Church and Modern Criticism*. Crestwood, NY: St. Vladimir's Seminary Press, 1972.

Kesich, Veselin. "Research and Prejudice." *SVTQ* 14:1–2 (1970): 28–47.

Kidd, I. G. *Posidonius*, 2 volumes. Cambridge, UK: Cambridge University Press, 1988.

Kidd, I. G. "Posidonius." In *The Oxford Classical Dictionary*, edited by S. Hornblower and A. Spawforth. 3rd edition. Oxford: Clarendon Press, 1996.

King, Martin Luther, Jr. *Stride toward Freedom: The Montgomery Story*. New York: Harper & Brothers, 1958.

Kittel, Gerhardt, and G. Friedrich, editors. *Theological Dictionary of the New Testament*, 10 volumes. Translated by G. Bromiley. Grand Rapids, MI: Eerdmans, 1964–1976.

Klawans, Jonathan. *Josephus and the Theologies of Ancient Judaism*. New York: Oxford University Press, 2012.

Kraftchick, Steven J. "An Asymptotic Response to Dunn's Retrospective and Proposals." In *Pauline Theology*, Volume 4, edited by E. E. Johnson and David M. May. Atlanta, GA: Scholars Press, 1997.

Kristof, Nicholas. "Cardinal Tobin, Am I a Christian?" *New York Times*, December 22, 2017.

Lachs, Samuel Tobias. *A Rabbinic Commentary on the New Testament*. Hoboken, NJ: KTAV and ADL, 1987.

Lampe, G. W. H, editor. *The Cambridge History of the Bible, Volume 2: The West from the Fathers to the Reformation*. Cambridge, UK: Cambridge University Press, 1969.

Lane, Anthony N. S., editor. *The Unseen World: Christian Reflections on Angels, Demons, and the Heavenly Realm*. Grand Rapids, MI: Eerdmans, 1996.

Lane, W. L. "Corinth." In *Major Cities of the Biblical World*, edited by R. K. Harrison. Nashville, TN: Thomas Nelson, 1985.

Lang, M. *Cure and Cult in Ancient Corinth: A Guide to the Asklepieion*. Princeton, NJ: ASCSA, 1977.

Latham, R. E. Introduction to Lucretius, *The Nature of the Universe* (De rerum natura). Translated by R. E. Latham. Baltimore, MD: Penguin, 1951.

Lean, Garth. *Frank Buchman: A Life*. London: Constable, 1985.

Levin, S. "The Old Greek Oracles in Decline." *ANRW* II/18.2 (1989) 1599–1649.

Levine, Lee I. "The Nature and Origin of the Palestinian Synagogue Reconsidered." *Journal of Biblical Literature* 115:3 (Fall 1996): 425–448.

Levinskaya, Irina. *The Book of Acts in Its Diaspora Setting. Volume 5 of The Book of Acts in Its First Century Setting*, edited by Bruce W. Winter. Grand Rapids, MI: Eerdmans/Paternoster, 1996.

L'Huillier, Archbishop Peter. "Authority in the Church." *SVTQ* 39:4 (1995): 325–337.

Liddell, Henry George, Robert Scott, and Henry Stuart Jones. *A Greek-English Lexicon*, 9th edition, with revised supplement. Oxford: Clarendon Press, 1982.

Lieberman, Saul. *Hellenism in Jewish Palestine: Studies in the Literary Transmission, Beliefs and Manners of Palestine in the I Century B.C.E.–IV Century C.E.*, 2nd edition. New York: Jewish Theological Seminary of America, 1962.

Linebaugh, Jonathan A. "Debating Diagonal δικαιοσύνη [Dikaiosynē]: The Epistle of Enoch and Paul in Theological Conversation." *Early Christianity* 1:1 (2010): 107–128.

Livy. *History of Rome, Volume 1: Books 1–2*. Translated by B. O. Foster. Loeb Classical Library 114. Cambridge, MA: Harvard University Press, 1919.

Longenecker, R. *Biblical Exegesis in the Apostolic Period*. Grand Rapids, MI: Eerdmans, 1975.

Louth, Andrew. *Discerning the Mystery: An Essay on the Nature of Theology*. Oxford: Oxford University Press, 1983.

Lucan. *The Civil War (Pharsalia)*. Translated by J. D. Duff. Loeb Classical Library 220. Cambridge, MA: Harvard University Press, 1928.

Lucretius. *De rerum natura*. Translated by William Ellery Leonard. London: E. P. Dutton, 1916.

Lucretius. *The Nature of the Universe* (De rerum natura). Translated by R. E. Latham. Baltimore, MD: Penguin, 1951.

Lucretius. *On the Nature of Things*. Translated by W. H. D. Rouse. Revised by Martin F. Smith. Loeb Classical Library 181. Cambridge, MA: Harvard University Press, 1924.

Luhrmann, Tanya. *Persuasions of the Witch's Craft: Ritual Magic and Witchcraft in Present-Day England*. Oxford: Oxford University Press, 1989.

Mabry, John R. (ed.). *Spiritual Guidance across Religions: A Sourcebook for Spiritual Directors and Other Professionals Providing Counsel to People of Differing Faith Traditions*. Nashville, TN: Skylight Paths, 2014.

Maccoby, Hyam. *Early Rabbinic Writings*. Cambridge, UK: Cambridge University Press, 1988.

MacMullen, Ramsay. *Paganism in the Roman Empire*. New Haven: Yale University Press, 1981.

MacMullen, R., and E. N. Lane, editors. *Paganism and Christianity, 100–425 C.E.: A Sourcebook*. Minneapolis, MN: Fortress Press, 1992.

Manseau, Peter. *Vows: The Story of a Priest, a Nun, and Their Son*. New York: Free Press, 2005.

Marcus Aurelius. *Meditations*. In *Marcus Aurelius* edited and translated by C. R. Haines. Loeb Classical Library 58. Cambridge, MA: Harvard University Press, 1916.

Margalit, Ruth. "Israel's Jewish-Terrorist Problem." *New Yorker*, August 4, 2015. Online: https://www.newyorker.com/news/news-desk/israels-jewish-terrorist-problem.

Marrou, H. I. *A History of Education in Antiquity*. Translated by G. Lamb, 3rd edition. London: Sheed and Ward, 1956.

Marshall, I. H. *The Acts of the Apostles: An Introduction and Commentary*. Leicester, UK: Inter-Varsity Press, 1980.

Marshall, Peter. *Enmity in Corinth: Social Conventions in Paul's Relations with the Corinthians*. Tubingen: Mohr, 1987.

Martinez, Florentino Garcia. *The Dead Sea Scrolls Translated: The Qumran Texts in English*. Translated by W. Watson. Leiden: Brill, 1992.

May, Herbert G., and Bruce M. Metzger, editors. *The New Oxford Annotated Bible with the Apocrypha* (Revised Standard Version). New York: Oxford University Press, 1977.

Matassa, Lydia D. *Invention of the First-Century Synagogue*. Atlanta, GA: Scholars Press, 2018. Online: https://www.sbl-site.org/assets/pdfs/pubs/9780884143208_OA.pdf.

Meeks, Wayne A. *The First Urban Christians: The Social World of the Apostle Paul*. New Haven, CT: Yale University Press, 1983.

Merrit, B. D., editor. *Corinth: Results VIII/I*. Princeton, NJ: ASCSA, 1931.

Metzger, Bruce. *An Introduction to the Apocrypha*. New York: Oxford University Press, 1977.

Metzger, Bruce M., editor. *The Oxford Annotated Apocrypha*. Oxford: Oxford University Press, 1977.

Meyendorff, John. *St Gregory Palamas and Orthodox Spirituality*. Crestwood, NY: St. Vladimir's Seminary Press, 1974.

Milliker, E. J. "Three Heads of Serapis from Corinth." *Hesperia* 54 (1985): 123–124.

Moffat, James. *The First Epistle of Paul to the Corinthians*. London: Hodder and Stoughton, 1938.

Momigliano, Arnaldo. *On Pagans, Jews and Christians*. Middletown, CT: Wesleyan University Press, 1987.

Montefiore, C. G., and H. Loewe. *A Rabbinic Anthology*. London: Macmillan, 1938.

Mortley, Raoul. "The Past in Clement of Alexandria." In *Jewish and Christian Self-Definition*, Volume 1, edited by E. P. Sanders. London: SCM Press, 1980.

Mulder, M. J., editor. *Mikra: Text, Translation, Reading and Interpretation of the Hebrew Bible in Ancient Judaism and Early Christianity*. Minneapolis, MN: Fortress, 1990.

Müller, Ulrich B. *Prophetie und Predigt im Neuen Testament: Formgeschichtliche Untersuchungen zur urchristlichen Prophetie*. Gutersloh: Mohn, 1975.

Munck, J. *The Acts of the Apostles*. Garden City, NY: Anchor Bible, 1967.

Murphy-O'Connor, Jerome. "The Corinth That Paul Saw." *Biblical Archeologist* 47 (1984): 147–153.

Murphy-O'Connor, Jerome. *Paul: A Critical Life*. Oxford: Oxford University Press, 1997.

Murphy-O'Connor, Jerome. "Sex and Logic in 1 Corinthians 11:2–16." *Catholic Biblical Quarterly* 42 (1980): 482–500.

Murphy-O'Connor, Jerome. *St. Paul's Corinth: Texts and Archeology*. Wilmington, DE: Michael Glazier, 1983.

Nathan, G. S. *The Roman Family in Late Antiquity: The Endurance of Tradition and the Rise of Christianity*. Ann Arbor: University of Michigan, 1996.

"A Nation Bound by Faith." *Newsweek*, February 23, 2003, 21–23.

Neusner, Jacob. *The Classics of Judaism: A Textbook and Reader*. Louisville, KY: Westminster John Knox Press, 1995.

Neusner, Jacob. *The Mishnah: A New Translation*. New Haven, CT: Yale University Press, 1988.

Neusner, Jacob. *Rabbinic Literature and the New Testament: What We Cannot Show We Do Not Know*. Valley Forge, PA: Trinity Press, 1994.

Neusner, J., and W. S. Green, editors. *Dictionary of Judaism in the Biblical Period: 450 BCE to 600 CE*. 2 volumes. New York: Macmillan, 1996.

Niditch, Susan. *Oral World and Written Word: Ancient Israelite Literature*. Louisville, KY: Westminster John Knox Press, 1996.

Nwaubani, Adaobi Tricia. "A Voodoo Curse on Human Traffickers." *New York Times*, March 24, 2018. Online: https://www.nytimes.com/2018/03/24/opinion/sunday/voodoo-curse-human-traffickers.html.

Oden, Thomas C. *Ancient Christian Commentary on Scripture*. Downers Grove, IL: InterVarsity Press, 1998.

Ogilvie, R. M. *The Romans and Their Gods in the Age of Augustus*. New York: Norton, 1969.

Oikonomos, Elias. "The Significance of the Deuterocanonical Writings in the Orthodox Church." In *The Apocrypha in Ecumenical Perspective*, edited by S. Meurer. Translated by P. Ellingworth. United Bible Society Monograph Series, No. 6. New York: United Bible Society, 1991.

Origen. *Homilies on Joshua*. Translated by Barbara C. Bruce. Edited by Cynthia White. Fathers of the Church Patristic Series 105.Washington, DC: Catholic University of America Press, 2010.

Origen. *Homilies on Leviticus 1–16*. Translated by Gary Wayne Barkley. Fathers of the Church Patristic Series 83. Washington, DC: Catholic University of America Press, 2005.

Orr, W. F., and J. A. Walther. *1 Corinthians, a New Translation*. Garden City, NY: Doubleday, 1976.

Osiek, C., and David Balch. *Families in the New Testament World: Households and House Churches*. Louisville, KY: Westminster John Knox, 1997.

Osler, R. E. "Use, Misuse, and Neglect of Archeological Evidence in Some Modern Works on 1 Corinthians." *ZNW* 83 (1992): 52–73.

Ovid. *The Metamorphoses of Ovid*. Translated by Mary Innes. Harmondsworth, UK: Penguin, 1955.

Ovid. *Tristia. Ex Ponto*. Translated by A. L. Wheeler. Revised by G. P. Goold. Loeb Classical Library 151. Cambridge, MA: Harvard University Press, 1924.

Pagels, Elaine. *Beyond Belief: The Secret Gospel of Thomas*. New York: Random House, 2004.

Pagels, Elaine. *The Gnostic Gospels*. New York: Random House, 1979.

Pagels, Elaine. *Why Religion: A Personal Story*. New York: Harper Collins. 2018.

Paige, T. P. "Spirit at Corinth: The Corinthian Concept of Spirit and Paul's Response as Seen in 1 Corinthians." PhD diss., Sheffield University, 1993.

Papahatzis, N. *Ancient Corinth: The Museums of Corinth, Isthmia and Sicyon*. Athens: Ekdotike Athenon, 1994.

Parke, H. W., and D. E. W. Wormell. *The Delphic Oracle*. 2 volumes. Oxford: Blackwell, 1956.

Pausanias. *Description of Greece, Volume 1: Books 1–2 (Attica and Corinth)*. Translated by W. H. S. Jones. Loeb Classical Library 93. Cambridge, MA: Harvard University Press, 1918.

Pelikan, Jaroslav. *Credo: Historical and Theological Guide to Creeds and Confessions of Faith in the Christian Tradition*. New Haven, CT: Yale University Press, 2003.

Pelikan, Jaroslav. *The Emergence of the Catholic Tradition (100–600)*. Chicago: University of Chicago Press, 1971.

Pelikan, Jaroslav, and Valerie Hotchkiss, editors. *Creeds and Confessions of Faith in the Christian Tradition*. 4 volumes. New Haven, CT: Yale University Press, 2003.

Pentiuc, Eugen J. *The Old Testament in Eastern Orthodox Tradition*. New York: Oxford University Press, 2014.

Petit, P. *Pax Romana*. Translated by J. Willis. London: Batsford, 1976.

Petrochilos, N. K. *Roman Attitudes to the Greeks*. Athens: S. Saripolos' Library, 1974.

Peterson, Eugene H. *The Message: the New Testament in Contemporary English*. Colorado Springs: NavPress Publishing, 1993.

Petronius, Seneca. *Satyricon. Apocolocyntosis*. Translated by Michael Heseltine and W. H. D. Rouse. Revised by E. H. Warmington. Loeb Classical Library 15. Cambridge, MA: Harvard University Press, 1913.

Pew Research Center. *America's Changing Religious Landscape*. May 12, 2015. Online: http://assets.pewresearch.org/wp-content/uploads/sites/11/2015/05/RLS-08-26-full-report.pdf.

Pew Research Center. "Attendance at Religious Services." *America's Changing Religious Landscape*, May 12, 2015. Online: https://www.pewforum.org/religious-landscape-study/attendance-at-religious-services/.

Pew Research Center. "Frequency of Prayer." *America's Changing Religious Landscape*, May 12, 2015. Online: https://www.pewforum.org/religious-landscape-study/frequency-of-prayer/.

Pew Research Center. "The Age Gap in Religion Around the World," June 13, 2018. Online: https://www.pewforum.org/2018/06/13/how-religious-commitment-varies-by-country-among-people-of-all-ages/.

Philo. *Every Good Man Is Free. On the Contemplative Life. On the Eternity of the World. Against Flaccus. Apology for the Jews. On Providence*. Translated by F. H. Colson. Loeb Classical Library 363. Cambridge, MA: Harvard University Press, 1941.

Philo. *On Abraham. On Joseph. On Moses*. Translated by F. H. Colson. Loeb Classical Library 289. Cambridge, MA: Harvard University Press, 1935.

Philo. *On the Cherubim. The Sacrifices of Abel and Cain. The Worse Attacks the Better. On the Posterity and Exile of Cain. On the Giants*. Translated by F. H. Colson, G. H. Whitaker. Loeb Classical Library 227. Cambridge, MA: Harvard University Press, 1929.

Philo. *On the Confusion of Tongues. On the Migration of Abraham. Who Is the Heir of Divine Things? On Mating with the Preliminary Studies*. Translated by F. H. Colson, G. H. Whitaker. Loeb Classical Library 261. Cambridge, MA: Harvard University Press, 1932.

Philo. *On the Embassy to Gaius. General Indexes*. Translated by F. H. Colson. Index by J. W. Earp. Loeb Classical Library 379. Cambridge, MA: Harvard University Press, 1962.

Philo. *On Flight and Finding. On the Change of Names. On Dreams*. Translated by F. H. Colson and G. H. Whitaker. Loeb Classical Library 275. Cambridge, MA: Harvard University Press, 1934.

Pietersma, Albert, and Benjamin G. Wright, editors. *A New English Translation of the Septuagint*. Oxford: Oxford University Press, 2007.

Plato. *Euthyphro. Apology. Crito. Phaedo*. Edited and translated by Christopher Emlyn-Jones and William Preddy. Loeb Classical Library 36. Cambridge, MA: Harvard University Press, 2017.

Plato. *Euthyphro. Apology. Crito. Phaedo. Phaedrus*. Translated by Harold North Fowler. Loeb Classical Library 36. Cambridge, MA: Harvard University Press, 1914.

Plato. *Lysis. Symposium. Gorgias*. Translated by W. R. M. Lamb. Loeb Classical Library 166. Cambridge, MA: Harvard University Press, 1925.

Plato. *Theaetetus. Sophist*. Translated by Harold North Fowler. Loeb Classical Library 123. Cambridge, MA: Harvard University Press, 1921.

Plato. *Timaeus. Critias. Cleitophon. Menexenus. Epistles*. Translated by R. G. Bury. Loeb Classical Library 234. Cambridge, MA: Harvard University Press, 1929.

Plaut, Gunther, editor. *The Torah: A Modern Commentary*. New York: Union of American Hebrew Congregations, 1981.

Pliny. *Natural History, Volume 1: Books 1–2*. Translated by H. Rackham. Loeb Classical Library 330. Cambridge, MA: Harvard University Press, 1938.

Plutarch. *Lives, Volume 1: Theseus and Romulus. Lycurgus and Numa. Solon and Publicola*. Translated by Bernadotte Perrin. Loeb Classical Library 46. Cambridge, MA: Harvard University Press, 1914.

Plutarch. *Moralia, Volume 2: How to Profit by One's Enemies. On Having Many Friends. Chance. Virtue and Vice. Letter of Condolence to Apollonius. Advice about Keeping Well.*

Advice to Bride and Groom. The Dinner of the Seven Wise Men. Superstition. Translated by Frank Cole Babbitt. Loeb Classical Library 222. Cambridge, MA: Harvard University Press, 1928.

Plutarch. *Moralia, Volume 5: Isis and Osiris. The E at Delphi. The Oracles at Delphi No Longer Given in Verse. The Obsolescence of Oracles.* Translated by Frank Cole Babbitt. Loeb Classical Library 306. Cambridge, MA: Harvard University Press, 1936.

Plutarch. *Moralia, Volume 7: On Love of Wealth. On Compliancy. On Envy and Hate. On Praising Oneself Inoffensively. On the Delays of the Divine Vengeance. On Fate. On the Sign of Socrates. On Exile. Consolation to His Wife.* Translated by Phillip H. De Lacy and Benedict Einarson. Loeb Classical Library 405. Cambridge, MA: Harvard University Press, 1959.

Plutarch. *Moralia, Volume 8: Table-Talk, Books 1-6.* Translated by P. A. Clement and H. B. Hoffleit. Loeb Classical Library 424. Cambridge, MA: Harvard University Press, 1969.

Plutarch. *Moralia, Volume IX: Table-Talk, Books 7-9. Dialogue on Love.* Translated by Edwin L. Minar, F. H. Sandbach, W. C. Helmbold. Loeb Classical Library 425. Cambridge, MA: Harvard University Press, 1961.

Polybius. *The Histories, Volume 1: Books 1-2.* Translated by W. R. Paton. Revised by F. W. Walbank and Christian Habicht. Loeb Classical Library 128. Cambridge, MA: Harvard University Press, 2010.

Propertius. *The Elegies of Propertius.* Edited with an introduction and commentary by H. Butler and E. A. Barber. Oxford: Clarendon Press, 1933.

H. Rackam. introduction to Cicero, *On Fate* in *On the Orator: Book 3. On Fate. Stoic Paradoxes. Divisions of Oratory.* Translated by H. Rackham. Loeb Classical Library 349. Cambridge, MA: Harvard University Press, 1942.

Rahlfs, Alfred, and Robert Hanhart, editors. *Septuaginta.* Stuttgart: German Bible Society, 2006.

Rajak, T., and D. Noy. "Archisynagogoi: Office, Social Status in the Graeco-Roman World." *Journal of Roman Studies* 83 (1993): 75–93.

Rice, D. G., and J. E. Stambaugh, editors. *Sources for the Study of Greek Religion.* Missoula, MT: Scholars Press, 1979.

Roberts, Louis. "Reliefs votifs et cultes d'Anatolie." *Anatolia* 3 (1958): 103–136.

Robinson, Edward, editor. *This Time-Bound Ladder: Ten Dialogues on Religious Experience.* Oxford: Religious Experience Research Unit, Manchester College, 1977.

Robinson, Zoe. "Lobbying in the Shadows: Religious Interest Groups in the Legislative Process." *Emory Law Journal* 64:1041 (2015). Online: http://law.emory.edu/elj/_documents/volumes/64/4/articles/robinson.pdf.

Roebuck, Carl. *Corinth XIV: The Asklepion and Lerna.* Princeton, NJ: ASCSA, 1951.

Romano, D. G. "Post 146 B.C. Land Use in Corinth, and Planning of the Roman Colony of 44 B.C." In *The Corinthia in the Roman Period,* edited by T. E. Gregory. Ann Arbor: University of Michigan Press, 1993.

Runia, David, *Philo of Alexandria and the Timaeus of Plato.* Leiden: Brill, 1986.

Sacks, Rabbi Jonathan. *Not in God's Name: Confronting Religious Violence.* New York: Schocken, 2015.

Saebo, Magne, editor. *Hebrew Bible/Old Testament: The History of Its Interpretation, Vol. 1, From the Beginnings to the Middle Ages, Part I: Antiquity.* Gottingen: Vandenhoek and Ruprech, 1996.

Safrai, S. "Relations between the Diaspora and the Land of Israel." In *The Jewish People in the First Century,* Volume 1, edited by S. Safrai and M. Stern. Assen: Brill, 1974.

Safrai, S., and M. Stern, editors. *The Jewish People in the First Century.* 2 volumes. Assen: Van Gorcum, 1974 (Volume 1), 1976 (Volume 2).

Sampley, J. Paul, and Peter Lampe, editors. *Paul and Rhetoric.* New York: Continuum, 2010.

Sanders, E. P., editor. *Jewish and Christian Self-Definition, Volume 1: The Shaping of Christianity in the Second and Third Centuries.* Philadelphia: Fortress, 1980.

Sanders, E. P. *Paul and Palestinian Judaism: A Comparison of Patterns of Religion.* Philadelphia: Fortress Press, 1977.

Sanders, E. P. *Paul: The Apostle Paul's Life, Letters, and Thought.* Minneapolis, MN: Fortress Press, 2015.

Sanders, Guy D. R., Jennifer Palinkas, and Ioulia Tzonou-Herbst, with James Herbst. *Ancient Corinth: Site Guide.* 7th edition. Princeton, NJ: ASCSA, 2018.

Sandmel, Samuel. *Philo of Alexandria: An Introduction.* New York: Oxford University Press, 1979.

Schaffer, Alice. "Pete the Leper Pig." *Moth Radio Hour,* February 9, 2019. Online: https://themoth.org/radio-hour/bearing-witness.

Schama, Simon. *The Story of the Jews: Finding the Words, 1000 BC–1492 AD.* London: Bodley Head, Random House, UK, 2013.

Schmemann, Alexander. *Celebration of Faith: I Believe.* Translated by John A. Jillions. Crestwood, NY: St. Vladimir's Seminary Press, 1991.

Schmemann, Alexander. *Great Lent.* Crestwood, NY: St. Vladimir's Seminary Press, 1969.

Schnackenburg, R. *Baptism in the Thought of St. Paul.* Translated by George R. Beasley-Murray. Oxford: Basil Blackwell, 1964.

Schreiber, Aaron M. *Jewish Law and Decision-Making: A Study through Time.* Philadelphia: Temple University Press, 1979.

Seneca. *Epistles, Volume 3: Epistles 93–124.* Translated by Richard M. Gummere. Loeb Classical Library 77. Cambridge, MA: Harvard University Press, 1925.

Seneca. *Moral Essays, Volume 1: De Providentia. De Constantia. De Ira. De Clementia.* Translated by John W. Basore. Loeb Classical Library 214. Cambridge, MA: Harvard University Press, 1928.

Seneca. *Moral Essays, Volume 2: De Consolatione ad Marciam. De Vita Beata. De Otio. De Tranquillitate Animi. De Brevitate Vitae. De Consolatione ad Polybium. De Consolatione ad Helviam.* Translated by John W. Basore. Loeb Classical Library 254. Cambridge, MA: Harvard University Press, 1932.

Sherwood, Harriet. "Attendance at Church of England Sunday Services Falls Again." *The Guardian,* November 14, 2018. Online: https://www.theguardian.com/world/2018/nov/14/attendance-church-of-england-sunday-services-falls-again.

Singer, Isidore, editor. *The Jewish Encyclopedia,* 12 Volumes. New York: Funk and Wagnall, 1906. Online: http://www.jewishencyclopedia.com.

Slane, K. W. *Corinth XVIII.2: The Sanctuary of Demeter and Kore: The Roman Pottery and Lamps.* Princeton, NJ: ASCSA, 1990.

Spawforth, A. J. S. "Corinth, Argos, and the Imperial Cult: A Reconsideration of Pseudo-Julian Letters 198 Bidez." *Hesperia* 63:2 (1994): 211–32.

Sperling, D. "Akkadian Egerru and Hebrew Bat Qwl." *Journal of the Ancient Near Eastern Society of Columbia University* 4 (1972): 63–74.

Spitzer, D. C. "Roman Relief Bowls from Corinth." *Hesperia* 11:2 (1942): 162–192.

Statista. "Number of Football Attendances in the United Kingdom (UK) in 2017, by League (Aggregate Attendance in Millions)." Online: https://www.statista.com/statistics/686981/football-aggregate-attendance-by-league-united-kingdom/.

Stern, David. "Introduction." In "The Anthological Imagination in Jewish Literature." Special issue of *Prooftexts* 17, no. 1 (January 1997): 1–7.

Stern, Jessica. *Terror in the Name of God: Why Religious Militants Kill.* New York: HarperCollins, 2003.

Stern, M. "The Greek and Latin Literary Sources." In *The Jewish People in the First Century*, Volume 2, edited by S. Safrai and M. Stern. Assen: Van Gorcum, 1976.

Stern, M. "The Jewish Diaspora." In *The Jewish People in the First Century*, Volume 1, edited by S. Safrai and M. Stern. Assen: Brill, 1974.

Strabo. *Geography, Volume 1: Books 1–2.* Translated by Horace Leonard Jones. Loeb Classical Library 49. Cambridge, MA: Harvard University Press, 1917.

Stroud, R. S. "The Sanctuary of Demeter on Acrocorinth in the Roman Period." In *The Corinthia in the Roman Period*, edited by T. E. Gregory. Ann Arbor: University of Michigan Press, 1993.

Stulmacher, P. "The Significance of the Old Testament Apocrypha and Pseudepigrapha for the Understanding of Jesus and Christology." In *The Apocrypha in Ecumenical Perspective*, edited by S. Meurer. Translated by P. Ellingworth. United Bible Society Monograph Series, No. 6. New York: United Bible Society, 1991.

Suetonius. *Lives of the Caesars, Volume 1: Julius. Augustus. Tiberius. Gaius. Caligula.* Translated by J. C. Rolfe. Introduction by K. R. Bradley. Loeb Classical Library 31. Cambridge, MA: Harvard University Press, 1914.

Suetonius. *Lives of the Caesars, Volume 2: Claudius. Nero. Galba, Otho, and Vitellius. Vespasian. Titus, Domitian. Lives of Illustrious Men: Grammarians and Rhetoricians. Poets (Terence. Virgil. Horace. Tibullus. Persius. Lucan). Lives of Pliny the Elder and Passienus Crispus.* Translated by J. C. Rolfe. Loeb Classical Library 38. Cambridge, MA: Harvard University Press, 1914.

Sullivan, J. P. *The Satyricon of Petronius: A Literary Study.* Bloomington: University of Indiana Press, 1968.

Syme, Ronald. *The Roman Revolution.* Oxford: Oxford University Press, 1939.

Tacitus. *Histories: Books 4–5. Annals: Books 1–3.* Translated by Clifford H. Moore and John Jackson. Loeb Classical Library 249. Cambridge, MA: Harvard University Press, 1931.

Tarazi, Paul Nadim. *1 Thessalonians: A Commentary.* Crestwood, NY: St. Vladimir's Seminary Press, 1982.

Tarazi, Paul Nadim. *The Old Testament: An Introduction, Historical Traditions,* Volume 1. Crestwood, NY: St. Vladimir's Seminary Press, 1991.

Tarazi, Paul Nadim. *The Rise of Scripture.* St. Paul, MN: OCABS Press, 2017.

Taylor, Justin. *Les Actes des deux apotres.* Paris: Gabalda, 1996.

Tertullian. On Modesty. Translated by S. Thelwall. In *The Ante-Nicene Fathers*, Volume 4, edited by Alexander Roberts, James Donaldson, Arthur Cleveland Coxe, Allan Menzies. New York: Scribner's, 1926.

Theissen, G. *The Social Setting of Pauline Christianity: Essays on Corinth.* Philadelphia: Fortress Press, 1982.

Thompson, Cynthia L. "Hairstyles, Head-Coverings, and St Paul: Portraits from Roman Corinth." *Biblical Archeologist* 51:2 (June 1988): 99–115.

Toy, Crawfor Howell. "Tobit, Book of." In *The Jewish Encyclopedia*, edited by Isidore Singer. New York: Funk and Wagnall, 1906. Online: http://www.jewishencyclopedia. com/articles/14422-tobit-book-of.

Treves, P. "Posidonius." In *The Oxford Classical Dictionary*, 2nd edition, edited by N. Hammond and H. Scullard. Oxford: Oxford University Press, 1970.

Underhill, Evelyn. "A Letter from Evelyn Underhill to Archbishop Lang of Canterbury." 1930. Online: http://intotheexpectation.blogspot.com/2013/07/god-is-interesting-thing-about-religion.html.

Urbach, Ephraim. *The Sages: Their Concepts and Beliefs*. Translated by Israel Abrahams. Jerusalem: Magnes, 1979.

van der Valk, M. "The Homeric Quotations or the Indirect Tradition of the Homeric Text." In *Researches on the Text and Scholia of the Iliad*, edited by van der Valk. *Part 2*. Leiden: Brill, 1963.

Vassiliadis, Petros. *Charis, Koinonia, Diakonia*. Thessaloniki: Pournara, 1985.

Vassiliadis, Petros. "Equality and Justice in Classical Antiquity and in Paul: The Social Implications of the Pauline Collection." *SVTQ* 36:1–2 (1992): 51–59.

Vassiliadis, Petros. *Prolegomena stē Theologia tēs Kainēs Diathēkēs*. Thessaloniki: Pournara, 2000.

Vassiliadis, Petros. "ΣΤΑΥΡΟΣ: Centre of the Pauline Soteriology and Apostolic Ministry." *Epistēmonikē Epetērida Theologikēs Scholēs, Thessalonikē* 27 (1982): 251–259.

Vassiliadis, Petros. *Stavros kai Sotēria*. Thessaloniki: Pournara, 1983.

Velleius Paterculus. *Compendium of Roman History: Res Gestae Divi Augusti*. Translated by Frederick W. Shipley. Loeb Classical Library 152. Cambridge, MA: Harvard University Press, 1924.

Vermes, Geza. *The Complete Dead Sea Scrolls in English*. 7th edition. Harmondsworth, Middlesex, UK: Penguin, 2012.

Vermes, Geza. *Scripture and Tradition in Judaism*. Leiden: Brill, 1961.

Vermes, Geza. *The Story of the Scrolls: The Miraculous Discovery and True Significance of the Dead Sea Scrolls*. Harmondsworth, Middlesex, UK: Penguin: 2010.

Virgil. *The Aeneid*. Translated by C. D. Lewis. Introduced by Jasper Griffin. Oxford: Oxford University Press, 1986.

Walbank, M. H. "The Nature of Early Roman Corinth." *American Journal of Archeology* 90 (1996): 220–221.

Walbank, M. H. "Pausanias, Octavia and Temple E at Corinth." *Annual of the British School at Athens* 84 (1989): 361–394.

Waltke, Bruce. *Finding the Will of God: A Pagan Notion?* Grand Rapids, MI: Eerdmans, 1995.

Wan, S. K. "Charismatic Exegesis: Philo and Paul Compared." *Studia Philonica Annual* 6 (1994): 54–82.

West, A. B., editor. *Corinth: Latin Inscriptions 1898–1927 VIII/2*. Cambridge, MA: ASCSA, 1931.

Wevers, John W. "The Interpretative Character and Significance of the LXX." In *Hebrew Bible/Old Testament: The History of Its Interpretation, Volume 1, From the Beginnings to the Middle Ages, Part I: Antiquity*, edited by Magne Saebo. Gottingen: Vandenhoek and Ruprech, 1996.

Williams, C. K. "The City of Corinth and Its Domestic Religion." *Hesperia* 50 (1981): 408–421.

Williams, C. K. "The Refounding of Corinth: Some Roman Religious Attitudes." In *Roman Architecture in the Greek World*, edited by S. Macready and F. H. Thompson. London: Thames and Hudson, 1987.

Winter, Bruce W. *After Paul Left Corinth: The Influence of Secular Ethics and Social Change.* Grand Rapids, MI: Eerdmans, 2001.

Winter, Bruce W. *Philo and Paul among the Sophists.* Cambridge, UK: Cambridge University Press, 1996.

Winter, Bruce W. "Rhetoric." In *Dictionary of Paul and His Letters,* edited by Gerald F. Hawthorne and Ralph P. Martin. Downer's Grove, IL: Inter-Varsity Press, 1993.

Winter, Bruce W. *Seek the Welfare of the City: Christians as Benefactors and Citizens.* Grand Rapids, MI: Eerdmans, 1994.

Winter, Bruce W., and Andrew Clarke, editors. *The Book of Acts in Its Ancient Literary Setting.* Grand Rapids, MI: Eerdmans, 1993.

Witherington, Ben, III. *Conflict and Community in Corinth: A Socio-Rhetorical Commentary on 1–2 Corinthians.* Grand Rapids, MI: Eerdmans, 1995.

Wiseman, J. "Corinth and Rome I: 228 B.C.–A.D. 267." *ANRW* II.7.1: (1979): 438–548.

Withrow, Brandon. "Does Jesus Want Gun-Toting Christians." *Daily Beast,* April 28, 2018. Online: https://www.thedailybeast.com/does-jesus-want-gun-toting-christians.

Witmer, Stephen E. "θεοδίδακτοι in 1 Thessalonians 4.9: A Pauline Neologism." *New Testament Studies* 52 (2006): 239–250.

Witmer, Stephen E. "Taught by God: Divine Instruction in Early Christianity." *Tyndale Bulletin* 58:2 (2007): 313–316.

Wright, C. J. H. "Family." *ABD* 2:761–769.

Wright, N. T. "Learning from Paul Together: How New Insights into Paul's Teaching Can Help Move Us Forward in Mission." *SVTQ* 62:4 (2018): 317–332.

Wright, N. T. *Paul: A Biography.* New York: HarperOne, 2018.

Young, Frances M. "The God of the Greeks and the Nature of Religious Language." In *Early Christian Literature and the Classical Intellectual Tradition in Honorem Robert M. Grant,* edited by W. R. Schoedel and Robert L. Wilken. Paris: Beauchesne, 1979.

Zanker, Paul. *The Power of Images in the Age of Augustus.* Translated by Alan Shapiro. Ann Arbor: University of Michigan Press, 1988.

Index